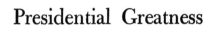

Presidential Greatness

Presidential Greatness

THE IMAGE AND THE MAN FROM
GEORGE WASHINGTON TO THE PRESENT

Reissued with a new Preface

by THOMAS A. BAILEY

BYRNE PROFESSOR OF AMERICAN HISTORY, EMERITUS

STANFORD UNIVERSITY

IRVINGTON PUBLISHERS INC., New York

Library of Congress Cataloging in Publication Data

Bailey, Thomas Andrew, 1902-
    Presidential greatness.

    Reprint of the ed. published by Appleton-Century,
New York.
    Bibliography: p.
    Includes index.
    1. Presidents—United States. I. Title.
[E176.1.B17   1978]   973'.0992   77-27551
ISBN 0-89197-356-7
ISBN 0-89197-642-6 pbk.

PRINTED IN THE UNITED STATES OF AMERICA

Preface to the Reissue

This book was originally published in 1966, while Lyndon Johnson was still president. I then indicated that he had a chance to attain greatness if he managed to get into a really big war and then win it. But the Vietnam conflict proved to be long rather than big and the United States did not win it.

Nixon will certainly not go down in history as a great or even a near-great President. The irony is that in his secretive efforts to strengthen the presidency he greatly weakened it for himself and his successors. In justifying his misconduct he blackened the reputation of some of his predecessors by pointing out that they also had used the F.B.I. and wiretaps to invade the privacy of honest citizens. His argument was that he had only been acting in what he conceived to be the national interest and hence his conduct was not unlawful. He claimed that in the area of domestic division over Vietnam he had only done what Lincoln had done in taking liberties with civil liberties under the Constitution. But in equating his problem with that of Lincoln he did not point out that the dangers from internal turmoil during the two periods were not even remotely comparable. Further, all Nixon had to do was to bring the boys home and end the bombing and quiet would return.

Nixon was only throwing dust in the eyes of the public when he claimed that he had only been doing, in the national interest, what Johnson and Kennedy had done. Admittedly a "credibility gap" had developed under Johnson. But clearly no man in history has ever told more lies to more people on television than Nixon, all in the "national interest" (meaning his own interest as well). The President is supposed to be the servant of the people, not its enemy, yet his "enemies lists" indicated that he regarded many citizens as his foes subject to the harrassment and persecution that only the Chief Executive can initiate.

Ironically, Nixon's downfall brightened the image of some of his predecessors and one of his successors. Ford's greatest achievement was to restore respectability to the tarnished Republican government in Washington, and this was no mean feat. As for Nixon's predecessors, the legend to Truman's greatness was sharply revived, while people forgot about his mink-coated "dynasty." Eisenhower and his eight years of peace looked better by contrast with the Nixon record.

The Presidential image grows or declines even after death. Packets of old letters are found, scandals are exposed or revived, offspring write books, and money-hungry paramours employ imaginative ghost writers to net millions. Most or all of these affairs, if true, have had little or no relation to the conduct of the office. Also ironically, nothing convincing of a sexual nature has been hung on Nixon. He has major sins to answer for.

Thomas A. Bailey
January 1978

Foreword

Next to a child's version of the Bible, the first book I remember is a juvenile *Lives of Our Presidents*, which my mother read to us children while we were grouped at her knee. The present volume reflects a lifelong interest not only in the Presidents but also in the relation of public opinion to American history. It is a new look at old stereotypes rather than a dirt-farming piece of research. Even so, I have developed more than a nodding acquaintance with the published writings of many of the Presidents. Additionally, and in connection with preparing other books, I have examined substantial parts of the manuscript collections of Presidents Cleveland, Mc-Kinley, Theodore Roosevelt, Taft, Wilson, and Hoover.

If the reader suspects me of partisan bias, I can only reply that I am an independent in politics. I cast my first presidential vote in 1924 (with misgivings), and beginning with that election have supported the nominee of one major party six times and that of the other major party five times (each time with misgivings). Perhaps 1968 will even things up.

I offer this book with more humility than its contents suggest. If the reader is startled by my boldness in challenging the judgments of scores of fellow historians, I can plead in my defense that they do not agree among themselves. Even the late Dr. Arthur M. Schlesinger, Sr., who conducted two famous polls among experts, has pointed out that he himself did not concur completely in their findings.

Some readers whose knowledge of the American presidency is hazy may wish to straighten out the chronology by reading my last three chapters first.

Dozens of individuals have proved helpful, either through correspondence or in person, including a former President, three former presidential candidates, and two ex-Secretaries of State, one presidential assistant, and one justice of the Supreme Court. I herewith express my sincere thanks without implicating them. Several of my friends (also without incrimination, I hope) have read all or substantial parts of the manuscript: Dr. Clarence C. Clendenen, Dr. Alexander DeConde, Dr. Frank Freidel, Dr. Rodney G. Minott, Dr. Raymond G. O'Connor, and Dr. E. Berkeley Tompkins. I acknowledge their helpfulness with gratitude and thanks.

Thomas A. Bailey

Contents

PART II. The Testing of Presidential Reputations

PART I

The Making of Presidential Reputations

"Reputation is an idle and most
false imposition; oft got without merit,
and lost without deserving."

WILLIAM SHAKESPEARE (*Othello*), 1604

CHAPTER I

Presidential Cults and Cultists

> "A nation reveals itself not only by the men it produces but also by the men it honors, the men it remembers."
>
> JOHN F. KENNEDY, 1963

THE WASHINGTON-LINCOLN DEIFICATION

A statesman is often cynically defined as a dead politician. The American people are prone to place their Presidents—especially the dead ones—on a pedestal rather than under a microscope. One result has been the formation of cults, which immensely complicate the task of trying to arrive at a true appraisal of presidential greatness. The cultists, with their excessive devotion to heroes, are instinctively involved in a conspiracy to hide the warts, moles, and other blemishes.

The George Washington cult, intimately associated with the Constitution cult, is the oldest. Its hero personifies the American Revolution—a glorious achievement of world-shaking importance. Unlike all other Presidents, he preceded political parties, largely rose above them, and hence can be claimed by all Americans. Conspicuous among the outward trappings of his cult is the cloud-piercing monument in the city which bears his name but which he modestly called the Federal City. In many ways more attractive than this marble obelisk are the residence and tomb at Mount Vernon, by far the most visited of the presidential homes. The im-

3

mortal name of Washington is also attached to one state and thirty-one counties, to say nothing of cities, towns, townships, islands, parks, sounds, lakes, mountains, schools, and colleges.

The Lincoln cultists have one bond in common with the Washington cultists: they regard criticism as unholy. If the Father of his Country is godlike, the Great Emancipator is Christlike—"the mystic mingling of star and clod." The Lincoln cult sprang into existence overnight, spawned by the martyrdom at Ford's Theater, which is now a Lincoln Museum. Across the street stands the house where the victim died, now administered by the National Park Service. We also have the Lincoln Boyhood Memorial in Indiana, consisting of two hundred acres, and the New Salem State Park in Illinois, with its reconstruction of the village in which Lincoln once lived. More important are the house in Springfield (the only one he ever owned) and the birthplace cabin near Hodgenville, Kentucky, now piously enclosed in a marble memorial building and dignified as a national historic site. Above all stand the impressive tomb in Springfield and the magnificent Lincoln Memorial in Washington, D.C.

The Lincoln cult boasts other trappings as well. Numerous names on the land include sixteen counties, plus the capital of Nebraska, as well as cities, parks, mountains, highways, schools, and colleges. Countless millions of schoolchildren are required to memorize the deathless Gettysburg Address and the peroration, among other immortal Lincoln passages, of the second inaugural, beginning "With malice toward none. . . ." There is in addition an incredible flood of adulatory Lincoln literature, including countless apocryphal sayings and anecdotes.

JEFFERSON'S BELATED CANONIZATION

The Jefferson cult is less formidable than Lincoln's but real. It is partially embodied in the monument in Washington and, perhaps more important, in the baronial home at Monticello, where stands the simple tombstone with its moving inscription. The cult is further bolstered by the names of twenty-six counties, not to mention the capital of Missouri and other cities, plus summer resorts, mountains, rivers, schools, and colleges. Nor can we overlook the resounding Declaration of Independence, which used to be read annually at

Fourth of July gatherings and was memorized—at least its sonorous preamble and peroration—by a host of rebellious schoolboys.

But Jefferson, unlike the central figure of some other cults, can be criticized with relative impunity. This may partially explain why his monument in Washington was not erected until the 1940's, the era of sympathetic New Dealers. During his lifetime his enemies were numerous, outspoken, and influential. As a deist, he antagonized the orthodox clergy. As an aristocrat who helped wipe out aristocratic privileges in Virginia, he alienated the well born. As a peace lover and anti-militarist, he irked the advocates of preparedness. As a Democratic-Republican, he offended the Federalists. As an idealist, he estranged the hardheaded. As a long-time and admiring resident of Europe, he provoked the America-firsters. Many of his most quotable statements, often penned in private and with obvious exaggeration, seem like the ravings of an unbalanced mind, such as "A little rebellion now and then is a good thing." He would be investigated if he were here today. And he left office under something of a cloud, not as a martyr to a cause, but as one who had crucified himself on his ill-starred embargo policy.

THE ENSHRINEMENT OF WILSON

The Wilson cult is vigorous and vocal, though it boasts few visible tabernacles. The birthplace at Staunton, Virginia, though imposing for a Presbyterian manse, is not a palatial residence. The home that Wilson built in Princeton, now privately owned, features Tudor architecture, thus reflecting his ingrained Anglophilism. The three-story brick residence on S Street in Washington, where he died, now a memorial, is not pretentious. There is as yet no national monument, and there were few unnamed places of importance left when he attained fame. (His name is attached to a dam in the Tennessee Valley project.) His remains were entombed in the unfinished National (Episcopalian) Cathedral in Washington, beside those of Admiral George Dewey, and awaiting those of his beloved second wife, who joined him in 1961. The campaign to turn this imposing Gothic edifice into a kind of Westminster Abbey has made little headway.

But the memory of Wilson is cherished, almost fanatically, by the thousands who recognized him as a martyr to a glorious cause.

Battling for a League of Nations that would lift the curse of war from mankind, he broke himself down and suffered a living martyrdom for nearly four and one-half years. Criticism of the fallen warrior seemed to be unsporting, even sacrilegious. Numerous adulatory books and pamphlets have honored his vision and courage. The Woodrow Wilson Foundation of New York was launched in 1922 with financial contributions from devoted followers, headed by the recently crippled Franklin D. Roosevelt. It proved to be an effective agency for keeping alive the name of the far-visioned Princetonian and the ideals for which he fought. At times he seemed to be almost a religious, rather than a political, issue.

The Wilson cult—a secular cult—has sunk deep roots. For many years the Woodrow Wilson Foundation maintained a Wilson Library in New York, from which it issued approved book lists. The early ones tended to omit titles that were critical, in the manner of a papal index in reverse. In 1963 the Foundation decided to concentrate its funds on the publication of the vast collection of Wilson papers, and this is now being done at Princeton University under the auspices of the leading Wilson scholar, Dr. Arthur S. Link.

In recent years several thousand Woodrow Wilson fellowships have been awarded by another foundation to gifted college students to finance their graduate work, especially if they aspire to be university teachers. The recipients of these stipends presumably entertain kindly feelings toward the President who is thus honored by the benefaction they enjoy. If they ultimately teach American history, their goodwill toward the professor-President may well be reflected in the classroom. Certainly many beneficiaries of the Rhodes scholarships feel well disposed toward England and Cecil Rhodes, just as their donor intended.

HEROES ON HORSEBACK

The Jackson cult is much less formidable. This is rather surprising when one considers the heroic military figure, the flamboyant man-on-horseback statue in Washington, the splendid Tennessee home at the Hermitage, and the simple tomb in the garden graveyard. Even so, the popular Old Hero's name is attached to twenty-two counties, in this respect ranking behind thirty-one for Washington and twenty-six for Jefferson. It is also attached to the capital of Mississippi and to numerous other towns and cities, to say nothing of mountains and lakes.

Until recent decades, Jackson has generally been downgraded by historians. His ruthless crushing of the Bank of the United States, an eminently sound if arrogant "Monster," raised grave doubts as to his statesmanship.

Foremost among Jackson's critics were the Whigs and Republicans of the 19th century. As fate would have it, they were the men who wrote most of the nation's history. Jackson's lack of scholarly attainments, marked by poor spelling and grammar, rasped the intellectuals, who did and still do most of the teaching and writing. His birthday is generally ignored. The annual Jackson Day dinners of the Democrats commemorate not his birth but his devastating victory over the British at New Orleans, January 8, 1815.

Theodore Roosevelt was the last great American on horseback, but his cult has not shown the vigor that the Rough Rider displayed during his overvigorous lifetime. One reason is that he was partially overshadowed by a younger scion of the Roosevelt clan. "Our Teddy" was shot in the chest by a fanatic during the presidential campaign of 1912, while "battling for the Lord" (and a "third term") as a Bull Moose. If he had only died, the cult could have boasted a glorious martyr—one fighting the good fight for Progressivism. But the tough old Bull Moose survived, and his anguished bellowings at President Wilson from 1913 to 1919 were often more embarrassing to his friends than bothersome to his foes.

The Rough Rider's centennial in 1958 excited much less interest than that of Wilson. Even so, his name is attached to two Western counties, a borough, a town, a mountain range in Greenland, the giant dam on the Salt River in Arizona which he had sponsored, and the Brazilian River of Doubt. The foolhardy exploration of this stream in 1914 nearly cost him his life, but resulted in the Rio Roosevelt, now officially the Rio Teodoro.

THE ROOSEVELT-KENNEDY MARTYRDOMS

We are today witnessing the formation of cults to honor our two most recently martyred Presidents: Franklin D. Roosevelt and John F. Kennedy. What a cult needs perhaps more than anything else, as was notably true of Lincoln, is a martyr.

Franklin Roosevelt was a martyr in the sense that he died in the harness and on the eve of victory over the fearsome forces of aggression. He sacrificed his life, in a manner of speaking, not to make the world safe for democracy but to make the world safe against dictatorship. He is still too controversial a figure for us to expect an elaborate monument in Washington. Ironically, the anti-third-term "Franklin Roosevelt Amendment," adopted in 1951, was something of a monument in reverse—a kick at his corpse. But he still commands the admiration, not to say adoration, of now-old New Dealers. The history of the era is being taught in our colleges and universities by men and women who, in many instances, approved of him and even voted for him. The impressive presidential library at Hyde Park in itself serves as a kind of shrine. Grateful Britishers have also erected a statue of him in Grosvenor Square, London, opposite the American Embassy with its thirty-five-foot eagle. His own countrymen, in 1965, dedicated a modest marble memorial to him, on a site near the Pennsylvania Avenue in Washington that he knew so well.

John F. Kennedy was martyred, in the same sense as Lincoln, and in a way that presents amazing parallels to the Lincoln assassination. His funeral was witnessed, both in person and on television, by many more millions than reverently viewed the Lincoln bier. His tomb, with an eternal flame, is to be erected at Arlington, overlooking the Lincoln Memorial. The library museum for his presidential papers, a kind of secondary shrine, is to be constructed by popular subscription at Harvard University, at a site on the banks of the Charles that he had chosen. An airport, a cape, a mountain, streets, and many other places have been named or renamed in his memory.

President Kennedy, chopped down in his prime, was an attractive young man—intelligent, articulate, vibrant, idealistic. But he will probably be honored more for what he sought—the ideals of world peace and human brotherhood—than for what he actually accomplished. The assassin killed not only a President but the promise of a President. As Woodrow Wilson demonstrated, a martyr with unrealized ideals of a universal nature is prime material for an enduring cult. Some cynic has remarked that there is one thing worse than ideals unattained, and that is ideals attained.

NATAL DAYS AND HOLIDAYS

Birthday observances, especially those designated as legal holidays in the various states, are intimately associated with national cults and serve to strengthen them.

A glance at the year 1900 is revealing. George Washington's birthday was a legal holiday in every one of the then forty-five states, except Mississippi. Lincoln's birthday was similarly recognized in only eight of the states, all of them in the North. Robert E. Lee was thus honored in five states, all in the South, and Jefferson Davis in two states, both in the South.

By 1965 all of these celebrities had gained ground, except George Washington. Two of the now fifty states—Louisiana and Nevada—either did not honor his birthday as a legal holiday or had no provision for proclaiming it as such. Lincoln's birthday was legally observed or observable by governor's proclamation in thirty-three of the states. Significantly, Tennessee was the only one of the eleven states of the Confederacy that recognized Lincoln's birthday as a legal holiday, although Arkansas authorized its observance by proclamation of the governor. Tennessee is a maverick probably because it was the only one of the "wayward eleven" that came back into the fold in time to escape the bitterness of military reconstruction.

The Lincoln cult has obviously not sunk as deep roots into Southern soil as it has elsewhere in the Republic. George Washington, a national heritage, was essentially a non-partisan; Abraham Lincoln, a Northerner, was a Republican—and a "black Republican" at that. Not every Southerner can forget that if Lincoln had not held on with bulldog grip, the Confederacy would have made good its gamble to establish an independent republic. The blood of several hundred thousand Southern boys stained his hands, and his assassination was greeted with shortsighted cries of satisfaction by many dyed-in-the-wool Confederates.[1]

Anti-Lincolnism is long adying. A generation or so ago the first task of Southern pupils at the beginning of a new year was to rip the picture of Old Abe out of their textbooks. Harry Truman's

---

[1] President Kennedy's murder was similarly applauded in 1963 by some Southern extremists who resented his efforts to force racial integration on them.

Missouri grandmother, who had suffered from Yankee raiders, scolded him for entering the house in the blue uniform of the National Guard. His mother, who had approved of Lincoln's assassination, rebuked him when, as President, he laid a wreath at the Lincoln Memorial. The bitterness of the Civil War had largely subsided when the controversy over desegregation, triggered by the Supreme Court decision of 1954, tore open old wounds. One hundred years after the Emancipation Proclamation tens of thousands of white Southerners—some in white sheets—were dug in to thwart the fruition of the Great Emancipator's work.

Other American Presidents receive similar but scattering recognition. Thomas Jefferson's birthday is observed or observable in four states, all south of the Mason-Dixon line, and including his native Virginia. Andrew Jackson, the Carolinian, is so honored by his adopted state, Tennessee. Kentucky is the only state thus far formally to observe the birthday of Franklin Roosevelt.

THE CAPITOL'S PANTHEON

Each state is privileged, by Congressional act of 1864, to place two statues of its most distinguished citizens in the nation's Capitol, in either Statuary Hall or the Rotunda. Most of the states now have two, although some have only one, and a few none. The varying sizes and types of statues, as well as their jumbled placement, have led to the quip "Chamber of Horrors."

Little significance can be attached to these choices. Many seem to have been made on a hit-or-miss basis, often by politically motivated legislatures responding to sectional passion or pride. Virginia chose the immortal George Washington but passed over the hardly less exalted Thomas Jefferson in favor of the beloved war hero, General Robert E. Lee. Woodrow Wilson, Virginia-born but domiciled in New Jersey, came along too late in the day. Tennessee selected its transplanted son, Andrew Jackson, and Ohio chose its assassin-martyred President James A. Garfield.

Priorities explain some of these presumed oversights. In a few cases two luminaries were already honored before the more eminent figures emerged. This apparently was the case with New York, which selected George Clinton, Father of the Erie Canal, and Robert R. Livingston, co-purchaser of Louisiana, before President

Grover Cleveland and the two Roosevelts came along. We are rather surprised to find that the illustrious Lincoln is claimed by neither Kentucky, Indiana, nor Illinois. Perhaps he fell among three stools. The two presidential Adamses, for reasons not altogether clear, were rejected by Massachusetts in favor of two other celebrities: Samuel Adams, the master propagandist of the Revolution, and John Winthrop, stalwart founder of the Old Bay Colony.

An assessment of eminence is thus too often left to chance, caprice, or prejudice. Much depends on the frame of mind of the person or persons making the final judgments. And here we encounter a labyrinth of legend, tradition, patriotism, sectionalism, sentimentalism, politics, and plain ignorance.

Greatness, by its very nature, is difficult if not impossible to define. An indefinable aura clings to a great poem, a great statue, a great painting, a great cathedral, a great statesman. By definition, an aura cannot be seen; it can only be sensed. But some critics manage to see it; others sense it, even when it is not present; and still others fail to sense it when it is there.

CHAPTER II

The People's Choice

"To add brightness to the sun or glory to the
name of Washington is alike impossible."

ABRAHAM LINCOLN, 1842

BORGLUM'S BIG FOUR

Towering majestically over all other monuments erected to the
Presidents are the sixty-foot granite busts in Mount Rushmore Memorial Park, in the Black Hills of South Dakota. Completed in 1941,
they honor Washington, Jefferson, Lincoln, and Theodore Roosevelt.
Viewed each year by tens of thousands of awed tourists, they have
helped crystallize the impression that these were the four greatest
Presidents.

Much misunderstanding persists as to the selection of the colossal
quartet. The final choice was not made by a commission of historical
experts, but by the sculptor himself, Gutzon Borglum. An individualist of the old school and a temperamental prima donna as
well, he heatedly defended his choices against all comers. The
devotees of Woodrow Wilson were distressed not to find their hero
there, in the place of his gadfly, Theodore Roosevelt. Much later,
after the advent of Franklin Roosevelt, some agitation developed
to add the dynamic New Dealer. But Borglum resisted any addi-
tions, alleging, among other arguments, that there was not enough
granite left in the grouping.

Of the four finally chosen, the selection of the tempestuous "Teddy" Roosevelt evoked the most debate. Many critics argued that he was of such recent vintage that proper perspective was lacking. But Borglum stuck grimly to his guns. His choice was probably not unrelated to the fact that both he and Senator Peter Norbeck of South Dakota, a prime pusher of the project, had been ardent Roosevelt Bull Moosers in 1912.

Borglum was clever enough not to label his choices *the* four greatest Presidents. Nor did he claim that they were the four greatest Americans. He was merely honoring the four eminent statesmen who, in his view, best represented the growth of the United States and its ideals during its first century and a half. George Washington symbolized the founding of the nation. Thomas Jefferson, whose Louisiana Purchase actually embraced the Mount Rushmore site, represented the expansion of the Republic and the spirit of its continental growth. Abraham Lincoln best portrayed the preservation of the Union. Theodore Roosevelt reflected the emergence of America as a great world power in the 20th century, as highlighted by his acquisition of the Panama Canal Zone. He also exemplified the need for conserving the nation's natural resources, especially in the West. If Roosevelt seems like a maverick in this group, his presence may be further justified by his experience as a cattleman and ranch owner in the Badlands of the Dakotas, some two hundred miles away.

Whatever Borglum's merits as a sculptor—and they are hotly disputed—he took a narrow and imperialistic view of American history. He proposed also to etch in bronze a five-hundred-word history of the Republic to be written by President Coolidge about eight epochal events.[1] These were the Declaration of Independence, the framing of the Constitution, the purchase of Louisiana, the annexation of Texas, the settlement of the Oregon boundary dispute, the admission of California as a state, the conclusion of the Civil War, and the construction of the Panama Canal.

If expansion was Borglum's main theme, as it evidently was, then President Polk had stronger claims to a place of honor than Roosevelt. He had secured Oregon and California and had validated the nation's claim to Texas. All these territorial gains, though achieved

[1] This part of the scheme was dropped after Borglum undertook to rewrite Coolidge's version, and an unseemly dispute resulted.

by dubious means, were more impressive than Roosevelt's precarious ten-mile-wide leasehold in Panama, also achieved by dubious means.

But Borglum, sculptor-turned-historian, was not to be shouted down. If he made an error in including the Rough Rider, it will not be easy to erase. Geologists estimate that the granite faces will withstand the elements for tens of thousands of years. Countless Americans will meanwhile be persuaded that this gigantic quartet is the choice of the experts as the four most distinguished Presidents.

THE NEW YORK UNIVERSITY HALL OF FAME

A highly publicized attempt to separate eminent Americans from their lesser fellows came with the opening of the Hall of Fame for Great Americans at New York University. It was formally dedicated, literally with much fanfare, in 1901. Bronze busts of the elite were appropriately displayed in a curving, open-air colonnade, looking out on the pleasant vista of the Harlem and Hudson River valleys.

The selection system was elaborate, and initially involved a panel of about one hundred experts, chosen from most of the states. There were fifteen categories of eminence, including "Rulers, Statesmen." One oddity was that while there were historians on the panel to choose statesmen, there were also experts on music, painting, and other unrelated fields. All the electors were asked to vote, and most of them presumably voted on personages outside the area of their competence. One is reminded of Herbert Spencer's sour jibe: "A jury is a group of twelve people of average ignorance."

The first election, that of 1900, enshrined five former Presidents among the twenty-nine celebrities chosen. They were George Washington, John Adams, Thomas Jefferson, Abraham Lincoln, and Ulysses S. Grant. General Grant, as the Hero of Appomattox, was included more appropriately in the category of "Soldiers, Sailors," rather than "Rulers, Statesmen." (He was joined by his foeman at Appomattox, General Robert E. Lee, whose selection stirred up a storm of criticism in the North, even though thirty-five years had passed since the "late unpleasantness.") George Washington, not unexpectedly, amassed the unanimous vote of all ninety-seven electors. Abraham Lincoln, quite surprisingly, garnered ninety-six votes, as the Southerners on the jury rose above sectional prejudices. Thomas Jefferson polled ninety-one votes and John Adams sixty-two.

The Hall of Fame later honored other Presidents: John Quincy Adams and James Madison in 1905, Andrew Jackson in 1910, and James Monroe in 1930. Grover Cleveland achieved recognition in 1935, after having received votes once and having been passed over twice in the five-year elections. Theodore Roosevelt made the roster in 1950, on the second try, and Woodrow Wilson also in 1950, on the first try.

Certain observations are warranted. The suspicion arises that many of the distinguished electors of the Hall of Fame ("Hollow Fame," wrote one unintentional punster) are not well posted on what the most recent scholarship has uncovered about these Presidents. Statesmanlike achievements before attaining the presidency, or after leaving it, were taken into account, as they properly could be in this competition. Such inclusiveness naturally boosts the stock of less highly regarded Presidents like James Madison (Father of the Constitution), James Monroe (co-purchaser in France of Louisiana), and John Quincy Adams (later Old Man Eloquent of the House of Representatives).

GAUGING THE GREATEST AMERICAN

Arthur H. Vandenberg, a prominent Michigan newspaper man and later an outstanding United States Senator, published in 1921 the results of a different poll. In preparing his spirited book, *The Greatest American: Alexander Hamilton,* he solicited the views of one hundred and eight prominent personages as to who was the greatest. The pollees ranged from generals and governors to lawyers and clergymen.

About ten replied that an intelligent answer was impossible, partly because greatness was a "relative matter" and because it applied "to lines of life of a great variety." President W. H. P. Faunce of Brown University demurred that too much depended on one's definition of "greatness." "It is somewhat like asking which is the most beautiful flower or which is the best country to live in. . . ." Admiral W. S. Sims, stormy petrel of the Navy, objected that an answer could not be given because greatness comprised many different qualities. Ex-President Taft, who had sweated out four unhappy years in the White House, protested that an opinion was impossible, "first, because it is a question of definition upon which there is a great dif-

ference, and, second, because there might be difference as to the
facts, and, on the whole, as to the merits." George B. Cortelyou, who
had worked intimately with Presidents Cleveland, McKinley, and
Roosevelt in various capacities, insisted that "there is no common
basis of comparison." Dr. David Jayne Hill, former Ambassador to
Germany, declared that there was "no aristocracy of Americanism"
and that "whoever is the greatest of them would not like being
considered the greatest."

Although ten of the Vandenberg pollees were unwilling to name
the greatest American, ninety-eight responded. Abraham Lincoln
came out well ahead with fifty votes; George Washington ran second
with thirty. Washington and Lincoln, or either of these two in
combination with one or two others, netted nine votes. Theodore
Roosevelt polled three and Thomas Jefferson one. Five additional
votes were scattered among five non-presidential figures.

On the basis of these returns, Vandenberg concluded that
probably a majority of Americans regarded Lincoln as the greatest
man they had yet produced. But we should keep in mind several
relevant facts. Only five of the fifty pro-Lincoln votes came from
respondents born in the South, where the so-called Emancipator was
least revered. Fifteen of the Lincoln supporters were avowed Republicans or Independent Republicans. Such results are not surprising when we remember that these men were expressing a
preference not only for the first Republican President but also for
the patron saint of their party. Five of the pro-Lincoln voters were
Democrats, but only one of these was Southern-born or Southern-
domiciled.

George Washington, a distinguished son of Virginia, ran best in
his native South. Of the thirty persons voting for him, ten were
Southern-born, fourteen were Southern-educated, and thirteen were
Southern-domiciled. (In some cases these were the same people.)
Of the thirty who chose Washington, eleven were Democrats, and
eight were Republicans; of the eleven Democrats, seven were
Southern-born. We must conclude that sectional and partisan
considerations, in 1921 at least, were influential in choosing the
"greatest American."

The crowning paradox of Vandenberg's poll must now be revealed. After its sponsor had failed to secure a single vote for

Alexander Hamilton as the "greatest American," he proceeded to make out an eloquent and rather persuasive case for the brilliant young émigré from the West Indies. Such are the curiosities involved in assessing greatness.

LINE-SPACE PROMINENCE

A rule-of-thumb test of eminence is to measure the line-inches accorded the celebrity in the various biographical dictionaries and encyclopaedias. We should bear in mind that although such tests are mechanically precise, they are in a high degree subjective. The space-recognition accorded a man is often the arbitrary decision of the editor, who may know little about the biographee, or by a committee, which may know more but whose decision often is a compromise. In addition, many a long-winded author exceeds the space allotted him for his sketch. If he is persistent, and if the publication deadline is too near at hand to permit judicious cutting, he may gain inches for his hero. One of the editors of the *Dictionary of American Biography* advises me that although the contributors often exceed their wordage, their essays are frequently so admirable that they are accepted without question.

One of the most laborious exercises in measuring distinction was unveiled in 1903 by a psychologist, Professor J. McKeen Cattell of Columbia University, in the *Popular Science Monthly*. His self-imposed task was to single out the one thousand outstanding figures in world history by measuring the space they occupied in six different biographical dictionaries or encyclopaedias published in four countries: England (2), France (2), Germany (1), and the United States (1). No effort was evidently made to determine to what extent the encyclopaedists copied from or were influenced by one another.

Eight American Presidents made Cattell's rather mechanical honors list. Washington, Lincoln, and Jefferson, in that order, appeared among the top one hundred. General U. S. Grant and John Adams made the second one hundred, Andrew Jackson the third, and James Madison and John Quincy Adams the fifth. The high ranking given General Grant points up the fact that the entire career, not just the presidential tenure, was included in the entry. The final list results in the absurdity of comparing warriors with poets, statesmen with painters, politicians with playwrights. Few exercises are more futile than the comparison of unlikes.[2]

More revealing, but still misleading, is the space accorded the Presidents in the monumental *Dictionary of American Biography*, initially published in twenty volumes between 1928 and 1936. Only dead persons were eligible, but two supplementary volumes, completed in 1944 and 1958, undertook to accommodate the more recently deceased figures to December, 1940. Calvin Coolidge appeared in the first supplement, but Hoover, Franklin Roosevelt, Truman, Eisenhower, and Kennedy have thus far not been included.

If one measures the line-inches allotted to each of these Presidents, the following are the most significant rankings:

Ranking based on space given entire career	*Ranking based on space given the Presidency*
1. Jefferson	5 or 6 (ties with Washington)
2. Washington	5 or 6
3. Lincoln	2
4. Wilson	1
5. Madison	17 [3]
6. Grant	10
7. J. Quincy Adams	22
8. John Adams	7 or 8
9. Andrew Johnson	3
10. Theodore Roosevelt	4
11. Jackson	7 or 8
12. Coolidge	12
13. Buchanan	9
14. Cleveland	5

This table illustrates strikingly some of the difficulties involved in evaluating the Presidents. Jefferson's overall line-space is not surprising, although one may observe in passing that the editor of the *Dictionary*, Dr. Dumas Malone, contributed the sketch himself. He may not have felt under the same restraints as the other authors.

[2] The folly of taking this kind of rating too seriously is revealed by noting the first forty: Napoleon, Shakespeare, Mohammed, Voltaire, Bacon, Aristotle, Goethe, Julius Caesar, Luther, Plato, Napoleon III, Burke, Homer, Newton, Cicero, Milton, Alexander the Great, Pitt, Washington, Augustus, Wellington, Raphael, Descartes, Columbus, Confucius, Penn, Scott, Michelangelo, Socrates, Byron, Cromwell, Gautama [Buddha], Kant, Leibnitz, Locke, Demosthenes, Mary Stuart, Calvin, Molière, Lincoln.

[3] To save space, this table is cut off at fourteen, although all twenty-nine Presidents through Coolidge were graded.

The influence of the non-presidential career in shaping the presidential image is underscored by the appearance of General Grant high on the list: he is widely regarded as one of the poorest Presidents. James Madison, John Quincy Adams, and James Buchanan also rank high, though, as we shall soon note, the professional historians do not generally give them a high rating as Chief Executives. The prominence accorded Andrew Johnson is surprising, particularly in view of his protracted quarrel with Congress and his subsequent impeachment. We are reminded anew that troubled nations have the longest history. Calvin Coolidge fares well in the space test, partly because he is the only one to appear in the supplements, where more elbowroom was evidently allowed the authors.

Two-term Presidents obviously have a heavy advantage over one-termers in consuming line-space. James K. Polk, who in recent decades has come to be regarded as a strong Executive, fares poorly in the *Dictionary of American Biography*, partly because he was a single-termer. Nor does the space allotted a President necessarily mean achievement: much may have been happening without his being able to do anything about it. This was painfully true of James Buchanan, who rates relatively high in space but low in accomplishment.

One can only repeat that space measurement is about the crudest possible form of assessment. In the last analysis, it rests only on a number of highly subjective judgments which, when added together, do not make objectivity.

THE CAPRICIOUS PUBLIC

Several of the national public opinion polls have touched on the problem of judging eminence. Thus far, none has published an attempted rating of *all* the Presidents.

Nearly a year after Pearl Harbor, *Fortune* magazine did some probing. It asked a national cross section of high-school students, both white and Negro: "Can you name two or three living Americans you would really call great?" The incorrigibly cheerful Franklin Roosevelt was then the war President; General Douglas MacArthur had recently conducted a vain but heroic defense of the Philippines; and Colonel James H. Doolittle had electrified the nation by a surprise carrier-bomber raid on Tokyo. Henry Ford, who had "put America on wheels," was contributing to the prodigies of production.

The white students named Roosevelt as the greatest (59.9 percent); General MacArthur second (58.2 percent); Colonel (by now General) Doolittle third (6.4 percent); and Henry Ford fourth (6.1 percent).

The Negro students evidently had different ideas and ideals. Roosevelt came first (37.3 percent); Joe Louis (a Negro), the current heavyweight boxing champion, second (28.2 percent); General MacArthur third (22.7 percent); and George Washington Carver fourth (20.0 percent). Dr. Carver, the gifted Negro scientist at Tuskegee Institute, was beginning to receive belated recognition for discovering hundreds of new uses for peanuts, sweet potatoes, soybeans, and other farm products.

Dr. George H. Gallup has also skirted the question of presidential distinction. He asked a cross section of the adult public in 1945: "Who do you think was the greater man, George Washington or Abraham Lincoln?" The respondents were not asked to limit their judgment solely to the presidential career, although in the case of Lincoln they did not have much choice.

The results were as follows:

Abraham Lincoln	42%
George Washington	22%
Equally great	28%
Uncertain	8%

Those positive souls who plumped for either Washington or Lincoln were then asked the reasons for their choices. The response revealed a curious mixture of myth, fact, and textbook clichés. Lincoln was most generally judged the greater man because he had been more democratic, had freed the slaves, had preserved the Union, and had come up "the hard way." Washington was judged the greater primarily because he "had won independence for us," had been the father of our country, the "first President," and had worked "under more trying conditions." A few naive souls voted for him because he had "never told a lie."

THE FRUITS OF POPULAR IGNORANCE

In July, 1945, shortly after Franklin Roosevelt's unexpected death, the National Opinion Research Center of the University of Denver took a hand in the game. It asked a nationwide cross section: "In

all the history of the United States who[m] do you regard as two
or three of the greatest men who have ever lived in this country?"
The question made no mention of Presidents, and the pollees were
not asked to pick the greatest man but the two or three greatest men.
This invitation threw the door wide open for multiple voting, with
the following curious results:

Franklin D. Roosevelt	61%
Abraham Lincoln	56%
George Washington	46%
Thomas Edison	11%
Woodrow Wilson	8%
General Eisenhower	7%
Thomas Jefferson	6%
General MacArthur	5%
Theodore Roosevelt	5%
Henry Ford	4%
Benjamin Franklin	4%
Harry Truman	3%
	216% [4]

This poll prompts certain reflections. One is that the public is
always influenced by "presentism." The war was not yet won in the
Pacific, and the current crop of heroes was still much in the head-
lines. Another not surprising conclusion is that the man in the street
has an extremely foggy knowledge of American history if this is
the best he can do in singling out the giants of the past. Finally, as
could have been predicted, the public preference runs heavily to
men of deeds: those who win battles or invent gadgets or make
machines, like the Eisenhowers, Edisons, and Fords. The Americans,
as a pioneer people on the go, have always been more impressed by
the doers than by the dreamers. Even so, in this particular poll
idealists like Wilson and Jefferson fared remarkably well.

An abortive Gallup poll of 1956 throws considerable additional
light on the complexities of our problem. The question was, "What
THREE United States Presidents do you regard as the GREAT-
EST?" The plan was to canvass some eighteen hundred respondents,
but the venture was abandoned after only a partial sample. The

---

[4] Percentages add to more than 100 because some respondents gave more
than one answer.

incomplete and unofficial results, hitherto unpublished, are as
follows:

F. D. Roosevelt	69%
Lincoln	64%
Washington	47%
Eisenhower	34%
Truman	16%
Wilson	14%
Theodore Roosevelt	9%
Jefferson	5%
Hoover	4%
Coolidge	2%
McKinley	1%
Others	1%
No answer, don't know	8%

This poll was probably abandoned when evidence mounted that
the workaday American does not know enough about our past to
give a meaningful response. Some of the pollees obviously could not
name three Presidents, aside from the incumbent. Others, presumably to conceal their ignorance, gave the only three names that
popped into their heads, including the reigning Eisenhower. Aging
beneficiaries of Social Security checks no doubt cast a grateful vote
for Franklin Roosevelt. Again we are impressed with the influence
of "presentism" in any historical judgment by the rank and file. "We
cannot escape history," declared Lincoln in his second annual
message to Congress. We certainly cannot escape the consequences
of it, as he indicated, but we do manage to escape a knowledge of it.

The historians themselves will have to be summoned for a less
vulnerable evaluation. But before turning to them we should observe
that the ill-informed pollee, as far as the top six Presidents are concerned, was not too badly out of line with the experts, except for
the inclusion of Eisenhower and Truman, and the exclusion of
Jefferson and Jackson. Paradoxically, Andrew Jackson, a Tennessee
horse racer of wide repute, ran out of the percentage money. The
hero tales of the grade-school readers and history texts evidently
did better by Washington and Lincoln, who were bound to come
out on top. Not to know that these two were the two greatest
naturally brands one an ignoramus—and an unpatriotic ignoramus
at that.

The Experts' Choice

"Do your duty and history
will do you justice."

HARRY S TRUMAN, 1948

THE SCHLESINGER SURVEYS

By far the most impressive polls relating to presidential greatness are the two that were conducted by Professor Arthur M. Schlesinger, Sr., of Harvard University. The first came in 1948; the second in 1962. The first solicited the views of fifty-five experts; the second, employing the same techniques, solicited the views of seventy-five experts, who included most of the original fifty-five. Of the seventy-five, fifty-eight were professional historians, six were political scientists, three were historians and political scientists, two were journalists, and the remainder represented scattered callings. Felix Frankfurter, a long-time friend of Dr. Schlesinger, was a justice of the Supreme Court. Commendably, the polls attempted to provide a geographical cross section of the country, and to attain even greater objectivity by seeking the opinions of three Britishers, including the well-informed Denis W. Brogan.

The instructions on the Schlesinger ballot were simple. All Presidents who had served an appreciable time were listed, including the recent incumbent, Dwight D. Eisenhower. Omitted were William H. Harrison and James A. Garfield, both of whom had served much less than a full year. After each President's name appeared a square designated A, B, C, D, and E. A signified Great; B, Near Great; C, Average; D, Below Average; and E, Failure. The pollees, most of whom were academicians long familiar with this letter-system of grading, were advised that, in the customary manner, they might shade their estimates by the addition of a plus or minus sign.

The only yardstick that Dr. Schlesinger set up was a partially negative one. "The test in each case," read the instructions, "is *performance in office,* omitting anything done before or after." Each respondent was advised, "If you care to state your criteria, do so." Some did.

THE SCHLESINGER POLLS

	1948 Poll		*1962 Poll*
		GREAT	
1.	Abraham Lincoln	1.	Abraham Lincoln
2.	George Washington	2.	George Washington
3.	Franklin D. Roosevelt	3.	Franklin D. Roosevelt
4.	Woodrow Wilson	4.	Woodrow Wilson
5.	Thomas Jefferson	5.	Thomas Jefferson
6.	Andrew Jackson		
		NEAR GREAT	
7.	Theodore Roosevelt	6.	Andrew Jackson
8.	Grover Cleveland	7.	Theodore Roosevelt
		8.	James K. Polk
			[Harry S Truman]
9.	John Adams	9.	John Adams
10.	James K. Polk	10.	Grover Cleveland
		AVERAGE	
11.	John Quincy Adams	11.	James Madison
12.	James Monroe	12.	John Quincy Adams
13.	Rutherford B. Hayes	13.	Rutherford B. Hayes
14.	James Madison	14.	William McKinley
15.	Martin Van Buren	15.	William Howard Taft
16.	William Howard Taft	16.	Martin Van Buren
17.	Chester A. Arthur	17.	James Monroe
18.	William McKinley	18.	Herbert Hoover
19.	Andrew Johnson	19.	Benjamin Harrison
20.	Herbert Hoover	20.	Chester A. Arthur
			[Dwight D. Eisenhower]
21.	Benjamin Harrison	21.	Andrew Johnson

BELOW AVERAGE

22. John Tyler		22. Zachary Taylor
23. Calvin Coolidge		23. John Tyler
24. Millard Fillmore		24. Millard Fillmore
25. Zachary Taylor		25. Calvin Coolidge
26. James Buchanan		26. Franklin Pierce
27. Franklin Pierce		27. James Buchanan

FAILURE

28. Ulysses S. Grant		28. Ulysses S. Grant
29. Warren G. Harding		29. Warren G. Harding

POLITICAL PREJUDICES

The party affiliation of the Schlesinger pollees is relevant, because the question of objectivity inevitably raises its bothersome head.

The political preference of scholars is apparently not so easy to discover as it once was; those celebrities who appear in *Who's Who in America* seem to be increasingly reluctant to list their party affiliation. Of the seventy-five persons consulted in the second Schlesinger poll, ten declared themselves to be Democrats; two, independent Democrats; and five, Republicans. If we may assume that this is a fair sampling, the Democrats outnumbered the Republicans slightly more than two to one. Roughly the same proportions hold for the fifty-five consulted in the first Schlesinger poll.

The pro-Democratic bias of the respondents is reflected in the results. Only two Republicans (Lincoln and Theodore Roosevelt) appear among the Big Eleven; the only two flat "Failures" (Grant and Harding) are both Republicans.

The truth is that an overwhelming majority of those who teach American history in our colleges and universities are Democrats,[1] and one should not be surprised to find this bias among the Schlesinger pollees. Their generally low grading of Republican Presidents was perhaps not so much an indictment of the men themselves as it was of the Republican philosophy, namely, that the Chief Executive must be an executor or caretaker of the rather passive type, rather than a strong activist or reformer of the type attractive to Democratic liberals. Beginning with Lincoln's death we have elected

[1] For a detailed explanation, see Appendix A, pp. 337–339.

twelve Republican Presidents and only six Democrats. At least five of the six Democrats were pronounced activists, unlike all twelve Republicans, except of course the superactive Theodore Roosevelt and possibly Herbert Hoover.

This ticklish question of political prejudice is closely tied in with the age and actual voting record of the respondents. Among the seventy-five scholarly participants in the 1962 poll, two were old enough to have voted for William McKinley and the Full Dinner Pail in 1900. Twenty could have voted for Theodore Roosevelt at least once; twenty-seven for ex-Professor Woodrow Wilson at least once; and over seventy, as far as age qualification was concerned, for ex-Governor Franklin Roosevelt at least once. One wonders if these experts, when filling out their questionnaires, had left these political preferences completely at the polling booths.

This blue-ribbon panel of seventy-five experts contains the names of a number of citizens who had actively entered the noisy arena of politics. Some had been outspoken champions of the New Deal and/or the New Frontier. Some had been conspicuous "Volunteers for Stevenson" or "Eggheads for Stevenson" in 1952 and 1956; others had been "Eggheads for Eisenhower" in 1952 and 1956. Professors are people, whatever their students may think, and again one wonders if a man can quickly switch a partisan's derby for a scholar's mortarboard without getting the two mixed. A justice of the Supreme Court will disqualify himself from sitting in judgment on a case which he has earlier passed upon in the lower courts. A strict regard for objectivity would suggest a similar course in a presidential poll.

HARVARDIAN HISTORY

Other features of the Schlesinger polls, relating to their objectivity, invite comment.

Birth, residence, and education, all of which may reveal sectional bias, should be noted. (We have already observed that white Southerners were prone to pick George Washington over Abraham Lincoln.) On the basis of population alone, the South of the Old Confederacy was entitled to nearly one-fourth representation in the Schlesinger polls. Actually, only one fifth of the pollees were born in the South, but this proportion is not badly out of line. Most of the respondents were concentrated in New England, the Middle Atlantic States, and the Middle West.

All of the seventy-five Schlesinger experts, except five, were college or university instructors. Only one eleventh of these were located in the Old South, and these figures point up the "brain drain" from the South to the generally more prestigious institutions of the North. Fourteen of the illustrious seventy-five had received their baccalaureate degrees in the South, but only seven had earned their Ph.D. degrees there. These statistics are not surprising because most of the high-quality graduate schools are to be found outside the South. The Northeast was represented by thirty-two Ph.D.'s, twenty of them from Harvard. All told, about half of the seventy-five respondents either had received degrees of one kind or another from Harvard, or had served on its faculty, either on a permanent or a temporary basis.

The heavy representation of Harvard University on this list is not strange. With its topflight faculty and other splendid facilities for graduate work, it attracts and hence trains a disproportionate number of brilliant young minds. And since Dr. Schlesinger served for thirty years as a member of this distinguished faculty, he naturally turned to colleagues, friends, former students, and other Harvard-connected scholars when he came to make up his panels.

But the strong Harvard coloration of the two groups probably accounts in part for the pro-Democratic slant. The American historians on the Harvard faculty, as is generally true in other leading universities, are overwhelmingly of a liberal or liberal-Democratic persuasion, and have been for many years. Dr. Schlesinger himself, in his autobiography published in 1963, states plainly that he has long had a strong preference for liberal or Democratic presidential candidates. A number of the former students whom he consulted in his polls had probably crystallized some of their judgments at his feet.

Nearly half of the historians whom Dr. Schlesinger polled, including six of his Harvard colleagues, are the authors or co-authors of college texts or high-school texts in American history, in some cases both. These volumes represent a substantial percentage of all basic guides published in the field. One would indeed be surprised if the liberal viewpoint of the Harvard history faculty, in a trickle-down fashion, had not in some degree influenced the responses of the non-Harvard pollees.

THE POLLSTERS' PITFALLS

The ratings of the two Schlesinger polls, as already presented in parallel columns (see pp. 24–25), are most revealing. We should observe that the list was expanded during the intervening fourteen years by the inclusion of Harry S Truman [2] and Dwight D. Eisenhower. Despite the shortness of perspective, Truman won a high ranking among the Near Greats. President Eisenhower, with even less perspective, appeared at the bottom of the Average group, alongside hapless Andrew Johnson, who narrowly escaped removal from office on trumped-up impeachment charges. One wonders whether the five-star General Eisenhower would have fared a bit better if the panel had not consisted so largely of Democrats, and if the alleged shortcomings of the Eisenhower administration, including the mythical "missile gap," had not been so recently attacked by Democratic orators. Dr. Schlesinger reported that some of his pollees, possibly Democrats, rated Eisenhower a Failure, while some, possibly Republicans, voted him a Near Great. A two-thirds majority put him much lower.

Good old American democracy consequently prevailed. Those Presidents who finally wound up in the various categories won their place by either a majority or a plurality. If, for example, Grover Cleveland received twenty votes as a Great, twenty-one as a Near Great, twenty as an Average, ten as a Below Average, and four as a Failure, he was rated a Near Great. Harrison the Elder was omitted from the polling on the ground that his one-month tenure was too short, and the same rule was applied to James A. Garfield, with his tragically shortened six months. If these two men were eliminated because their terms were too short, then perhaps the most recent incumbents should have been excluded because perspective was too short.

The Schlesinger experts are sometimes referred to as a jury, but the analogy is not altogether sound. Twelve jurors are asked to

[2] The "S" in Harry S Truman is not an abbreviation. One side of the family wanted the middle name Shippe; the other, Solomon. They compromised on a plain "S."

determine, on the basis of the evidence, whether the accused is guilty or innocent. They are not supposed to decide whether George ("Machine Gun") Kelly was a greater gangster than "Scarface" Al Capone. The panel of historians was faced with a more demanding task: they were not only asked to determine greatness but the degree of greatness.

REVERSIBLE JUDGMENTS

The two Schlesinger polls reveal a degree of consistency that is not at all remarkable when we remember the partial duplication of respondents. There was only one change which involved a shift from one broad category to another. Andrew Jackson, by a narrow margin, was dropped from the august company of the Great in 1948 to that of the Near Great in 1962. The readiest explanation is that in 1945 Arthur M. Schlesinger, Jr., had published his best seller and Pulitzer-prize winner, *The Age of Jackson,* a brilliant but controversial book which made a tremendous splash. It presented Old Hickory, the brawler and duelist from Tennessee, in a more favorable light than usual. Jackson even seemed to be a kind of John the Baptist for the recent New Deal. In particular, he was represented as having received massive voting support, hitherto little suspected, from the laborers of the Eastern cities. But a series of subsequent studies by other scholars, conducted on a city-by-city basis, challenged this particular thesis. The consequent dimming of *The Age of Jackson,* together with the fading of the New Deal, evidently was reflected in the dimming of the Jacksonian image in the 1962 Schlesinger poll.

Surprising fluctuations also developed within the five categories. Grover Cleveland, a sterling Democrat, dropped two notches, and barely hung on among the Near Greats. This change is difficult to explain, except possibly that by 1962 the bloom had worn off Allan Nevins' admiring interpretation in a Pulitzer-prize biography, *Grover Cleveland: A Study in Courage* (1932). Perhaps the 19th-century rugged individualism of stubborn Old Grover did not fit into the hope-freighted atmosphere of Kennedy's New Frontier. On the other hand, James K. Polk, in keeping with the tendency to upgrade the first "dark-horse" President in recent biographical studies, rose two notches.

Within the Average group, James Monroe, the Last of the Cocked Hats, unaccountably dropped five places. The Monroe Doctrine, to which his name is imperishably attached, had lost some of its potency, with the Soviets defiantly entrenched in Cuba, and perhaps some of Monroe's glamor had sunk in the Caribbean.

James Madison, traditionally portrayed as weak Little Jemmy, rose three notches, probably as a result of Irving Brant's monumental six-volume biography. There is a subtle implication that any man worthy of six volumes, in this age of high-cost publication, must have been a high-quality statesman. In any event, the theme of the Brant volumes was that their hero had been unfairly represented (as indeed he had been to some extent), and that he should rank with the more masterful and aggressive of the Presidents. One need only add that the author's heroic effort is generally regarded by the experts as having fallen somewhat short of proving his thesis. The miserably botched War of 1812, which Madison both welcomed and directed, is a classic example of how wars should not be fought, even though the blame was not all his.

Other shifts in Dr. Schlesinger's Average group are interesting. The dudish Chester A. Arthur, one of the surprisingly able "accidental" Presidents, dropped three points, for reasons not altogether clear. William McKinley, once branded as Wobbly Willie, rose an impressive four places, probably as a result of the efforts of scholars in recent years to show that he was a remarkably effective manager of Congress. Far from being the spineless tool of Mark Hanna, he displayed commendable decisiveness in arriving at some important decisions. Andrew Johnson, the tormented tailor, dropped two points —perhaps he should have dropped more. He suffered from the correctives applied by Eric L. McKitrick in his study of Andrew Johnson, to say nothing of the findings of other scholars. Drab Benjamin Harrison, the Centennial President, unaccountably rose two places, except that a worthy two-volume biography was published in the 1950's by Harry J. Sievers, bringing the story of his life through the election of 1888.

Herbert Hoover, the erstwhile boy-wonder, also rose two points. He had published prolifically since leaving the presidency, including some observations on fishing which revealed a rather unsuspected sense of humor. (". . . All men are equal before fish.") After World War II he had undertaken the coordination of food supplies to dozens of countries impoverished by the war, and his travels in unpressurized aircraft had brought on severe deafness. Under President Truman he was made head of the Hoover Commission to study the reorganization of the Executive branch of the government, and his memorable report resulted in President Eisenhower's asking him to head the second Hoover Commission to make recommendations as to policy.

Time heals all wounds, including those of the Great Depression, which gradually fades into ancient history. Many Americans have a slightly guilty feeling that they booed Hoover unjustly, and this disquietude, together with his subsequent public service, probably has influenced some historians unduly. Certainly they treat him more gently than the voters did in 1932.

Dr. Schlesinger's Below Average group contains few surprises. Sober-visaged Calvin Coolidge, who left office as one of our most popular prosperity Presidents, has never been a favorite of scholars. His stock continued to drop here by two points, though not as drastically as the Big Bull Market of 1929. Roughhewn and tobacco-spitting Zachary Taylor unaccountably rose three places, possibly because several recent biographies have revealed him more fully. To know all is to forgive all, as the proverb has it. Or perhaps better, the more publicity, the more stature.

The two Failures of the first Schlesinger poll were still Failures in the second—the bewildered Grant and the harassed Harding. To give the Devil his due, something can be said for both scandal-beset men. They were both obvious misfits, but so, to some extent, were Andrew Johnson, John Quincy Adams, William H. Taft, and Herbert Hoover. As for scandals, we have never had an administration completely free of them, although the political vultures never had it so good as in the era of good stealings presided over by Grant and Harding.

PROFESSORIAL FALLIBILITY

The Schlesinger polls, both published in nationally circulated journals—*Life* and *The New York Times Magazine*—provoked widespread comment and considerable dissent. Newspaper editorials, as well as scores of letters and postcards mailed to the author, "registered anguish or assent—mostly anguish," wrote Dr. Schlesinger of the first poll. The foes of Franklin Roosevelt objected bitterly to his being placed above Wilson, Jefferson, and Jackson and only slightly below Washington, the great father image. One New Yorker wrote, "I will agree that FDR was great if by that is meant great liar, great faker, great traitor, great betrayer." Franklin Roosevelt had died only three years earlier, and bitterness against That Man in the White House was still gnawing the vitals of countless anti-New Dealers. The Schlesinger poll was published almost simultaneously with the presidential election of 1948, when "Give 'em Hell" Harry Truman, who had been Roosevelt's Vice President, engineered the upset of the century by defeating an overconfident Thomas E. Dewey. The frustration of many Republicans, who had seen defeat "snatched from the jaws of victory," was directed at Dr. Schlesinger's scholarly appraisal.

The second Schlesinger poll likewise became something of a storm center, though a less violent one. Dissatisfaction was voiced, chiefly by Republicans, against rating peppery Harry Truman a Near Great and downgrading the perennially popular Eisenhower to the near bottom of the Average group. But such are the occupational hazards if one chooses to deal with recent political combustibles.

These two scholarly polls are certainly the most impressive and highly publicized attempts thus far made to assess presidential performance. One would be hard pressed, with geography in mind, to assemble a more distinguished panel of historical scholars. It is a veritable honor roll of American historians, and includes five past presidents of the American Historical Association, and a dozen or so winners of Pulitzer prizes. Most of the weaknesses of the two polls were built in and hence unavoidable. Such a group of experts could not be assembled without including members of the two political parties. No one would want pollees so little interested in their government that they had not voted in past presidential elections. We could solicit the views of Australian scholars, if we wished to run objectivity into the ground. But their objectivity would verge on know-nothingness, and that would be even less desirable than a tolerable amount of subjectivity.

The brilliance of the Schlesinger panels casts a warmer glow over their votes than the facts warrant. Americans tend to be unduly impressed by big names. The results of the two polls reflect opinions, not facts. The opinion in most cases was a relatively well-informed one, but it was an opinion nevertheless. As Dr. Schlesinger himself concedes, "A judgment of historians is not necessarily the judgment of history, but at any given moment it is the best available without awaiting the sifting process of time." There is an element of truth in the observation of Bertrand Russell: "Even when the experts all agree, they may well be mistaken." The Schlesinger polls represent a jury of historians standing before the bar of history, but we must remember that juries sometimes hang the wrong man.

The rule of the majority or plurality in these polls introduces a necessary but disquieting element. One is reminded of Horace Mann's remark: "We go by the major vote, and if the majority are insane, the sane must go to the hospital." The differences between the poll of 1948 and that of 1962 illustrate the fallibility of human judgment. Some of the Presidents rose or fell by five or six notches, often for no clearly discernible reason. Let us suppose that a similar poll is conducted after a similar gap of fourteen years, that is to say in 1976, with many of the survivors of both polls included. We may get another differential of four or five points, for a total of eight or ten. Yet the achievements of the past Presidents remain unchanged.

"God cannot alter the past," wrote Samuel Butler, "that is why He is obliged to connive at the existence of historians." In this instance, all that changes is the opinion of the scholars, and that is controlled by many forces, many of them subjective. Included are party biases, personal experiences, sectional prejudices, one's information or lack of it, one's philosophy of government, the findings of recent scholarship, new fashions in interpretation, and the current atmosphere. In some respects the Schlesinger polls revealed more about the professors than about the Presidents.

THE GREAT GAME OF GREATNESS

Presidential polls are something of a parlor game, and as such should not be taken too seriously. A former official of the American Historical Association relates how a group of historians, when they gathered informally, would play the game of selecting the one hundred greatest historians of all time. This no doubt was useful as an icebreaker or for stimulating dinner table conversation, especially if wives were not present. As time wore on and reputations were ruptured or revived, names would be dropped or added. But it was still a game, much like the game of picking the greatest Presidents or pinning the tail on the donkey.

The Schlesinger polls, probably much more than their originator anticipated or wished, are now widely regarded as the law and the gospel. Various treatises by political scientists and others accept the ratings at their face value, and then take off from there. In 1961 Dr. Morton Borden edited a book of ten essays entitled *America's Ten Greatest Presidents.* He conceded in his preface that "rating America's Presidents is as personal and as difficult as handicapping thoroughbreds." But he accepted the Schlesinger ten because the pollster had found "a large measure of agreement among the experts" within the several categories.

All this suggests that rating the Presidents is not only a game that we can play with others but also with ourselves. Closed-mindedness leads to rigidity; open-mindedness, to constant revision. But we must never forget that comparing eminent figures is only a game, and a frustrating game at that. "Every great man is unique," observed Ralph Waldo Emerson in 1841. And what is in a class by itself can hardly be compared with something else in a class by itself.

CHAPTER IV

Measuring the Unmeasurable

"Make no Comparisons and if any of the Company be Commended
for any brave act of Vertue, Commend not another for the Same."

GEORGE WASHINGTON, *Rules of Civility*, 1748

THE QUEST FOR YARDSTICKS

A major stumbling block in assessing presidential greatness is
the impossibility of agreeing upon yardsticks.

Dr. Schlesinger, in both of his polls, neatly ducked this problem—
and with good reason. The only rule that he laid down was that the
pollees should ignore everything that the President had done before
or after attaining his high office. No one can quarrel with this exclusion, for some of the incumbents would rate higher as public
figures if they had never entered the White House. This is certainly
true of the egregious Grant and the glad-handing Harding. It is also
true of genuine statesmen like John Quincy Adams and Herbert
Hoover. Both of these men spent an agonizing four years in their
respective "hair shirts" (Hoover's phrase), although both were
internationally known figures before they were elevated to what
Jefferson called the "splendid misery" of the Presidential Palace.

But blotting out of mind everything that happened to a man before or after he became President is a neat trick. In the case of
Lincoln, Franklin Roosevelt, and Wilson, the task is fairly simple
because they had accomplished comparatively little before taking

the inaugural oath. Of the three, Wilson alone lived out his elected terms, only to retire to pathetic obscurity. But who can completely disassociate Jefferson from the authorship of the Declaration of Independence, the statute of Virginia for religious freedom, and the founding of the University of Virginia? As a man of enduring ideals rather than transient deeds, he requested the enshrinement of these three achievements on his tombstone. None of them related to the presidency. He completely ignored the record of his two administrations, including the fantastically fortunate Louisiana Purchase.

Jefferson's generally high standing among fellow scholars is no doubt due in part to such irrelevancies. Academicians are inclined to admire Minerva more than Mars, and they are probably less swayed than the ordinary citizen by Andrew Jackson's triumph at New Orleans or by Theodore Roosevelt's derring-do on Cuba's San Juan Hill. But this may be all that the workaday citizen remembers about them.

COMPARING THE NON-COMPARABLE

A more basic pitfall in attempting to measure presidential achievement is that we must compare unlikes. This is one of the reasons why some of the experts approached by Dr. Schlesinger declined to participate in his polls. Judging Presidents is not like judging those who play duplicate bridge; no two incumbents were ever dealt the same hand.

Back in my grade-school days we used to debate the question: Which is the more useful animal, the horse or the cow? We also used to debate the question: Who was the greater President, Washington or Lincoln? Not until later years did the absurdity of this whole business dawn on me. A good case could be made out for the horse in those smog-free days of the horseless carriage, but even today the sensible answer would be a cow for milk and meat but a horse for transportation and recreation. As for Washington and Lincoln, each was confronted in different eras by different tasks that called for different talents exercised at different tempos. Washington had to build the Union on solid foundations; Lincoln had to glue the pieces together again. One task was constructive, the other restorative.

We must also bear in mind that the presidency of today is not the presidency of yesterday. The Constitution of today, with its sheaf of amendments and Supreme Court interpretations, is not the Constitution of yesterday. The vast interlocking economy of today is not the barnyard economy of yesterday. The budget of each of the present-day states is far larger than Alexander Hamilton's in the 1790's, and many of our fifty commonwealths can now boast more wealth and population than some of the important European nations at the end of the 18th century.

When Washington took the inaugural oath in 1789, the population numbered nearly 4 million souls; when Lyndon Johnson took the inaugural oath in 1963, it numbered over 180 million souls. There were more people on the federal payroll in the days of Lyndon Johnson (some 5.3 million, counting the armed services) than there were inhabitants of the entire country at the beginning of Washington's administration. The few executive offices of 1789, which would rattle around in today's Pentagon, have swelled to a bulky bureaucracy. Even as recently as the 1880's a conscientious Grover Cleveland answered the White House telephone himself, although one must add that there were few such newfangled instruments in the land.

We honor Jefferson and Polk for adding vast and virgin vistas to the contiguous territory of the United States. But no President in the 20th century can duplicate these coups, unless by conquest of Canada and Mexico, and this is unthinkable. Perhaps he can acquire the moon or Mars, but such a feat would be out of this world. We are reminded anew of the absurdity of attempting to compare statesmen of different eras.

The powers and responsibilities of the presidential office have also expanded enormously. Andrew Jackson, who came along some forty years after Washington's inauguration, was the first President to veto bills in quantity—"government by veto." He regarded himself as the only official in the whole legislative process who represented the people of the entire nation, rather than those of a district or a state. He was also the first to veto bills not solely because he found them unconstitutional but because he found them unpalatable: he did not like them and would not have voted for them if he had been a member of Congress. The veto is now used so routinely and so effectively that the President in effect is a one-man "third house of

Congress." In this role he is equal to two thirds of both houses of Congress—or 66 Senators and nearly 300 Representatives.

In the 19th century the Chief Executive was supposed to be a "constitutional President," more or less a presiding officer of the "caretaker Buchanan type." He was expected to honor the delicate checks and balances by not treading on the toes of the legislative or judicial bodies. His function was to give Congress its head and not try to run the government uphill. All this, symbolically, was before the coming of the automobile. But most of the 20th-century Presidents, beginning with Theodore Roosevelt and Woodrow Wilson, undertook to lead Congress, and on occasion to drive or dominate it. The public came to regard them as remiss in their duty if they did not.

NEW ERAS, NEW RESPONSIBILITIES

The most spectacular expansion of presidential authority in recent decades has occurred in the arena of foreign affairs. As the Executive's powers have expanded at home, the theater in which he has exercised them has expanded abroad. Generally speaking, the bigger the jurisdiction, the bigger and hence more powerful the President.

In the pubescent period of the Republic all we asked for was to be let alone to pursue our peculiar destiny—later called Manifest Destiny (Manifest Desire?). We were wedded to isolation, neutrality, non-involvement, and non-entanglement. Monroe's now-famous warning of 1823, issued when we had only a tiny naval force in the vast Atlantic Ocean, was greeted with sneers and jeers by the crowned heads of Europe. The outside world scarcely knew we existed. Minister James Buchanan, while serving in St. Petersburg in the 1830's, met a well-educated Russian princess who asked if the United States still belonged to Britain, and if the English language was spoken there.

The oxcart era has long since creaked into the past. In Woodrow Wilson's day, the fate of Europe and of much of the rest of the world depended on White House decisions. In Franklin Roosevelt's day, the salvation of the world from the steely hand of dictatorship depended on presidential commitments and leadership. Beginning with the days of Truman, the halting of Communism and the bolstering of the free world against aggression became overwhelming preoccupations of the Chief Executive.

Some of the *new* functions exercised by President Truman (many of them also by his successors) are simply astounding. They would include Custodian of the Atomic Bomb, Backer-in-Chief of the United Nations, Prosecutor-in-Chief (War Crimes trials in Germany and Japan), Propagandist-in-Chief (Voice of America), Good-Samaritan-in-Chief (Truman Doctrine, Marshall Plan), Protector-in-Chief of the Free World (containment policy), Wager-in-Chief of the Cold War (Berlin Blockade, Korean intervention), Bolsterer-in-Chief of Backward Nations (Point Four), and Coordinator-in-Chief of an Alliance Network (Rio Pact, NATO, ANZUS). Today the President of the United States, now Space-Race Leader-in-Chief, is constantly confronted with decisions that involve the life and health of every inhabitant of the globe. He has a world constituency; if he sneezes, mankind catches cold.

Not only have presidential responsibilities increased in magnitude and multitude but the time factor has been correspondingly accelerated. Even President Wilson complained that in Washington's day the Chief Magistrate had time to think. In the pre-cable days of the 1850's and 1860's, grave international questions could simmer on the back burner. But today decisions of the gravest consequence must be made on a few hours' notice, without mature reflection, as was notably true of Truman's momentous decision to reverse the field and go into Korea in 1950.

In Washington's day the disquieting question was: Will the rest of the world let us live? Today the question is: Will the United States assume its responsibilities so that the rest of the free world can live?

Even if we could summon from their graves all the past Presidents, and administer the same tests to them, the results would still be misleading. If we are going to measure presidential achievement with any degree of precision, we shall need dozens of yardsticks, not one. We must ask ourselves, among other questions, how well the man did in view of the problems that faced him, the responsibilities that vexed him, the handicaps that shackled him (including an uncooperative Congress), the concept of presidential powers that limited him, and the current political and economic philosophy that restricted him. To compare Presidents of different centuries is somewhat like comparing a skilled oxcart driver of 1789 with a skilled jet-plane pilot of our time. We must conclude that without training neither man could do the job of the other, that the jet pilot needs vastly more training to do his job, and finally that the two jobs are simply non-comparable.

Another possible approach is suggested by the world of athletics. After intersectional football games, the sportswriters used to vote for the outstanding star of each contest. The honor usually went to a spectacular backfield man, while the burly lineman who cleared the path for the touchdowns was slighted. In more recent years the sportswriters have voted in several categories: backfield star, line star, or possibly defensive star. The scintillating Franklin Roosevelt was the quarterback type: in fact, he liked to describe himself in these terms. Rugged "Old Grover" Cleveland was more the defensive tackle. A high-quality tackle may be a more gifted player than a flashy halfback.

In short, we cannot properly compare the non-comparable—draft horses with thoroughbreds, veterinarians with surgeons, apples with oranges, pumpkins with peaches, British prime ministers with American Presidents, or the smile of "Mona Lisa" with that of Calvin Coolidge.

THE TEST OF TIME

If we decide that achievement is to be the ultimate test of presidential greatness, we run head on into other snags.

What about perspective? Many historians give Harry Truman a high mark for his decisive intervention in Korea, which presumably saved the United Nations from going down the old League of Nations drainpipe. But the last chapter has yet to be written. The Korean armistice is an uneasy one, and could explode overnight, with the ultimate loss of South Korea. Should this tragedy occur, the numerous critics of "Mr. Truman's War" would redouble their charges that billions of dollars and thousands of lives were all flung away fruitlessly. If the United Nations should collapse—and this is quite possible—then the bloody war in Korea to save it would seem to be all the more useless.

In 1964 Truman remembered that a reporter had asked him about the second Schlesinger poll, in which he ranked a surprising ninth—a Near Great. "I told the reporter I didn't think the poll meant a thing insofar as recent history is concerned; the historians didn't know any more than the pollsters did when they said I wouldn't win in 1948. Nobody will be able to assess my Administration until about 30 years after I'm dead. . . ."

Perspective has certainly inspired second thoughts about various Presidents. We sometimes wonder about Polk's seizure of the Mexican cession, which led to the Civil War. We sometimes doubt the wisdom of Theodore Roosevelt's "taking" Panama, which is still an explosive issue. We are now somewhat appalled by Truman's decision to drop the atomic bomb, which established a backfiring precedent. We even have misgivings about Truman's Marshall Plan, which ultimately led to the economic backlash of the European Common Market. This list could be impressively lengthened, but many of these now-questionable achievements, once widely acclaimed, are chalked up to the credit of the administration then in power.

Conversely, blunders once denounced sometimes take on a different hue and throw a retrospective glow on the administration responsible for them. For many years cynics condemned the purchase of Alaska—"Johnson's Polar Bear Garden"—as a woeful waste of $7.2 million. But now that Alaska has panned out with gold, fish, and furs, and has become a state of enormous economic and strategic value, we think more highly of Andrew Johnson's floundering administration for having brought off the coup. It will probably stand as the most significant single act of the ex-tailor's troubled four years, even though it was conceived and carried through by his expansionist Secretary of State, William H. Seward.

What about alternatives? Critics who have assailed President McKinley's decision to annex the Philippines have usually been less energetic in examining the awkward alternatives before him in 1898, and the probable outcome of each choice. Statesmanship is the science of alternatives, and Presidents all too often have to choose, as Woodrow Wilson did at Paris in 1919, not between the good and the bad but between the bad and the less bad.

Who deserves the credit for the President's achievements and the discredit for his mistakes? Much of the success of Washington's administration was due to Hamilton, although the role of the General himself is usually underplayed. Two of Grover Cleveland's most questionable decisions appear to have been unduly influenced by Richard Olney, a tough-fisted and ultra-conservative Cabinet member. These were, first, sending federal troops into Chicago to crush the Pullman strike and, second, intervening belligerently in the boundary dispute between Britain and Venezuela in 1895–1896. Yet Cleveland is roundly blamed, as perhaps he should be, for permitting himself to be misled.

THE ACCOLADE OF ACHIEVEMENT

How shall we balance accomplishments in domestic affairs against those in foreign affairs? President Grant, whose administration was branded "eight long years of scandal," scored two signal successes in foreign affairs. Or rather, his long-suffering Secretary of State Hamilton Fish did, specifically in negotiating with Britain the Treaty of Washington in 1871 and in implementing the Geneva arbitral tribunal. But how many of Grant's "Black Friday" and "Whiskey Ring" scandals are needed to cancel out these triumphs?

What weight shall we assign to purely negative achievements? President Eisenhower passed up an opportunity to wrap the world in atomic flames when he backed off from a proposal to intervene in French Indochina at the time of the disaster to French arms at Dien Bien Phu in 1954. Presidents often deserve more credit for what they did not do than for what they did do. Yet such negative decisions seldom bulk as large on the checkered pages of history as the positive decisions.

And how do we balance the totality of error against the totality of achievement? Take any one of the so-called Greats, say Jefferson, and make parallel lists of his failures and accomplishments, his weak points and strong points. In the case of all of Dr. Schlesinger's Big Six or Big Seven, except George Washington, one could draw up assessments, depending on one's biases and ingenuity, that are as long on the negative side as on the positive.

With this kind of refinement, we can begin to wonder if there ever were any really great Presidents or, for that matter, any really complete failures. The activist in the White House will obviously make more positive errors than the passivist, whose errors may be purely negative but more disastrous. Misleading indeed is the old saying that the man who never did anything never made a mistake.

Do-nothingism, like that of Harding, Coolidge, and Hoover, can be disastrous. The purblind ostrichism of the 1920's and 1930's toward ominous trends in Europe helped prepare the slippery path down which the nation later slid into the abyss.

An arresting case in point is the experience of President Kennedy, as reported by Arthur M. Schlesinger, Jr.[1] Invited to participate in the 1962 Schlesinger poll, Kennedy began to fill out his ballot and then stopped, concluding that the exercise was "unprofitable." As he wrote to the pollster, "A year ago I would have responded with confidence ... but now I am not so sure. ... There is a tendency to mark the obvious names. I would like to subject those not so well known to a long scrutiny after I have left this office." He later remarked to the younger Schlesinger, "How the hell can you tell? Only the President himself can know what his real pressures and his real alternatives are. If you don't know that, how can you judge performance?" Some Presidents, Kennedy perceived, received credit for an achievement when there was nothing else they could do; only the most careful study could reveal what weight their personal participation carried.

EXPERT IGNORANCE

Beclouding this whole complex problem is simple ignorance. No panel of experts, no matter how learned, knows enough about all the Presidents to render a satisfying verdict. Here, as elsewhere in a democracy, an ignorant vote cancels out an informed vote. Dr. Dumas Malone is a recognized authority on Thomas Jefferson, and when he speaks about the versatile Virginian, we sit up and listen. But is he comparably well informed about Millard Fillmore and other lesser lights? In fairness to all these Presidents, he ought to be, if he is going to pass comparative judgment on them.

More than thirty years ago—shortly after I began my formal teaching of American history—I learned a painful lesson. A graduate student in psychology at Stanford University, seeking human guinea pigs, requested my cooperation in administering a questionnaire to my basic lecture course. Naively, I acquiesced. Every President of the United States was paired off with every other President in some nine hundred different combinations. The student was to

[1] Schlesinger, *A Thousand Days* (1965), p. 674.

indicate which man in each pair was the greater President. My class of some two hundred sophomores almost mutinied when they found that this seemingly simple chore would require about four hours or so of conscientious if ill-informed application. But I sternly held them to their task. Today I marvel at my folly. The results established absolutely nothing, except what two hundred Stanford sophomores, out of the depths of their ignorance and resentment, happened to jot down.

A panel of seventy-five experts runs into much the same difficulty, though admittedly at a higher level. In the broad field of history, as in many fields of learning, we are all ignorant, though some of us are much less so than others. An opinion is not a fact, as we have seen, except that its existence, however mistaken, is a fact. Whatever we may happen to think about President Grover Cleveland will not in the slightest degree alter the failures and accomplishments of that roughhewn individualist.

The sad case of Andrew Johnson is illuminating. Fifty years or so ago, thanks to the appraisals of historians like James Ford Rhodes and John W. Burgess, his stock had sagged. He was regarded as a tactless blunderer, an uncomfortable square peg in a round hole—the only President ever to be impeached and the one who escaped by the margin of a single vote in the Senate being removed from his high office. We almost began to feel sorry for the poor man who was nearly railroaded out of the White House.

Then in the late 1920's Johnson's stock rose sharply. This bullishness resulted from adulatory biographies by Robert W. Winston and Lloyd P. Stryker, the brilliant attorney who later also defended Alger Hiss. An added coat of whitewash was applied by the impassioned Democratic orator and journalist, Claude G. Bowers, whose colorful and best-selling *The Tragic Era* (1929) portrayed the bedeviled President as more sinned against than sinning—the victim of a foul conspiracy by partisan Radical Republicans. Johnson's stock among scholars remained fairly high until 1960, when it took a nose dive following Eric L. McKitrick's critical analysis, *Andrew Johnson and Reconstruction* (1960).

The tempestuous tailor is now back more or less where Rhodes and Burgess left him, after having enjoyed a dizzy swing around the circle. He now appears to have been a narrow, vindictive, bungling, bullheaded, hot-tempered misfit. His stubborn insistence on his own way, in the teeth of a contrary-minded majority in Congress, delayed the closing of the "bloody chasm" and visited untold woes on Southern whites and emancipated Negroes alike.

Every year or so a new study is published, biographical or otherwise, about one or more of the Presidents. In some years a dozen or more scholarly tomes roll off the presses, to say nothing of picture book potboilers and other non-books. How can the scholar, slaving away on a thirty-volume edition of the manuscripts of one of the Presidents, possibly find time to read, digest, and evaluate all these current publications? A just appreciation of many of these leaders lies buried under an avalanche of manuscripts or submerged in a sea of words.

The Barriers of Bias

"That you have enemies you must not doubt, when
you reflect that you have made yourself eminent."

THOMAS JEFFERSON, 1782

BRAINWASHED POLLEES

Once we set up measuring rods for Presidents, with emphasis on achievement, we run squarely into the problem of applying such devices objectively.

Almost every American is in some degree brainwashed before he reaches maturity. At a tender age he hears and reads hero tales about Washington and Lincoln, complete with the cherry-tree-and-hatchet fabrication of Parson Weems. He sees the future Father of his Country crossing the ice-clogged Delaware standing majestically but perilously erect in a boat, or praying at Valley Forge in the snow (though there is no credible evidence that he ever did either). The pubescent patriot envisions Abraham Lincoln stretched out before the fireplace, ciphering with chalk on the back of a shovel or reading by the flickering light to acquire the mastery of English which he revealed in his Gettysburg Address. (According to his stepmother, he went to bed early, arose, and read in the morning.)

Other factors, including birthday celebrations, exert a subtle influence on plastic young minds. The annual commemoration of Washington and Lincoln, often with joyful respite from the boredom of classrooms, inspires fond memories of these heroic figures. There are also statues of Washington and Lincoln decorating public parks and granite cliffs; and who is to quarrel with the judgment of those sterling patriots who enshrined these worthies, to say nothing of other Presidents. Washington's Mount Vernon and Jefferson's Monticello, among various hallowed homes, are visited by busloads of schoolchildren, with those under twelve often admitted free.

Elsewhere the impressionable youth is not allowed to forget our most illustrious leaders. For many years we have had the Lincoln penny, the Jefferson nickel, the Washington quarter, and the Franklin Roosevelt dime. Now we have the Kennedy half dollar. Paper currency has long honored a number of the Executives, including Washington on the one-dollar bill, Jefferson on the two, Lincoln on the five, and Jackson on the twenty. But the Jefferson two-dollar bill, popularly regarded as a bad-luck item, has probably done nothing to enhance the Virginian's fame.

The Presidents, notably Washington and Lincoln, have also appeared on postage stamps. When the Democrats are in power, the Post Office Department tends to honor Democrats; when the Republicans are in power, it tends to honor Republicans. Cynics have dubbed this philatelic favoritism the "battle of the postage stamps."

The total buildup for Washington and Lincoln is thus overwhelming. To doubt that they were our two greatest Presidents, not to say our two greatest men, is a form of atheism.

THE IMPRESSIONABLE CITIZEN

Even less exalted presidential heroes have their day. Andrew Jackson's incredible balancing act on a bronze steed near the White House no doubt leaves a favorable impression on those passersby who recognize who he is supposed to be. Grant's massive tomb on the Hudson does something to obscure the fumblings and bumblings of the General's eight scandal-seared years. An imposing white marble memorial even commemorates President Harding in his home town Marion, Ohio, although to some imaginative cynics it suggests the outlines of Teapot Dome.

No statue in Washington honors Harry Truman, but his palatial presidential library in Independence, Missouri, serves a better purpose. The people of Greece, remembering their salvation in 1947 by the Truman Doctrine, erected a twice-lifesize bronze likeness of their benefactor in the main square of Athens in 1963. The object of their devotion, aware that the ultimate outcome of many of his acts lay in the laps of the gods, was quoted as saying with becoming modesty: "I have never been in favor of erecting statues of people who are still alive. You never know when you have to turn around and tear it down." The next year, when Greek bitterness against the United States flared forth during the Cyprus crisis, the statue was daubed with whitewash and a warning, "Go Home, Yankee."

Centennials also leave their marks. The observance in 1956 of the birth of Woodrow Wilson brought a flood of articles, eulogistic speeches, and lectures, most of which followed the ancient Roman admonition, "Concerning the dead, nothing but good." The Theodore Roosevelt centennial in 1958 touched off a similar but less widespread outpouring for the departed Rough Rider.

Also unmeasurable is the impact of dinner table conversations, especially on adolescent minds. One wonders what picture of Franklin Roosevelt remains with countless citizens, reared by "economic royalists," who nightly heard a red-faced father berate the allegedly dictatorial New Dealer. Such prejudices may later be softened by instruction and reading, but in some cases they are only deepened.

Another subtle influence is that of cartoons. Sometimes the image is rather favorable, as when a jaunty Franklin Roosevelt oozes confidence with his outthrust jaw and upturned cigarette holder. Theodore Roosevelt's ever-restless Big Stick can be interpreted as commendable vigor rather than excessive energy. Taft's portly figure, Hoover's youthful chubbiness, and Truman's owlish glasses may all be regarded as slightly amusing rather than malicious.

But the cartoonist, whose stock-in-trade is an exaggeration of physical features, can often leave an unfavorable impression. Lincoln traditionally appeared with homely face and scarecrow frame. The professorial Wilson, with his pinched-on spectacles and cap and gown, did not show to the best advantage in an America that exalts the hardheaded businessman above the dreamy egghead. Year after year the diabolically clever cartoonist Thomas Nast hammered at President Grant in *Harper's Weekly*. The General's image was already badly enough tarnished by scandals, but these pictorial exposés further stoked the fires of public indignation.

Homer Davenport, of Hearst's New York *Journal*, consistently portrayed "Willie" McKinley as a puppet being manipulated by bloated "Dollar Mark" Hanna. Only in recent years, following the publication of revealing biographical studies, has substantial justice been done to one of the least appreciated Presidents—one who was his own man.

The memory of departed Presidents is also kept green by other literary media. We have numerous historical novels, such as the American novelist Winston Churchill's portrayal of Lincoln in *The Crisis* (1901), Irving Stone's tribute to Andrew Jackson in *The President's Lady* (1951), and Samuel H. Adams' characterization of the Jackson era in *The Gorgeous Hussy* (1934) and of Warren G. Harding in *Revelry* (1926).

Playwrights have likewise sensed the dramatic potential of presidential heroes. Especially memorable are plays like John Drinkwater's *Abraham Lincoln* (1918), Robert E. Sherwood's Pulitzer prize-winning *Abe Lincoln in Illinois* (1938), and Dore Schary's *Sunrise at Campobello* (1958), which portrays Franklin Roosevelt's agonizing fight back from infantile paralysis. We also have numerous radio and television dramas, as well as moving pictures, like *Johnson of Tennessee* and *Wilson*. The latter did not turn out to be a noteworthy box-office success but it further cast the plucky Princetonian in an heroic mold.

Few of the Presidents have prompted memorable poems, yet many of them have been the subject of so-called verse. The *New York Times* reported that it received about three hundred poetical tributes to John F. Kennedy within a few days after his murder. Woodrow Wilson, the dedicated Covenanter, was the inspiration of many poems but none stands out from the ruck. George Washington, both in life and in death, was honored by much verse, little of which is especially meritorious.

Abraham Lincoln, customarily voted the greatest President, inspired the greatest poems. This was altogether fitting and proper, because he was himself something of a poet, and his tragic death stirred profound emotions. We especially remember Walt Whitman's two noble elegies "O Captain! My Captain!" and "When Lilacs Last in the Door-yard Bloom'd." We also treasure Edwin Markham's "Lincoln, the Man of the People," and Vachel Lindsay's "Abraham Lincoln Walks at Midnight."

JAUNDICED JUDGMENTS

The adult citizen is swayed by a number of subjective influences when he scans the presidential lineup. He is inclined to think more highly of the activist who puts on a colorful show, as did Theodore Roosevelt, than of the passivist, who sits lumpishly at the other end of Pennsylvania Avenue, as did William H. Taft. If the pollee is a progressive who likes to see progress being made in the fertile fields of social and economic reform, he is disposed to give Theodore Roosevelt, Woodrow Wilson, and Franklin Roosevelt high marks. If he comes from the lower rungs of the economic ladder, he is liable to have a liberal bent and to appreciate Franklin Roosevelt's concern for human suffering and the neglected man. If he is of a conservative cast of mind—in the Federalist-Whig-Republican tradition—he is more likely to deplore than to praise Andrew Jackson's attack on the Second Bank of the United States.

Morality likewise warps opinions. If the respondent is straight-laced, he may unconsciously give Grover Cleveland a black mark for having fathered (admittedly) an illegitimate son, and another black mark to Warren G. Harding for having fathered (allegedly) an illegitimate daughter. If he has high ethical standards, he may give James K. Polk a black eye for the seizure of the Mexican cession (including California) and Theodore Roosevelt another for the so-called rape of Panama.

Nor does the trail of subjective influences end here. If the respondent is a Virginian, he may harbor an unconscious bias for fellow Virginians (and Southerners) like Thomas Jefferson and Woodrow Wilson. If he is an idealist, especially a Southern idealist, his regard for these two virtuous Virginians may melt into hero worship. If his maternal grandfather died defending Richmond and his paternal grandfather lost his fortune when the slaves were freed, he may still curse President Lincoln. If he is a pacifist, he may have a fellow feeling for Thomas Jefferson and Woodrow Wilson, both avowed pacifists in the broader sense.

Economic influences also sway judgment. If the pollee is a hard-fisted businessman devoted to "hard money," he will probably damn Franklin "Deficit" Roosevelt and his dollar tinkering. If he is pro-labor, he will perhaps have a warm spot in his heart for Woodrow Wilson and Franklin Roosevelt, both of whom sponsored epochal labor legislation. If he is anti-labor, he will perhaps react the other way and feel kindly toward Eisenhower for pressuring through Congress the Landrum-Griffin Bill, designed to curb labor racketeering.

Politics likewise inserts an unsettling hand. If the good citizen is an active Republican, he will be impressed with the virtues of that great trinity: Abraham Lincoln, Theodore Roosevelt, and Dwight D. Eisenhower. If he is a Democrat, he will revere the memory of that immortal quartet: Jefferson, Jackson, Wilson, and especially Franklin Roosevelt, who in the 1930's elbowed aside the corpulent Grover Cleveland. Indeed, the pictures of these political giants have traditionally been displayed on banners, placards, badges, and tickets at the quadrennial madhouses known as nominating conventions. "If you eliminate the names of Lincoln, Washington, Roosevelt, Jackson, and Wilson," observed Will Rogers, "both conventions would get out three days earlier."

THE WILSON WORSHIPPERS

Political passions linger with astonishing tenacity. One has to be careful about mentioning the names of recent Presidents in a casual smoking-room conversation, for fear of stirring up the animals.

The heat generated by the Wilson-Lodge feud over the League of Nations has cooled only slowly. In 1941, at the annual meeting of the American Historical Association in Chicago, a session was held on the Peace Conference at Paris in 1919. Several learned scholars read learned papers. Then the chairman of the session, as customary, threw the meeting open to discussion from the floor. A half-dozen or so speakers sprang to their feet to proclaim, "I, too, am a Wilsonian" —and thereupon to deliver a spirited defense of the Schoolmaster President. Then the chairman remarked, "Is there anyone present who is Henry Cabot Lodgical minded?" Dead silence. The meeting adjourned with the ark of the covenant still in the hands of friends.

This episode should have warned me to praise Wilson, if I wrote about him at all. But during World War II, no doubt taking myself too seriously, I concluded that I could best serve my country by trying to discover what went wrong last time so that we would not make the same ghastly mistakes all over again. To whitewash Wilson would only mislead; besides, the brush had already been wielded by experts. But my emphasis on mistakes was anathema to worshipful Wilsonians. At the annual meeting of the American Historical Association in New York in December, 1943, I brashly read a paper discussing the twenty-two mistakes or *alleged* mistakes made by Wilson in connection with the Treaty of Versailles. My conclusions were that eight of his so-called blunders were not blunders at all, and that some of the others were either unavoidable or not vital.

If man bites dog, that is news. If a professor bites Wilson—a fellow academician who made good—that is also news.[1] The press promptly picked up the story, and heeding the ancient journalistic principle that one must never exaggerate unless one improves the story, reported that I had accused Wilson of having made twenty-two outright blunders.

A storm of denunciation burst about my head. I was condemne.: by idealists, Democrats, academic Wilsonians, and clergymen. (Wilson was a lay preacher and the son of a clergyman.) One professor of history in a Massachusetts college wrote to *Time* saying that a majority of scholars did not agree with me at all. This may have been true, but I do not know how he found out. A majority of scholars, not having seen my manuscript, did not know what I had said. Even so, the majority is not always right: if it were, we might still be back in the pre-Galileo era. As for the professor who wrote to *Time*, I doubt that he was present when the paper was read, and certainly he did not see my manuscript. All this was a little odd, since the trained historian presumably teaches his students to work only from authentic documents and not from garbled reports in the press.

My views on Wilson as a peacemaker were later published in two volumes during the war years. The first one was reviewed—and not flatteringly—in a leading historical journal by the same historian who had already prejudged my findings in his letter to *Time*. The scholarly world in general was critical of me, primarily because I had been critical of Wilson. Perhaps I had been unduly critical. But in the succeeding two decades the opening of the papers of Lodge, Lansing, and Tumulty, among others, has further revealed that

---

[1] Journalist Arthur T. Hadley writes that fellow historians cover "for him as policemen do for policemen who go wrong." *Power's Human Face* (1965), p. 142.

Wilson himself, a sick and broken man, must share a considerable part of the responsibility for deadlock and ultimate failure in the fight for the League of Nations. This view, though voiced by Republican partisans in 1919–1920, was not original with me, but it is now far more acceptable than it was before I volunteered to make myself the sacrificial goat. Partisan accusations often turn out to contain at least a kernel of truth.

This disturbing experience proved to be an eye-opener. It taught me that one should not be surprised to find a pro-Wilson bias among idealists, academicians, clergymen, Southerners, and Democrats—all told, a rather wide and vocal spectrum. Generally found in this group were the old League of Nations advocates, the new United Nations supporters, plus the United World Federalists, One-Worlders, Atlantic Communitarians, and other sponsors of international cooperation. In a special category was the small army of experts who, at Paris, had advised or had tried to advise Wilson. The survivors, many of whom had been extremely critical of his failure to heed their recommendations, rather resented having a young whippersnapper trespass on their special preserve.

The "current eventists" were also heard from. They had lived through this feverish period, had read the daily newspapers, and consequently knew all about it. They were not going to have any nosey scholar dig up material from the archives to disprove their convictions. In my "pan mail" was a letter from a woman in Massachusetts—the wavering script indicated an elderly woman—who told me that I was wrong in not putting all the blame on Senator Henry Cabot Lodge. She wished that I were there so she could slap my face.

HYSTERICAL HISTORIANS

Investigators who conduct polls among academic experts assume that these scholars, schooled in objectivity, will return objective answers. In short, they can speedily cast aside the garb of the patriotic citizen and don the gown of the unbiased judge. Dr. Schlesinger records that his first group of fifty-five pollees were "admonished by their professional consciences against partisan bias. . . ."

On the basis of sad experience and observation, I am prepared to challenge this assumption. In time of national crisis scholars of various kinds, including historians, do not seem to be conspicuously able to keep their heads when all about them are losing theirs. During World War I, a number of distinguished but patriotic American historians prostituted their high calling by twisting the historical record in such a way as to cause Germany to be far more malevolent than the facts warranted. The record of American historians during World War II was much better, when the real Hitlerian wolf was loose in the world.

The annual meeting of the American Historical Association was held in Chicago late in December, 1941, about three weeks after the gigantic surprise party at Pearl Harbor. A better name for the organization at this time would have been the American Hysterical Association, because these presumably objective scholars were sharing generously in the anti-Japanese hysteria sweeping the country. One of the luncheon speakers was the Chief of the Division of Far Eastern Affairs of the Department of State, and an influential adviser of President Roosevelt in the anxious weeks before the blowup. A Rhodes scholar, a Ph.D., and a former member of the Harvard faculty, among numerous honors, he said in effect, "I address you today, not as an official of the Department of State, but as a scholar speaking to fellow scholars." He then proceeded with an historical analysis of Japanese-American relations, enumerating in detail the acts of aggression and other sins allegedly committed by the Tokyo regime. He conspicuously avoided presenting a list of American actions which the Japanese had found objectionable.

The speaker's one-sided indictment was no doubt patriotic, given the current Japanese assault on the Philippines, but it was not balanced scholarship. When he sat down, he received the usual round of applause. But as we were leaving the banquet hall, a Canadian historian remarked to me, "My God, if that represents the mentality of the State Department, I don't wonder that the Japanese kicked over the applecart at Pearl Harbor."

MEN AND MANUSCRIPTS

The availability of relevant documents tends to color the judgment of scholars, perhaps more subtly than they realize. A bibliographical law is at work: the bigger the collection of presidential papers, the bigger the President. The Schlesinger Big Five—Washington, Jefferson, Lincoln, Franklin Roosevelt, and Wilson—left exceptionally voluminous collections. The presidential papers of lesser fry like McKinley and Coolidge are disappointingly thin, and so in general are the reputations of their authors. From the standpoint of sheer bulk, Theodore Roosevelt deserves to rank among the Greats. With an eye to his future image, he was at pains to write numerous "posterity letters." When a controversial episode occurred, he would select a correspondent likely to preserve papers for the historian, and dash off a fifty-page or so brief of explanation. A copy was carefully preserved in his official papers as a dual safeguard against loss to the future biographer.

The cubic footage of Franklin Roosevelt's papers is enormous. He not only served some four years longer than anyone else, but the arms of the federal government in the heyday of the New Deal proliferated into many tentacles. We must also remember that mechanisms for turning out documents—the typewriter, the mimeograph, the dictaphone, the tape recorder, and various photographic processes—have all been introduced or perfected in more recent decades. All Executives until near the end of the last century had to rely on quill and ink or pen and ink.

Not surprisingly, the unavailability of manuscripts has hurt certain presidential reputations. For many years the rumor circulated that Mrs. Harding had burned all of her husband's papers, and the sinister implications of this act further besmirched the Harding name. Information released to the press in 1964 revealed that some 350,000 pieces of Harding correspondence were to be deposited with the Ohio Historical Society, and when these are fully explored we may think somewhat better of the dupe of the Ohio gang. By a perverse quirk of fate, later in the same year new scandal emerged in the form of a packet of 250 Harding love letters. Written to the wife of a fellow townsman in Ohio between 1909 and 1920, they turned up among her effects after her death. They lend damning support to the widely bruited rumors that Harding, at least in his pre-presidential days, was less than a faithful husband.

The Adamses collected papers with pack-rat assiduity, but their heirs hoarded them with mulish obstinacy. Not until the 1940's and 1950's was a gifted scholar, Dr. Samuel Flagg Bemis, able to do justice to John Quincy Adams. Not until 1962 was Dr. Page Smith able to bring out two humanizing volumes on John Adams. The two

Adamses might today be more highly regarded if they had been more fully revealed—and yet the reverse may be true.

SLAVERY-POLLUTED PRESIDENTS

Historical bias against certain Presidents is also related to sectionalism. In the 19th century particularly, the writing of American history suffered from a made-in-New-England prejudice—the legitimate but unlovely offspring of Federalists, Whigs, Republicans, abolitionists, and sectionalists. New England produced a disproportionate number of prominent historians, largely because it boasted leading cultural centers, an illustrious literary tradition, a community of scholars with leisure time, and document-rich libraries. New England also harbored an ill-concealed bias against Southerners and slaveholders, both before and after the Civil War, and partly as a heritage from anti-slavery forebears.

In the hands of such jaundiced gentry, Southern statesmen usually fared ill. President Polk is a prize example. He was portrayed by made-in-New-England history as an unscrupulous and conniving "unknown" who deliberately picked a war with Mexico so as to create bigger slavepens for the chattels of his fellow Southerners. James Bryce, doubtless influenced by such indictments, rated him as having been as insignificant as Franklin Pierce. Some of the charges of deviousness were well founded, but by no means all of them. Then in 1910 Polk's four-volume White House diary was published, and his stock, responding like Wall Street to a bullish impulse, rose sharply. In 1919 Dr. Justin H. Smith, though himself a New Englander, published his two-volume *The War with Mexico,* a Pulitzer-prize winner. From it Polk emerges with a remarkably clean bill of health—overclean, in the view of many scholars.

Today Polk's reputation is perhaps unduly inflated, though as late as 1957 Dr. Edward S. Corwin of Princeton University could refer to him as "slavery's tool—the sly, pious Polk. . . ." The presidential diary reveals that Polk kept all of the reins of the administration in his own hands. He almost literally worked himself into the grave by taking on the burdens of his subordinates, as well as his own, in the Turkish-bath Washington summers. Sympathy tends to merge with admiration.

Made-in-New-England history was generally rough on other

Southern politicos, especially slaveholders. The list would include Thomas Jefferson, who acquired slave territory in Louisiana; James Madison, who pressed for a war with Old England over the opposition of New England; and John Tyler, who engineered the annexation of Texas with its additional slavepens.

The slaveholding Andrew Jackson, despite near-hysterical popularity when he retired from Washington, was no hero to New England historians. Their section had deplored the War of 1812, from which he emerged as the number-one hero. The legislature of Massachusetts, sanctimoniously thanking God for the successful termination of the conflict at New Orleans, refrained from thanking Andrew Jackson or even mentioning his name. Yet the Almighty was evidently permitting events to unfold themselves in an alarming way until Old Hickory arrived on the scene. At any rate, the genteel New England historians probably would never have ranked the Wild Man of the West as a Great or a Near Great.

New England prejudice was not directed solely at Southern slaveholders. It extended likewise to Northern Presidents with Southern exposures or sympathies—the malleable gingerbread men or "doughfaces" of the 1850's who presumably did their bidding. The so-called do-nothing trio—Fillmore, Pierce, and Buchanan— consequently felt the prick of their pens. A contemporary jingle reflected a widespread Yankee view of "doughfaced" tools of the Southern slavocracy:

> The dough! the dough! the facial dough!
> The nose that yields when you tweak it so!
> It sighs for the spoils—it sells its soul
> For a spoonful of pap from the Treasury bowl.

New England historians were likewise inclined to be harsh on Andrew Johnson, the accidental heir of Lincoln, because of his soft-on-the-South policies.

PRESIDENTIAL LIBRARY-SHRINES

Presidential library-shrines, which now dot the country, have added new complexities. Ideally, the scholar's convenience would be best served in many cases if all papers of the Presidents were concentrated in one immense depository, as was to have been the case with the Library of Congress. But the practice of diffusion was begun, perhaps unwittingly, when Herbert Hoover arranged to send his presidential papers to the War Library that he had established in 1919 at Stanford University, his alma mater.

An individualized presidential library, visited as a kind of temple by thousands of tourists, is gratifying to the great man's ego. From his standpoint such a depository is preferable to having his papers submerged in a morass of manuscripts in the Library of Congress. We now have the Franklin Roosevelt Library at Hyde Park, New York; the Truman Library at Independence, Missouri; and the Eisenhower Library at Abilene, Kansas. In 1962 Herbert Hoover, seeking to honor the place of his birth, had his White House papers removed from the Hoover Library at Stanford University to the embryonic presidential library at West Branch, Iowa.

Scholars are only human, and their judgments are perhaps unconsciously swayed by the pleasant, air-conditioned accessibility of presidential manuscripts. Franklin Roosevelt was wise enough to make his papers fully and conveniently available to historians as soon as possible. A generation of researchers, grateful for the splendid facilities at Hyde Park, has not been unduly critical of the fast-shuffling New Dealer. Harry Truman has not only opened his papers as completely as feasible to qualified students, but has given generously of his time in interviews and in voluminous correspondence. The generation of historians writing about his era, and beholden to Mr. Truman for numerous favors, will presumably not go out of their way to bite the hand that befriended them.[2]

President Kennedy, who himself had authored two creditable volumes of history, early established an excellent rapport with historians. One of his presidential assistants and close advisers, Arthur M. Schlesinger, Jr., was a widely known Harvard historian. Kennedy himself, some little while before his death, had made preliminary plans for the housing of his papers in a library-museum at Harvard University.[3] Speaking to a group of scholars in Washington during the first year of his administration, he remarked that

[2] In May, 1965, when The Organization of American Historians met at nearby Kansas City, Mr. Truman spoke briefly and graciously to about two hundred of them in the auditorium of his Library. He received a rousing standing ovation both before and after his appearance.

[3] In 1965 President Johnson accepted an offer from the University of Texas to house his papers after he leaves office.

"some of us think it wise to associate as much as possible with historians and cultivate their good will." He whimsically recalled Winston Churchill's prophecy during World War II that "history would deal gently with us" because he intended to write it himself.

THE HOOVERIAN BLACKOUT

The Hoover papers are another story. Until the 1930's the ex-engineer enjoyed an exalted reputation as a miracle worker. The Great Depression was enough to ruin anyone's reputation, and Hoover, the most-booed incumbent in American history, was swept out in an unprecedented landslide. His ego suffered a shattering blow, and he could hardly be blamed for wanting to refurbish his reputation. His presidential memoirs suffer from excessive self-justification. He portrays the Hawley-Smoot Act, the highest peacetime tariff since the Civil War, as moderate; the evicted bonus army as heavily Communist; and the apple sellers on street corners as men who had quit good jobs to make more money.

Mr. Hoover was trained as an engineer, not as an historian. When he came to publish certain of his pre-presidential documents, he undertook to alter the text in the light of the intervening years. Several of those scholars who worked with him have informed me that when they protested against this irregularity, he replied that since he had written the original version, it was his and he was at liberty to change it. In fairness to Mr. Hoover one must add that he permitted a number of documents to be printed that he did not approve of, but the historian can only shudder at such willingness to tamper with the evidence.

More than thirty-three years after the event, the Hoover presidential papers are still not freely available to scholars, though in some instances they have been examined under severe restrictions. Mr. Hoover, despite his undoubted services to historical scholarship, developed a deep suspicion of historians. After they studied the documents they tended to come out with an account that did not square with what he remembered—or what he wanted to remember.

About twenty-five years ago, also to my personal knowledge, a scholar was granted permission to consult the papers relating to Mr. Hoover's foreign policy. Some months later, without warning and without explanation, word came down that the permission was withdrawn. At least three book-length manuscripts, prepared from the Hoover papers, proved distasteful to the ex-President and none of them has as yet attained the immortality of print. The impression does not seem unwarranted that pressure from the Chief had at least some bearing on the negative result.

During the 1950's and 1960's Mr. Hoover repeatedly denied scholars permission to examine his presidential papers. If he was concerned with his image—and his memoirs indicate that he was to an inordinate degree—such a policy was self-defeating. The story of the Hoover-Roosevelt years is now being written by high-grade historians, and little is to be gained by offending them. A Hoover side of the controversial issues no doubt exists, and presumably the ex-President's stature would be enhanced if it were told. The suspicion arises that these papers contain secrets which, in unsympathetic hands, would further damage his reputation. At all events, Mr. Hoover not only antagonized a generation of historians but he deliberately created an image which in substantial part they will have to tear down—with a certain amount of secret satisfaction.

SHIFTING WINDS OF OPINION

The current national mood also sways historical judgments. If the scholar lost his textbook royalties in the stock-market crash of 1929, he may feel bitter toward both Coolidge and Hoover, who are now widely, if somewhat unfairly, condemned for permitting the speculative bubble to expand. If he applauds the Good-Neighbor policy, he may think ill of Theodore Roosevelt's Big-Stick tactics in the Caribbean, especially in Panama and Santo Domingo. If he is a champion of Negro rights, he would perhaps downgrade Woodrow Wilson (who believed with many fellow Southerners that a Negro was all right in his place—down), and upgrade Harry Truman (who risked renomination and re-election in 1948 by his forthright stand on civil rights). If he believes that Negro rights have been pushed too far and too fast in recent years, he might think less well of Presidents Eisenhower and Kennedy for having sent federal troops into the South.

The mood of the 1930's is highly illustrative. The nation was isolationist, neutralist, and non-interventionist. The Senate, responding to popular pressures, appointed the Nye committee to investigate the international arms racket. This little group of politicians, misreading the evidence, concluded that America had in large part been dragged into World War I by the munitioneers, the profiteers, the sloganeers, the racketeers. In the light of these findings, an increasing majority of Americans believed that the nation had made a ghastly mistake by allowing itself to be "suckered" into a useless conflict. Wilson had asked Congress for the unnecessary war, or so it seemed, and consequently his stock fell. On the floor of the Senate his most vehement defenders, Senator Glass of Virginia and Senator Connally of Texas, pounded their desks so violently that the one emerged with a bleeding hand and the other with a permanently deformed knuckle. But their wrath was unavailing.

After World War II erupted in 1939, the issues were distorted by new passions. If the pollee was an isolationist, he would deplore Franklin Roosevelt's destroyers-for-bases deal, lend-lease, and other acts of unneutrality, while damning the White House "warmonger" for having sponsored them. This certainly was the reaction of the well-known historian and political scientist, Dr. Charles A. Beard. He went so far in his *President Roosevelt and the Coming of the War, 1941* (1948) as in effect to accuse the New Dealer of having deliberately exposed the fleet at Pearl Harbor so that he might have his war with Japan and the European dictators. In short, this distinguished scholar and polemicist, without proper evidence, was convicting the Commander-in-Chief of having plotted the murder of some three thousand American servicemen and the destruction of the entire Pacific fleet on the first day of the war. And the war was one which Roosevelt wanted to win in the interests of world freedom and his own place in history.

We must reluctantly conclude that historical judgments are sometimes as much visceral as cerebral.

Pre-Presidential Happenstance

"A pound of pluck is worth a ton of luck."

JAMES A. GARFIELD

THE RAGS-TO-RICHES SHEEN

Many irrelevancies are bound to enter into the assessment of a President, whether at the popular or scholarly level. Prominent among them are pre-White House experiences, which in turn are often shaped by purely fortuitous events. The irony is that many of these occurred before the future statesman ever dreamed of entering politics.

Humble birth was once regarded as a powerful political asset, and three of the Schlesinger Big Six—Jackson, Lincoln, and Wilson— enjoyed no silver-spoon upbringing. Lincoln and possibly Jackson were born in log cabins, as were some four other future Presidents. Jackson was a posthumous child, and his mother left him an orphan (and a juvenile delinquent) when he was only fourteen years old. Lincoln was born to a Kentucky family of poor whites; they lived barely above the subsistence level in a crude, dirt-floored log cabin in which a bath was hardly possible during the winter months. Lincoln's mother, who died in his youth, was an illegitimate child; his father was essentially illiterate. Wilson was born to a minister's family, which was much better off than in the case of Jackson and Lincoln, but he was hardly cradled in the lap of luxury. Jackson and

Lincoln, beneficiaries of "Alger's law" at its best, are striking examples of the American success story, and as a result stand out from their compeers all the more conspicuously.

Other Executives, less highly rated, represent in dramatic form the rise from rags to riches—or to relative riches. Much of the presidential appeal of Herbert Hoover lay in his background as an orphan in Iowa, his upbringing by an uncle, and his working his way through Stanford University. He then worked his way up from the bottom of a Nevada mine shaft with pick and shovel to a position of prominence and munificence as a mining engineer. Made a junior partner of a prominent British firm at age twenty-seven, he was put in charge of some twenty mining ventures in various parts of the world.

Andrew Johnson, a veritable diamond in the rough, was reared under conditions even more wretched than those of Abraham Lincoln. Apprenticed to a tailor as a half-orphan, and once advertised for as a runaway, he was the only artisan by vocation ever to reach the White House. Whatever else may be said of the temperamental tailor, he had come a long way when he was suddenly enthroned by Booth's bullet. A self-made man, he was distressingly proud of his maker, and he had the bad taste to remind audiences that Jesus, the carpenter, had also worked with his hands.

THE DECAYING LOG CABIN

Log-cabin symbolism definitely colors popular evaluations of the Presidents. It was first used on a nationwide scale in the hard-fought hard-cider campaign of 1840, when William H. Harrison defeated little "Matty" Van Buren, who was pilloried as a simpering aristocrat. Harrison, though moderately wealthy, was palmed off on the public as a poor, homespun farmer who not only lived in a log cabin but had been born in one. Actually Harrison was one of the F.F.V.'s (First Families of Virginia), and the college-educated son of a signer of the Declaration of Independence. Born in a manorial Virginia home, he lived in an Ohio Valley mansion at the time he ran for the presidency. The only kernel of truth in the log-cabin legend is that there had once been a cabin on his broad acres, and that his impressive abode had been built around it. But by 1840 the log cabin had become so important as an anti-aristocratic symbol that Daniel Webster half apologized in public for not having been born in one. He proudly added that his elder brothers and sisters could claim that honor.

The day when the flickering fireplace of the log cabin cast a favorable shadow on the President has vanished. Both of the Roosevelts were born to patrician homes, and neither seems to have suffered politically from a solid-silver upbringing. Nor has the acquisition of wealth—whether through patrimony, matrimony, or parsimony—left a black mark, at least not in recent years. Yet this was not always true. George Washington, who had both inherited and married money (to the vast annoyance of John Adams), was one of the wealthiest men of his day. But his assets were mostly in non-liquid real-estate holdings; at times he was "land poor" and badly pinched for cash.

Few of the Chief Magistrates before the present century were regarded as wealthy men, much less millionaires. Herbert Hoover appears to have been the first authentic multi-millionaire, but he had pulled himself up by his own bootstraps in the approved luck-and-pluck tradition. President Kennedy was a multi-millionaire, although his money had come from a fabulously rich father. Even so, his wealth was not held against him; it definitely helped him by enabling him to campaign in a private airplane and enjoy other advantages not available to less affluent candidates. His running mate, Lyndon B. Johnson, was likewise a millionaire: the press reported in mid-1964 that his holdings (and his wife's) were then valued at some nine million dollars.

Millionaire status is now acceptable, provided that the money was inherited, married, or made honestly in enterprises unconnected with the candidate's possible shenanigans as a Senator or other public servant. Yet we should not forget that as recently as 1920, when the millionaire newspaperman James M. Cox ran for the presidency as a Democrat, he soft-pedaled his misfortune in having a fortune. Among other precautions, he was careful to make no noisy display of his imposing home, Trailsend, in Ohio.

SONS OF THE SOIL

Whatever the statesman's bank balance, a farm background was a decided political asset until recent decades, and helped enhance his presidential image. We are prone to forget that George Washington was America's foremost farmer. Not until Chester A. Arthur was elevated by Charles Guiteau's bullet in 1881 did we have in the White House a big-city man, in this case from New York. In the 20th century only William H. Taft, with his home in Cincinnati, and John F. Kennedy, with his Boston antecedents, were prominently identified with big-city life. President Lyndon B. Johnson's ranch, with its high-heeled boots and tall Texas hats, was more in the earthy American tradition.

A British diplomat in Washington reported that President Jefferson looked like a "tall, large-boned farmer." If the Virginian had read this sneer, he would probably have felt complimented, because that was what he was and wanted to be. The fresh-air Jeffersonian view long prevailed that life on the farm was pure and wholesome, in contrast with life in the festering cities. Besides, in the dawning days of the Republic the farmers represented about 90 percent of the population. Today they are one of many minority groups in a society that is rapidly becoming 90 percent urban or suburban.

Of Dr. Schlesinger's Big Seven, only two were not rooted in the soil. A parsonage was the cradle of Woodrow Wilson and the Hyde Park manor was the playpen of Franklin Roosevelt. The latter became by inheritance the Squire of Hyde Park, and while President informed Congress in a famous veto message (February 22, 1944) that he was a "grower and seller of timber." Actually, much of the business of this gentleman lumberman was raising and marketing Christmas trees, which may have accounted, as one cynic observed, for his giveaway, Santa Claus complex. His fifth cousin, the red-blooded blue blood Theodore, though reared in metropolitan New York, became a ranch owner in the Badlands of the Dakotas, where he punched cattle and (occasionally) cowboys. He lost much of his patrimony in those blizzardly winters but gained much of his physique.

President Calvin Coolidge, a lawyer and Amherst graduate, was fully aware of the farmhouse-to-White-House tradition. "The greatest man ever to come out of Plymouth Corner, Vermont," in the words of Clarence S. Darrow, he returned to the ancestral farm often enough to be photographed in bucolic poses. A photograph widely used in his campaign of 1924 shows him perched on a hay wagon, clad in brand-new overalls, and displaying a white shirt and polished black shoes.

WHAT'S IN A NAME?

A good name, especially a good old Anglo-Saxon name, can help the presidential candidate and his subsequent image. "Harding," for example, is a simple name with a hard, solid ring. We are not yet quite ready for a tongue-twisting Teutonic or Polish name, like "Woiciechowicz." The quadrisyllabic "Eisenhower" was a little hard to swallow, but it is not especially difficult to pronounce, and the universally used nickname, "Ike," which rhymed beautifully with "like," was seductively simple. The sloganeers fairly outdid themselves with:

> The man of the hour
> Is Eisenhower.

Adlai E. Stevenson, Eisenhower's opponent in two campaigns, was not helped by his unusual first name, which millions of people enthusiastically mispronounced. One New York newspaper dubbed him "Adelaide," thus adding the burden of effeminacy.

The magic name "Roosevelt" was definitely not in the mainstream of the American tradition, even though two generations of Americans got used to it. The correct pronunciation—Rose-velt (rō'-zĕ-vĕlt)—was never mastered by millions of voters, many of whom shouted themselves hoarse while incorrectly mouthing the name of their hero.[1]

The glamorous surname "Roosevelt" was a major asset to the relatively little-known Franklin Roosevelt when he ran for the White House in 1932. Ill-informed admirers in the crowds would call out, "You're just like your Old Man," or "I voted for your Pappy, and I'm going to vote for you, too." After Franklin Roosevelt was elected in 1932, the widowed Mrs. Theodore Roosevelt received letters from many voters rejoicing that they had voted for her husband in 1904, 1912, and again in 1932. FDR once remarked to Frances Perkins that one of his political assets was the belief of some back-country folk that he was Theodore.

Even the Rooseveltian initials were an asset. TR became the popu-

---

[1] President Buchanan's name was commonly pronounced "Buck-anan," and this accounts for his having been called "Old Buck" and cartooned as a horned buck.

larized initials of Theodore, and FDR the popularized initials of Franklin. No other presidential initials before their time enjoyed such widespread use, and few if any since then. The New Frontiersmen, with their contrived pioneer imagery, did their best, with considerable success, to promote JFK. Lyndon B. Johnson's LBJ, already famous as the initials of the entire family and of the luxurious Texas ranch, quickly gained popular acceptance.

The political potency of a distinguished name is widely recognized. At various times politicos have made serious attempts to groom or boom for the White House the son of a former President. One need only mention Robert Todd Lincoln, Frederick Dent Grant, and Senator Robert A. Taft. Taft was the only one who came even close to a major nomination.

Sometimes the famous name can be a liability as well as an asset. It invites comparisons, some of them not altogether flattering to the latecomer. Many voters felt at the outset, and some no doubt still do, that Franklin Roosevelt was a pale imitation of his colorful cousin. Perhaps a determination to prove them wrong helped spur the New Dealer on to higher heights.

THE RELIGIOUS HALO

Religion has also played its role. The presidential image is affected by the church that the future President was born into, or the one that he joined, or the type of faith, if any, that he embraced. Until 1960, when John F. Kennedy shattered a tenacious tradition, Catholicism was regarded as about as formidable a bar to the presidency as a black skin. This conclusion was seemingly reinforced by the defeat of the "wet" Catholic Al Smith in 1928, although he almost certainly would have lost had he been a teetotaling Methodist deacon. Most of the Presidents—indeed an overwhelming majority—have been orthodox churchmen or WASPS (white Anglo-Saxon Protestants).

Two of the Big Six—Jefferson and Lincoln—were non-church members and free thinkers. Such unorthodoxy was a black mark against them, especially Jefferson. Although a deist, he was branded an atheist, partly because he had helped to lead the fight to separate church and state in Virginia. Lincoln was a non-denominational Christian, and the absence of religious affiliation hurt him politically.

But his martyrdom and presumed ascent to Heaven, in a manner suggestive of Elijah, caused him to appear more conspicuously religious than he actually was.

The barrage of books on Lincoln has tended to gloss over the Great Emancipator's individualized methods of communing with his Maker. One of the many ironies of American history is the fact that a man who had so little truck with organized religion should have been bracketed with Christ as the central figure in the American passion play. The cultists have not failed to point out that Jesus, born in a manger, died on a cross on Good Friday, and that Lincoln, born in a log cabin, died under an assassin's bullet on Good Friday. Both were redeemers (of those in bondage), saviors (the one of sinners, the other of the Union), and martyrs (to their objectives).

LOOKS MAKE THE MAN

An impression of greatness is enhanced if the Chief Executive looks like a great man.

All of the Schlesinger Big Six were imposing men physically, except Woodrow Wilson, who was about average. Until Lyndon B. Johnson (six feet three inches) fell heir to the office in 1963, the six tallest were Lincoln, at six feet four inches; Jefferson, at six feet two and one-half inches; Washington, at six feet two inches; Chester A. Arthur, at six feet two inches; Franklin Roosevelt (before infantile paralysis) at six feet two inches; and Jackson, at six feet one inch. Wilson, at best, ranks about sixteenth, among a group of five men at five feet ten inches.

One should note that the American male in recent generations has become markedly taller. In an era when basketball is a national sport, a youth of six feet two inches is not regarded as remarkably tall, but in the days of Washington and Lincoln he towered over his fellows. The two men commonly regarded as the two greatest Presidents were almost certainly the two strongest. Washington could crack nuts between his fingers; the youthful Lincoln was the champion weight lifter of his community.

In the fiercely competitive world of business administration, the imposing man has a distinct advantage over his undersized rival. Psychologists have long since proved that topflight bankers and corporation executives are generally bigger men physically than lesser bankers and corporation executives. Yet physical size is due to the accidents of heredity, nutriment, and possibly climate. Stature bears no demonstrable relationship to one's innate ability. By the "inches test" Chester A. Arthur, the Dude President, should rate higher (as perhaps he deserves to), and Woodrow Wilson should rate lower (as perhaps he deserves to when one takes into account his crippled year and a half at the end). Perhaps the towering Lyndon Johnson, the second tallest of all, is destined for greatness.

Arresting indeed is the fact that five of the six shortest Presidents rise no higher than the Average group in the second Schlesinger poll. The exception is John Adams, who rates Above Average but who on several counts deserves no higher ranking than Average. This is not to say that the short President cannot become a top-drawer President, but he is handicapped. Nor must we conclude that a short man cannot become a dynamic leader. Napoleon is the prime example of an undersized man who developed enormous drive (Napoleonic complex), which is often seen in those who strive to compensate for their physical handicap. William McKinley, in whom cartoonists found a resemblance to Napoleon (the Napoleon of Protection), added to his short stature by several inches of dignity.

Good looks seem to have been less important than size in affecting the popular image of the President. Of the Big Seven, Franklin Roosevelt alone could be deemed a handsome man. Two of the handsomest were two of the weakest: Franklin Pierce, an alcoholic, and Warren G. Harding, a glad-hander and philanderer.

Handsomeness, which is a matter of opinion, is clearly not an indispensable asset. The American people, even women, are prone to give their highest rating to the rugged-appearing man rather than the handsome one. Washington was an impressive figure, whether on foot or on horseback, but his deep pockmarks and ill-fitting false teeth would eliminate him today in a Mr. America contest. A youthful Thomas Jefferson, sandy-haired and freckled-faced, won fame as the homeliest scholar at William and Mary College. The emaciated Andrew Jackson looked like a broken-down refugee from an old-soldiers' hospital. A stooped and shambling Abraham Lincoln, commonly voted the greatest of all, was perhaps the ugliest of all—so ugly as almost to be handsome. The jokes about his homely face and scarecrow frame were legion, and he delighted in telling them. Theodore Roosevelt, with his squinty, myopic eyes and his walrus mustache (covering horsey teeth), would never have won any prizes in a beauty contest. Woodrow Wilson, keenly conscious of his lantern jaw, admitted that his face was against him until he began to speak. One of his favorite limericks, by Anthony Euwer, ran:

> As a beauty I'm not a great star.
> Others are handsomer far;
> But my face—I don't mind it
> Because I'm behind it;
> It's the folks out in front that I jar.

Most of these men fortunately held office in an era before the television camera could mercilessly expose to tens of millions of viewers their warts and blemishes, their poor teeth and articulation. The coming of the One-eyed Monster has forced nominating conventions to place a high priority on telegenic qualities as they scan the stable of presidential hopefuls. More than ever the kingmakers are seeking a clean-cut jaw, a glamorous grin, or a toothpaste-advertisement smile. With many voters molars are more important than minds.

WHITE HOUSE OR REST HOME?

Closely connected with physique is the man's health before he entered the Executive Mansion. Most Americans would be more charitable of his shortcomings if they had before them his detailed medical record. His pre-presidential health problems, especially in the early days, were often aggravated by the conditions in Washington. The capital city was once a marsh, only partially reclaimed; and mosquitoes and malarial fevers, combined with intestinal disturbances caused by bad drinking water, took their toll. The damp, timber-warped White House for long periods was rat-infested and in a scandalous state of disrepair. The boon of air-conditioning did not come to the capital until the 1930's, and before that time the cruel summers added to the bodily wear and tear.

As we scan the medical record, we wonder how the nation muddled through as well as it did. George Washington suffered from severe toothache and recurrent malarial fever (the ague), first contracted during his youthful surveying. Jefferson, during much of his life, was afflicted with dysentery, rheumatism, migraine headaches, malarial fever, crippling backaches, and the pain resulting from a poorly set broken wrist. Lincoln was cursed with such overwhelming melancholia that at times his friends despaired of his sanity. He called these attacks "the hypos"—from "hypochondria."

As for other members of the Big Seven, Jackson was virtually a one-man clinic. Even before coming to the presidency he had long suffered from chronic dysentery and intestinal cramps, malarial fever, abscess of the lung with chronic bleeding, probable tuberculosis, serious tooth and gum troubles, bone infection, and possible lead poisoning from the two bullets that he carried in his body from his near-fatal duels. All these disabilities, which would have been enough to hospitalize a less willful man, no doubt accounted in part for his irascibility and shortness of temper. The wonder is that he preserved as creditably as he did the dignity of his high office.

Woodrow Wilson, like Andrew Jackson, suffered most of his life from ill health. He had been forced to drop out of college for a year because of recurrent illness. Before he became President a catalog of his ailments would include neuritis, prostrating headaches, partial blindness in one eye as the result of a thrombosis, and chronic nervous indigestion, with the discomfort of heartburn and intestinal distress. He entered the White House in 1913 with a stomach pump and a generous supply of headache pills. His subsequent physical collapse dimmed his fame and frustrated the far-visioned work on which he was embarked.

We marvel that Washington, Jefferson, Jackson, Lincoln, and Wilson performed as well as they did, dragged down as they were by these disabilities. Franklin Roosevelt, the last in point of time of the Big Seven, was a cripple throughout his twelve years. If we were to handicap Presidents as we handicap horses—and perhaps we should—these illnesses would have to be taken into account. If they are, most of the Greats emerge all the greater; great men seem to rise above great afflictions.

Paradoxically, physical handicaps are sometimes assets. Two of the more eminent Presidents were helped rather than hurt by being "fortunate" enough to incur serious physical disabilities earlier in their careers.

Theodore Roosevelt, later famed for his robustness, probably would never have reached the White House if he had not been born a sickly, spindly, asthmatic, myopic child. Determined to build his body, he toiled in a homemade gymnasium until he became the apostle and exemplar of furious, red-blooded manhood. All his life he seemed to be trying to overcompensate—to prove something—and the most striking manifestation of this desire was his volcanic display of energy. If he had been born the normally healthy and lazy lad, he probably would never have developed the dash and color that endeared him to the voters. These assets brought him to the highest office, and then kept him there, Big Stick and all, for an elected term in his own right.

Franklin Roosevelt possibly would never have been elected President in 1932 if he had not been felled by infantile paralysis in 1921. He had earlier been regarded as a patrician lightweight, even though burning with ambition for high political office. As late as January 8, 1932, the pundit Walter Lippmann could publish the classic miscalculation that he was "no crusader . . . no tribune of the people . . . no enemy of entrenched privilege . . . a pleasant man who, without any important qualifications for the office, would very much like to be President." But paralysis, agony, and near despair, combined with the long and humiliating fight to work his way back to hobbling mobility, put additional steel in Roosevelt's soul while putting steel braces on his legs. He forced himself to cultivate to an even greater degree his innate cheerfulness, self-assurance, and optimism. He once remarked that after one had spent two years in bed trying to move a big toe—the hardest thing he ever had to do—"anything else seems easy." His disability also cut him down to the level of the forgotten man, whose champion and idol he became.

THE DYNAMISM OF YOUTH

Closely related to health and energy is the age at which the President happens to be elected. Seventeen of the thirty-five—or almost precisely one half—were over sixty when inaugurated. The older a man is, the more likely he is to have accumulated the ills that human flesh is heir to. With increasing age, he normally suffers a diminution of energy and alertness. It is often revealed in forgetfulness, lassitude, and even sleepiness, as well as in an excess of caution. This lack of dynamism was evident to a considerable degree in Buchanan and also in Eisenhower—the two oldest incumbents.

In politics, as in athletics, many a potential star never gets his real chance until he is over the hill,[2] and senile delinquency can be even more harmful to a nation than juvenile delinquency.

Young men often protest that old men should not govern the world; old men do not have to live so long with their mistakes. Young men are inclined to be liberal, old men conservative. As the saying goes, if a man does not have liberal inclinations in his youth, something is wrong with his heart; if he does not have conservative inclinations in his autumnal years, something is wrong with his head. Young men, with their superior energy and physical stamina, are more inclined to push Square Deals, New Freedoms, New Deals, and New Frontiers.

All of the Big Five came into office in their fifties: Washington and Jefferson at fifty-seven, Wilson at fifty-six, Lincoln at fifty-two, and Franklin Roosevelt at fifty-one. Significantly, all of them (except Lincoln) served at least two terms, and in every case (except Lincoln) left office in their sixties. Dropping two notches to include the Big Seven, we have Jackson coming in at sixty-one and Theodore Roosevelt, an accidental incumbent, at forty-two. But we must note that a man of fifty-seven in the 18th and 19th centuries was presumably older and tireder than a man of the same age in the 1960's; life expectancy at birth has virtually doubled since 1789. On the other hand, if life expectancy has increased markedly, the burdens and responsibilities of the office have increased overwhelmingly.[3]

The four oldest at inauguration were William H. ("Old Tippecanoe") Harrison at sixty-eight, James Buchanan at sixty-five, General Taylor at sixty-four, and General Eisenhower at sixty-two. General Harrison died after only thirty-two days in the harness, but he showed no signs of becoming an outstanding President. To the probable good fortune of the nation, General Taylor suffered the same fate after less than a year and a half in office. Buchanan's so-called timidity during the critical secession months is customarily blamed on the weakness of his character. But he was almost seventy when the storm broke, and a man of seventy in those days, especially a lame duck, was normally well past his peak.

General Eisenhower assumed his awesome office at age sixty-two.

---

[2] Winston Churchill did not receive his call to the prime ministership until he was sixty-five, a common retirement age in America.

[3] See Appendix B, "Is the Presidency a Killing Job?"

By living out his eight years—almost miraculously it seemed—he left the White House the oldest man ever to have occupied it. He achieved this all-time record despite three major illnesses while in office, including a near-fatal heart attack. His advanced age may have had something to do with his middle-of-the-road philosophy of government.

MARRIAGE AND MORALS

Marital status, ordinarily established before the White House is attained, can have an important bearing on the incumbent's reputation.

Only one President, the low-ranked James Buchanan, never married. His hysterical fiancée had died after a youthful lovers' quarrel, and for various reasons he never took unto himself a wife. His single blessedness somehow seemed offbeat. When he ran for the presidency in 1856, a banner paraded by a group of women declared "Opposition to Old Bachelors."

No divorced man has ever been elevated to the White House. Andrew Jackson had married a divorced woman, or one whom he believed to have been divorced. Subsequently he was horrified to discover that she had not been granted her final papers, and that he was technically though innocently guilty of having lived in adultery for over two years. "Do we want a whore in the White House?" was the cry of his political foes in the gutter-low campaign of 1828. Such charges probably contributed to the heartbreak of his beloved Rachel, who died shortly after the election and before she could be greeted as First Lady. Jackson believed that his enemies had killed her, and bitterness gnawed at his vitals during his stormy eight years in office.

Lurid tales of post-marital but pre-presidential infidelity have leaked out from time to time. President Harding's afterimage, already scalded by Teapot Dome, was further besmirched by Nan Britton's book *The President's Daughter*. Miss Britton charged, with much circumstantial detail, that Harding, then Senator, had fathered her child. With much less persuasiveness, scandalmongers accused Thomas Jefferson of not only having begotten Negro children by his own wenches but, even more incredibly, of having sold them under the hammer.

The capital's whispering gallery has often clucked over tales of sex derelictions by a number of other Presidents, before and after they reached their exalted office. If such affairs did occur, the principals seem to have been unusually discreet. At any rate, we demand a higher standard of morality in the Chief Executive than, for example, in a Senator. The President sits on a pedestal, the object of emulation, and the entire nation expects both Caesar and his wife to be above reproach. When he falls from grace, as Harding did, he falls farther and harder.

THE ROYAL FAMILY

Some of the leaders-to-be married wiser than they knew when they went to the altar, not realizing that they were about to embrace a future First Lady. A gracious hostess can do much to brighten the White House image; an ungracious one can blacken it.

If we scrutinize the Big Six, and exclude the widowers Jefferson and Jackson, we note that the charming Martha Washington was a definite asset. But Mary Todd Lincoln was a dubious helpmeet. A high-strung woman who was ultimately committed to an institution for the mentally deranged, she added immensely to the harassments of an already bedeviled man. As the belle of a family of Kentucky slaveholders, she was maliciously accused, among other crimes, of being a Confederate spy. Lincoln subjected himself to the humiliation of voluntarily appearing before the Senate members of the Committee on the Conduct of the War, and there declaring "that it is untrue that any of my family hold treasonable relations with the enemy." As Richard Armour [4] has put it:

> His face was lined, in part, by God,
> In part, they say, by Mary Todd.

Towering above all other First Ladies as a public figure was Eleanor Roosevelt (Mrs. Franklin D. Roosevelt). She was certainly the most written about and the most written to, with the mountainous White House mail running heavily in her favor. Energetic, liberal-minded, and public-spirited, she traveled widely, spoke frankly, wrote voluminously for the press, and otherwise kept in the headlines as "Public Energy Number One." Robert Moses, a New York Republican, criticized the presidential "immunity" which

[4] Richard Armour, *Our Presidents* (1964), p. 40. By permission of the author.

"protects her when she uses the immense prestige of the White House to market scribblings which a college freshman would hesitate to hand to the professor."

Gallup polls in later years repeatedly rated Eleanor Roosevelt the nation's most admired woman. But during her husband's lifetime she was condemned for parading too much in the public eye, prescribing "quack remedies for economic ills," and promoting "pinko" causes. Many critics felt that the place of the President's spouse was in Washington, not out on the soapbox. The official in charge of the White House mail later wrote of the steady "stream of letters to FDR demanding to know why in hell he didn't put his foot down and stop this habit his wife had of being constantly on the run somewhere or other and of always poking around in other people's business." But many of these critics were anti-New Dealers who would not have approved of her, even if she had been completely self-effacing. An anti-Roosevelt slogan in the fourth-term campaign of 1944 was "We Don't Want Eleanor Either."

The family that the new Executive brings to the White House, aside from his wife, can project a favorable or unfavorable image. Theodore Roosevelt had his troubles with "Princess" Alice, who persisted in being shockingly unconventional, even to the point of smoking cigarettes in public and gadding about unchaperoned.

The large and active family of Franklin Roosevelt was much in the limelight. The philosophy of the parents, embarrassingly enough, was to let the children lead their own lives, including divorces. The younger Roosevelts, the quip ran, did not marry "forgotten women." Critics further charged that the sons traded on their father's influence to promote business schemes, and used their high connections to secure commissions in the armed forces. We now recognize that there are two sides to these stories, but anti-Roosevelt literature featured this sneer: "I pledge allegiance to the Democratic Party, and to the Roosevelt Family for which it stands. One Family Indispensable—with divorces and Captaincies for all."

If a man is known by the company he keeps, a President in some measure is known by the family that he happens to bring to the White House. If their conduct is above reproach, he receives no credit: nothing less is expected. If it is not, the mudslingers move in, and some of their slime is bound to stick. From such happenstance is the presidential image fashioned.

CHAPTER VII

Pre-White House Career

"The necessary and wise subordination of the military
to civil power will be best sustained . . . when lifelong
professional soldiers, in the absence of some obvious and
overriding reasons, abstain from seeking high political office."

GENERAL DWIGHT D. EISENHOWER, 1948

WARRIORS IN FROCK COATS

Irrelevant though it may be, the previous career of the President
is closely related in the public mind to his excellence as Chief
Executive. A glamorous military record, for example, has swept a
number of men into the White House and kept a halo over them, no
matter how blatant their bunglings.

This affinity for military heroes in the United States is a disturbing
sign of political immaturity. It stems in part from the New Democracy of the Jacksonian era, when every man was supposed to be
as good as every other man. Accordingly, he could wear all kinds
of different hats. The best bear shooter (Davy Crockett) would
naturally make the best Congressman, and the best Indian fighter
(Andrew Jackson) would naturally make the best President.

Such a naive view of the interchangeability of talents still persists.
It made General Eisenhower, a lifelong soldier, a misfit president
of Columbia University. No one would dream of asking a professional educator to lead our armies in battle—the results would be

77

too costly—but we apparently do not grasp the absurdity of asking a professional soldier to lead a distinguished university. His miscues are less conspicuous.

Only two West Pointers, General Grant and General Eisenhower, have yet reached the White House. The Schlesinger experts ranked Grant a Failure and Eisenhower, despite the shortness of perspective, near the bottom of the Average group. Zachary Taylor, though not a West Pointer, was the only other professional military man, although his incredibly sloppy appearance belied military discipline of the spit-and-polish school. A hero of the Mexican War but a political rookie, Taylor had never before held civilian office or voted for President, and his elevation was no boon to the Republic.

Alarmists have often expressed the fear that the war hero in the presidential chair may become the dictatorial Man on Horseback. The military mind is suspect because it is accustomed to giving orders and having them obeyed with heel-clicking celerity. It does not accord well with the inevitable price we pay for democracy— back talk from Congress, the judiciary, the press, and the public.

To the professional soldier the presidency can be profoundly exasperating. After General Eisenhower was nominated in 1952, President Truman mused, "He'll sit here, and he'll say, 'Do this! Do that!' *And nothing will happen.* Poor Ike—it won't be a bit like the Army. He'll find it very frustrating." And "poor Ike" did find it infuriatingly frustrating on a number of occasions.

But the overgrown and bureaucratic American government has proved much too impregnable to be captured by a mere general, no matter how laurel-bedecked. The three professional soldiers— Grant, Taylor, Eisenhower—were not "strong" Presidents. Without a taste for politics, and unsure of themselves in a new job, they were often content to sit at their command post in the White House and let Congress map the strategy and execute the tactics. Sometimes they become prisoners of the wheelhorse politicians. Eisenhower, "The Captive Hero," was captured by the Old Guard Republicans, declared the Democrats—something that Hitler's best generals could not do.

CITIZEN SOLDIERS

The only other military men on the presidential roster were not professional soldiers at all, or were so only in a limited sense. George Washington, perhaps the most famous of all, was a surveyor-planter who answered the call of duty in the French and Indian War and in the War of Independence. He gladly returned to civilian life as the Cincinnatus of the West, after having exercised quasi-dictatorial powers. Although known as the Sword of the Revolution, the Deliverer of America, the Savior of His Country, he had lost more pitched battles than he had won. His name is not associated with a major victory like Saratoga; he had to share the glorious triumph at Yorktown with the French. Yet his cunning and tenacity won for him acclaim as the Old Fox and the American Fabius.

General Andrew Jackson—lawyer, planter, duelist, politician—was primarily a militia officer, not a lifelong professional soldier. Yet he emerged as a Grade-A military hero, reflecting the glamor of three wars. Captured by the British during the War of Independence when only fourteen years old, he had sustained a saber cut across the face when he defiantly refused to polish a redcoat officer's boots. Unlike the cherry-tree-and-hatchet yarn, this story is true; the scar which Jackson took to his grave bore visible testimony. His political foes, weary of the story, insisted that any red-blooded American boy would have acted with similar spirit.

As a militia general, Jackson crushed the Southeast Indians in 1814 at the bloody Battle of Horseshoe Bend in Alabama. The redskins came to fear and respect him as Pointed Arrow and Sharp Knife, while his men came to fear and respect him as a leader who shared their hardships. Tough as hickory—Old Hickory was the nickname that helped inflate his image—he commanded in one engagement when the ravages of dysentery forced him to have his arms tied between two trees so that he could stand.

But Jackson's finest hour came at New Orleans on January 8, 1815. Placed in command of a motley collection of backwoodsmen, militiamen, Creoles, and pirates, he at first showed inexplicable lethargy in preparing his defenses. He was almost caught by complete surprise. And if the British had only thrown a strong force across the river to his rear—they sent a small detachment which was successful—they could have wiped him out. But the veteran redcoats, contemptuous of his ragtag army, assaulted his prepared position frontally and suffered frightful losses, while the American losses were negligible.

New Orleans, though necessary for Jackson's buildup, was an unnecessary battle. The peace treaty had already been signed at Ghent two weeks earlier. The war had gone badly for the United States, and Jackson's triumph proved to be the only smashing land victory that was not set up by naval power. If a nation is going to win only one decisive engagement, a better taste is left in the mouth if it is the last one, especially against an hereditary and hated foe that had recently burned the nation's capital.

The country had half expected Jackson to be crushed at New Orleans. Then the glorious news reached Washington that the British had been crushed—the selfsame army that had recently vandalized Washington. Shortly after that the Treaty of Ghent arrived, and three indestructible legends were born. One was that America had won the war; another was that Jackson had won it; and another was that the British, following their humiliation at New Orleans, had hastened to sign the Treaty of Ghent. So Jackson was on his way not only to the presidency but to a "great" presidency as the Old Hero, the Hero of New Orleans, and the Land Hero of 1812. Of such fortuities is greatness made. To give him his due, Jackson was the only soldier-general of the 19th century with reasonably valid claims to a high rank as a President.

CIVIL WAR CELEBRITIES

Lincoln's stature was not enhanced by military service, although he had a controlling hand in the management of the Civil War. His brief stint as a volunteer captain in the Black Hawk Indian fracas was bloodless, except, as he jocosely remarked in Congress some years later, for his "bloody struggles with the mosquitoes." During the Civil War he confided to a friend, with perhaps mock frankness, that he was a "great coward" and that if he were a soldier he would "run at the first fire."

Ulysses S. Grant—the strong, silent, cigar-puffing man—undoubtedly became President because he was the ranking hero of the Civil War (in the North). His shortcomings as President have been glossed over to some extent because of his services to the nation while in uniform. Although he was educated at West Point and had served for eleven years as a professional soldier, he was nevertheless something of a citizen-soldier in the American tradition. Having drunk himself out of the Army, he had returned to civilian life, quite unsuccessfully, seven years before the guns began to boom at Fort Sumter. At that time he was an incompetent employee (he forgot the prices) in his father's leather store in Galena, Illinois, at fifty dollars a month—hardly a Horatio Alger success story. He was later dubbed the Fighting Tanner, the Galena Tanner, and the Tanner President.

Grant's bad luck turned suddenly when, having won a brigadier general's commission, he forced the Confederates to yield Fort Donelson, in Tennessee. When asked what his terms would be by the commander (a classmate from whom he had earlier borrowed money), he unsportingly replied "unconditional and immediate surrender." Grant, the Hero of Fort Donelson, was now a made man. His was the first significant victory to crown Northern arms after a series of stinging setbacks, including the rout at Bull Run. Grant's given names, Hiram Ulysses and Ulysses Simpson,[1] had earlier been against him; in fact, Ulysses led to the rather relevant nickname "Useless." But the initials U.S. now stood for many pleasing concepts, notably Unconditional Surrender but including Union Safeguard, Unprecedented Strategist, Unquestionably Skilled, and Uncle Sam Grant. After he began pounding at Lee in the Virginia war of attrition, he was dubbed the Great Hammerer, Butcher Grant, and the Butcher from Galena.

Undismayed, Grant reported to Washington, "I propose to fight it out on this line, if it takes all summer." It took other lines and all summer, plus all winter and a part of the following spring, but his laconic words gripped the public imagination. At long last Grant became the Hero of Appomattox, the Great Peacemaker, and the Man Who Saved the Nation.

So potent was Grant's stature as a war hero that (like Eisenhower) he probably could have received the presidential nomination by either the Democrats or the Republicans at the next election.

---

[1] At birth Grant was named Hiram Ulysses; by a mistake in the records he became Ulysses Simpson when he was appointed to West Point. The initials H.U.G., for an obvious reason, never appealed to him.

A political tyro, he had only once before voted for a President and that had been for the Democrat Buchanan. He chose the Republican party, and it elected him in 1868, after he had declared in his acceptance speech, "Let us have peace." These welcome words are engraved on his Hudson River tomb.

From Lincoln to Taft—nine Presidents—all were military men or heroes of sorts, except the Democrat Cleveland. To his lasting political hurt, he sat out the Civil War. Needed at home to support his widowed mother and two sisters while two brothers went to the front, he took advantage of the draft law and hired a substitute for $150 to go in his place. When he ran for the presidency in 1888 resourceful Republicans rewrote the words of "Marching Through Georgia":

> Grover Cleveland sent a substitute where he did not dare to go,
> Into the Union Army to face a rebel foe;
> There he left this poor old German to die of death and woe
> While he was boasting of our Union victory.

The substitute in question was a Pole, not a German; he was young, not old (thirty-two); he was never in an important battle as a combatant; and he survived the war. Truth is one of the first casualties in politics.

Previous military service, though undeniably a political asset, added little to the image of the Presidents (except Grant) who came in after the Civil War. At least four of them had highly creditable fighting records, and one of them, Rutherford B. Hayes, was wounded in action on four separate occasions.

FROM COLONEL TO GENERAL

Colonel Theodore Roosevelt, flamboyant hero of the Spanish-American War, was a special case. Craving action and eager to squeeze all the glory possible out of what promised to be a short war, he managed to transport to Cuba a part of his regiment of Rough Riders (without their horses). He outflanked his colleagues in getting into action, and he became president, said "Mr. Dooley" [Finley Peter Dunne], "of the society of the first man up San Juan Hill." He wrote a book entitled the *Rough Riders*, which the same Mr. Dooley felt should have been entitled *Alone in Cubia* [sic]. In it Roosevelt boasted about having killed "his Spaniard." (His political foes infuriated him by charging that he had "got" his Spaniard by shooting him in the back.) He privately urged that he be awarded the Congressional Medal of Honor as the capstone on his exploits but never managed to get it. At all events, he was the most glamorous hero to come out of the war. His colorful antics, involving bravery to the point of recklessness and self-advertising to the point of immodesty, brought him temporary entombment in the vice presidency, from which Czolgosz's bullet exhumed him. His role as the number-one hero of the Spanish-American War, at a time when the Civil War was largely forgotten, undoubtedly magnified his stature as President. Such sobriquets as the Rough Rider and the Hero of San Juan Hill would let no one forget.

Then came a long succession of non-warriors—Taft, Wilson, Harding, Coolidge, Hoover (a Quaker), and Franklin Roosevelt. Roosevelt had served nearly eight years under Wilson as Assistant Secretary of the Navy but, though desiring action, had become involved in no heroics reminiscent of "Uncle Ted." Harry Truman, who participated creditably in some of the heaviest fighting of World War I as an artillery captain in France, no doubt attracted some veteran votes. But his war service had no appreciable bearing on his presidential image: in fact many irreverent people were disposed to laugh when they heard a reference to "Captain Truman of Battery D."

As regards popular appeal, Dwight D. Eisenhower was the glamor-general hero of World War II. But the two West Pointers, Grant and Eisenhower, are hardly comparable, and one should be careful not to damn Eisenhower because of Grant. Eisenhower's background was far broader than Grant's, and his unusual talents for persuading balky elements to pull together were widely recognized. They won for him the command of the Allied forces in Europe during World War II, and the command of the NATO armies in Europe after the war. His responsibilities were diplomatic and administrative, on an enormous scale, and involved high-level dealings with top-ranking civilians like Winston Churchill. He was also "demilitarized" for several years as president of Columbia University. His political backers evidently reasoned that he would be more acceptable to the dictator-wary electorate if he first donned a cap and gown instead of his five-starred uniform.

Eisenhower was a man of quick intelligence who soon grasped the usual platitudes and proved more willing to listen, learn, and adjust than the ordinary old soldier of sixty-two. He consequently did a far better job than might have been expected. His admirers claimed that the troubled times demanded a conciliatory man with his special gifts and training. They stuck to their guns, even though he had written a persuasive letter in 1948 explaining why a military man should not ordinarily occupy the White House. But, in an atomically triggered world, military problems and civilian problems had become so intimately intertwined that they were often inseparable. A knowledge of military affairs, far from being a handicap, is today often an asset.

Eisenhower's military record also blunted the charges of Communism in government. So redoubtable a hero could hardly be expected to sell out to Moscow, or even be guilty of "appeasement." When he brought the stalemated fighting to an end in Korea— a peace without victory—the Democrats were distressed. They charged that they had long been willing to settle on these terms, but that if they had done so, they would have been traduced as traitors.

GRADE "C" WAR HEROES

America has produced many eminent admirals, but Lieutenant (junior grade) John F. Kennedy was the first authentic naval hero, of any rank, to reach the White House. His decoration for bravery was well deserved. After his plywood PT boat was cut in two by a Japanese destroyer in World War II, he swam several miles to save the lives of his crew. One injured seaman he towed for five hours with his teeth. These heroic exploits were widely advertised in magazine articles, books, television shows, and in a full-dress Hollywood production. They undoubtedly contributed to his appeal, both as a candidate and President, especially with the veterans. He was properly entitled to burial in Arlington Cemetery, alongside other martial heroes. This honor, combined with the tomb and the eternal flame, will no doubt help cast a brighter afterglow on his tragically truncated administration.

But unlike Theodore Roosevelt, the lone ranger of San Juan Hill, Lieutenant Kennedy was modest about his heroism. After reaching the presidency, he was asked by a small boy how he became a war hero. He replied, "It was absolutely involuntary. They sank my boat." Without detracting in the slightest from his life-saving exploits, one must conclude that if he had been more skillful or more lucky, he would not have lost his craft and would have remained one of the many unknown sailors of World War II.

Lyndon B. Johnson, the latest President-by-assassination, was the first member of the House of Representatives to don his uniform after Pearl Harbor, as a Lieutenant Commander in the Naval Reserve. He received the Silver Star after the patrol plane in which he was flying suffered damage from a Japanese fighter craft. But his seven-month war record was clearly not a major consideration in placing him on the ticket as vice presidential candidate with Kennedy in 1960. He had other political assets, including his influence in the South and his remarkable record as Senate majority leader.

In sum, while prior military service may not be especially good preparation for being Commander-in-Chief, it often adds to the glamor and hence the stature of the Commander-in-Chief. In the first year of his tenure, President Kennedy good-humoredly told an audience at the University of North Carolina, "Those of you who regard my profession of political life with some disdain should remember that it made it possible for me to move from being an obscure Lieutenant in the United States Navy to Commander-in-Chief in fourteen years with very little technical competence." Lieutenant (j.g.) John F. Kennedy was clearly marked by the finger of destiny for noteworthy deeds.

NON-MILITARY RENOWN

Among the so-called Greats and Near Greats, George Washington, Andrew Jackson, and Theodore Roosevelt were best known for their pre-presidential military exploits. But all the Presidents, especially the Greats and Near Greats, achieved some distinction in previous civilian life, often after initial or repeated failures. This circumstance, though irrelevant, has added to their stature as Chief Executives.

A rundown of Dr. Schlesinger's Big Eleven, aside from war heroes Washington and Jackson, is most revealing. Thomas Jefferson, Penman of the Revolution, had won renown as chief author of the

Declaration of Independence, as sole author of *Notes on the State of Virginia* (1782), as Minister to France, as Secretary of State, and as Vice President of the United States. Honest Abe Lincoln had been in the limelight, chiefly as a result of his much-publicized debates with Senator Douglas. Woodrow Wilson, the battling Princetonian, had attained national prominence as the reform Governor of New Jersey. Franklin Roosevelt had been in the public eye as an unsuccessful candidate for the vice-presidency in 1920, and then as the Depression Governor of New York.

Among the Near Greats, the story is much the same. John Adams, the Father of American Independence, was perhaps second only to George Washington as a Founding Father of the Republic. Young Hickory Polk, erroneously regarded as an unknown, had been Governor of Tennessee and twice Speaker of the House of Representatives. Grover Cleveland had attained both notoriety and fame as the "hangman" Buffalo sheriff, the Veto Mayor of Buffalo, and the Veto Governor of New York, all before he became the Veto President of the United States. Theodore Roosevelt, aside from his derring-do in Cuba, had been in the public eye (how could he have kept out of it?) as a member of the Civil Service Commission, as head of the New York City Police Board, and notably as Governor of New York and successful vice presidential candidate.

Harry Truman, the peppery Man from Missouri, shares with Polk the distinction of being the least known of the so-called Near Greats before attaining the presidency. He was perhaps even less conspicuous than Polk. But we must remember that he was initially elected only to the vice presidency, and largely because he had served ably during World War II as chairman of the special Senate Committee to Investigate the National Defense Program. Credited with saving the taxpayers more than a billion dollars (his own estimate later became fifteen billion), he emerged as one of the civilian heroes of the conflict.

CONGRESSMEN AND GOVERNORS

Previous experience in public life has done much more in most cases than merely bring a man into the limelight. It has contributed to his success while in the White House, and consequently to his reputation. Service in Congress, especially the House, has been valuable in enabling an Executive to familiarize himself with the temper and viewpoint of that balky body, and in helping him to establish harmonious relations with its members. This was conspicuously true of ex-Congressman McKinley but certainly not of ex-Senator Truman. Much was expected of President Lyndon Johnson in the light of his spectacular record as Senate majority leader, and the pressure that he brought on his former colleagues, whether in conference or by telephone ("the fourth branch of government") made the Congressional wheels grind more rapidly. Even so, he probably was able to manipulate the Senate with greater ease as majority leader than while sitting at the other end of Pennsylvania Avenue.

Aside from Truman, Jackson was the only one of the Greats or Near Greats ever to serve in the Senate, and there, as a young man, he made something of an ass of himself. The presiding officer, Thomas Jefferson, later recalled that his passions were so "terrible" that when he rose to speak his voice would choke up, and he would have to sit down. The combined experience in Congress of the eleven Greats and Near Greats averages less than two years for each man.

The record also reveals that prior experience as governor of a state, despite the focus on local interests, is a better guarantee of presidential greatness than service in Congress. Seven of the eleven men in Dr. Schlesinger's top two groupings had been elected governors of their respective commonwealths. Yet Jefferson, as Governor of Virginia, never completely lived down the ignominy of having to flee, prudently but seemingly disgracefully, to avoid capture by thundering British cavalrymen.

Developments in recent decades have placed an additional premium on governorships. The so-called Modern Presidency, with its emphasis on energetic leadership of Congress, was largely the creation of three men who had served vigorously as governors of their respective states: Theodore Roosevelt in New York, Woodrow Wilson in New Jersey, and Franklin Roosevelt in New York. Franklin Roosevelt brought to the White House much of the administrative routine that he had devised at the State House in Albany. His famous fireside chats evolved naturally from his direct radio appeals to the voters of New York; his two-a-day press conferences in Albany became twice-a-week press conferences in Washington.

Lincoln stands in a special category. Alone among the Presidents, he had never served as a governor, or as a senator, or as a cabinet officer, or as a Vice President, or as a general. At the national level, he could point to only two routine years in the House of Representatives.

AUTHORS-TURNED-POLITICIANS

Previous literary output has helped or hurt the image of some of the Presidents; in a few instances it has done both.

Neither Washington nor Lincoln ever published a book, and in a narrow sense neither can be regarded as an author. But both wrote voluminous letters and public documents; both are imperishably associated with famed addresses or messages of high literary quality. The published papers of Washington now occupy many volumes, as do those of Lincoln. Franklin Roosevelt could hardly claim distinction as an author, but the numerous presidential speeches and messages which he prepared, usually with ghostly assistance, have been published in thirteen volumes.

Andrew Jackson, a fighting man rather than a writing man, could boast of no literary gifts. Yet he could express his ideas vigorously, despite difficulties with spelling and syntax. His enemies charged, with considerable exaggeration, that he applied Jacksonian democracy to the parts of speech, regarding all adverbs and verbs as being created free and equal.

Three of the Big Seven were authors of genuine distinction: Thomas Jefferson, Theodore Roosevelt, and Woodrow Wilson. Many of Jefferson's letters are model essays, such as his latter-day estimate of Washington's character. His *Notes on the State of Virginia* (1782) and his majestic Declaration of Independence brought him well-merited acclaim at home and abroad.

From the standpoint of sheer bulk, at least, Theodore Roosevelt ranks as an eminent author. All told, and excluding long-winded official messages, he wrote some forty volumes of prose, all of it vigorous and much of it muscular. Sixteen of these books appeared before he came to the Executive Mansion. But he was much too biased and violent in his judgments ever to be an objective historian of high rank. His first book, published when he was only twenty-four years of age and before he became deeply involved in politics, was probably his soundest historical contribution. It still ranks as a standard monograph on America's naval role in the War of 1812.

Woodrow Wilson, the scholar-turned-politician, published some thirteen volumes before coming to Washington. Many of his presidential papers are classics, including his Peace Without Victory Speech, his War Message of 1917, and his Fourteen Points Address. Of the thirteen volumes, one was a textbook, one was a frequently reprinted doctoral dissertation on Congressional government, and five comprised a popular and profusely illustrated history of the United States. He later confessed that he wrote it "to instruct myself" and "to find out which way we were going." His multi-volume history was essentially a potboiler, but it has received more recognition from historians than it merits, largely because its author went on to higher things—the making of American history rather than the writing of it. Such are the vagaries of backward reflected glory.

Sometimes a man's pre-presidential writings are enhanced by his having become President, and these in turn inflate his presidential image. John F. Kennedy's *Profiles in Courage* (1956), which had faded from the best-seller lists, regained vigor after his election, and then shot back to the top shortly after his assassination. The book remained there many weeks, bringing total sales beyond the three-million mark.

THE PERILS OF PUBLICATION

The Old Testament author of Job desired "that mine adversary had written a book." The Duke of Richelieu remarked, "If you give me six lines written by the most honest man, I will find something in them to hang him." Whenever a politician becomes a candidate for high office, he lays himself open to all the brickbats that the opposition can fling. He may be sure that his past life, including his writings, will be worked over with a fine-toothed comb. Happy is he if in sowing his wild oats he left no crop of tares to haunt him, as was notoriously not the case with the beer-drinking, wenching Grover Cleveland. Happy is the potential President if he has safeguarded himself in his writings against attack by minorities and other pressure groups. The more a man writes, the greater the danger of a slip. If these indiscretions catch up with him as President, his popular image is bound to suffer.

In his *Notes on the State of Virginia*, Jefferson had declared, "The mobs of the great cities add just as much to the support of pure government as sores do to the support of the human body...." Federalists used this passage to turn urban artisans against the Virginian. The red-corpuscled Theodore Roosevelt, in his early years, wrote some scornful things about spineless pacifists and Quakers, who could be as "undesirable" citizens as duelists. When he became a prominent political figure these barbs were exhumed to plague him.

Professor Woodrow Wilson, when he prepared his conservative five-volume *A History of the American People*, evidently did not have the White House in view. He expressed his dislike or contempt for advocates of cheap money, strikers, radical farm organizations, pensioners, the unemployed, small office seekers, and particularly the "sordid" Polish, Hungarian, and Italian immigrants. Most of this "coarse crew," he felt, were less desirable in some respects than the Chinese. After Wilson had achieved national political prominence in 1912, a hostile press opened fire. It assailed him for "Tory" and "Federalist" prejudices that were clearly rasping to millions of voters, especially the foreign-born. Wilson wrote numerous letters to immigrant spokesmen, either apologizing abjectly or squirming somewhat dishonestly, and promising to take steps to remove the objectionable passages from future editions. Even the most high-minded of politicians usually have to stoop a bit to conquer.

HANDPICKED PRESIDENTS

By some queer kind of political rhythm, the strongest Presidents are ordinarily followed by weaker ones. This is especially true if the outgoing idol chooses—or handpicks—his own successor. Andrew Jackson, his popularity at a heady level, not only dictated the presidential nominee, Martin Van Buren, but also the vice presidential nominee, Colonel Richard M. Johnson. Jackson's roughshod tactics appear all the more remarkable when we note that Colonel Johnson acknowledged a Negro mistress.

In 1908 President Theodore Roosevelt, still enormously popular, decided (temporarily) that he was not an indispensable man. He handpicked Taft, a faithful "yes-man" lieutenant, and virtually dictated the platform. The only real uncertainty at this Chicago convention was that the delegates might shake off the reins and stampede to Roosevelt.

A handpicked candidate is invariably weakened at the outset. For one thing, he inherits the enemies of his predecessor. This was especially true of Martin Van Buren, who was accused of being smuggled into office under the military folds of General Jackson's greatcoat. The "crown prince" also suffers by contrast with the departing king, under whose shadow he lives. Such comparisons are inevitable under ordinary succession; they become more pointed when the incumbent is something of an artificial flower.

The handpicked President, moreover, is not completely his own man. He is in some degree shackled by the desires and policies of his creator, however mistaken. If he turns against his benefactor, as Taft finally did against Roosevelt, he suffers from embarrassing charges of ingratitude, disloyalty, and even treachery. If he is a servile "yes-man," he suffers from charges of being a stooge. Jackson was credited, rather unfairly, with being the first President to serve three terms: his own and Martin Van Buren's. He not only gave unsolicited advice to Van Buren but also to President Polk, who angered him by ignoring much of it.

NEAR-MISS INCUMBENTS

A President likewise loses some face if he is Mr. Second Best— that is, not the clear first choice of the convention that nominated him. Lincoln and Wilson both fall into this category, and to the credit of both they rose above the stigma. Lincoln was emphatically a second choice; William H. Seward, a more famous man with more enemies, led him on the first two ballots. "Success rather than Seward" was the slogan of the Lincolnites.

Woodrow Wilson won the nomination in 1912 on the forty-sixth ballot over the wisecracking, hard-drinking Missourian, Champ Clark. Clark garnered a simple majority during much of this time, but never quite scraped together the requisite two thirds. Fortunately for Wilson, the present majority rule was not adopted until 1936. If it had then existed, Clark would have been the nominee and probable next President of the United States.

James K. Polk was the first, but not the last, dark horse. Though numbered by the experts among the Near Great, he has never fully recovered from this onus. When the Baltimore convention first met in 1844, he was not even considered; he received no votes at all on the first seven ballots. Only when deadlock developed was he trotted out as a compromise candidate, and this unexpected twist led to the unfair jeer by his opponents, "Who is James K. Polk?"

Even worse in some respects than a dark-horse handicap is a disputed election. On a technicality, vice presidential candidate Aaron Burr tied with Thomas Jefferson for first place in 1800, even though the Electoral College presumably had Thomas Jefferson in mind for the presidency. After a bitter and protracted contest in the House of Representatives, Jefferson triumphed. But his administration began—and also ended (the embargo)—under a cloud.

John Quincy Adams suffered from a disputed election in 1824–1825 (the "Corrupt Bargain"), and Rutherford B. Hayes experienced a similar fate in 1877. The Democrat Samuel J. Tilden, who had polled some 250,000 more popular votes than the Republican Hayes, was elbowed aside. A special compromise Electoral Commission, consisting of eight Republicans and seven Democrats, voted 8 to 7 in favor of the Republican Rutherford ("Rutherfraud") B. Hayes. From the very outset honest "Granny" Hayes was showered with such epithets as Old-Eight-to-Seven, Fraud President, His Fraudulency, President De Facto, Usurper, and Boss Thief. In the face of such abuse and passion, he deserves high praise for having served creditably. But his later image was undoubtedly damaged by the controversial nature of his election.

Most of the Greats or Near Greats, on the other hand, could boast a majority of the popular vote.[2] But Lincoln and Wilson were both elected initially by about 40 percent of the total, which meant that 60 percent of the voters preferred someone else. This black eye apparently did no irreparable harm to the image of either man, though both probably have suffered to some extent. Both were re-elected, Lincoln with a majority vote (eleven Southern states were still out) and Wilson with a fraction under a majority vote.

The Vice Presidents who climb into the White House over the

---

[2] In a day before careful records were kept of the popular vote, John Adams was elected President by the close electoral margin of three votes. The resulting sneer, "President by three votes," rasped his pride, which was inordinate.

deathbed are usually not so highly regarded as those who are initially elected in their own right. In the 19th century, Tyler, Johnson, and Arthur were all dropped at the end of their partial terms. But in the 20th century all of these accidental legatees received the accolade of an elected term: Theodore Roosevelt, Coolidge, Truman, and Lyndon B. Johnson. Two of this quartet attained the exalted status of a Schlesinger Near Great.

LANDSLIDE VICTORS

Obviously the President who is swept into office by a strong popular majority, as Franklin Roosevelt was all four times, brings with him added prestige. He was the only Democrat since Franklin Pierce in 1852 to be elected by a popular majority, not a plurality. John F. Kennedy, who squeaked through by the narrowest of margins, received only 49.7 percent of the popular vote. But he naturally claimed, as politicians are prone to do, a mandate for his program—the New Frontier. Actually he had not received a mandate for anything, even though he had come much closer to receiving one than Wilson had for his New Freedom.

Landslide victories in particular add luster to a presidential reputation. George Washington was the only President ever to receive the unanimous vote of the Electoral College, and he was so honored twice. The landslide victories of Andrew Jackson and the two Roosevelts no doubt added further sheen to already illustrious names, and may in some degree sway the experts who give them high ranking. On the other hand, two of the low Average Presidents rode in on landslides: Hoover in 1928 and Eisenhower in 1952 and again in 1956.

The two so-called Failures, depressingly enough, were conspicuous successes as vote getters. When General Grant ran for reelection against the preposterous Horace Greeley, he received an overwhelming popular endorsement. Not surprisingly, he interpreted it as a mandate to keep on misgoverning. No less depressing is the fact that Harding was elected by the greatest popular landslide up to that point in American history. One wonders where Harding, already in last place with the experts, would have landed if he had not received what prestige he could glean from his electoral triumph.

Oddly enough, Abraham Lincoln, the President popularly judged the greatest, was the weakest at the polls, with an all-time low percentage of the popular vote—39.9 percent, except for John Quincy Adams in 1824. In ten Southern states the Emancipator-to-be did not receive a single popular vote; his name was not permitted on the ballot. He even failed to carry his own county in Illinois. To paraphrase the Great Galilean, a prophet is often more honored outside his home town than in it.

Presidential Fortuities

"The only thing you have to worry about
is bad luck. I never have bad luck."

HARRY S TRUMAN, 1950

THE WHEEL OF FORTUNE

Once we have risen heroically above all subjective influences—
assuming such perfection possible—we may evaluate what the man
actually achieved. But even this nuts-and-bolts approach can be misleading. The successes or setbacks of an administration have often
had little or no relation to what the incumbent did or failed to do.

Some men were plain lucky. Prosperity continued during the era
of George Washington, thanks in part to the outbreak of war in a
Europe hungry for American foodstuffs. Otherwise Hamilton's
elaborate financial structure might have come crashing down,
leaving the Father of his Country with a stillborn Republic on his
hands. Jefferson was supremely lucky during his first administration
when the Louisiana windfall dropped into his lap; his luck ran out
during his second administration when his self-destructive embargo
collapsed. Acid-tongued John Randolph sneered that the four years
of Jefferson's second term ate up the four years of his first term, just
as the seven lean cattle had eaten the seven fat cattle in Pharaoh's
dream. The "Roosevelt luck" was proverbial for both Theodore

and Franklin; both had exceptionally high batting averages, even though both struck out occasionally.

Other men have run into adversity, especially when the cyclical blight of a depression descended. James Monroe, imperishably associated with the somewhat mythical Era of Good Feelings, was the only President ever to be re-elected after a major panic (that of 1819) had burst forth during his term. Lincoln, happily for his reputation, was shot just as the Reconstruction Era began. The hapless and tactless Andrew Johnson was left to wrestle with vexations that would have taxed the ingenuity of a Bismarck.

Ill fortune often comes in highly personal guises. McKinley was distraught by a scandal at the time he had to make the crucial decision to take or not to take the Philippines. (His wife's brother was shot by the woman he had "betrayed.") Wilson's beloved first wife died just as the titanic war was erupting in Europe in 1914. "God has stricken me almost beyond what I can bear," he wrote. The emotional upset through which he passed may partly explain his faltering development of a neutrality policy, as well as his dangerously belated espousal of a preparedness program.

Wilson's overpowering grief gave way to a rapturous love affair. A lonesome and uxorious man, he married the charming widow of a Washington jeweler some eighteen months after he had become a widower. All the world loves a lover, but preferably not an elderly occupant of the White House who wrote daily letters to his lady love, some of them many pages long. He was widely criticized (especially by Republicans) for having remarried at all, and particularly for not having waited a more seemly interval after the death of his first beloved. "My wife is dead. Long live my wife," jeered ex-President Theodore Roosevelt. Colonel House, Wilson's intimate adviser, who was worried about the impending election of 1916, urged a postponement of the nuptials. For this interference the bride-to-be evidently never forgave him. Her continuing hostility appears to have further shielded Wilson from a valuable adviser at the time of the fight over the League of Nations, and to have contributed to the tragic outcome.

On the other hand, "Coolidge luck" (he was born on July Fourth) held until the vinegary Vermonter left office early in 1929. Indeed, a premonition of the crash that came late in 1929 may have partially prompted his laconic "I do not choose to run in 1928." Herbert

Hoover, who probably would have gone down in history as one of our ablest Executives if he had served in the early 1920's, has simply gone down in history. During World War I, as a miracle-working food administrator, he had become a verb ("to Hooverize"); during the presidency he sank to a noun ("Hoovervilles" were the Depression shantytowns).

John F. Kennedy ran into misfortune on the very outposts of the New Frontier. Needing a strong vice presidential running mate in 1960 to carry the South, he turned to the towering Texan, Lyndon B. Johnson. As luck would have it, Johnson was also the highly effective majority leader of the Democrats in the Senate. His skillful hand was removed at a time when masterful leadership was needed, especially in steering New Frontier legislation past the tomahawks of the conservatives on both sides of the aisle. Then "Mister Sam" Rayburn, the highly respected Speaker of the House, suddenly died, leaving his gavel in the hands of a less able and less cooperative man. The somewhat disappointing legislative record of the three Kennedy years can be traced partly to such mischances.

The Chief Executive must also be fortunate enough to have a temperament and outlook that harmonize with his era. Nationalism was an energizing force following the gloriously concluded War of 1812, and John Quincy Adams was a burning nationalist. But by 1825, when he came to the White House, the nation was veering toward sectionalism, and his nationalistic proposals fell on barren soil. Yet in his successor, Andrew Jackson, the man and the times blended perfectly. Decades later the mood of the early 20th century favored reform; the American people were willing to be spurred forward by the impetuous Rough Rider, Theodore Roosevelt. Woodrow Wilson, with a high sense of duty and destiny, administered a heady dose of domestic reform (New Freedom) and foreign intervention (League of Nations). But by the 1920's the national mood had changed: the people, weary of being prodded into global dogoodism, simply wanted to be let alone.

Harding and Coolidge, whatever their other shortcomings, chimed in admirably with the times. One cynic said of Cautious Cal Coolidge, the country "wanted nothing done and he done it." Theodore Roosevelt, with his noisy impetuosity, might have been a failure in the prosperity-drugged days of Coolidge, and Coolidge, with his calculated do-nothingness, might have been a failure in the

strenuous days of Progressivism. In short, a quiet man for quiet
times; a vigorous man for troubled times.

CRISES MAKE THE MAN

To be reckoned great, a President should be "lucky" enough to
serve in a time of intense crisis.

All of the Big Five held office during a critical era. Three of them
—Lincoln, Wilson, and Franklin Roosevelt—got us into our three
biggest wars. Perhaps one could more fairly say that these men
occupied the White House when war erupted. The crisis in all three
cases was not of their making, but by one line of argument each
could have kept out of the ensuing conflict—at least temporarily—
if he had steered a different course. Both Abraham Lincoln and
Franklin Roosevelt were accused of having diabolically goaded
the enemy into attacking, the one at Fort Sumter, the other at Pearl
Harbor.

Two of the three celebrities—Lincoln and Roosevelt—were "lucky"
enough to have had their crises last through their entire tenure.
General Lee surrendered at Appomattox on the Palm Sunday before
the Good Friday on which the Emancipator was shot. Franklin
Roosevelt, who was not doing so well with the Depression, was
"lucky" enough to have it merge with World War II. He died less
than a month before Germany surrendered. Wilson was much less
fortunate: the acute phase of the war crisis passed on November 11,
1918, when the Germans signed the Armistice. The next sixteen
months were anti-climatic, and the nationwide letdown accounts in
large part for the failure of Wilson and his program.

As we survey the other Greats and Near Greats, we note how the
absence of war or near war affected their standings. George Washington kept us out of a conflict with England in 1794–1795, but his
reputation, though already exalted, would probably be even more
impressive today if he had got us into the war—and had won it.
John Adams is praised for having pulled back the nation from the
brink of full-dress hostilities with France in 1798. But can anyone
doubt that his rating would be higher today if, as a kind of early-day
Polk, he had gone to war and had seized vast chunks of territory
to the south and west, as Hamilton planned? Jefferson kept us out
of a clash with England in 1807 after the *Chesapeake* outrage. But

can anyone doubt that he would stand higher today in popular esteem if he had gone to war—and had won it? In fact, the armed conflict would probably have cost less in 1807, would have been prosecuted with more unity after the *Chesapeake* indignity, and would have caught England more deeply mired in the Napoleonic struggle.

Polk and Truman rank among the Near Greats, primarily because they were both crisis Presidents. The showdown that Polk provoked with Mexico resulted in rich territorial booty, for which we praise him. The crises that the Cold War thrust upon Truman forced him to take resolute action, which few had thought him capable of before the presidency fell on him like a "load of hay" in April, 1945.

All this raises the chicken-versus-egg question: Do great men make great times or do great times make great men by shoving them forward on the stage of history? Sidney Hook, in *The Hero in History*, draws an interesting distinction between the "event-making man" and the "eventful man." Someone has said, with obvious exaggeration, that statesmen make the occasion but the occasion makes politicians.

Whatever the merits of this argument, we must conclude that the times have much to do with creating a reputation, and here again we encounter Lady Luck. If Lincoln had averted the Civil War, he undoubtedly would appear less glamorous today: arbitrators seldom receive the acclaim of subjugators. If he had lost the South, as at times he almost did, his standing today would probably approximate that of a victorious Jefferson Davis, if the latter had won. But the emergency finally compelled this improbable Rail Splitter to take resolute steps, including the issuing of the Emancipation Proclamation, which contributed to his enduring fame.

We must further conclude that if the President craves preeminence, he should be "lucky" enough to get the nation not into just any war but into a large-scale war. In general, the bigger the conflict the bigger the President—witness Lincoln, Wilson, and Franklin Roosevelt. The medium-sized Mexican War and the Korean "police action" leave Polk and Truman with the Near Greats. The miserable little War of 1812 and the "squalid little" Spanish-American War (with subsequent Philippine hostilities) leave Madison and McKinley in the Average group. No war President drops below the Schlesinger Average.

The man who was luckless enough to serve in times of piping peace is handicapped in popular esteem and even in expert ratings. From 1815 to 1914, Europe avoided a general conflict—the so-called and semi-mythical "peaceful century." For these years the Schlesinger panels found no Great President, except for Lincoln and his home-brewed hostilities. In the face of crisis even the cautious leaders, like Madison in 1812 and McKinley in 1898, are normally forced to take action that reflects some credit on them.

THE LUCK OF THE DRAW

Some men have been lucky enough to be the beneficiaries of a peaceful overturn. The rising tide of manhood-suffrage democracy, to which Andrew Jackson contributed little or nothing personally, swept him into the White House and enthroned him there for eight years. Scholars still debate whether he led the so-called Jacksonian revolution or was led by it; whether he understood it or merely capitalized on it; whether he supported it because he believed in it or because it supported him. In short, was he the product or prophet of his times? Certainly, he was one of the few Executives, except those who departed in a coffin, who left the White House more popular than when he entered.

Franklin Roosevelt was the beneficiary of the desperate mood, born of the Great Depression. It enabled him to bring off a peaceful revolution under the aegis of the New Deal. On the other hand, John F. Kennedy was bedeviled by a revolution (the "Third American Revolution") resulting from the demands of the submerged Negro population for long-sought equality. Some four months before he was murdered the Gallup pollsters found, for the first time in five and one-half years, that a domestic problem—in this case the race issue—overshadowed Cold War worries.

The simple happenstance of succession—of who followed whom—can also help to make or break a reputation. Van Buren had the misfortune to follow a noisy and domineering figure, Andrew Jackson, and he suffered by comparison. Andrew Johnson had the misfortune to follow a recently martyred national hero, Abraham Lincoln, whose death a few extremists accused the ex-tailor of engineering.[1] The amiable, good-natured, subthyroid Taft had the misfortune to follow the crusading, club-brandishing, hyperthyroid Roosevelt, much as a dim star follows a blazing comet. The nation felt let down.

Sometimes the process is reversed, and men of hardly better than average attainments appear ten feet tall when contrasted with the mediocrities who preceded them. Between Jackson and Lincoln there were eight rather ordinary Presidents ("the eight dwarfs," they have been dubbed), and Polk was the only reasonably "strong" one. He stands out like a white crow among the three undistinguished men who preceded him and the four undistinguished men who succeeded him. Between Lincoln and Theodore Roosevelt, we find another eight rather ordinary men, except for the subordinary Grant. The pedestrian Grover Cleveland looks rather impressive when compared with his five drab predecessors and his two drab successors. He may or may not have been great, but he was probably the best these humdrum times had to offer.

The two most scandal-besmirched administrations, though giving the Republic a bad name, helped give their successors a good name. The public pillaging under Grant ground to a halt with the high-minded Hayes and his straightlaced wife, whose non-alcoholic convictions earned her the nickname "Lemonade Lucy." We accord the administration of "His Honesty" Hayes a high mark for integrity. The wholesale thievery under Harding coasted to a stop under Calvin Coolidge, whose regime won praise for its probity. Somehow the grim-faced, penny-pinching Vermonter did not seem like one who would rob the Treasury or permit it to be robbed.

It is a sad commentary on our democracy that we should upgrade public men for simply being honest and for doing their plain duty.

GREATNESS BY CONTRAST

The most eminent leaders, without exception, have looked even better by comparison with their predecessors. The "easy boss" Thomas Jefferson contrasted favorably with the pompous, quarrelsome, and aristocratic "Duke of Braintree," John Adams; the head-strong Andrew Jackson, with the politically inept John Quincy

[1] This charge has also been made by the mean-minded against other beneficiaries of presidential assassinations, from Johnson to Johnson.

Adams; the rather irresolute Abraham Lincoln, with the even more irresolute James Buchanan; the dynamic Woodrow Wilson, with the easygoing Smiling Bill Taft.

Most spectacular of all is the case of Franklin Roosevelt. We tend to forget that he was widely regarded as something of a good-natured playboy when nominated and elected in 1932. As Governor of New York, he had handled corruption in New York City with kid gloves. He seemed to promise all things to all men. He touched in only the vaguest way upon a New Deal, partly because he did not have one specifically in mind. Millions of jobless voters were presented with a choice of evils: the vague, tooth-flashing, airily optimistic Roosevelt or the gloomy, dour, colorless Hoover. Little was expected of the gladsome New Yorker, and this was one of his strongest assets as far as his reputation was concerned. But he put on a spectacular exhibition of leadership, declared what amounted to financial martial law, unveiled a New Deal (albeit off the cuff), and pulled rabbits out of his hat (some rather sickly). The contrast between what the people got and what they had feared rebounded strongly in his favor. He had the "Roosevelt luck" to take office vastly underrated. The same was true of Lincoln and Polk ("a pig in a polk," he was called).

All of the five Greats were fortunate enough to come to the White House after a party overturn, except George Washington. He took office before parties were born. In the other four cases the new-comers were elected after the opposition had wielded power for at least eight years, and while a head of steam for overdue reform was building up. They were not the prisoners of a party program already in operation: they came into power after attacking that of their predecessors.

But when a Republican succeeds a Republican, as Taft did Roosevelt and as Hoover did Coolidge, his hands are partially tied. He is guilty not only of bad politics but of bad manners if he re-pudiates what the party has laboriously installed and then sub-stitutes an entirely new deal. More favorably situated were Jefferson and Lincoln, both of whom headed new parties, and Franklin Roosevelt, who headed a party that had been out of power for twelve years. These men were entirely free to unveil ambitious programs that clashed sharply with the principles of their foemen predecessors.

All of the five Greats began their terms with favorable Congressional majorities, which accounted in large part for their initial legislative momentum. Beneficiaries of a party overturn, these new Presidents also had available for distribution coveted new offices. The patronage bludgeon expedited New Freedoms and New Deals through "dummy" Congresses that were relatively young, green, and confused. Freshman legislators were especially amenable to party discipline and leadership after many years of wandering in the wilderness without post offices to dispense.

SURPRISE-PACKAGE PRESIDENTS

Deathbed succession introduces another significant fortuity, especially when it results in an agreeable surprise. Vice President Arthur, the slightly spoiled spoilsman, is a classic illustration. This "pothouse politician," guilty of excessive political activity, had been dismissed from the only civilian office he had ever held before going to Washington. His unexpected accession was greeted with much hand wringing and with such groans as "Good God! Chet Arthur President of the United States!" Yet he rose commendably to the occasion and gave the American people a far more effective administration than they had any right to expect or deserve after having elected a candidate with his tainted background. His stature expanded accordingly.

Vice President Theodore Roosevelt, the wild-eyed "damned cowboy," was only one heartbeat away from the presidency. When President McKinley's heart stopped beating, "the madman" turned out to be much more rational and much less radical than many people had feared. The welcome relief was translated into higher popular esteem.

Two other surprise-package Presidents were Vice Presidents Coolidge and Truman. The virtuous Vermonter cautiously fumigated the Harding leftovers and restored confidence in the integrity of the Republican regime. Truman, the bewildered ex-haberdasher and protégé of the notorious Pendergast machine, likewise suffered from serious handicaps. Following a glamorous predecessor, and unbriefed as to Roosevelt's secret dealings at Yalta and elsewhere, he quickly regained his equilibrium. Little was expected of him—

which in itself was a bit of luck—and when he turned out far better than expected, his image improved accordingly.

If the agreeable surprise provided by these abler Presidents-by-inheritance magnified their standing, the process was sharply reversed in the cases of the others. John Tyler and Andrew Johnson simply did not rise to the occasion. Stubborn and self-willed, each tried to bull his way through obstacles like a rhinoceros through a jungle. One result was that both were ostracized by the party that had put them on its ticket to catch votes for the President—but not to catch the presidency for the second-place man.

In somewhat the same category of disagreeable surprises are the overinflated Presidents. These were the men who came to the Executive Mansion with exalted reputations, so exalted in fact as to lead the voters to expect more of them than they were able to deliver. Such was the fate of world-renowned figures like John Quincy Adams, Ulysses S. Grant, and Herbert Clark Hoover, who was notably the victim of the "supersell." Blessed is he of whom the people expect little, for they shall not be disappointed.

WINDFALL PRAISE AND BLAME

Luck, good or bad, comes in still other guises. Some Presidents, for example, were the beneficiaries of programs launched by their predecessors for which they just happened to get credit.

Genial William H. Taft is praised for having actually "busted" more trusts in four years than his predecessor, the trust-busting Theodore Roosevelt, had "busted" in over seven. The statistics are on Taft's side but they are somewhat deceptive. Some of the most important court actions concluded in the days of Taft were actually initiated in the days of Roosevelt, notably the illusory Standard Oil dissolution. The size and importance of the trusts "busted" are more important than sheer numbers. We must also credit Roosevelt with breathing new life into the Sherman Anti-Trust Act at a time when it had become virtually a corpse.

On the other hand, a man is often praised for an achievement with which he had little or nothing to do. The Reconstruction Finance Corporation, "a breadline for bankers," was finally approved by a Democratic Congress in the closing phases of the Hoover administration, even though Hoover had opposed it for some four months. One of the shining gems in the diadem of the New Deal is the Federal Deposit Insurance Corporation. In his first press conference Franklin Roosevelt expressed his opposition to such a measure, but it finally passed Congress and is often cited as a splendid example of New Deal planning.

Conversely, some men have had the misfortune to receive discredit for what they have not done or what they could not control. Woodrow Wilson was accused of having "lost" Russia by not intervening wholeheartedly to aid the Allies in overthrowing the Bolsheviks. (Public opinion would not have supported such a large-scale intervention.) Harry Truman was accused of having "lost" China by not intervening with powerful forces to bolster Chiang Kai-shek against the Communists. (Public opinion would have recoiled from such action.) No one can lose something he does not possess. Neither Wilson nor Truman ever had either of these "lost" nations to lose. Yet blame, often of a bitterly partisan nature, is showered generously on their heads.

A similar type of partisanship is the charge by Republicans that the Democratic party is "the party of war." They point an accusing finger at Wilson's World War I, Roosevelt's World War II, and Truman's Korean War. The Democrats, after arguing that all these conflicts were necessary and would have occurred if patriotic Republicans had been in power, countercharge that the Republicans are "the party of depression." They are referring, of course, to the desperate days of Herbert Hoover. The truth is that the Republican-prosecuted Civil War resulted in about as many soldier deaths (wounds and disease) as in all the rest of our wars combined, and that more of our major depressions have occurred under Democratic than Republican auspices.

Many vexations, including the panics of the Van Buren and Cleveland terms, have been unlucky heritages from previous administrations, sometimes of the opposition party. But the incumbent is normally blamed for them. McKinley inherited the Cuban crisis from Cleveland; Wilson inherited the Mexican muddle from Taft; and Eisenhower inherited the Korean conflict from Truman. (Eisenhower alone was lucky enough to turn the Korean settlement heavily to his political advantage.) At an early meeting of the National Security Council, President Kennedy reportedly opened a folder of briefs on current problems and said, "Now, let's see. Did we inherit these or are these our own?"

HARASSED HONEYMOONS

Some Presidents have been unlucky enough to suffer from an interruption of their "honeymoons"—that is, the period between inauguration and the time when they had Congress "on their hands." Often this embarrassment came as a result of summoning a special session of Congress, well in advance of the ordinary nine-month breathing spell.

The politically naive Herbert Hoover, for example, blundered badly. Panicked by impatient spokesmen for agriculture during the campaign of 1928, he promised to summon Congress in special session to revise the tariff in the interest of the farmers. The members assembled only five weeks after his inauguration, and after many long months of wrangling brought forth the Hawley-Smoot monstrosity. It got the administration off on the wrong foot and dimmed the luster of the magic Hoover name.

But not all special sessions of Congress have turned out badly for the incoming President. Woodrow Wilson enjoyed only thirty-four days of honeymoon before his special session and Franklin Roosevelt only five days. But each had a crash program to drive through, and each operated in something of a panic atmosphere. After the firing on Fort Sumter in April, 1861, Lincoln was forced to call a special session of Congress, but he set it for the following July. During this three-month interval—"the ten-week dictatorship" —he had a free hand to take the precedent-breaking steps which contributed so much to his towering stature. Congress, when it finally convened, was more or less committed to rubber-stamping his interim decisions.

Other men had the misfortune to be in office when, through no fault of their own, the Supreme Court handed down a highly unpopular decision. The luckless bachelor James Buchanan enjoyed only a two-day honeymoon. Hardly had he taken the oath when the Supreme Court released the reverberating Dred Scott decision, which re-aroused the slavering dog of slavery. Nearly one hundred years later, in 1954, the Supreme Court brewed a fresh kettle of racial troubles when it handed down the epochal desegregation decision, to the acute embarrassment of President Eisenhower. He was ultimately forced to send troops to Little Rock, Arkansas, in the first federal military intervention in the South since the hate-charged days of Reconstruction.

The vexations of the Kennedy-Johnson administration were compounded by the liberal and controversial "Earl Warren" Supreme Court. Ultra-conservative elements reacted violently against a series of decisions, handed down on "Red Monday," that seemed to shield Communists and to ban God from the public schools. The John Birchers and other extreme right-wingers not only demanded the impeachment of Chief Justice Warren but were disposed to blame the decisions on the White House. Actually, Kennedy was still a college undergraduate when some of the Supreme Court justices first donned their black robes.

THE SUPREME COURT ROADBLOCK

Most of the Greats, being strong Presidents, had the misfortune to cross swords with the Supreme Court. The conspicuous exceptions were George Washington and Woodrow Wilson. Washington was the luckiest of all: he enjoyed the unique privilege of appointing to the entire body—ultimately a total of thirteen—men of his own Federalist outlook. The first President of the United States to "pack" the Supreme Court was the first President of the United States.

Jefferson, Jackson, Lincoln, and Franklin Roosevelt all clashed with the Supreme Court. The anti-Federalist Jefferson had the ill luck to encounter a Federalist Court, headed by the redoubtable and long-lived John Marshall. The President came off second best when he suffered a judicial setback in the case of *Marbury v. Madison*, and when he failed in his attempt to remove Associate Justice Chase by impeachment. To rub salt in the wounds, the doughty Chief Justice shielded Aaron Burr behind judicial robes during the famous treason trial in Richmond.

President Jackson fared decidedly better. His defiance of John Marshall's unpopular decision favoring the land claims of Georgia's Cherokee Indians probably did not hurt his popular standing. Seemingly the red man had no rights the white man was bound to respect. But Jackson's scorn for the judiciary, spectacular though it was, undermined the mutual respect which is essential for the smooth operation of the three branches of government.

The New Dealing Franklin Roosevelt had the ill fortune to run headlong into an Old Dealing Supreme Court. It shot down his high-flying Blue Eagle (National Recovery Administration) and plowed under his Triple A (Agricultural Adjustment Administration), among other fatalities. Roosevelt encountered incredibly bad luck in his ill-tempered and ill-advised attempt in 1937 to "pack"— or rather "unpack"—the Supreme Court. Perhaps the most shocking setback came when Joseph T. Robinson, the hard-working Senate leader of the Roosevelt forces, suddenly died of a heart attack. The net result was a short-run political disaster for the administration but a hollow long-run victory in bringing the Court more into line with 20th-century thinking. It was hollow because after 1938 a now-balky Congress refused to pass any more major New Deal reforms for the Supreme Court to invalidate.

THE APPOINTMENT GRAB BAG

One qualification we insist on in the President is an ability to select top-grade men for appointive office. We also expect high quality in his unofficial advisers, whether in Woodrow Wilson's quiet and self-effacing Colonel House or in Franklin Roosevelt's less quiet but perhaps more effective Harry Hopkins. Each of these underlings in his heyday was widely regarded as the second most potent politician in Washington.

Advisers, whether official or unofficial, are often a matter of pure luck. The President must first discover able men, and then persuade them to serve. By sheer good fortune General Grant happened to select as his able Secretary of State a wealthy New Yorker, Hamilton Fish, at whose home he had dined amid impressively luxurious surroundings. Grant knew little about his background, and probably could not have evaluated it properly if he had known more. In any event, Fish's admirable achievements in diplomacy partially redeem the scandals of the Grant orgy.

Discouragingly often, the President is not fortunate enough to secure his first choice for an important post; he often has to settle for a fourth, fifth, or even lower. None of the major ambassadorial appointments of Wilson was as much as a second choice; the journalist Walter Hines Page, tapped for the London post, was a third choice. Turning out to be more British than the British, Page watered down American protests to London in such a way as to make more certain Washington's final break with Berlin and the alignment with Britain. Wilson finally became so disgusted that he simply ignored Page's pro-British preachments.

Increasingly, the President's problem is to persuade a prospective appointee to make the necessary financial sacrifices. Most men are not eager to leave a high-paying job in industry, dump their securities at a loss because of possible "conflict of interest," and subject themselves to public abuse and Congressional investigation—all for relatively modest remuneration. Defense Secretary Charles E. Wilson, under Eisenhower, had to leave the headship of General Motors Corporation, with a huge salary, rid himself of his stock in the company, and expose himself to criticism whenever he put his foot in his mouth, which he did with uncanny frequency.

If the appointee turns out well, as Secretary of the Treasury Hamilton did for George Washington, we tend to give the adviser undue credit. This we certainly have done in Hamilton's case. If he turns out badly, as the crooked Secretary of War Belknap did for Grant, we blame the Executive for not having exercised better judgment. There are now hundreds of thousands of people on the federal payroll, and if a handful of them are exposed as bad apples, the ancient cry is raised anew, "Throw the rascals out."

A President sometimes has the additional misfortune to be assailed for scandals which his own "scoundrels" did not create. The already besmirched Grant administrations were further blackened by the Tweed Ring and the Crédit Mobilier. The grafting Tweed Ring was a purely municipal racket in New York City, and although it reflected the moral measles of the era, Grant had nothing whatever to do with it. The Ring was forged while Andrew Johnson was President, and we could as logically (or illogically) blame him. The Crédit Mobilier railroad construction company, which bribed certain Congressmen to forestall investigation, did its dirty work more than a year before Grant came to the White House. But since the exposure occurred during his regime, some of the muck has rubbed off on him. We could as fairly blame President Benjamin Harrison for the Johnstown flood of 1889.

THE THIRD-TERM SHACKLE

The "lame-duck" President, like the "accidental" President, suffers from handicaps that can be labeled bad luck.

The sneer "lame duck" used to be applied most commonly to a public official who had been defeated for re-election—say, a member of Congress. He still had several months to serve, presumably without the same sense of responsibility that would guide him if he had been re-elected and was expecting to run again. Before 1933, when the Twentieth Amendment to the Constitution was adopted, the lame-duck period for the President and members of Congress was more dangerous than it is now. It then ran from early November, when the elections were held, to March 4, when the new term began, for a total of about four months. Now it extends from early November to January 20, less than three months, but still a perilously protracted period in an atomically triggered era.

In recent years the term lame duck has been twisted from its common meaning. It is now applied to a President who is triumphantly re-elected, as Eisenhower was in 1956, but who cannot aspire to a third term because of the Twenty-second Amendment, adopted in 1951. Critics of the amendment complained, and some still do complain, that every President elected thereafter would be a lame duck because he would be hopelessly crippled during his second term. Congress, knowing that the king was dead or about to die, would presumably go its own sweet way, completely irresponsive to the patronage bludgeon and other pressures. (Congress often went its own sweet way even before the anti-third-term amendment, as maladroit Andrew Johnson and many others discovered to their sorrow.)

But those critics of the Twenty-second Amendment who cry "lame duck" overlook certain basic facts. The Chief Magistrate now has relatively little patronage "pie" to parcel out, and most of this is eaten long before the end of his second term. He has various other ways of coercing Congress. He can appeal over its head to the voters—"going to the people"—as Wilson did dramatically through platform and press. He can make appeals on radio and television, as Eisenhower did on occasion. He can set forth his views in press conferences. He can withhold federal funds for public works from certain Congressional districts, or he can create a propaganda backfire against a Congressman in his district or a Senator in his state, as Kennedy did in pushing his Civil Rights program. He can "inspire" a letter-writing campaign directed at members of Congress, as Eisenhower did conspicuously in supporting teeth-equipped labor legislation. He can withhold public support from candidates for re-election, or openly oppose such candidates, as Franklin Roosevelt did in his ill-fated purge of 1938. He can have the Internal Revenue Service scrutinize income tax returns, or the F.B.I. investigate private lives. Finally, he can threaten a vigorous veto, as Eisenhower did with remarkable success.

Critics of the two-term restriction also ignore the fact that until 1940 almost every second-term President labored under the shadow of the unwritten Twenty-second Amendment. It had virtually the force of a constitutional prohibition. Critics likewise ignore the fact that a number of the stronger Presidents—notably Jackson, Polk, Cleveland, and Wilson—came into office favoring a single term or committed to one.

When General Eisenhower was elected as the first President under the Twenty-second Amendment, political wiseacres insisted that the poor man was condemned to be a lame duck. Wobbly at the start, he admittedly did not bestir himself much more than a caretaker during his first term. But in the latter part of his second term, when he should have been quacking like a crippled duck, he displayed more vigor and effectiveness than at any other time during his incumbency. He even aroused some criticism toward the end by breaking relations with Castro's Cuba and otherwise showing an excess of vigor which threatened to commit his successor to embarrassing courses. Evidently no one on his staff warned him that a lame duck is supposed to waddle like one.[2]

---

[2] Eisenhower later expressed himself as favoring the Twenty-second Amendment, declaring that the President has plenty of powers and that he had felt no diminution of power in his second term. Dwight D. Eisenhower, *Waging Peace* (1965), p. 643n; see also *Saturday Evening Post,* CCXXXIV (May 13, 1961), pp. 116–17 and radio statement, October 17, 1963. Kennedy as President likewise expressed his approval, arguing that "eight years are enough for any man." T. C. Sorensen, *Kennedy* (1965), p. 755; also White House press release, December 17, 1962 (rocking-chair chat).

LAME DUCKS: REAL AND PARTIAL

In the good old days, a lame duck was whimsically defined as a politician whose goose had been cooked at the recent election. Among the Presidents, the "Spurned Seven" were the two Adamses, Van Buren, Cleveland, Benjamin Harrison, Taft, and Hoover, all of whom ran for second terms and were defeated. During these four-month interregnums the power of the dying king was waning, and his troubles stemmed in part from his weakening hand on the scepter.

Hoover, bogged down in the Depression, sweated out his four months as a lame duck. He complained bitterly, then and later, that Roosevelt refused to cooperate with him in lessening the impact of the Depression, and anti-Rooseveltians have charged that the President-elect deliberately dragged his feet so that the crisis would worsen and he would appear all the more glorious as a savior. But Hoover privately wrote to Senator Reed of Pennsylvania that if Roosevelt had accepted his proposals, they would mean "the abandonment of 90 percent of the so-called New Deal."

The "Spurned Seven" were all double lame ducks: they and their party were both thrown out of the Executive branch. A similar kind of lame duck was the man who did not run for re-election but who was serving out his term after his own party had taken a beating at the polls. The prime example is Buchanan. His Democratic party had lost in November to the Lincoln Republicans, and his already aged hands were weakened by this vote of no confidence. Ordinarily a departing Democrat can work out a harmonious transfer of power with an incoming Democrat, just as Republicans normally can with Republicans. But when there is a party overturn, the lame duck in the White House finds himself doubly handicapped, as indeed Buchanan did.

Limited lame ducks include the "accidental" trio who did not stand for a second consecutive elected term: Theodore Roosevelt, Calvin Coolidge, and Harry Truman. In the case of Truman alone did the succession pass into the hands of the opposition party. But in a narrow sense these three men were all virtual lame ducks for a period of from three to four months. In their waning weeks, both

Theodore Roosevelt and Harry Truman had especially refractory Congresses on their hands.

All of the Schlesinger Big Six ran for re-election and triumphed, but Wilson presents a unique case. He was the only one of the Greats to be followed by a President of the opposition party, in this instance by the affable Harding. Although Wilson was partially paralyzed by a stroke and suffering from other disabilities, he coveted the honor of a third nomination. If he had received it, he might have run again, so deep was his devotion to the League of Nations. James M. Cox, the pro-League Democrat who won the nomination instead, was overwhelmingly defeated by Harding, who had erratically opposed Wilsonian policies.

Political pundits generally agreed that, figuratively speaking, the crippled Wilson and not the energetic Cox had run for the White House in 1920. Certainly the landslide for Harding was a resounding repudiation of the moral overstrain and disillusionment that Wilson had brought upon a nation that was both fickle and immature. In this sense, the ex-Princetonian was an authentic lame duck, and the futility and drift of his last four months in office were worsened by the backhanded slap at the polls.

All the world loves a winner. The presidential image shines all the brighter if the setting sun of the departing Chief is followed by the rising sun of a new administration by his own party.

CHAPTER IX

The Post-Presidential Glow

"... Those who have held the office of Chief
Magistrate should abstain, after their retirement, from
becoming partisans in subsequent elections to that office."

Ex-President Monroe, 1828

DEATH AND DEIFICATION

A former President's image is often colored by the circumstances of his death. Three of the Big Five were martyrs, of sorts, and this is one prime reason why they appear among the Big Five. John F. Kennedy reportedly remarked that to be a great President one must get the country into a great war or get assassinated.

Some men die at the right time for their reputations; others are less fortunate. Lincoln could hardly have picked a better moment if he had hired the assassin: he almost literally, like Nelson at Trafalgar, expired in the arms of victory, five days after Lee's surrender. His bier lay in state, witnessed by sorrowing thousands, and was then routed to Springfield by way of New York and Chicago. All told, the corpse was viewed by a million and a half mourners; the coffin or funeral train by some seven million more. Slain by a demented Southerner, and allegedly the victim of a Confederate plot, Lincoln seemed to be a martyr to the cause of freedom and democracy for which he had given his "last full measure of devotion."

114

Countless citizens had not regarded Lincoln before his death as an effective Chief Executive, much less a great one. In 1864, when he ran for a second term, nearly two million of his Northern countrymen voted against him. Yet the Booth bullet sped the Lincoln legend on its way. The cynic who today denies that Lincoln was our greatest President is liable to be regarded, at least in the North, as moronic, unpatriotic, pro-Communist, or all three. But if Lincoln had lived, he undoubtedly would have locked horns with the Radical-led Congress; in fact, he already had. His prestige and tact were such that he almost certainly would have escaped some of the woes that bedeviled Andrew Johnson, yet his laurels no doubt would have partially withered. If General Grant had accompanied Lincoln to the theater that night, as originally planned, and had been shot instead, his stature today would probably be greater and Lincoln's smaller. Victory or martyrdom is a potent ingredient in reputation making, but the two combined are irresistible.

Franklin Roosevelt died at the right time. He expired, like Lincoln, in mid-April, and, like Lincoln, in the arms of victory, almost. Some four weeks later, Hitler's Germany surrendered. If Roosevelt had lived on, the Cold War almost certainly would have heated up, and we would have been spared the Communist plaint, "If Roosevelt were only alive." His death in 1945 was almost certainly a boon to his reputation.

Woodrow Wilson died at the wrong time. If his spirit had fled at Pueblo, Colorado, the night he delivered the last of his impassioned speeches, his reputation today would doubtless be more exalted than it is. Ex-Senator Albert J. Beveridge later remarked that martyrdom "would have lifted him overnight to a position higher than Lincoln's." Vice President Marshall, who had presided over the Senate and had sensed its temper, would have taken command, and the Treaty of Versailles, with the Lodge reservations added, would probably have been approved. World War II might even have been averted. Certainly we would have been spared the never-ending debate over what would have happened if America had only joined the League of Nations.

But Wilson, his wings clipped, lingered on in impotence, a kind of living legend. He was strong enough to obstruct but not vigorous enough to construct. His place among the Big Five is based upon his amazing legislative achievements in 1913–1914, and upon his crusading war leadership in 1917–1918. But in so elevating him, we must overlook the peacemaking mistakes before his collapse and the virtual stagnation after his collapse. A President must be judged by his entire administration, not by just the first six years of an eight-year stint. The academicians who rate these statesmen would do well to remember that if a student does "A" work during the first three fourths of a course, and then fails the last part, including the term paper and the final examination, only an act of charity will permit him to receive the highest grade.

Other Executives died at the wrong time for their reputations. Theodore Roosevelt, having left the White House young and full of fire, developed into a common scold as he assailed both Presidents Taft and Wilson. We should probably think more highly of him today if the African lions had only "done their duty" and devoured him in 1909.

Other former Executives, living on usefully for decades, cast a more favorable backward light on their unhappy years in the White House. Conspicuous in this group were Taft (as Chief Justice), Hoover (as relief worker and government reorganizer until age eighty-one), and John Quincy Adams (as a savage anti-slavery battler for seventeen years on the floor of Congress). Eyes watering, hands shaking, voice cracking, Adams fell in the harness, and was accorded the most impressive funeral that the capital had yet witnessed.

MARTYRS ALL

Every President who dies in office, whether from bacteria or bullets, is regarded as a martyr to the public weal, at least in some degree. James A. Garfield, whose troubled six months were marred by officemongering, was probably helped, as far as reputation was concerned, by his assassination. One recalls George Bernard Shaw's cutting remark, "Martyrdom is the only way in which a man can become famous without ability." Even Harding was fortunate in dying just before the cesspool in Washington overflowed. He was laid reverently to rest by a sorrowful and unsuspecting nation.

The tragic death of John F. Kennedy likewise has resulted in spotlighting his achievements and overshadowing his shortcomings. Eulogists are forced to stress what he might have done, if he had lived and fulfilled his bright promise. The truth is that affairs of state, both at home and abroad, were not prospering conspicuously. But Kennedy was such a bright, vibrant, and likeable human being that attention was focused on the ideals that he stood for rather than the legislation that he had failed to drive through Congress.

The magnitude of the last rites honoring a martyred President is also related to the magnitude of his later stature. All those who died in office were accorded impressive funerals, including the bullet-martyrs Garfield and McKinley. Mrs. John F. Kennedy had a study made of the Lincoln rites before she perfected final arrangements for her murdered husband. About a million people in Washington viewed the funeral procession or the bier as Kennedy lay in state; tens of millions witnessed the obsequies on television. The Kennedy image, like Lincoln's, did not suffer from all this pomp and pageantry.

Among the non-martyrs who died after leaving office, George Washington occupies a unique place. His death released a flood of essays, obituaries, eulogies, elegies, orations, and black-bordered newspapers, almost to the point of idolatry. Some two hundred memorial services were held in towns all over the country. If partisanship had demoted George Washington from first place "in the hearts of his countrymen," the silencing hand of death surely restored him to his premier position.

THE DIFFICULT ROLE OF HAS-BEEN

Much depends on the President's behavior after leaving office. The problem of what to do with the ex-kings is ever before us; at one time we had as many as five, just before the Civil War. "Marse Henry" Watterson, the outspoken Kentucky journalist, is said to have proposed as his solution of the problem, "Take them out and shoot them." Grover Cleveland more reasonably declared, "The best thing to do with ex-Presidents is to leave them alone to make an honest living like other people." Most ex-Chiefs, after their turn at bat, have refrained from jogging the elbow of their successors.

Some Presidents emeriti, as we have just seen, lived to cast a better backward light on their stressful presidential years, notably John Quincy Adams, William H. Taft, and Herbert Hoover. The Southern farmer-planters generally retired to their plantations, there to give advice to their successors (not always taken) and thus graduate to the rank of "sages." The list includes Jefferson, the Sage of Monticello; Madison, the Sage of Montpelier; and Jackson, the Sage of the Hermitage.

Some has-beens are circumspect; others are not. Woodrow Wilson declared, "I am showing President Harding how an ex-President should behave," and he did so by remaining almost completely in seclusion. Others stir up controversy and varying amounts of turmoil by commenting publicly on the so-called blunders of their successors. Theodore Roosevelt, finally living up to his "madman" billing, pulled no punches in condemning both Taft and particularly Wilson, whom he branded a "damned Presbyterian hypocrite." Herbert Hoover, President-reject, dourly and sourly berated the creeping socialism of the New Deal throughout the 1930's, and thus invited a decade of brickbats and boos. So bitter was the resentment he aroused that President Franklin Roosevelt spurned his offer of public service after Pearl Harbor.

Ex-President Truman took potshots at President Eisenhower's "do-nothingism," and otherwise enjoyed himself shooting, as usual, "from the lip." (President Kennedy wittily remarked that Truman had shown "how interesting life can be for a fallen President.")

Truman undoubtedly hurt his image by some of his ill-considered remarks, especially when, in 1965, he reportedly condemned the Reverend Martin Luther King, the Negro who had won the Nobel Peace Prize, "as a rabble-rouser who hasn't got any sense." On the other hand, he starred in a series of television programs presenting his side of a number of the "great decisions"; in fact, he was named television personality of 1964.

Ex-President Eisenhower, the oldest incumbent who outlived the youngest elected incumbent (Kennedy), followed in Truman's footsteps by being openly critical of the left-leaning New Frontier. Some of his actions and attitudes, including his shilly-shallying regarding the Goldwater nomination in 1964, raised retrospective doubts as to his competence and decisiveness as Chief Magistrate.

Some of the former Executives, already low in public esteem, became involved in unpopular causes, and their standing suffered accordingly. John Tyler, finally putting his native Virginia above the Union, served as a member of the Confederate provisional Congress, which met in Montgomery and drew up the Confederate

Constitution. Elected to the permanent Congress in Richmond, he died before he could take his seat. With the taint of treason clinging to his name, invading Union soldiers ravaged his beautiful Virginia estate and home, Sherwood Forest. Fifty years after his death Congress voted a modest monument to his memory in Richmond.

Ex-President Fillmore also hurt himself. Favoring conciliation rather than coercion, he criticized Lincoln's conduct of the war and in 1864 supported the Democratic candidate, General McClellan. Branded a Copperhead, Fillmore antagonized his neighbors in Buffalo. At the time of Lincoln's assassination he was so busy at the sickbed of his wife that he was unaware of the request to drape private houses. He awoke one morning to find his home smeared with ink.

Franklin Pierce, the New Hampshire "doughface" of the 1850's, was similarly blackened. Lapsing pitiably into alcoholism after his wife's death, he condemned the Lincoln administration for its abuse of personal and property rights. Charges of treason were redoubled after he made a speech in Concord, New Hampshire, in which he warmly supported the "noble martyr" Clement L. Vallandigham, a notorious anti-war Copperhead. The Granite State has never been conspicuously proud of her only President—Young Hickory of the Granite Hills. Not until after fifty years of debate did the legislature erect an unpretentious monument to him in Concord.

RIGGING THE RECORD

Some men lived long enough to publish revealing memoirs. Most of these works in turn have had enough impact, either on the public mind or the world of scholarship, to help reshape the previous image.

Several ex-Presidents published their observations so late in the day, or in such fragmentary form, that they were of little consequence. John Quincy Adams' twelve-volume journal did not appear until 1874–1877. Historians have found it a veritable gold mine, and although Adams is revealed at his most envious and petulant worst, the scholar is so grateful for all this rich fare that he is disposed to overlook such failings.

James Buchanan, unlike his other two Southern-influenced predecessors, steered clear of Copperheadism. As a prominent War Democrat, he gave Lincoln strong moral support. But the ageing Sage of

Wheatland (his beautiful Pennsylvania farm) devoted the later years of his life to preparing a vindication of his alleged vacillation. Published as *Mr. Buchanan's Administration on the Eve of the Rebellion* (1866), while wartime passions were still high, the book unleashed a new torrent of abuse.

General Grant left no memoir of the presidency, although he did prepare two volumes dealing with his career in the Civil War. Dying of cancer of the throat, he pluckily strove to write his way out of severe financial difficulties by publishing this plainspoken, soldierly account. Sponsored by Mark Twain, the work enjoyed enormous popularity and the publishers paid the widow over $400,000 in royalties. One of the royalty checks was probably the largest thus far in American publishing history.

The irony is that the man who had failed at everything else in civilian life, finally succeeded spectacularly as an author after his death, and he died knowing that he would leave his widow in comfortable circumstances. His exhibition of raw courage, followed by sensational financial success, did something to raise him in the esteem of his contemporaries. The tragic-happy ending has probably persuaded some historians, whose royalty checks seldom equal Grant's, to think more charitably of the General's blunderings.

Beginning with the 20th century, the pattern has been to prepare full-blown memoirs relating to the White House years, and running heavily to apologia. All who left office alive and well did so, though Taft's effort, unlike his frame, was sketchy. Theodore Roosevelt, often called the first of the Modern Presidents, led off in 1913. His vigorous portrayal of the strength of righteousness and the righteousness of strength featured his brandishings of the Big Stick. The tale lost nothing in the telling—in fact gained some adornments—and probably helped inflate his image.

Calvin Coolidge came forth in 1929 with an autobiography. Like its author, it was dry and reserved, and, like the soil of his native Vermont, rather barren. These juiceless philosophizings did little, if anything, to boost his stock as a statesman. At the same time he dashed off syndicated columns for the newspaper press, reputedly at more than one dollar a word. ("The cluckings of Calvin," jeered the New York *Nation*.) He was responsible for such banalities as: "When more and more people are thrown out of work, unemployment results." No one but an ex-President could get such stuff published, let alone purchased.

More recent Presidents have been even more wordy than so-called Silent Cal Coolidge. Herbert Hoover published two volumes dealing with his four tormented years in the White House; they suffer from a determined effort to warp the record to his advantage. The public may be impressed, but the world of scholarship, generally more sympathetic with the pro-intellectualism of the New Deal, is less enthusiastic. Harry Truman's frank, informal, and personalized reminiscences, published in two volumes and supplemented by two other volumes of less solid off-the-cuff fare, will probably hold up better. Dwight D. Eisenhower has now brought out the two volumes of his best-selling memoirs. They deal with the presidential years, and while they are detailed, they are not as revealing as one might have hoped. The General's genial nature shines through, but he is more pleasing than penetrating. Critics have said essentially the same thing about his performance in office.

THE BIOGRAPHICAL BUILDUP

Much depends on the excellence of the biographers whom the retired President happens to attract.[1] Usually this is a matter of pure luck: he is at the mercy of any writer, trained or untrained, partisan or non-partisan, who comes down the pike. Notable exceptions occur when the former Chief chooses his own official chronicler, as Woodrow Wilson happily did in Ray Stannard Baker, and as Theodore Roosevelt did in Joseph B. Bishop. The ex-Rough Rider proved to be an active kibitzer-collaborator.

More recent Presidents have shared their secrets rather openly with well-disposed newspaper men; witness such officially inspired works as Jonathan W. Daniels' *The Man of Independence* [Truman] (1950) and Robert J. Donovan's *Eisenhower: The Inside Story* (1956). This type of biographer does not ordinarily bite the hand that feeds out the documents.

The so-called Greats and Near Greats, on the whole, have fared unusually well at the hands of biographers, and this is one reason why they repose in the exalted categories. Washington was early made into something of a plaster-of-Paris demigod by the cherry-

[1] See Biographical Appendix D for a full list.

tree-and-hatchet imaginings of Parson Weems, by the massive
scissors-and-paste five volumes of John Marshall, and by the five
volumes of literary artistry by Washington Irving. The debunking
attacks by W. E. Woodward and Rupert Hughes in the cynical
1920's made hardly a dent; and President Coolidge is said to have
twanged, "Washington Monument still stands." The monument
certainly does stand, especially when buttressed in more recent
years by the seven-volume life by Douglas S. Freeman and his
posthumous collaborators. Jefferson has outlived the slings of the
19th-century New England historians, has survived the laudatory
trilogy by Claude Bowers (1925–1945), and is now being further
enthroned by the multi-volume classic of Dumas Malone. Lincoln's
biographers, with the notable exception of Edgar Lee Masters, have
been generally favorable.

The two modern Greats have likewise been fortunate. Franklin
Roosevelt is treated fairly, to say the least, by gifted biographers
like James M. Burns, Frank Freidel, and Arthur M. Schlesinger, Jr.
Woodrow Wilson was overpraised by his handpicked Ray Stannard
Baker, for a total of eleven volumes, and by Dr. William E. Dodd's
one volume, whose every page voted Democratic. A reaction was
bound to set in. Dr. Arthur S. Link is now well along with a multi-
volume biography which, with scholarly objectivity, is as much
concerned with the debit as with the credit side of the ledger.

Some men have been blackened by their biographers. Conspicuous among them is Theodore Roosevelt, a Near Great, who
might well have landed among the Greats had it not been for the
Pulitzer-prize biography by journalist Henry F. Pringle, published
in the early depression year 1931. Reacting against the Rough
Rider's unbounded egotism and self-praise, Pringle cynically cut
him down to size—probably overcut him—to about the stature of a
boisterous Boy Scout who never grew up. Fairer studies since then
have helped to swing the pendulum back the other way.

Other men have suffered from silence. A meritorious biography of
Buchanan, by Philip S. Klein, did not appear until 1962, one
hundred and one years after that Old Public Functionary had left
Washington. There is still no first-rate biography of President Hoover,
partly because Hoover denied his papers to scholars. A maligned
McKinley had to wait more than a half century before Margaret

Leech and H. Wayne Morgan more fully revealed the mystery man of Canton, Ohio.

Great biographies—or at any rate Pulitzer-prize biographies—tend to add stature to their subject. We think at once of such books as Arthur M. Schlesinger, Jr.'s (a quasi-biography of Andrew Jackson), Allan Nevins' (Grover Cleveland), Samuel F. Bemis' (John Quincy Adams), Margaret Leech's (William McKinley), Robert E. Sherwood's (Franklin Roosevelt), and Arthur Walworth's (Woodrow Wilson). Some of these Presidents did not need their sheen brightened by such Pulitzer-prize treatments, and the authors probably gained more fame than their subjects. This seems to have been true of D. S. Freeman's *George Washington*, Carl Sandburg's *Abraham Lincoln*, and Ray Stannard Baker's *Woodrow Wilson*.

Several biographical laws seem to be operating. Distance lends enchantment: in general, the Greats are viewed more favorably by latter-day scholars than they were by many contemporaries. The most eminent Presidents, with their lush legacy of manuscripts, also attract the most biographers. Famous Presidents not only seem more heroic and more significant, but their biographies are more likely to sell. Hundreds of collectors routinely buy Lincolniana, but few, if any, gather Fillmoriana. Finally, the more objectively and intensively the great man is studied, the more the whitewash is flaked off, as certainly is true of all the Greats. But when this is done, enough eminence remains to leave their ranking virtually unimpaired.

TEXTBOOK STEREOTYPES

For most Americans the Presidents live, if they live at all, in the history textbooks. Here they are usually done to death by dullness. To be given any popular ranking at all, much less a high ranking, the statesman must lodge in the memory. He is more likely to endure if his personality and administration are colorfully associated with nicknames, symbols, slogans, and catchwords.

Lucky indeed was the man who became conspicuously associated with some kind of concrete imagery that lent itself to cartooning or other pictorial representation. Old Hickory Jackson, a tough veteran of the wars, was symbolized during his political campaigns by countless hickory poles and sticks. Old Tippecanoe Harrison still lives, as he has lived for a century and a quarter, in a non-existent log cabin, with a cider barrel nearby. Honest Abe Lincoln split some rails in his youth, and he became the Rail Splitter, with thousands of rails being paraded about that he never saw, much less split.

Nor does the 20th century lack presidential imagery. Theodore Roosevelt, the Rough Rider of the Spanish-American War, is remembered for his cowboy outfit, blazing six-shooters, and sleepless Big Stick, which sometimes turned out to be only a padded club. An even more popular symbol of esteem and affection was the Teddy bear, beloved by millions of children.[2] Similarly, we visualize ex-Professor Wilson with his gown and mortarboard, Franklin Roosevelt with his saucily upturned cigarette holder, John F. Kennedy with his covered frontier wagon and rocking chair, and Lyndon B. Johnson with his tall Texas hat.

All of the Greats and Near Greats are associated with nicknames, slogans, or sayings, some of which are erroneously attributed to them. We remember George Washington as counseling no "permanent alliances." We think of Thomas Jefferson as the foe of "entangling alliances," and of Andrew Jackson as standing firm for both "Our Federal Union" and "Spoils for the Victors." We see Franklin Roosevelt meeting his Rendezvous with Destiny by sponsoring the New Deal and the Good-Neighbor Policy, battling "fear itself," quarantining the aggressors, and serving as the Arsenal of Democracy, while espousing the Four Freedoms and the forgotten men, who were one third "ill-housed, ill-clad, ill-nourished."

Woodrow Wilson, the pedagogue in politics, is remembered for a series of teachings that turned sour, and his standing has consequently suffered. He preached "watchful waiting" regarding Mexico (and twice invaded that country). He urged his countrymen to be "impartial in thought" toward the war in Europe (though he himself was not impartial in thought and his counsel was one of perfection). After the *Lusitania* was torpedoed in 1915, the "Watchful Waiter" was "too proud to fight" (but he finally did with the clarion call "Force, force to the utmost, force without stint or limit"). He called for "peace without victory" early in 1917 (he ultimately

---

[2] While President Roosevelt was bear hunting in Mississippi, a newspaper dispatch reported that he had refused to shoot a small bear brought in for him to kill. After a cartoonist had depicted the supposed incident, the Teddy bear craze caught on.

settled for victory without peace). After trying "armed neutrality" (it was essentially unarmed unneutrality), he asked for a war to make the world "safe for democracy" (it ended with the world unsafe for democracy) and for "a war to end war" (there were twenty or so wars being waged after the big one jarred to a halt). At Paris, he fought desperately for his Fourteen Points, including "Open covenants of peace, openly arrived at" (he met secretly with the Big Four), but most of his points were blunted, bent, or brushed under the rug.

THE LINGERING AFTERGLOW

Some Presidents were lucky enough to have administrations which lent themselves to brand names. These linger favorably in the memory and generally indicate movement, if not greatness. We link Jeffersonian Democracy with the so-called electoral Revolution of 1800; Jacksonian Democracy or the coonskin New Democracy with the so-called electoral Revolution of 1828. The pleasant catchword, the Era of Good Feelings (only it was not), casts a mellow glow over James Monroe. We associate Manifest Destiny with Polk; the Great Barbecue with Andrew Johnson; the Gilded Age with Grant; the Agrarian Revolt with Cleveland and Harrison; the Full Dinner Pail and the Advance Agent of Prosperity with McKinley; the Square Deal with Theodore Roosevelt; Standpattism with Taft; the New Freedom with Wilson; Normalcy [3] with Harding and Coolidge; Rugged Individualism and the New Day with Hoover; the New Deal and the Good Neighbor with Franklin Roosevelt; the Fair Deal with Truman; Modern Republicanism with Eisenhower; the New Frontier with Kennedy; and the Great Society with Lyndon B. Johnson.

We have considered other post-presidential heritages in earlier chapters, but by way of summary certain questions are worth recalling. Did the former Executive leave a rich lode of manuscripts, which scholars might mine without annoying restrictions? Have his diaries and other private papers been published, or are they being published, in huge, multi-volume sets? (Only Great Presidents de-

---

[3] Legend to the contrary, Harding did not coin the word "normalcy." As a mathematical term it may be found in the language, according to the unabridged *Oxford Dictionary*, as early as 1857.

serve great sets, it would seem.) Did he become a patron saint of his party, as Jefferson and Jackson did for the Democrats and Lincoln for the Republicans? Are holidays observed in his honor, as is conspicuously true of Washington and Lincoln? Were monuments erected to his memory? Were his homes, actual or ancestral, preserved as shrines? Did myths cluster around him, as they do around Washington and Lincoln?

All of these items—many irrelevant, often inconsequential, and largely fortuitous—may be lumped under historical happenstance. They play their part, though backhandedly and belatedly, in shaping our conception of the eminence that the President actually attained while in his lofty office.

PART II

The Testing of Presidential Reputations

"No man will ever bring out
of the Presidency the reputation
which carries him into it."

THOMAS JEFFERSON, 1796

CHAPTER X

Body and Brain

"I am suffering many perplexities and troubles and this term of the Presidency has cost me so much health and vigor that I have sometimes doubted if I could carry the burden to the end."

GROVER CLEVELAND, 1893

PRESIDENTIAL PHYSIQUES

Thus far we have dealt with the making of presidential reputations, whether deserved or not. Henceforth we shall be primarily concerned with tests for determining whether or not that reputation was deserved. As the old saying goes, "Reputation is what people think we are; character is what we actually are."

We must first turn to certain qualifications or tests of a more personal nature. A President must possess these, or at least a substantial number of them, if he expects to achieve a high ranking.

Personal appearance or presence, as we have seen, is an important asset. A man must ordinarily look like a great President if he is to be deemed one. Even so, a few of the more imposing ones, like Pierce and Harding, had feet of clay. Harding, a kind of "living lie," was in fact handicapped because no man could possibly be as great as he looked.

Abounding physical and nervous energy may partially compensate for the lack of an impressive physique. If these qualities are added

129

to a robust body, as was strikingly true of Theodore Roosevelt, the image is by that much brightened. Certainly the suave, effeminate type suffers in the public esteem. President Van Buren, ousted by Harrison in the log-cabin-and-hard-cider campaign of 1840, was unfairly caricatured as an effeminate fop ("Sweet Sandy Whiskers") who wore corsets and ate exotic food with gold spoons. The sneering campaign slogan, "Van is a used-up man," still lives in our history texts.

The Executive Mansion needs a physically vigorous tenant, though Theodore Roosevelt went to extremes with his bullish ebullience and his hand-crushing "dee-ee-lighted." Ike Hoover, the long-time White House usher, reveals that at the end of a busy day the Rough Rider, still bursting with energy, would slip out the back door and run around the base of the Washington Monument until he had worked off excess steam.

The presidential office, with its burgeoning burdens, is clearly no place for the ailing man, the lazy man, or the sleepy man. The elephantine Taft, suffering from a voracious appetite and aching feet, fought a losing battle of the bulge most of his life. Constantly behind in his work, he often caused embarrassment by dropping off to sleep at conferences and on other occasions, while yearning for the golf links. Calvin Coolidge, afflicted with assorted ailments and lacking the bounce of a Harry Truman, was highly relaxed. His two- or three-hour afternoon naps were legendary, although H. L. Mencken was unfair when he jeered that Coolidge snoozed away his five or so years in office. As he slept, the country quietly slipped toward the abyss of economic catastrophe.

DISTINGUISHED INVALIDS

The White House is not—or should not be—a hospital, an out-patient clinic, or an old-soldier's home. President Eisenhower, the grievously wounded old warrior, was induced to run for a second term after a crushing heart attack, followed by a serious abdominal operation. He warned the voters on the radio and television that if they elected him, he could be only a part-time President, conserving his strength and indulging in frequent recreation. But so bedazzling was the glamor of his grin, so blinding was the glitter of his five stars, so comforting was the projection of his father image, that the

American voters continued their "national love affair" and took the distinguished semi-invalid on his own terms. They got for much of his administration precisely what he had promised—a part-time President. Nearly a year after his second inauguration, the *New York Times* reported that out of 1,777 days as President, Eisenhower had spent 583 days resting, vacationing, or recovering from his illnesses, for a total of a year and a half. Critical Democrats complained that there ought to be a law to protect the voters from themselves.

Some men become ill after they take office but Eisenhower is the only incumbent to be re-elected after having suffered a recent physical collapse. Fortunately, no earth-shaking emergency developed while he was completely incapacitated; the Suez crisis of 1956 came to a boil after he had returned to his desk on a limited basis. But small crises have a nasty way of ballooning into big crises. Critics have pointed out that three days after Eisenhower's near-fatal heart attack, the Egyptian government announced its arms deal with the Czechs. This coup not only alarmed Israel but upset the power balance in the Middle East and led eventually to the Suez blowup. The State Department could only respond with feeble protests and futile pressures. Perhaps this is all that it would have done anyhow, but decisive leadership is impossible when the leader is flirting with death in a hospital.

Andrew Jackson, the bullet-bearing old warrior, and Woodrow Wilson, the nervously high-strung academician, both brought serious physical disabilities with them to Washington. But with grim determination they rose above the flesh and discharged their duties with unusual vigor. Wilson kept on keeping on until 1919. Overworked at the Paris Conference, he developed a nervous tic on one side of his face and then fell victim to a severe attack of influenza. At the same time he may have suffered a mild stroke which changed his personality and clouded his memory. This is pure conjecture, but it is a possible explanation of his stubbornness in Washington after he had compromised so much at Paris. He collapsed completely in September, 1919, when prostrated by a major stroke which paralyzed the left side of his body and face. He lingered on until early 1924, when, "tired of swimming upstream," he died.

President Franklin Roosevelt was a special case. Even though his legs were shriveled by infantile paralysis, he was so robust that he managed to secure immense amounts of life insurance. His torso resembled that of a heavyweight wrestler. But even the fabled New Dealer faded and died under the strain of being anchored for more than twelve years to his demanding chair. He delivered his last personal message to Congress—the report on Yalta—sitting in a wheelchair, minus his ten-pound steel braces.

TENSION AND RELAXATION

Today the burdens of office are infinitely more crushing than they were in the days of George Washington. The Chief Magistrate can hardly gain the White House, let alone survive there, without an abundance of physical and nervous energy. While still a Princetonian, Woodrow Wilson suggested that future Presidents might have to be chosen from a small class of "wise and prudent athletes."

The incumbent must also have steady nerves as well as physical reserves. During the Cuban crisis of 1898, when Congress was clamoring for a war to free the oppressed Cubans, McKinley was so harassed that he had to resort to sleeping powders. He finally dumped the whole issue into the lap of Congress, which was hell-bent for blood and which hastened to give the nation the war that it was demanding.

During the Cuban crisis of 1962, when the Soviet Premier Khrushchev attempted to turn Cuba into a missile-launching pad, Kennedy's nerves held steady. He met the pudgy premier in an eyeball-to-eyeball confrontation, and the hardened Kremlinite blinked. The President needed an iron nerve, combined with skillful diplomacy, to face up to a nuclear holocaust that might well have wiped out hundreds of millions of people. "I saw at first hand," wrote Kennedy's confidant Theodore C. Sorensen some months later, "during the long days and nights of the Cuban crisis, how brutally physical and mental fatigue can numb the good sense as well as the senses of normally articulate men." Europe had burst into flames in the summer of 1914 partly because the leading statesmen, many of them elderly men, were so badly beaten down by the pressures and fatigues of anxious days and sleepless nights that their sound judgment took flight.

The ability to relax is likewise related to the ability to serve successfully as President. Lincoln found release in humorous stories and in the writings of professional humorists, even going so far as to open the Cabinet meeting that considered the Emancipation Proclamation with a reading from one of them. On doctor's orders Wilson went to the golf course routinely, using colored balls when snow carpeted the grass, but he played somewhat grimly and mechanically (about 115 was his average score). He also attended vaudeville with regularity, even, critics noted, when the casualty lists of World War I were mounting. Franklin Roosevelt swam frequently (partly for therapeutic purposes), and stole what little time he could spare for his valuable stamp collection. Theodore Roosevelt, a fresh-air fiend, hunted bears, played tennis with cronies (the Tennis Cabinet), and took dignitaries on grueling hikes through Rock Creek Park.

Other men, usually less successful than their more relaxed compeers, found little time for frivolity. John Adams had no real hobby (he lived to be the oldest of all), though his son John Quincy Adams played billiards in the White House (the ultra-Puritans were shocked) and swam nude in the Potomac (the prudes were shocked). Herbert Hoover, despite his labored sessions of tossing the medicine ball back and forth (the Medicine Ball Cabinet), was one of the least relaxed and one of the least effective Presidents, though admittedly his problems were unprecedentedly difficult.

James K. Polk, though successful in achieving his objectives by fair means or foul, was hard, humorless, and unrelaxed, tending strictly to business. He left the capital for only six weeks out of his four years, even enduring the hottest summers, and his worried wife could seldom persuade him to go riding in a carriage with her. Nearly two years after taking office he wrote in his diary, "In truth, though I occupy a very high position, I am the hardest working man in this country." Prematurely grey, he died about three months after leaving the White House; he almost certainly would have died in the harness if he had undertaken to serve a second term.

The president of a corporation is entitled to his vacations and weekends of relaxation. The President of the mammoth corporation known as the United States of America is certainly entitled to relaxation—that is, if he is to function efficiently or perhaps at all. Yet the taxpaying voters, especially those of the opposition party, tend to criticize. Many feel that he should spend virtually all of his waking hours at his well-paying job. President Eisenhower was widely condemned for his quail shooting and especially his golfing, to which he was dedicated. Yet this game was played by other incumbents with varying degrees of proficiency and assiduity; it may have been all that kept Eisenhower going through his eight onerous years in the White House pressure cooker.

FEATHERBRAINS NEED NOT APPLY

The effective Executive needs more than a sound body; otherwise we could happily elect a champion weight lifter. Brainpower is infinitely more important than horsepower.

Few men, including Harding, emerge from the dog-eat-dog competition of politics without revealing considerably better than average intelligence, combined with native shrewdness. The voters must think of the President as a "smart" man with the "gift of gab." Yet they will generally fight shy of one who is too brainy or too gabby (Clay, Webster, Blaine, and Bryan never made it). The masses are alienated by a man who reveals too much "book larnin' " (Woodrow Wilson, Ph.D., was handicapped here). They are repelled by one who talks down to them (there was a suggestion of this in the unsuccessful candidate Adlai Stevenson).

The President's mind must be active, alert, resourceful. He must be fertile in ideas (Hoover was perhaps more criticized for the inadequacy of his ideas than for the inadequacy of his behavior). He must be hospitable to the ideas of others (here Wilson fell down somewhat). He must have a vivid imagination. Such a gift involves a clear conception of the nation's needs, the capacity to perceive which reforms should be pushed first, and a talent for envisaging what will happen when corrective measures are enacted. Woodrow Wilson, with his breathtaking New Freedom program, brilliantly illustrates the application of constructive imagination to long overdue legislation.

Perceptiveness is a close cousin of imagination. The President must have insight enough to perceive the trends that are currently developing, vigilance enough to avoid simply reacting to the actions of others, and farsightedness enough to promote measures that may head off disaster. Coolidge in some measure failed the nation when he encouraged speculation to run its feverish course.

The Chief Executive must be intelligent enough to gain the respect, cooperation, and loyalty of his peers; to lead and even dominate them through his intellectual force. Franklin Roosevelt, with his New Deal, and John F. Kennedy, with his New Frontier, were unusually successful in enlisting the support of a group of younger men distinguished for their intelligence, energy, and dedication. Inspired by their Chief with crusading zeal, many of them served with stars in their eyes but with fewer dollars in their pockets.

The President must have the capacity to grasp, digest, and evaluate a vast body of information, as Kennedy did, even though at times he is dependent on "position papers" or staff-study summaries. He must be able to "pick brains" and store away multitudinous facts in a capacious memory. He must have the intellectual power and discipline to concentrate intensely on the essential problems of fifty American states and more than one hundred foreign countries, even though he may have had no previous knowledge of them. He must be able to analyze all facets of a problem, at home and abroad, and weigh the consequences of his decision. Like a skillful chess player, he must be prepared for all possible countermoves.

Foolhardy indeed is the statesman who stakes everything on one move. This blunder Eisenhower (and Dulles) committed in 1954 when they insisted that France adopt the integrated European Army (EDC), and, when finally rebuffed, found that they had no fallback position. Kennedy backed himself into a corner during the Bay of Pigs fiasco in Cuba, but in his crucial confrontation with the Soviets in 1962 he turned on the heat by degrees. First there was the naval "quarantine" of Cuba (which worked); then there were to be more strenuous measures, including an armed assault on the island. Kennedy had learned from his reading of history, according to his assistant Arthur M. Schlesinger, Jr., that "you should never get into a fight and deny your opponent a means of exit."

The superior President shows a sense of discrimination in seizing upon the essentials of a problem, in separating the significant from the insignificant, and then in fighting for the timeliest programs. He must choose the issues that are the most pressing, the reforms that the public is willing to support, and the proposals that have a reasonable chance of adoption. There is no point in asking for the sky. One of the secrets of Wilson's spectacular success with his domestic program in the Congress of 1913–1914 was that he picked issues—Federal Reserve, tariff reform, trust control—on which the public had been educated to the point where it was ripe for action.

PHI BETES AND NON-PHI BETES

Most of the Presidents have been men of superior intellectual endowment. George Washington, a man of practical wisdom, was a bit slow in his mental processes but sound in his conclusions. John Adams, Thomas Jefferson, and James Madison, all scholars in politics, were recognized for their published contributions, even before they became Presidents. John Quincy Adams, who graduated from Harvard, was elected to Phi Beta Kappa, the national scholarship fraternity, as was Theodore Roosevelt, who published his first scholarly book shortly after leaving college.

Several other Presidents were later elected to Phi Beta Kappa by their alma mater or by other colleges in recognition of their latter-day eminence. The list includes Woodrow Wilson and Franklin Roosevelt. Wilson was clearly the member of this group most worthy of belated kudos on the basis of his scholarly publications and other intellectual achievements. As a Princeton undergraduate, he had determined not to let grade-seeking interfere with his education, and he was more inclined to burrow into Burke and Bagehot than into fact-crammed textbooks. While still in college, he published a learned article on cabinet government in the *International Review*, of which Henry Cabot Lodge, later his archenemy, was then the junior editor. On the other hand, Franklin Roosevelt, while at Harvard, was one of the "activities men," whose grades ran to the "gentleman's C."

We may note in passing that only one of the four men regularly elected to Phi Beta Kappa as undergraduates was regarded by the Schlesinger experts as Above Average. He was Theodore Roosevelt, a Near Great; the other three lodged in the Average group. But we must not draw sweeping conclusions from this tiny sample. Sour-grapes critics of Phi Beta Kappa have often sneered that it is a society of the best memories rather than of the best minds. Hard work, which surprisingly often is accompanied by good luck, is usually one of the prerequisites for success in life. Good grades often indicate, though not necessarily, industry rather than exceptional mentality. Some of the Presidents did not enter college; some did not attend an institution that boasted a chapter of Phi Beta Kappa; and still others were not grade-seekers.

We must also remind ourselves that those who receive the best grades in medical school or law school do not always turn out to be the best doctors or lawyers. There is more to these professions, as there is to the presidency, than a superior intellect, assuming that grades reveal the superior intellect. Theodore Roosevelt, a Harvard Phi Beta Kappa, insisted with rare modesty and with obvious self-depreciation, "I am only an average man but, by George, I work harder at it than the average man."

COLLEGIANS AND NON-COLLEGIANS

A college education is clearly not a guarantee of greatness. A total of twenty-three of the thirty-five Chief Magistrates graduated from college. Some of the least effective, notably Pierce and Buchanan, were college graduates; some of the strongest, notably Washington, Jackson, and Lincoln, were not. Neither Lincoln nor Jackson was formally instructed in as much as the rudiments of a grammar-school education.

The more distinguished non-college men have generally been awarded honorary degrees. George Washington, whose formal education ended before age seventeen, was the recipient of five such degrees from the nation's leading institutions, including Harvard College. This ancient seat of learning even conferred the degree of doctor of laws on the unlettered President Jackson when he toured New England. John Quincy Adams lamented in his diary, "Myself an affectionate child of our Alma Mater, I would not be present to witness her disgrace in conferring her highest literary honors upon a barbarian who could not write a sentence of grammar and hardly could spell his name."

Adams was less than fair. It is true that "Dr. Jackson" (so Adams sneered in private) was apparently the only President to believe that the earth was not spherical. It is also true that his spelling was unorthodox—"logg" for "log," "oragagon" for "Oregon," "potant" for "potent," "paralel" for "parallel." But even Washington wrote "oyl" for "oil," "blew" for "blue," "lye" for "lie," and "ploo Reese" for "pleurisy." Yet Jackson, as well as Washington, could rise above mere spelling and not only think straight but write vigorously.

Academically untutored men like Abraham Lincoln and Andrew Johnson were far from obtuse. But the two so-called Failures, Grant and Harding, obviously lacked the mentality, adaptability, and interest to comprehend fully what was going on about them, much less to chart a farseeing and purposeful course. Grant was acclaimed a great general, but his amateurishness in political life was pathetic. President Harding was in beyond his depth, and he floundered about unhappily knowing it, especially at first. On one occasion he reportedly moaned that somewhere in the country there was an expert who knew the truth, but "I don't know where to find him. I don't know who he is, and I don't know how to get him. My God, but this is a hell of a place for a man like me to be!" Unfriendly critics have suggested that Harding not only had feet of clay but a head of clay.

The American people, with their tradition of anti-intellectualism, are innately suspicious of the "overeducated" egghead who sits in his ivory tower. Theodore Roosevelt had solid claims to scholarship, but his he-mannishness obscured the taint. Intellectuals like Jefferson and Madison, both deemed closet philosophers, may have been injured politically, but in the days before manhood suffrage such learning was not fatal. Dr. Woodrow Wilson, who had to live down his professorial antecedents, never succeeded completely, as evidenced by the numerous cartoons depicting him in academic garb.

The instincts of the ordinary voter are not completely unsound. The presidency calls for caution in council and decisiveness in deed, once all the facts are gathered and the alternatives are duly weighed. The more a man knows, the more alternatives he perceives and the more he is inclined to hesitate—"the paralysis of analysis." The more lively the imagination, the more horrendous the dangers. We are reminded of Mark Twain's cruel remark that all one needs in life is ignorance and confidence and success is sure. Adlai Stevenson was hurt in 1952 by his apparent indecisiveness, underscored by his hesitation about becoming a candidate. The voters sensed in General Eisenhower a more dynamic leader, in part because he had made many military decisions, including the timing of the D-day strike in France.

A man is known by the cronies he keeps. President Eisenhower, though an ex-university president, sought the company of military men and big-business moguls rather than intellectuals. A non-bookish man of deeds rather than words, he relied heavily on oral reports and capsulated summaries rather than on an extensive reading of newspapers and official documents. Such shortcuts may have enabled him to sharpen his golf game, as critics concluded, but they engendered grave doubts as to his competence in high office.

THE BALANCED BRAIN

A keen mind by itself it not enough; it must have breadth and balance. Washington was eminently judicious but not intellectually brilliant. Hamilton, his youthful Secretary of the Treasury, was sparklingly brilliant but erratically balanced. The two men complemented each other. Ideally, the President should be both balanced and brilliant, but if we can have only one of these qualities, we should certainly settle for balance.

He must also be open-minded—that is, teachable. He must give ear to criticism, even if he does not welcome it. The Kennedy administration seemed both petty and petulant when the White House temporarily cancelled subscriptions to the New York *Herald Tribune* after that journal had allegedly misrepresented facts. "Love your enemies," someone has quipped, "for they are the only ones who will tell you the truth about yourself." President Kennedy later saw some humor in the situation when he remarked, "Karl Marx used to write for the *Herald Tribune* [actually *Tribune*], but that isn't why I cancelled my subscription."

The incumbent must likewise listen patiently to the arguments of both sides. George Washington solicited the views of Secretaries Hamilton and Jefferson for and against the Bank of the United States, but the final decision was his. A President must especially guard against the temptation to gather around him only yes-men who will feed him merely what he wants to hear and agree with him on every point of view. "No-men" can be more useful. Andrew Jackson, who seemed to regard disagreement as a species of disloyalty, turned from his regular Cabinet to a Kitchen Cabinet of more like-minded intimates.

Woodrow Wilson found a perfect counselor in the soft-spoken and self-effacing Colonel House, in what has been called "The

Strangest Friendship in History." House, with his "passion for anonymity" and his relish for the power behind the throne, agreed with his Chief most of the time. A faithful bird dog and an ingrained yes-man, he learned to express dissent by merely remaining silent. Wilson sought information from many sources on which to base his judgments, but generally he made up his mind on the basis of the facts rather than permitting others to tell him how he should decide. He was especially annoyed when advisers would retrace their ground; he evidently felt that such repetition was not only time-consuming but also a reflection on his capacity to grasp the point when first expressed. Wilson's chief adviser was Wilson.

The other extreme is a man with such an open mind that, in Shaw's figure, only a draft blows through it. Franklin Roosevelt, while desperately seeking a way out of the Great Depression, grasped at all kinds of straws with bewildering changes of direction. But there was usually more long-range calculation in his "jumping-jack mentality" than his critics were willing to concede.

MACHIAVELLIAN MANIPULATORS

Before the manhood-suffrage days of Andrew Jackson, a presidential candidate could be a statesman without having to stoop to the lower arts of the professional politician. Now the President must reveal shrewdness and cleverness—cunning not unmixed with guile. Indeed, except for the bedazzlement of an occasional military hero like Eisenhower, he can hardly reach his high office, much less stay there, unless he is something of a political manipulator. Martin Van Buren was so adroit that he honestly won such titles as the American Talleyrand, the Little Magician, the Wizard of Kinderhook (his New York home), and the Red Fox of Kinderhook (the little that remained of his hair was red). His enemies charged that he rowed toward his objectives with "muffled oars."

Theodore Roosevelt was not above implementing secret plots, as in the case of the Panama revolt of 1903, or resorting to cheap tricks. In 1904, for political effect, he authorized Secretary Hay's cablegram to Morocco demanding the release of an American citizen by the bandit Raisuli: "Perdicaris alive or Raisuli dead." The resulting public cheers were gratifying; but before the message was sent arrangements had already been made for the prisoner's release.

Grave doubts even existed at that time as to whether Perdicaris was a bona fide naturalized American citizen.

Sometimes the President can be so clever as to overreach himself. In 1937 Franklin Roosevelt came up with a plan to rejuvenate the Supreme Court that he regarded as "the answer to a maiden's prayer." But the scheme was too sly, his support of it too slippery, and the Court too much of a sacred cow. The whole affair backfired disastrously, at least as far as its short-run effects were concerned.

Shrewdness, cleverness, and a native cunning are ordinarily the natural earmarks of a first-rate intelligence. But the President who possesses these gifts must not appear to be too slick, for he will arouse suspicions that may not be groundless. The voters admire a smart man but not a smart aleck.

The Test of Character

MEN OF BACKBONE

The nation's leader must, above all, be a sterling character. Harding, with a spongy interior, was not; Washington, with an Olympian grandeur, was. Almost without exception, the so-called strong Presidents were strong characters. Witness the iron self-discipline of a Washington, the hickory-tough fiber of a Jackson, the steely stubbornness of a Cleveland, the Scotch-Irish obduracy of a Wilson.

Tenacity of purpose, which the Greats all possessed, is but one manifestation of a strong will. Washington persisted in a policy of neutralism and non-involvement during the critical period of the French Revolution. Jefferson clung overlong to his ill-advised embargo on American exports in his frantic efforts to find a substitute for shooting. Lincoln hung on with a drowning man's grip to the ideal of preserving the Union, whatever the cost in gore and gold. Wilson tried desperately to preserve both peace and American rights, until finally forced into the abyss by the ruthless German submarine. Franklin Roosevelt labored through long years of strain, pain, and drain to conquer the Great Depression and reduce unemployment. Not all of these policies proved to be the ultimate in wisdom, but they were all pursued over prolonged periods in the face of persistent and often savage criticism.

Courage is so essential a part of the President's character as hardly to need elaboration. Washington displayed his animal courage on many a bloody field; his moral courage, when he withstood the clamor of the crowd and insisted on peace with Britain in 1793–1794. Legend has it that a century or so later Rudyard Kipling was inspired to write his poem "If" after reading of Washington's coolness at this critical juncture.

Grover Cleveland, attempting to separate the greedy from the needy, displayed rare courage when he offended the potent veteran vote by vetoing the Dependent Pension Bill. He also insisted on sending his explosive tariff-reform message to Congress in 1887, thereby doubly jeopardizing his chances of re-election. "What's the use of being elected or re-elected unless you stand for something," he insisted. Subsequent generations have probably honored him more for his forthrightness than did contemporary voters.

Yet fortitude in standing up for one's personal philosophy, especially an outmoded one, can run into callousness. Grover Cleveland, ever rugged and stubborn, revealed shocking insensitivity when he vetoed a bill that would have provided federal money to purchase seed for drought-stricken farmers in Texas. Depression-cursed Herbert Hoover, a kind of throwback to Grover Cleveland, was bitterly condemned for his 19th-century concepts of rugged individualism. During the drought of 1932 he urged a federal handout of $45 million to feed Kansas cattle, but balked at a dole of $25 million to feed the stricken owners of the cattle. The cattle themselves presumably had no character to undermine.

PROFILES IN COURAGE

The Schlesinger experts accorded a high rating to a number of men who are perhaps best known for courageous acts, especially those decisions that were bound to offend a host of vocal and vengeful voters. Harry Truman, John Adams, and Grover Cleveland are exalted to the Near Greats, in whose august company they probably would not appear if conspicuous acts of stouteartedness did not cancel out serious shortcomings. The combative Jackson would certainly not rank as high as he does if he had not stood up for his convictions, first in defying the plutocratic Bank of the United States and then the Calhounite nullifiers of South Carolina. Wilson likewise revealed commendable courage. He battled the big bankers, while pushing through the Federal Reserve Act; he routed the tariff lobbyists, while ramming through the Underwood-Simmons Tariff Act. After he had rather impulsively ordered an attack on Vera Cruz in 1914, he was deeply disturbed by the deaths of nineteen young American servicemen. At the funeral services in Brooklyn he confessed: "I never went into battle; I never was under fire, but I fancy that there are some things just as hard to do as to go under fire. I fancy that it is just as hard to do your duty when men are sneering at you as when they are shooting at you. When they shoot at you, they can only take your natural life; when they sneer at you, they can wound your living heart. . . ." Someone has well said that we admire courage in direct ratio to the infrequency with which we see it in our public servants. Animal courage, often found in the lowest savages, is probably a commoner virtue than moral courage.

Nor can we overlook the hardihood of those Executives who had to expose themselves to the hazards of their office, including the constant and well-founded fear of an assassin's bullet. In recent years we have expected the incumbent to undergo the additional risks of travel by ship and aircraft to far distant continents—Franklin Roosevelt, Truman, Eisenhower, Kennedy—with all the dangers involved. The battleship *Iowa*, on which Franklin Roosevelt journeyed part way to the Teheran meeting with Stalin, was almost hit accidentally by a torpedo from an American warship.

Yet we should note, however, that so-called acts of political courage have often been politically profitable. When John Adams resolutely, if belatedly, chose peace rather than war with France in 1798, he probably did so in the knowledge that such a course would be popular with a majority of the voters. Yet he knew that it would not be with the warhawk (Hamilton) wing of his own party, whose support he needed for re-election. Almost certainly the rank-and-file voter applauded Jackson's demagogic attack on the Bank of the United States. It became the paramount issue in the election of 1832, which Jackson won by an overwhelming margin. As for Wilson's antagonists, we should observe that big bankers, tariff lobbyists, and pro-German agitators were not then, nor are they now, popular with the American masses.

Overloyal support of one's subordinates, on the other hand, may result in an exhibition of backbone that can be politically harmful. Harry Truman showed misplaced courage by defending his sticky-fingered cronies, and in so doing no doubt hurt himself with many voters, chiefly of the opposition party.[1] More commendably, he had the fortitude to pull the rug from under the headstrong war hero, General Douglas MacArthur, when civilian control over the military was frontally challenged in Korea. The "S" in Harry S Truman may have stood for nothing but the same could not be said of the mulish Missourian himself.

PLIABLE PRINCIPLES

Making enemies of the unsavory sort by standing up for principle can be a distinct political asset. If a man is known by the company he keeps, he is perhaps even better known by the enemies he makes. Grover Cleveland, to his credit, had antagonized Tammanyites and other unsavory elements as Governor of New York. When his name was placed before the Democratic National Convention in 1884, the orator proclaimed that the young men of his state "love him most for the enemies he has made."

The experts probably would give President Eisenhower a higher ranking today if he had only made more enemies. Everybody seemed to "like Ike," even those who did not like him well enough to vote for him. If great Presidents make many powerful enemies, Eisenhower is not marked for greatness.

Yet politics doth make cowards of us all. Even those sterling characters rated among the Great or Near Great occasionally re-

---

[1] Truman had come up through a Missouri political machine (Pendergast) which inculcated up-and-down loyalty: loyalty to one's superiors and loyalty to one's subordinates. In 1940 President Roosevelt opposed Truman for re-election to the Senate in the Missouri primaries, but Truman continued his loyal support of his Chief.

vealed flexible backbones in delicate situations. Lincoln's Emancipation Proclamation, much overpraised and much misunderstood, is a case in point. Issued after much travail of spirit, and with due regard to the pressures from highly vocal zealots, it is a classic example of fence straddling. Where Lincoln presumably could emancipate the slaves, he would not; where he could not, he professedly would as an act of military necessity. The Emancipation Proclamation was stronger on proclamation than emancipation.

Grover Cleveland, the prototype of jut-jawed firmness, betrayed uncharacteristic weakness during his campaign for re-election in 1888. Sir Lionel Sackville-West, the British minister in Washington, had indiscreetly written a private letter (subsequently published) advising in effect that a vote for Cleveland was a vote for England. In a transparent attempt to salvage the fast-slipping Irish vote, the President asked him to leave Washington without even waiting for the red-taped London Foreign Office to recall him. Five days later the voters asked Cleveland to leave Washington.

Franklin Roosevelt, despite his many undeniable gifts, was at times hardly a devil-may-care leader. Rather than go to the mat with his adversaries or with a hostile public opinion, he much preferred indirection, not to say guile. His famed Quarantine Speech of 1937—that is, his demand for quarantining the dictator-aggressors of Japan, Italy, and Germany—was an act of audacity. Pointedly, he delivered it in Chicago, the so-called isolationist capital of the then most isolationist section of the nation. The result was a furious outcry, including the demand of the *Wall Street Journal*, "Stop War Mongering, Mr. President." Rocked back on his heels, Roosevelt abandoned his head-on approach and sought to curb the dictators by destroyer-base swaps and other dubious dealings which risked war and finally helped bring it on. He regarded his clever maneuvers as in the public interest, but millions of his isolationist critics disagreed.

President Kennedy was impaled on the prongs of a not-dissimilar dilemma. Fearing to alienate Southern votes in Congress that were needed for his proposed New Frontier, he did not push forward with civil rights in the South as rapidly as many Negroes wished. A placard carried in a San Francisco demonstration proclaimed: "Less Profile, More Courage"—an obvious reference to Kennedy's best-selling book on courageous Senators, *Profiles in Courage*.

HONESTY THE BEST POLICY

Integrity is another acid test. Its absence in the Grant and Harding administrations accounts primarily for their cellar ranking. Grant was personally honest, but gullible, naive, politically obtuse, and fanatically loyal to the blowsy, horsy, cigar-smoking crowd that swarmed around him and took full advantage of his befuddlement. The slimy trail of corruption, which directly implicated his brother-in-law, led perilously close to the White House door.

Harding, a political wheelhorse, was less naive but no less fully victimized, in this case by his unscrupulous associates of the Ohio gang. Poker chips clicked shamelessly and liquor flowed freely in the private quarters of the White House, despite the Eighteenth Amendment to the Constitution which Harding had sworn to uphold. "In this job," he groaned, "I am not worried about my enemies. I can take care of them. It is my friends who are giving me trouble."

Both of these presidential misfits—Grant and Harding—were evidently incapable of detecting moral halitosis in those around them. But both men were to some extent victims of the debased moral tone which normally follows bloody wars and which certainly followed the Civil War and World War I. In the Chicago stockyards one can hardly detect whether one's associates are bathed or unbathed.

President Jackson suffered at times from nasal blockage, and for this he deserves more censure than he has generally received. The spread of the spoils system was in itself a scandal, but it was inevitable and had in fact been introduced on a substantial scale under President Jefferson. Spoilsmen can be honest, but some of Jackson's definitely were not, and he should never have tolerated them. The worst nest of iniquity was the New York Custom House, through which flowed about two thirds of all American imports. To the lucrative post of Collector of the Customs at New York President Jackson appointed Samuel Swartwout, a loyal friend but a questionable character whose speculative bent had caused Martin Van Buren to warn the General against him. Nearly nine years later Swartwout "swartwouted out" to England, leaving his accounts a million and a quarter dollars in arrears. He was the first man, but alas not the last, to steal a million dollars from the federal government.

On a small scale, fortunately, were the scandals of the Truman era, which also followed a costly and demoralizing war. Like Grant before him, the doughty Missourian revealed a dogged loyalty to his buddies of the Missouri gang. As 5-percent "influence peddlers," they were enjoying too many dubiously earned deep freezers and mink coats ("Mink Dynasty"). The natural instinct of the professional politician—and Truman certainly would qualify as a pro—is to cover up when one's intimates are caught with their hands in the cooky jar. "The mess in Washington" was an effective war cry of the Republicans in the Eisenhower-Stevenson presidential campaign of 1952.

No presidency is ever completely untainted by scandal, usually at the lower levels. Hundreds of thousands of civilians are now on the federal payroll, and small-scale sins, ranging from homosexuality to conflict of interest, are inevitable. One could hardly expect better ethics when we find members of Congress shamelessly voting for legislation to protect their own oil wells and other lucrative holdings.

Even the Kennedy administration, which ended in a deluge of eulogies, was not unsmirched by scandal. Secretary of the Navy Korth, was had used his high office to promote private business in Texas, was forced to resign. President Kennedy, as was natural, hushed up the sordid affair without the show of indignation that he would have betrayed if he had been a candidate for the presidency. Ironically, he had told Congress in the fourth month of his administration, "No President can excuse or pardon the slightest deviation from irreproachable standards of behavior on the part of any member of the Executive Branch."

Then came the Bobby Baker embarrassment during the closing months of the Kennedy years. Young Mr. Baker, a Senate employee and a protégé of Senator Lyndon B. Johnson, had become a mystery millionaire on a relatively small salary in a remarkably short time. Allegedly he had been an "influence peddler." The subsequent Senate investigation, tightly controlled by Democrats, dredged up the fact that President Lyndon B. Johnson, then Senate majority leader, had received a free stereophonic console worth some $500 at the suggestion of Mr. Baker. Under pressure from the White

House, the Senate committee temporarily choked off the investigation while additional witnesses were yet to be called. President Johnson was eager for election in his own right in 1964, and the sooner the Bobby Baker business was dropped, the better for the LBJ image. The console was swept under the White House rug, but the bulge still showed. In 1966 Mr. Baker was indicted by a federal grand jury on nine counts.

PRESENTS FOR PRESIDENTS

The Eisenhower administration, dedicated to cleaning up the "mess in Washington," actually created a mess of its own. The bestarred general, though seemingly the soul of integrity, was deeply embarrassed by the imprudence of his near-autocratic presidential assistant, Sherman Adams. The efficient Adams was found to be exerting his influence to secure favors from the federal government for industrialist Bernard Goldfine, who in turn was making expensive gifts to him, including a vicuña coat and some $3,000 worth of hotel bills. Eisenhower, displaying the Grant-like loyalty of an old soldier and the usual protective coloration of a politician, tried to shrug off the unfortunate affair as a simple case of bad judgment. "I need him," declared the General—and no doubt he did. But when the Maine election in September, 1958, went heavily against the Republicans, the need became less apparent. Mr. Adams, though still protesting that he had done no wrong, was forced out on the wrong grounds—political rather than moral. Cynics rewrote the ancient saying, "As Maine goes, so goes the nation," to read, "As Maine goes, so goes Adams."

General Eisenhower himself was not above taking gifts. Here again following in the unfortunate footsteps of General Grant (the other West Pointer), he accepted a large number of valuable donations, including stock and other expensive equipment for his Gettysburg farm. Muckraking journalists like Drew Pearson claimed that such largesse was worth more than half a million dollars.

The Constitution wisely forbids the President to accept presents from foreign potentates, although even these are often kept, frequently for the non-personal White House "chamber of horrors." Article I, Section 9 stipulates that any federal official holding a position "of profit or trust," may not accept "any present, emolument, office, or title of any kind whatever from any king, prince, or foreign state," without the express "consent of Congress." The obvious intent was to prevent undue foreign influence. The Constitution might also be properly concerned with undue internal influence. A public official is embarrassed to say a needed "no" after he has accepted costly presents, many given in the lively expectation of favors to come.

Some of the early Presidents drew a commendable distinction between gifts of nominal value and those of substantial value. Polk, rather than embarrass both the giver and the receiver, would accept a cane or a book, but nothing more valuable. He persuaded his wife to abide by the same rule. Andrew Jackson, not sharing this sense of delicacy, accepted a valuable French piano with indecent enthusiasm. Even more questionably, the Tafts collected hundreds of silver gifts on their twenty-fifth wedding anniversary.[2]

Integrity invariably brings up the name of Honest Abe Lincoln, who was personally untouched by any stain. But scandals did occur in the War Department under Secretary Simon Cameron, while outside the government an unsavory brood of "shoddy millionaires" mushroomed into being. Desperately determined to preserve the Union, Lincoln ordered his generals to furlough soldiers home, where they sometimes voted for the absent members of their company. The Boys in Blue, generally Republicans, played an important part in making up the majorities without which Lincoln could not have been re-elected over war hero General McClellan in 1864. Stark necessity overruled ethical niceties.

THE SMELL OF SCANDAL

Shockingly enough, the contemporary atmosphere is often such that what would be a ruinous scandal in one era is condoned in another.

The oily stench whistling out of Teapot Dome after Harding died should have been enough to drive the Republicans out of office in 1924. But they were overwhelmingly returned to power in an

[2] The legend is widespread that Washington, Hoover, and Kennedy all refused to accept their presidential salaries, but the records of the Treasury Department show otherwise. Washington appears to have used his stipend for necessary expenses, and Hoover and Kennedy, also wealthy, reportedly donated their salaries to charity.

election which cynics hailed as a mandate to go on
faced Calvin Coolidge seemed like the quintessen<
Vermont farmer, but the painful fact is that he
explicable slowness in fumigating the infected areas
death. The prosperity-drugged voters took an incredibly tolerant
view of this public plundering, which, confusingly enough, also
involved some leading Democrats.

Only one incumbent, the lay preacher and spellbinding orator
James A. Garfield, seems to have become involved in a pre-White
House scandal involving his official position. The evidence is more
than suggestive that, as a Congressman, he accepted a bribe of $329.
The alleged briber was a lobbyist anxious to head off an investigation of the nauseous Crédit Mobilier railroad construction company,
which was underhandedly milking millions out of railroad building.
Although Garfield denied this charge under oath, his protestations
were not altogether convincing. The telltale $329 was chalked on
countless fences and rocks during the heated Garfield-Hancock
presidential election campaign in 1880. The scandal undoubtedly
did Garfield's reputation no good, though he won by a slim margin,
and it certainly did nothing to improve his standing when he entered
upon his duties.

Garfield spent a tortured six months in the White House. "My
God!" he burst out. "What is there in this place that a man should
ever want to get in it." He was so kindly that he hated to disappoint
people by returning a blunt "no," and in this way resembled Franklin
Roosevelt. One of his friends wrote: "One thing thou lackest yet,
and that is a slight ossification of the heart." His death by an
assassin's bullet was no doubt a boon to his fame, as it has been to
all incumbents, for in his case scandals were breaking in the Post
Office Department. The worst of these were slop-overs from the
previous administration, but the public is usually more shocked by
their exposure than by their inception.

Anyone seriously engaged in politics can hardly escape becoming
involved in political deals of one kind or another. The public
generally accepts these as a part of the game, while recoiling in
horror when the dollar sign is directly involved. President Hayes,
the soul of integrity, was declared elected by a special Electoral
Commission in 1877, following wholesale fraud, intimidation, and
murder during the campaign of 1876. Shortly thereafter he rewarded

with federal offices all four members of the Louisiana Returning Board that had high-handedly, not to say corruptly, put the state in the Republican electoral column and Hayes in the White House.

INTELLECTUAL INTEGRITY

Herbert Hoover was wont to draw a sharp distinction between "money honesty," which we find in bank tellers, and "intellectual honesty," which we find in sterling characters. Many a man who would not dream of stealing a penny from a piggy bank does not scruple to twist the truth to promote his political ambitions, the fortunes of the party, or the welfare of the country. (Frequently all three become one in his thinking.) In the strictest sense, no professional politician who has reached the highest office can be deemed 100 percent intellectually honest. George Washington, who was not above an occasional deception, would seem to be an exception. But he was never a professional politician; he did not want the job; and he was the only incumbent who did not in some way pull wires to secure it.

Hoover's record, for all of his concern about "intellectual honesty," is spotty. Preaching "rugged individualism," he came out for prohibition and a high tariff, both of them the antithesis of individualism. By a manipulation of statistics, he represented the towering Hawley-Smoot tariff as one of the most reasonable in American history. By giving out misleading figures on unemployment, and issuing cheery statements about the imminent end of the Depression, he was doing essentially what the doctor does when he tells the patient little white lies to speed recovery.

The stock-in-trade of the professional politician is half-truths and quarter-truths, if not actual lies. If he is a dedicated politician, he has presumably convinced himself that his party is the repository of all the virtues, and that there is no rectitude in the opposition camp. The one is infallible; the other is insufferable. His party platform views with alarm or points with pride, often at alleged misdeeds that are not alarming or at alleged achievements unworthy of pride or even non-existent. The dyed-in-the-wool politician is like the prosecuting attorney who possesses evidence helpful to the defense but who conceals it. A democratic election is all too often a species of mass deception. Little wonder that fond parents do not want their children to become politicians—gentry who shake one's hand before election and one's confidence afterward.

The American system of open debate tends to bring out both sides, as long as there is reasonably full coverage in the press, on the platform, on radio, and on television. But the Chief Executive, in the interests of his own prestige and the future success of his party, often fails to present both sides with complete candor.

President Polk, branded a chronic liar by the Whigs, took serious liberties with the truth in his formal addresses. In his inaugural, he declared that "our title" to Oregon was "clear and unquestionable" when he knew it was not. After he had provoked the Mexicans into crossing the Rio Grande and attacking United States troopers, he informed Congress that war had come "notwithstanding all our efforts to avoid it" (which was not true). He further stated that Mexico had "invaded" our territory and had shed "American blood on the American soil" (the "American soil" was at least as rightfully Mexico's as America's). He subsequently told Congress that the Mexican War "was neither desired nor provoked by the United States" (which is hardly true), that it was not a war of "conquest" (he ultimately seized about one half of Mexico), and that his administration was dedicated to "peace" (unless war became necessary to achieve his objectives). Polk's own Vice President, George M. Dallas, disturbed by his chief's practice of announcing one policy publicly and pursuing another privately, complained bitterly of the "frauds and falsehoods" and "crooked politics" of the administration.

Theodore Roosevelt, free to brand other men liars,[3] would on occasion fall from grace himself. His loud protestations of innocence about the "taking" of the Panama Canal Zone do not have a convincing ring, and his later magnification of his heroic deeds as President has left historians with much to set straight. In the campaign of 1904 he condemned what he came to call the "malefactors of great wealth," but secretly he was putting pressure on them to enrich his campaign fund. One of the heaviest contributors, who had sought to take the "heat" off the trusts, later complained bitterly, "We bought the son of a bitch, and then he did not stay bought."

Woodrow Wilson, for all of his Presbyterian upbringing and

[3] In 1907 Abe Martin defined a liar as a "person who disagrees with Roosevelt."

devout Christianity, would lie on occasion. The month before taking office, he told Colonel House that a man was justified in lying to protect the honor of a woman or to promote public policy. As president of Princeton he testified emphatically that he had not read the manuscript of a certain book before writing a preface for it, and this statement was untrue. As President of the United States, he twice told a Senate committee that he had not known of the notorious secret treaties among the Allies before going to Paris in 1919. This was patently an untruth. Perhaps he was experiencing a loss of memory as a result of the minor stroke that he may have suffered at Paris. More probably, he shied away from a damaging admission that would hurt the League of Nations for which he was prepared to give his life.

Lloyd George, the British prime minister, once remarked that the successful politician must learn to keep his conscience under control. He himself proved that greatness and guile can co-exist in the same man.

TWISTING THE TRUTH

Franklin Roosevelt, as a history-maker and not an historian, was prone to twist the record to achieve his ends. In 1939, when he urged Congress to repeal the arms embargo in the interests of the embattled democracies, he solemnly informed the assembled members that an economic embargo and commercial non-intercourse had brought on the War of 1812. Not only that, but it had resulted in the burning by the British of the very Capitol building, or rather its predecessor, in which the Congressmen then sat. Shocked by such vivid language and the deepening crisis, Congress lifted the arms embargo. But the truth is that the Jeffersonian embargo had been repealed more than three years before the United States, not Great Britain, declared war. Far from bringing on hostilities, it was the first in a series of economic sanctions that came heartbreakingly close to averting armed collision altogether.

Roosevelt may or may not have known better, but his tactics were to use precedent and statistics to bolster policies that he deemed desirable for the welfare of the nation. After the unnerving experience with the Quarantine Speech in Chicago, he was reluctant to disturb the public with disagreeable truths. While glossing over the backward state of American military preparedness after Hitler broke loose in 1939, he would report glowingly on the number of airplanes and tanks "on hand" and "on order." He was careful not to categorize the numbers "on hand" and those "on order," or to explain that the numbers "on order" vastly outnumbered those "on hand."

In the crisis of September, 1940, Roosevelt swapped fifty "overage" destroyers with Britain for a string of potential base sites off the Atlantic Coast. These craft may have been relatively old but they were still highly serviceable. The transaction overrode at least two statutes, but was justified by Roosevelt's Attorney General on dubious premises. Roosevelt, in an off-the-cuff press conference, likened the acquisition of the bases to the Louisiana Purchase as a defense measure. In kind, if not degree, he was roughly correct. The Louisiana Purchase was also of dubious constitutionality, but, like the destroyer deal, it was tolerated by Congress and accepted by the people because it seemed desirable. The President is often able "to do good by stealth."

As the fiery breath of Mars came closer to America, Roosevelt became even less cautious. Campaigning for a third term, he ringingly told an audience in Boston, late in October, 1940, that their boys were not going to be sent "into any foreign wars." He was correct in the sense that the conflict which finally came was America's, though fought on foreign soil. In September, 1941, he reported to the nation by radio that a German submarine had fired a torpedo at the American destroyer *Greer* in the North Atlantic. He conveniently failed to add that the destroyer had been trailing the submarine for three and one-half hours and radioing its position to nearby British patrols. In 1944 the outspoken Mrs. Clare Boothe Luce ran true to form when she charged in a campaign speech that Roosevelt was "the only American President who ever lied us into war because he did not have the political courage to lead us into it."

SILENCE IS GOLDEN

"The truth should not be spoken at all times," runs the proverb. This does not necessarily mean that a statesman should lie; it means that there are times when the less said the better. Undue candor can be harmful to the President, his party, and his country. Grover

Cleveland, deaf to the pleas of the politicians who had put him in office, insisted on telling the American people the blunt truth about the tariff and the Treasury surplus in his memorable message of 1887. Whether correctly or not, many observers attributed his defeat in 1888, and that of his party, to this supercandid approach. A slave of conscience, who was determined to let the chips lie where they fell, he fell out of office.

An incredible instance of undue candor involved President Eisenhower's handling, or mishandling, of the U-2 spy-plane incident in May, 1960. When this high-flying American craft was shot down deep in the Soviet Union on May Day, the appropriate response from Washington at the time could well have been "We are investigating," or "Regrettable, if true." But needled by the press, the official spokesmen in Washington became involved in a tangled web of denials and outright lies. The Paris summit conference was about to be held, and Premier Khrushchev of Russia gave Eisenhower an "out" by declaring he did not believe that the President was personally privy to these numerous spying forays. But in an unprecedented move General Eisenhower, who could have axed some underling, assumed full responsibility for the overflights. Khrushchev thereupon wrecked the summit conference, as perhaps he had planned to do all along.

The ugly truth is that all the great powers (and many lesser ones) engage in espionage; they must for their own security. But none ever admits it, certainly not the head of state, and most certainly not the President of the United States. This was not one of America's finest hours. The cherry-tree-and-hatchet complex of a legendary George Washington may be well enough in the world of Parson Weems, but it can do irreparable damage in the harsh arena of diplomacy.

CHAPTER XII

The Presidential Personality

"No President has ever enjoyed himself as much as I
have enjoyed myself, and for the matter of that I do not know
any man of my age who has had as good a time."

PRESIDENT THEODORE ROOSEVELT, 1908

WHITE HOUSE WARMTH

The personality of the Chief Magistrate has much to do with his success, indeed with his attaining high office. An ingenious psychologist could no doubt work out a personality-test scale for Presidents. Among various features, it would list and weigh the qualities that no candidate should lack.

The incumbents have ranged from cold to captivating. Among the coldest were John Quincy Adams, Benjamin Harrison, and Herbert Hoover, who nevertheless was noted for his quiet humor in small private gatherings. Critics said of Harrison ("The White House Iceberg") that he could make an impressive speech to ten thousand people, but that if he met them afterward individually, he would freeze them out of the room. Hoover, with his shyness and double-breasted dignity, was no hail-fellow-well-met, and the resulting gloom provided a depressing backdrop for the depressed 1930's. After a session with him, Senator Ashurst wrote, "Neither President John Quincy Adams nor President Benjamin Harrison could have refrigerated callers more quickly than President Hoover." None of these ultra-reserved gentry is ranked among the Greats or even the Near Greats, partly because of personality handicaps.

But most of the Greats were hardly glad-handers. George Washington, unwilling or unable to "unbutton himself," was dignified and aloof. The humorist Artemus Ward, referring to the proneness of public men to "slop over," rejoiced that "Washington never slopt over." He did not invite the arm on the shoulder or the friendly slap on the back. But his prestige was so towering that his august presence did not invite slaps on the back. Thomas Jefferson, though shy in public appearances, was a gracious host and a brilliant conversationalist. This talent was not altogether unrelated to his formidable White House wine bill.

Homespun Abraham Lincoln, when not suffering from one of his periodic spells of melancholia, was relaxed, whimsical, approachable —eminently endowed with the common touch. He wasted much time with casual visitors, and even in the White House would stand up to measure himself back-to-back with callers who might be taller than he. Yet he possessed a quiet dignity that did not invite undue intimacy.

Woodrow Wilson could be the life of the party—a small party— with limericks, mimicry, dialect stories, and hornpipe dances. But in public he gave the impression of cold and academic standoffishness. The masses called Roosevelt "Teddy" but they did not call Wilson "Woody." Even at Princeton his enormous success as a teacher lay in lecturing to large classes rather than in communing with seminar groups. William Allen White, no friendly critic, remembered that Wilson's handshake was "like a ten-cent pickled mackerel in brown paper," and that "when he tried to be pleasant he creaked." Like God, he could command fear and respect, but hardly mass personal affection. He loved humanity in the large and at a distance rather than people as individuals. When he embarked on his fateful speaking tour in 1919, associates urged him to unbend and become more warm and human. He replied that it was impossible for him to make over his personality at age sixty-two.

PERSONALITY-PLUS PRESIDENTS

Franklin Roosevelt, fairly oozing infectious confidence, was a geyser of warmth, buoyancy, cheerfulness, friendliness, and captivating personal magnetism. He would first-name important men at their first meeting. Observers said, with pardonable exaggeration, that with his dazzling smile he could charm the birds out of the trees. Fully aware of this marvelous talent, he delighted in turning it on and off, much as one would manipulate a perfume flagon. He enjoyed sending people away so spellbound that they forgot the complaint they had brought. He was eager to meet Joseph Stalin, the hardened old conspirator of the Kremlin, and charm him out of his nasty Communist ways. "I can handle that old buzzard," he is said to have remarked privately. He finally managed to meet the Russian premier at Teheran and then at Yalta, but the record does not reveal that he succeeded in melting his steely adversary.

Yet personal charm is no guarantee of greatness; it may even be a sign of weakness. "Handsome Frank" Pierce, one of the least successful Presidents, radiated charm. Warren Harding was one of the warmest, friendliest, and folksiest men ever to occupy the Executive Mansion, one who loved dogs ("Laddie Boy") and people, yet he was one of the least forceful. He hated so much to say "no" that his father gave thanks that Warren was not born a girl.

One of Franklin Roosevelt's major faults was that he likewise hated to disappoint people or otherwise to hurt their feelings. A good listener, as every President should be, he seemed to be nodding agreement when he was merely listening attentively. When the supposed promise was not kept, his cordial indefiniteness led to angry accusations of double-dealing. Senator Huey P. Long, the Louisiana Kingfish, complained, "I wonder if he says 'Fine!' to everybody." Roosevelt himself was free to admit that at times he was an easy mark, though when toughness was demanded he could be completely ruthless.

As for personal magnetism, General Eisenhower is probably the only other President who can be mentioned in the same breath with Franklin Roosevelt. His engaging grin was so much in evidence that critics often wondered aloud if he had anything behind and above the teeth. They were afraid that there was less there than met the eye. But the General's admirers, who were legion, hailed his gregarious grin as one of the great natural assets of resources-rich America. They were thinking especially of his ability to electrify enormous crowds during his spectacularly successful goodwill safaris in foreign lands.

GLADHANDER-IN-CHIEF

The ceremonial aspects of the presidency are now so demanding that the cold-fish personality is at a serious disadvantage. In this era of television, an aloof Benjamin Harrison could probably never be nominated, much less elected. If the incumbent wishes to be re-elected—and who does not want this stamp of approval on his first term?—he must wave and smile at the cheering crowds and grasp thousands of eagerly groping hands. A ready smile, which is not so permanent as to suffer from overexposure, is an undeniable asset, especially if it flashes toothpaste-advertisement teeth.

A warm handshake, especially the double clasp of an Abraham Lincoln or a Lyndon Johnson, must not be discounted. On certain official occasions the President must stand before a line, a smile frozen on his face, and pump the hands of thousands of visitors, many of them just rubbernecks. Theodore Roosevelt, whose ebullient vigor was a part of his colorful personality, once shook over six thousand hands in one day, and while he apparently emerged none the worse for the experience, the same probably could not be said for all the guests.

The President must meet an increasing flow of visiting dignitaries, often heads of state, now that the United Nations glass skyscraper is located in New York. A friendly personality can help clear the path for later diplomatic conversations and understandings. Lyndon Johnson, with his Texas breeziness, appears to have made a favorable impression on the scores of eminent visitors who came to Washington in 1963 to honor the recently assassinated John F. Kennedy.

On occasion the President must journey to summit conferences, as Eisenhower did to Geneva in 1955 ("The Spirit of Geneva"). There he was photographed, grin and all, in the company of the smiling Russian Premier Bulganin. Soviet propagandists, cutting out the other statesmen present, scattered this photograph broadcast to dishearten their captive satellites by demonstrating that the United States evidently beamed on Russian oppressors.

After his heart attack in 1955, Eisenhower was forced to restrict his schedule. He cut down on ceremonial duties, even though these are an important part of the office. The premier of Italy visited Washington in 1958, but a vacationing Eisenhower did not manage to meet him. The distinguished visitor must have returned home with some feeling of resentment.

A popular incumbent does not need to be a glad-hander so much as he needs to be colorful, even flamboyant—a good showman. Theodore Roosevelt, who suffered from autointoxication, was too much wrapped up in himself to be genuinely folksy. But his razzle-dazzle personality endeared him to the masses, and contributed to the success of his leadership. He genuinely liked people of all sorts, especially voters. He was wont, at the end of a railroad trip, to rush up to the engineer, shake his hand, and compliment him on his skill. All this did not offend the numerous and powerful members of the Brotherhood of Locomotive Engineers.

In the drab days before television reruns and singing commercials, personal color—one might almost say political sex appeal—was less essential than today. Washington lacked it. Poised without being oppressive, self-possessed without being objectionably self-assured, he revealed a gravity of manner and serenity of spirit that one associates with gentlemen of the old school. His earnestness and sincerity were beyond dispute—and these are qualities that we like to see in our Chief Magistrates.

An aura of sincerity was perhaps General Eisenhower's most attractive political asset. Franklin Roosevelt, for all his other magic gifts, implanted doubts as to his sincerity, especially when he engaged in flippant, not to say frivolous, banter with newsmen over deadly serious issues. The official published records of the Yalta Conference even reveal him as expressing the hope "that Marshal Stalin would again propose a toast to the execution of 50,000 officers of the German army." The unpublished records have him proposing, no doubt banteringly, that the king of Saudi Arabia might have "the six million Jews in the United States."

DYNAMIC MODESTY

The occupant of the White House today cannot afford to be a shy violet. He has to be an extrovert if he wishes to remain in the head-lines, as he must for political survival. He lives in a goldfish bowl, or perhaps better a monkey cage. He is expected to be the center of attention, and the sooner he adjusts to this bothersome reality the better. If he does something, he is news; if he does nothing, he is news, even if he only gets sick. If he develops ileitis, as Eisenhower did, X-ray pictures of his intestines appear nationwide in popular magazines.

We agree that Lincoln was a great President, if not the greatest, and then we note that one of his chief attributes was a Christlike humility. Logic suggests that we should seek statesmen with the same degree of humility, but politics has a different answer. There was only one Lincoln, and only one Civil War. What was good for Lincoln in a Civil War may not be good for another leader in the Cold War.

Herbert Hoover was quiet and unassuming, on the whole a modest man who abhorred the faintest suggestion of showmanship or demagoguery. He refrained from taking up many inches in *Who's Who in America* with a detailed list of his "honorary degrees from 85 institutions in U.S. and abroad," in addition to numerous other honors. But what the nation needed during an era of depression was not modesty and humility but aggressive and dynamic leadership— a willingness to break with the past and seek drastic new medicines for grave new ills.

At the other extreme, we do not need arrogance. Franklin Roosevelt, usually more discreet, overstepped the bounds in his re-election campaign of 1936. Stung by Republican attacks on his proposed social reforms, he welcomed the hatred of the "economic royalists," of "economic dynasties thirsting for power," of "entrenched greed," and of "the resolute enemy within our gates." At the climax of the campaign, in New York's Madison Square Garden, he proclaimed that he would like to have it said that in his first administration these forces of greed had met "their match" and in his second administration "their master." He remarked privately to one of his brain trusters, "There is one issue in this campaign. It's myself, and people must be either for me or against me." His head swollen by his landslide re-election in 1936, he revealed a disturbing cockiness. Pride goeth before a fall; and this was just before the Supreme Court "packing" debacle.

Yet confidence in one's self is an attribute usually found in our most effective leaders. Oddly enough, several of the ablest did not reveal this quality before taking office. Thomas Jefferson—shy, retiring, and with a slight speech defect—did not impress observers as being prepared to ride in the whirlwind and direct the storm.

Andrew Jackson, spurning a premature boom in 1821, burst out: "Do they think I am such a damn fool! No sir; I know what I am fit for. I can command a body of men in a rough way: but I am not fit to be President." In 1858, during the days of the Lincoln-Douglas debates, Lincoln laughed aside rumors of the White House with the reported statement, "Just think of such a sucker [1] as me being President!"

Self-assurance added to the appeal of Woodrow Wilson, and particularly of the two Roosevelts. Wilson, with his Presbyterian concepts of predestination, displayed confidence from the outset, notably in his inaugural address and in appearing before Congress to urge banking reform—the first time an Executive had so appeared since the days of John Adams. In marked contrast with Abraham Lincoln, who had sneaked into rebellion-racked Washington, Franklin Roosevelt exhibited confidence to a superlative degree during his inauguration in 1933. Standing before the vast assemblage while bank doors all over the country were clanging shut, he proclaimed in resonant tones, "The only thing we have to fear is fear itself." [2]

Undue self-confidence, or an unseemly display of it, can of course lead to public criticism. Woodrow Wilson, speaking to a New York crowd before returning to the Paris Conference in 1919, became disturbingly boastful. He declared that when he brought the Treaty of Versailles back, it would have the League of Nations firmly riveted in, and that the Senate would not dare break the heart of the world by tearing it out. Such strategy may have been clever (even this is debatable) but boasting about it was not.

The White House tends to engender confidence. Harry Truman was humble and bewildered when the office, without prior briefing, came down on him like "the moon, the stars, and all the planets." But, employing the power of positive thinking, he quickly developed a high degree of confidence, not to say self-righteousness. He was widely criticized for his cockiness, especially by opposition Republicans.

Conversely, a lack of confidence can be ruinous to national leader-

---

[1] Illinois was known as The Sucker State.

[2] Like many other presidential aphorisms, this one is not original. It goes back to Francis Bacon ("Nothing is to be feared but fear") and Thoreau ("Nothing is so much to be feared as fear"). Wilson's "The war to end war" was claimed by the English novelist H. G. Wells.

ship. A man must give the impression that he knows what he is doing, even though, like Grant, he may not. Taft had served so long under Theodore Roosevelt as a troubleshooter and yes-man that he never fully recovered from the subordinate experience. He relates that after he first became Chief, he kept asking himself what "Theodore" would do in a given situation. When someone addressed him as "Mr. President," he would instinctively turn around to see where Roosevelt was. Quite understandably, Taft did not provide the aggressive leadership that was demanded by a nation about to be caught up by a progressive tidal wave.

TACTFUL SELF-ASSURANCE

Self-confidence often manifests itself most conspicuously in an unwillingness to concede that one has made errors. Franklin Roosevelt, in one of his famed fireside chats, candidly admitted that he could not make a hit every time he came to bat, and Abraham Lincoln was even less reassuring. But Theodore Roosevelt seems to have been plagued by no such misgivings. His voluminous "posterity letters" and his back-patting autobiography are ample evidence of an ingrained cocksureness, particularly in defending his "taking" of Panama.

Harry Truman, like Theodore Roosevelt, was never given to self-reproach. Forced to make an incredible series of soul-wrenching decisions, he was convinced that they were the right ones, given existing conditions and the facts available to him. His long and active life since leaving Washington was probably due in part to his not being eaten by remorse. His habit was to make a decision with promptitude and to the best of his ability, and then not tie himself up in mental knots with second guessing.

Self-confidence, on the other hand, does not preclude tact, which most of the Presidents have possessed, some of them to a consummate degree. A politician cannot ordinarily get very far in his calling, much less to the Executive Mansion, unless he tells the people what they want to hear and unless he strokes their fur the right way. President McKinley was so gracious that he could turn down an office seeker, place a red carnation in the applicant's buttonhole, and send him away almost as happy as if he had received the coveted post.

The thorny crown of several of the less successful Executives may be traced largely to their lack of tact. John Adams' brusqueness and prickly temper were notorious long before he became President. Short chimneys catch fire the quickest, and John Quincy Adams inherited his father's short stature (both were five feet seven) and short temper. President Hoover's strongest suit was not tact. Though the bungling mismanagement was not all his fault, he contrived to run a demonstrating bonus army of veterans out of Washington in 1932 with torch, tear gas, and bayonets. A smaller force of ex-doughboys again invaded the capital the next year. President Franklin Roosevelt rode gaily out to welcome them, waved his hat, and arranged for gallons of free coffee to cheer them up. The veterans went home with a better taste in their mouths.

Some of the ablest leaders, on the other hand, have been notorious for their tactlessness. Andrew Jackson, whose spirit and body were evidently buoyed by controversy, was not averse to using temper tantrums, whether simulated or real, to achieve his ends. His successful handling of the French claims crisis had all of the finesse that one would employ in discharging an insolent janitor. Grover Cleveland was short-tempered and brusque, especially in dealing with self-seeking politicians who recommended prison-stripers for public office. Theodore Roosevelt, whose boiling point was low, confessed that he did not behave like a "gentleman" in bringing an end to the crippling coal strike of 1902.

Woodrow Wilson, though ordinarily gracious and tactful before his collapse in 1919, had his lapses. Somewhat arrogant intellectually, he did not suffer fools gladly. He referred sneeringly to the "bungalow minds" of the Senators, and once told one of their leaders, in connection with approving the Treaty of Versailles, that their heads were only knots to keep their bodies from unraveling. These tactless sallies drifted back to the Senate, where they contributed to Wilson's unraveling.

FOOT-IN-MOUTH DISEASE

Most of the ablest incumbents have avoided making distressing public statements of the foot-in-the-mouth type, especially remarks that could be seized upon by alert adversaries. But this is partly a matter of accident, for the fragile pitcher goes to the well every time the President makes off-the-cuff remarks or even a speech. The more trips the pitcher makes, the more danger there is of breakage. The Schlesinger Top Eleven on the whole came off rather well, except for Woodrow Wilson and Harry Truman. Many of Wilson's noblest statements, as we have already seen, were torn out of context or otherwise used to harass him. (See pp. 124–125.)

Harry Truman's quick lip repeatedly got him into trouble. "I like old Joe [Stalin]," he ad-libbed in 1948. "He's a decent fellow, but he's a prisoner of the Politburo." Truman also referred later to the Congressional spy hearings directed at Communists in government as a "red herring" to divert attention from his anti-inflation program. Alger Hiss, the prominent State Department official who was found guilty of perjury in connection with charges of being an accomplice of the Communists, turned out to be one of the "innocent" red herrings.

Herbert Hoover, an inept politician, blundered into serious political pitfalls. In 1928 he wrote to Senator Borah that the prohibition of alcohol was "a great social and economic experiment, noble in motive and far-reaching in purpose." This was jeeringly shortened to "noble experiment." In the campaign of 1928 he championed "rugged individualism," which soon became "ragged individualism." He likewise prophesied, "We in America today are nearer to the final triumph over poverty than ever before in the history of any land"—all of which made ironical reading in a few months. He also declared that "the slogan of progress is changing from the full dinner pail to the full garage." This McKinleyesque statement helped inspire the slogan, "A chicken in every pot and two cars in every garage." The inevitable parody, once Wall Street collapsed, was "Two chickens in every garage" or "Two families in every garage."

In the depths of the Depression, Hoover again blundered. He periodically issued cheerily optimistic statements suggesting that the corner had just been turned; several of these were telescoped into "Prosperity is just around the corner." (It may have been "hoovering" "just around the corner," but unfortunately it took about ten years to make the turn.) When the Democrats predicted that mob rule would follow a Republican victory in 1933, Hoover clumsily replied in his St. Paul speech (presumably remembering his routing of the bonus army), "Thank God, we still have a government in Washington that knows how to deal with a mob." In the closing stages of the campaign of 1932 Hoover gloomily prophesied that "grass will grow in the streets of a hundred cities" if the much-condemned Hawley-Smoot tariff should be repealed. It was drastically modified, under Franklin Roosevelt, but the pavements did not turn green.

DIGNIFIED DIGNITARIES

Tactful or not, the incumbent must maintain the dignity of his illustrious office. This is a test which some have failed, notably Andrew Johnson. A rough-and-tumble stump speaker from Tennessee, where politicians addressed crowds from stumps in the clearings, he disgraced himself while President by making intemperate speeches. As the result of fortifying himself against an illness, he had appeared drunk when sworn in as Vice President in 1865, although he was not regarded as a heavy drinker. The sneer "the drunken tailor in the White House" soon became a stock slur. During his speechmaking tour of 1866, he responded to hecklers by exchanging insults with them, while the dignity of the high office sank to the gutter.

Other men have appeared too informal on occasion. During the whistle-stop campaign of 1948—"the miracle of '48"—President Truman would appear on the rear platform of the train in a bathrobe, together with his wife and daughter, whom he introduced respectively as "the boss" and "the boss' boss." Quick to "shoot from the lip," he would dash off scorching letters to those who angered him ("delirium Trumans"). But his courage and decisiveness in grappling with overpowering postwar problems did much to erase these unfavorable vignettes, assuming that they were unfavorable. As Dr. Clinton Rossiter has written, "He was distressingly petty in petty things; he was gallantly big in the big things."

President-General Eisenhower brought a new and refreshing standard of dignity to the White House, although he too had appeared in a bathrobe on the train in the campaign of 1952. Green on the job, deferential to the delicate checks and balances, reluctant to badger Congress, preferring civilian placidity to soldierly pugnacity, he was sensitive about the proprieties of his proud office. He flatly refused to engage in a mud-bespattering contest with Senator

Joseph R. McCarthy. "I'm not going to get into the gutter with that guy," intimates reported him as having vowed—and he kept his word.

A feeling for the dignity of the office has revealed itself in numerous other ways. Various incumbents, aware of the necessity of preserving the independence of the Executive, have repeatedly refused to send confidential papers to Congress. George Washington, deeply conscious of his precedent-creating role, declined to submit to the House of Representatives secret documents relating to Jay's Treaty. Others have ignored subpoenas designed to hale them into court as witnesses, as Jefferson did when subpoenaed by Chief Justice Marshall to appear at the Burr treason trial. The Chief of State has enough to do without spending time at inconvenient periods on the witness stand being raked over the coals by defense attorneys.

Some Presidents, deeply concerned about their public image, have refused to permit themselves to be photographed in informal attire or in informal situations. Most of them are not ordinarily camera-shy: exposure to the public is the free advertising that the politician gets and needs. Calvin Coolidge, on a visit to the Dakotas, posed for the photographer in an Indian costume presented to him. The net effect was painful; he looked much better pitching hay in Vermont. Theodore Roosevelt, though willing to be photographed as a huntsman, drew the line at tennis flannels: tennis was then regarded as a snob's game. William McKinley was a heavy smoker, but he kept his cigar away from the cameras for fear of corrupting the youth. Herbert Hoover, another inveterate cigar smoker, was similarly discreet: a darling of the Woman's Christian Temperance Union, he might destroy a favorable impression.

Presidents also have to watch their language, but some have not been too successful in concealing their emotions. Andrew Jackson's "By the Eternal [God]" became legendary. Lincoln's penchant for telling earthy stories was blown up until folklore portrayed him as a backwoods Boccaccio. Short-fused Grover Cleveland, who found much to annoy him, could swear vigorously in private. In a personal letter he wrote, "The d——d everlasting clatter for office continues to some extent, and makes me feel like resigning, and Hell is to pay generally."

Even the Modern Presidents have proved to be human. John F. Kennedy, a former naval person, habitually used salty language with intimates. Harry Truman, in private conversations, was famous for employing the scorching language of a Missouri mule skinner (his father was a mule trader). Franklin Roosevelt got into hot water during his 1944 campaign for re-election when the voting machine in his New York precinct jammed. "The God-damned thing won't work!" he was heard to have exclaimed, at least by some vigilant Republicans. Subsequent coverups explained that he had merely observed, "The damned thing won't work."

The Puritans are dead but there is still a large puritan vote. We somehow expect our Presidents to be more than human, and the language of the drill sergeant, while perhaps appropriate for the barracks, is clearly not appropriate for his Commander-in-Chief—at least not in public.

Tests of Temperament

"A second-class intellect. But a first-class temperament."

JUSTICE OLIVER W. HOLMES, 1933,
on Franklin Roosevelt

DEDICATION TO DUTY

The ideal President is gifted with certain traits of temperament, which of course are intimately related to traits of personality.

The ablest men have been those most thoroughly dedicated to their job. A smilingly optimistic Franklin Roosevelt was not only dedicated to it, but he obviously enjoyed it, especially in the early years. Theodore Roosevelt had a "corking time" branding people liars, cracking heads, herding emperors and kings, and meddling in everything from conservation to "race suicide"—from earth control to birth control. After leaving the levers of power and going off to Africa to shoot lions, he made the mistake of deciding that after all he was an indispensable man. Finally sidetracked, he lived out his remaining years a furiously frustrated man.

The most reluctant ones in fact have been among the less successful ones. Taft did not want the job, but was prodded into it by an ambitious wife and his no less ambitious brothers. Irked by the silly business of politics, he sarcastically concluded that "the major part of the work of President is to increase the gate receipts of expositions and fairs and bring tourists to town." General Grant, obviously bored by politics and civilian administration, was induced to run for the presidency by designing men. He had displayed a keen intelligence as a general-in-chief, and he certainly would have done much better than he did as Commander-in-Chief if his heart had only been in it.

All of the five Greats, except possibly Franklin Roosevelt, probably got more sorrow than satisfaction out of bearing the burdens. Yet a man who does not enjoy power—or rather the pleasure of exercising power for the public good—has no business in the presidential chair. The popular fear has often arisen that the incumbent may like his job too well, and the bogey of dictatorship had much to do with spurring the anti-third-term Twenty-second Amendment to ratification in 1951.

The so-called Virginia dynasty—Washington, Jefferson, Madison, Monroe—were a remarkable quartet. They evidently served less in response to a burning ambition than to a sense of dedication to the public service—noblesse oblige. (As John F. Kennedy later remarked, paraphrasing the New Testament, "Of those to whom much is given, much is required.") George Washington, a truly indispensable man, heeded the call of duty, after reluctantly leaving his placid Potomac for the pressures of public office. He later regretted his decision.

Other men have also done their duty grim-faced. Even Lincoln found "this damned old [White] House," earlier known as the Presidential Palace, a house of black tragedy. He once remarked, "If to be head of Hell is as hard as what I have to undergo here, I could find it in my heart to pity Satan himself." Grover Cleveland and Herbert Hoover, a tormented duo, battled depressions through short lunches and long hours. When Cleveland later met the five-year-old son of his friend James Roosevelt, he reportedly said, "Franklin, I wish for you that you may never be President of the United States."

The mystery is why any man should break his back seeking this backbreaking job, unless he is consumed with ambition, or unless he has a deep sense of dedication to the public service, or both. He should be buttressed by the inner satisfaction of using the enormous powers of his office to promote programs for human betterment.

John F. Kennedy was frank to admit that he wanted to go to the "center of action" because "that's where the power is," and there he could do the most good. Power is opportunity; it is something to be used, not hoarded.

Yet the presidency, in many respects, is an empty bauble. The salary of $100,000 is not overgenerous when compared with the salaries paid by giant corporations, while the public is generous with its abuse. The President and his family live in a "jail," as Harding put it, shadowed by Secret Service men, much as they would shadow a criminal. One price of fame is the loss of privacy, even in courting a bride, as Wilson unhappily discovered. The incumbent has to fight for his political life while shaping the nation's destinies—that is, if he desires the accolade of re-election. Besides, there is so much to be done. Yet he may be repudiated ingloriously by the electorate, as Hoover and others were; or he may die gloriously from an assassin's bullet, as four have died. Neither prospect is attractive. "The President pays dear for his White House," Emerson once remarked.

BOLDNESS AND FORBEARANCE

The able Executive knows when to be bold and when to be cautious; when to move and when to hold back or mark time. In these respects he is like a general, which frequently he has been.

Andrew Jackson acted with boldness in attacking the Bank of the United States, among assorted dragons, so much so in fact as to give his name to an age. Lincoln exercised his war powers with boldness, sometimes in disregard of the Constitution he had sworn to uphold, and the precedents he set were improved upon with similar boldness by Woodrow Wilson in World War I. Theodore Roosevelt, brandisher of the Big Stick, was bold to the brink of belligerency. Rumor had it that the printers kept their headlines permanently set with the words "ROOSEVELT FLAYS," followed by a blank space for whatever he happened to be flaying that day.

But boldness must be tempered with inner calmness and forbearance. "Genius is only great patience," wrote Buffon, and one might venture a step further and say that it is virtually synonymous with statesmanship. Washington's delaying tactics during the Revolutionary War justly earned him the title The American Fabius; he carried over the same prudence into the presidency while waiting for the French Revolution to blow itself out. Jefferson might easily have unleashed the hounds of war against Britain in 1807, following the *Chesapeake* outrage, but he calmly, if futilely, sought a substitute for conventional warfare in the economic warfare of the embargo. It was a compromise between submission and shooting. Lincoln exhibited patience to a superlative degree as he waited for the fires of civil war to burn themselves out, and as he imperturbably searched for a trial-and-error general who could manage the waterbuckets.

Woodrow Wilson was infinitely forbearing in the face of outrages at the hands of both Mexicans and Germans. He was in fact castigated for his mañana policy—for dragging his feet and not getting into step with infuriated public opinion. "He kissed the bloodstained hand that slapped his face," fumed Theodore Roosevelt as he assailed the Princetonian's Mexican policy.

Franklin Roosevelt, a master of political timing, possessed "enormous patience," according to his wife. Yet he liked to give the impression that he was a rather frivolous fellow who made snap decisions. He was in truth inclined to err on the side of procrastination. He patiently sweated out the Depression and prudently waited for the right moment to come to the aid of the embattled democracies. His tolerance of the Supreme Court finally evaporated in 1937, but only after three pro-New Deal victories at the polls. Many of his admirers claimed that he had shown remarkable forbearance in the face of the repeated and crippling Old Deal decisions handed down by the Nine Old Men.

Every one of the Big Five displayed equanimity to an unusual degree; that is one of the prime reasons why they are the Big Five. Andrew Jackson and Theodore Roosevelt, the next two in line—and perhaps that is primarily why they stand in line—were markedly impatient on critical occasions. Roosevelt precipitantly "took" the Panama Canal Zone in 1903, when he might have achieved the same results a few months later, without the scandalous black eye given the United States. But the election of 1904 was imminent, and he was fanatically determined to be elected in his own right, as indeed he was in a landslide.

THE BUCK STOPS HERE

Decisiveness, which is a blood brother of boldness, must take high rank among the qualities that we demand in an effective President.

Ordinarily a Chief Executive will not get very far if he cannot face up to his responsibilities, assemble the essential information, think clearly, and then act rapidly. Theodore Roosevelt used to say that a large part of the virtue of being right was being right in time; there is little satisfaction in being right after the opportunity has passed. Calvin Coolidge, according to his Secretary of Commerce, Herbert Hoover, had a more passive philosophy. He declared that if ten problems started to come down the road at once, nine would run harmlessly into the ditch. So why go to all the trouble of anticipating ten eventualities? The weakness of this policy is that the tenth problem, if unprepared for, may engulf the President, as the oncoming Depression began to engulf President Hoover later in the year that Coolidge left office.

The capacity to make crucial decisions without shilly-shallying has generally marked our ablest statesmen. But Lincoln, forced into a delicate balancing act between conflicting forces, revealed painful indecisiveness at times, notably in connection with the Emancipation Proclamation. He finally made up his mind by himself. Summoning his Cabinet, he informed them of his decision and of his desire to have their advice only on the wording of the Proclamation and other minor matters.

The primary reason why Truman is ranked with the Near Greats is that he acted decisively—he evidently enjoyed doing so—when faced with a dozen or so crises of earth-shaking significance. Among them were the decisions to drop the atomic bomb on Japan, to enunciate the Truman Doctrine for the salvation of Greece and Turkey, to support the Marshall Plan for the rehabilitation of postwar Europe, to inaugurate the airlift for beleaguered Berlin in 1948, to "dump" China in 1949, to intervene in Korea, to go beyond the 38th parallel in Korea, to keep the secret of the atomic bomb, and to manufacture the hydrogen bomb. Although seeking counsel from his top advisers, he did not rely on staff decisions, at least not to the extent that President Eisenhower did. Perhaps he remembered the admonition of Theodore Roosevelt, "A council of war never fights." The motto on Truman's desk read, "The buck stops here."

All this is just another way of saying, in McKinley's words, that "government is always a crisis," or as Eisenhower remarked, "A President never escapes from his office." As the departing General told the incoming Kennedy, "No easy matters will ever come to you as President. If they're easy, they will be settled at a lower level."

PRUDENTIAL PRESIDENTS

Impetuosity or impulsiveness is obviously not the same thing as decisiveness. Theodore Roosevelt on occasion was guilty of hasty "horseback judgments," painfully so when he summarily dismissed "without honor" an entire unit of nearly two hundred Negro troops, following a shooting affray in Brownsville, Texas. The few guilty men would not confess; the innocent men could not or would not inform on their comrades. So Roosevelt, with rough-handed justice, inflicted punishment (later softened) on a large number of worthy men, several of whom had won the coveted Congressional Medal of Honor. Perhaps belatedly remembering that in America men are presumed innocent until proved guilty, he ignored this disagreeable episode in his *Autobiography.*

The Rough Rider, though a direct actionist, usually knew better. While still Governor of New York he wrote, "Sometimes it is a sign of the highest statesmanship to temporize." With proper precautionary treatment, problems often solve or dissolve themselves. President Eisenhower's Secretary of State, John Foster Dulles, was inclined to be so overactive that critics reversed the adage to read, "Don't just do something, stand there!"

A decision to delay or do nothing is in itself a decision. It may result in epochal consequences, such as occurred, presumably as a partial result of American indifference in Truman's day, when China went down the Communist drain in 1949. On the other hand, ex-Presidential Assistant Sherman Adams believed that President Eisenhower acted with undue haste in landing American troops in Lebanon during the crisis of 1958, when the Eisenhower Doctrine for the Middle East was allegedly being challenged by Communists.

There are times when wisdom requires that the President remain calm but vigilant, and we must note that Eisenhower acted with more prudence in avoiding American armed intervention in Indo-China after the disaster to French arms in 1954. Statesmen also serve who only stand and wait—for the dust to settle. The dust often beclouds facts which are essential for a sound decision.

FIGHTERS UNDER WRAPS

But patience does not rule out persistence, nor does moderation rule out the desirability or necessity of fighting for a cause. The effective President must be willing to battle for his program—"angry for the right"—without making too many personal enemies. If he is cursed with a hot temper, he must keep it under control, as an iron-willed George Washington managed to do. All the other Greats have been conspicuously successful in avoiding unseemly public outbursts, although all of them at times emphatically expressed varying degrees of annoyance. Even the gladsome Franklin Roosevelt publicly lost his temper on occasion. In February, 1944, he vetoed a tax bill in such scathing terms as to bring about the tearful but temporary resignation of Senator Barkley as majority floor leader. Andrew Jackson, distinguished in his earlier years for an ungovernable temper, showed remarkable restraint while President. This is all the more noteworthy because official decorum forbade him to challenge his opponents to duels, as was his wont, and shoot them down.

Fighting styles of course vary. The President may be a "gut fighter" in the slam-bang tradition, like Jackson with his bull-in-a-china-shop methods, or like Theodore Roosevelt with his ever-restless Big Bludgeon. Or he can be a fighter in the lofty academic tradition, as Wilson was in battling for the tariff or the Federal Reserve. At the time of the struggle over the Federal Reserve Bill, Senator Glass came to him despairing of victory. "Damn it, outvote them, old man," shot back the austere White House Presbyterian in one of his rare exhibitions of non-Presbyterian language.

President Kennedy, also the academic fighter, displayed cold fury when the steel companies, after having led him to believe otherwise, concertedly raised their prices. Outraged that the interests of "185 million Americans" should have been subordinated to those of a few steel moguls, he allegedly remarked, "My father always told me they were sons of bitches, but I never really believed him until now." Questioned at a subsequent news conference (May 9, 1962), he in effect confirmed the statement.[1] Kennedy's Homeric wrath brought the so-called conspirators to their knees. The exhibition of raw power by the White House was frightening, especially when government agents, Gestapo-like, routed reporters out before dawn or swarmed into the offices of the steel companies in search of incriminating evidence. The next year the steel prices were quietly raised without overt evidences of collusion—and without presidential protest.

But the two-fisted President must not make an unseemly display of his bellicosity; he must be a fighter under wraps. He must avoid petty quarrels which mushroom into Cabinet schisms. Andrew Jackson, incurably chivalrous, stirred up a frightful row when he defended the dubious premarital virtue of Peggy Eaton, wife of his Secretary of War. Oddly enough, the pro-Democratic, pro-forgotten-man administration of Old Hickory was almost wrecked over an issue of high-society snobbery.

The President must not be vengeful or vindictive. "The Bank," said Jackson to Martin Van Buren, "is trying to kill me, *but I will kill it.*" With the single-mindedness of an Apache, he pursued Nicholas Biddle and his Bank of the United States to the bitter end. Jackson's alleged deathbed regret—apocryphal but in character—was that he had never had an opportunity to shoot Henry Clay or hang John C. Calhoun.

The effective Executive cannot be a persistent feuder. Wilson's early Mexican policy was largely a private vendetta with the murderous Indian Victoriano Huerta, whom the pacifistic ex-professor despised and finally managed to unseat after bombarding Vera Cruz. The feud with Huerta was followed by another and more disastrous one with Senator Henry Cabot Lodge—one which wrecked the League of Nations in the United States and with it Wilson's dream of a better tomorrow.

---

[1] Kennedy also remarked in the presence of Arthur M. Schlesinger, Jr., "They *are* a bunch of bastards—and I'm saying this on my own now, not just because my father told it to me." Schlesinger, *A Thousand Days* (1965), p. 636.

THE COMPROMISING BATTLER

A fighting President can hardly be commended unless he is a purposeful fighter. He must come into office with positive aims and goals, not with a policy of delay and drift. He must be a doer and not solely a dreamer. Polk is rated a Near Great because he entered the Executive Mansion—or is widely believed to have done so [2]—with four major planks on his "must" list, including the settlement of the Oregon dispute with Britain and the acquisition of California from Mexico. He fought for and achieved every one of them, at times by dubious means, but he achieved them. Early observers said of him, "What he went for he fetched."

Some Presidents have fought valiantly for short periods but have failed to follow through in long campaigns. John F. Kennedy won a widely acclaimed diplomatic victory in his trigger-tense confrontation with Khrushchev over Cuba in 1962. But when the smoke cleared off Castro was as much of a thorn in the underbelly of the United States as ever, and Cuba was still rotating in the Soviet orbit. Right-wing critics insisted that if Kennedy had pressed his advantage, he might have forced the Russians out of the island entirely. Yet, if he had overplayed his hand, we might all be dead.

The ablest Presidents, though men of backbone, were more than fighters. They knew when to stand fast and when to roll with the punch; when to hit back and when to compromise. Perhaps the worst black mark against Lincoln is his flat refusal to accept the Crittenden Compromise in 1860–1861, the last-ditch hope—and a faint one at that—of reconciling the quarrel between North and South over the extension of slavery. He probably would have proved more conciliatory if he could have foreseen the bloodbath that lay ahead.

Theodore Roosevelt was a fighter, but he was never one to batter his head against a stone wall. When he saw that he was roadblocked, he would on occasion execute a dazzling end run, while kicking up an obscuring cloud of dust. By demanding four battleships a year of Congress, he was able to compromise on two. By prosecuting the "bad" trusts, he was able to preserve the "good" trusts. By big-sticking undesirable big business, he bolstered desirable big busi-

[2] For a full explanation see pp. 282–283.

ness. As Mr. Dooley put it, on the one hand he would crush the hideous monsters, known as trusts, but "on th' other hand not so fast." Roosevelt rarely clung to a lesser advantage at the cost of a greater one; he raised "informed opportunism," in the words of one historian, "to a new level of national dignity."

Woodrow Wilson presents curious contrasts in firmness and flexibility. While at Princeton, he changed from a conservative to a liberal, with much eating of his own words. At Paris in 1919 he compromised perhaps too much to secure that bristling bundle of compromises known as the Treaty of Versailles. Returning home, he compromised too little, especially after his collapse, to secure its ratification. On the eve of the crucial fight in the Senate, Colonel House met Wilson and quoted Burke, "To govern is to compromise." Despite his lifelong admiration for Burke, Wilson disagreed: "I have found that you get nothing in this world that is worthwhile without fighting for it." A short time earlier he had told Senator Martin of Virginia, "Anyone who opposes me in that [the League], I'll crush." Obstinacy, even firmness, ceases to be a virtue when it defeats its own ends.

The gay and smiling Franklin Roosevelt is not ordinarily thought of as a fighter. But descended from early Dutch colonists, he could put up a tremendous struggle when he "got his Dutch up," as he phrased it. Few Presidents have battled as tenaciously for any one proposal as he did for his Supreme Court "packing" scheme. But in the end he settled for a judicious compromise which finally, and belatedly, brought him all he could have really hoped to gain. The true statesman must be able to compromise—but not too quickly and not too much.

An effective President, in short, must have the temperament and skill of a horse trader. He must be able to bargain and barter with Congress; to conciliate, to wheedle, and even to threaten. The phenomenal success of Franklin Roosevelt with Congress during the hectic One Hundred Days was due in large part to his deliberately withholding offices from patronage-starved Congressmen until his numerous legislative sheep were safely in the fold.

EXPERIMENTER-IN-CHIEF

The Chief Magistrate must be a man of independent judgment, and not at the mercy, as Harding reputedly was, of the last man he sees. Grover Cleveland was ruggedly independent, almost to a fault, and the public admired him for what was called his "you-be-damnedness." Wearing no man's collar, he could not be bullied or bought. At the time of the Pullman strike he declared, "If it takes the entire army and navy of the United States to deliver a post card in Chicago, that card will be delivered."

The President must be an experimenter, if the times demand experimentation, as they clearly did in the dismal days of the Great Depression. The threadbare clichés no longer fitted the crisis. But a statesman must not fly too frontally into the teeth of basic traditions. He must be something of a gambler, as George Washington was when he adopted Hamilton's daring financial schemes. He must be an improviser in the face of unexpected developments. He must be able to play by ear, as Franklin Roosevelt airily did during the New Deal days, when tumbling events demanded a decision before all the needed facts could be assembled.

The New Dealers were guilty of many inconsistencies in method and detail. This Roosevelt freely admitted, but he insisted that there was "a consistency and a continuity of broad purpose." On one occasion he reportedly tossed back his head, laughed, and re-marked to a delegation of silver Senators: "I experimented with gold and that was a flop. Why shouldn't I experiment a little with silver?" After the nation slithered into World War II, and the unemployment slack was taken up, Roosevelt rather casually changed directions and doctors. He debonairly dropped old "Doctor New Deal" in favor of new "Doctor Win-the-War," both of whom presented huge bills.

The President must be unorthodox on occasion. He cannot be corseted by precedent if he expects movement rather than stalemate, popular support rather than apathetic acceptance. Theodore Roose-velt, thoroughly unconventional, climaxed a circuslike administra-tion by sending the entire fleet of sixteen battleships all the way around the world on a 46,000-mile cruise. This was something that had never been done before and it has not been done since. The

Master of the Big Stick believed—and he probably was right—that his flamboyant flourish helped fan away the poisonous atmosphere that was besmogging Japanese–American relations.

Woodrow Wilson was almost Rooseveltian in his unconventionality. He cancelled the traditional and costly inaugural ball; he attended church during hot weather in a white linen suit; he inaugurated the presidential press conference; he went over to Congress to confer with members; and he personally addressed the Congressmen with important messages. For all or most of these departures from the norm he was the target of criticism, if not abuse. Accused by the Republicans of having developed a messiah complex, he insisted on going to Europe in 1919—the first President to establish this precedent—there to lock horns with the white-spatted European diplomats at America's first "summit conference."

Franklin Roosevelt exhibited daring unconventionality from the day that he flew to Chicago to accept his first nomination in person, rather than waiting to be formally notified. With a penchant for grandiose and expensive projects of dubious utility, he responded favorably when the proposed atomic bomb was broached to him, even though a leading admiral branded it "damned professors' nonsense." Roosevelt finally arranged for a hush-hush blank-check appropriation of some two billion dollars—and the rest is mushroom-beclouded history.

Many of the Presidents whom we label conservatives were really radicals, in the sense that they came into office with new programs for "getting the country moving again." We regard George Washington, the wealthy planter, as a conservative; but he was the most famous rebel of his times. He placed himself at the head of a government which seems ultra-conservative in our day but which was deemed radical in his day.

Yet few radical reformers, when faced with the meat-and-potatoes practicalities of politics, are ever as radical in public office as in the private study. This was conspicuously true of Thomas Jefferson—a radical while out of office, a mild conservative while in. Vice President Theodore Roosevelt was deemed a "madman" by the Republican Old Guard, and the financial community shuddered when McKinley was assassinated. But despite the ensuing noise and fury, he gave the country an essentially conservative administration.

He did not really go "mad" until after he had left office and tried to Bull Moose his way back in.

Other so-called radicals hardly deserve the name. Woodrow Wilson was assailed as a "college professor gone Bolshevik" by oilman E. L. Doheny (of Teapot Dome infamy). But the austere academician described himself, more accurately, as "a progressive with the brakes on." The so-called radical Franklin Roosevelt, castigated by the conservatives, should be revered as their patron saint. He devised heroic measures for saving the capitalist system, and with it the capitalists themselves.

HUMANITY AND HUMILITY

The White House requires equanimity of spirit: passionate outbursts seldom settle a question. Here Lincoln excelled. He possessed an inner calmness, without undue complacency. He was in the highest degree forbearing, conspicuously in tolerating the arrogance and insolence of General McClellan, who privately called him a "gorilla" and who never did win a decisive victory. Harry Truman was no Lincoln, but in the Lincoln tradition of putting up with headstrong officers he tolerated a good deal of balkiness from General MacArthur before he finally pulled the rug. He later regretted not having acted two years sooner.

The ideal President should be tolerant of everything except wrong —and Senator Joseph R. McCarthy was wrong. His wild accusations and star-chamber persecutions shamed the United States before the entire world, and provided the gleeful Communists with new grist for their propaganda mill. Here President Eisenhower gets a low mark. Claiming to be loftily above the battle and unwilling to lower the dignity of his high office by tangling with so unseemly a character-assassin, he refused to use his immense powers for a crackdown. But he did wound the Senator deeply by not inviting him to social functions at the White House. Meanwhile the whole nation suffered through several years of humiliating hysteria.

The presidential office calls for a high degree of humanity, compassion, and magnanimity. George Washington generously pardoned the ringleaders of the Whiskey Rebellion, to the acute dissatisfaction of Secretary Hamilton and other leading Federalists. But for

Christlike magnanimity Lincoln receives the highest mark of all. His rough-hewn frame shone like a lighthouse in a nation convulsed with hate. He possessed gentleness, combined with strength; a sense of justice, tempered with mercy; a feeling of sympathy for the mass of the people, whether slave or free. Thomas Jefferson and Franklin Roosevelt, though branded as traitors by the aristocratic class, also revealed a high degree of compassion for the so-called forgotten man. By contrast, Hoover strove to preserve traditional economic values, while Roosevelt strove to preserve basic human values.

The President must be hard-nosed at times, but in an era when brother was killing brother, Lincoln chose to be compassionate. Popular fancy has him repeatedly snatching from the firing squad exhausted recruits found sleeping at their posts. Admittedly, he was softhearted and did pardon a good many offenders, but his policy was not to intervene unless appealed to. He did not succumb to all tearful appeals, and he did approve the death sentence in nearly three hundred cases. The volleys of the firing squads at a nearby camp could be heard in the White House, where they jarred his sensitive soul. An excess of compassion can be ruinous to army discipline, and some of the generals believed that Lincoln's mistaken leniency delayed final victory. But he was using compassion as a weapon to weaken the will of the Confederates to fight, while actively promoting the procurement of more lethal weapons to bring the Confederacy to its knees.

There is also a time to be ruthless. When the President's cronies or associates betray him, they should be condemned, not coddled. "Let no guilty man escape," insisted General Grant when the grafting Whiskey Ring was exposed. But when he found that his friend General Babcock was one of the leading thieves, he used the enormous prestige of the office to free the accused culprit. Woodrow Wilson, the hater of war, was finally forced to present a war message to Congress. He came away from that harrowing experience saddened by the applause; to him it was the death knell of tens of thousands of young men. His sense of obligation to the dead may explain why he ungenerously permitted Socialist Eugene V. Debs, convicted under the Espionage Act as an obstructor of the war effort, to languish in a federal penitentiary long after the guns had grown cold.

Harry Truman was faced with the cruel decision to drop or not to drop the atomic bomb on Japan. The argument was that this blow would shorten the war and save hundreds of thousands of lives, both Allied and Japanese. Truman chose the short-run and ruthless course—a kind of "mercy killing" in a sense—and continued to defend himself vigorously in those terms. Lincoln had used forgiveness and magnanimity as weapons to weaken the will of the Confederates to fight. But such an exhibition of Christian charity would have been laughed to scorn by the totalitarian dictators of the 1940's and 1950's. All this suggests that a humane and magnanimous Lincoln might not have fared well as a leader in the 1940's and 1950's, while a tough-fisted Truman might have been a failure in the 1860's.

THE NATIONAL MOOD-SETTER

The general mood of the Chief Magistrate has often contributed to his success or failure; it tends to infect the country, for better or for worse. Mediocrity, dishonesty, complacency, provincialism, drift, uplift, reformism—all these leave their mark. The presidential example even plays its role in smaller things: Kennedy eschews hats, and the sales of hats fall off; Kennedy uses a rocking chair for his injured back, and the sales of rocking chairs boom.

The gravity and sobriety of George Washington befitted the touch-and-go task of launching the daring new experiment in republicanism on an even keel. The pessimism and gloom surrounding Herbert Hoover may have contributed to the deepening of the Great Depression; they certainly did not contribute to his campaign for re-election. As he wrote in his *Memoirs* and demonstrated in office, "Unless the President remains cheerful and optimistic, he becomes a depressant." The incurable optimism of Franklin Roosevelt, with his theme song "Happy Days Are Here Again," may well have helped the nation to surmount the worst years of the Depression. Yet optimism can be carried too far. A less optimistic (and less naive) Roosevelt would have throttled down lend-lease shipments to Russia in 1943, when it became painfully clear that the Kremlin had no intention of cooperating with the United States in creating a more tolerable postwar world. A less optimistic (and less naive) Roosevelt might well have reposed less confidence in Stalin's promises at Yalta.

Several of the Big Five were blessed with a keen sense of humor, which can be something of a lifesaver. Lincoln was the President most prone to tell amusing stories, in season and out. A resident of the White House described his high-pitched laugh as like "the neigh of a wild horse on his native prairie." So notorious was his penchant for telling stories at indelicate moments that contemporary cartoonists had a field day. In the most solemn circumstances they had him saying, "This reminds me of a little joke." Yet Lincoln's moments of relaxation were pathetically few during these doleful days, and the letdown afforded by a humorous tale, at a time when there was little else to laugh about, may have kept him from cracking under the strain.

Other eminent Presidents were similarly blessed. Franklin Roosevelt, gifted with a prankish sense of humor, found relaxation in those not-so-happy days with the lighthearted laugh and the crackling quip. His famous speech to the Teamsters during the campaign of 1944 is a classic in the anthology of American humor. Referring to the charge that he had used expensive public transportation for his Scottish terrier Fala, he declared that he did not mind if his enemies maligned him or his wife or his sons, but he did object to their dragging in his defenseless dog, whose economical Scottish soul was "furious."

Franklin Roosevelt also had the priceless gift, rare among self-important politicians, of laughing at barbs directed at himself. He delighted in framing clever cartoons, especially the one in *Esquire* showing a small girl blabbing to her mother that little brother had just written a dirty word on the sidewalk: "Roosevelt."

John F. Kennedy had a sophisticated Irish sense of humor, wry and often self-mocking. At the elaborate dinner honoring Nobel-prize winners of the Western Hemisphere, he remarked that so much talent had never before been gathered at the White House, except possibly "when Thomas Jefferson dined alone." On the last day of his life, he convulsed a Texas audience by observing that while the press had a lot to say about his wife's clothes, nobody paid any attention to what he or Vice President Lyndon Johnson wore.

Much as humor may serve as an outlet for pent-up emotions, it

can be a dangerous gift when used too freely and too publicly.[3] The
American people want wise men, not "wise guys," in the White
House. The nation's business is serious, and the taxpayers are pro-
viding a substantial salary for their President to take care of it. If
he wishes to issue a statement, he would do well to preserve a sober,
if not solemn, demeanor. Here Calvin Coolidge succeeded conspicuously, though in private even he would reveal his deadpan
Yankee humor. He was quoted as saying that the American people
wanted a "solemn ass" for President.

The politician who is too quick with the quip is usually regarded
as too clever for the presidency. Abraham Lincoln would probably
have died a little-known lawyer if the voters had earlier known of
his overfondness for jokes. One of the most fortunate turns of his
career was his inability to win a second term in Congress; he was
beginning to be regarded in Washington as something of a buffoon.
But he dropped back into private life without a splash before this
weakness could be too widely advertised. To be great is to be grim
—or at least many voters think so.

MEN OF IDEALS

We now come to certain personal characteristics that can perhaps
best be placed in the category of ideals or idealism.

All of the abler Executives, and many of the lesser lights, were
distinguished by their high-minded devotion to the democratic ideal
—as it was interpreted in their day. All of the Big Five were idealists.
We especially remember Washington, with his ideal of a republican
union of thirteen states; Lincoln, with his ideal of a democratic
union of all sections; and Wilson and Franklin Roosevelt with their
ideals of a collective-security union of all nations. All five had faith,
notably Jefferson and Wilson, in the basic aspirations of their people.
All five felt a strong obligation to provide moral leadership, and all
were inspired by a sense of mission. All glimpsed the exalted destiny
of the Republic, and some of them felt anointed, particularly Wilson,
to help it achieve that destiny. A lifelong Calvinist, he declared on

---

[3] Presidential humor is evidently now in better odor than it was once, and
Kennedy seems to have helped to achieve the breakthrough. At least two books
embracing his wit have thus far been published, to say nothing of phonograph
recordings.

the eve of his inauguration, "God ordained that I should be the next President of the United States."

The ablest incumbents have also revealed a deep-rooted love of country. This largely explains the personal sacrifice that many have made in shouldering the oppressive burdens of the office, especially when they could have enjoyed a pipe-and-slipper life of retirement, whether as a General Washington or a General Eisenhower. Lincoln must have loved his country deeply to have allowed it to suffer and bleed as long as he did, at a time when the easy course would have been to let it fall apart. Jefferson was falsely accused of loving France more than his native land. Although more friendly to the French than to the British, he was first of all an American. In 1785, while urging James Monroe to visit France so that he could better appreciate America, he declared, "My God! How little do my countrymen know what precious blessings they are in possession of and which no other people on earth enjoy."

All of the ablest Presidents, without exception, had a feeling for the traditions and history of their country. They also had an abiding appreciation of the unique experience and opportunities of the most favored among the most powerful of the democracies. Theodore Roosevelt and Woodrow Wilson were deeply enough interested in their country to write many volumes recording its history. Franklin Roosevelt was more than a dabbler in the nation's past: he was at pains to avoid the mistakes of Wilson in waging a coalition war and in making a coalition peace. John F. Kennedy, when asked during the campaign of 1960 in what respect he was better qualified for the presidency than his opponent, Richard M. Nixon, replied, "I think I have a better sense of history."

All those Presidents who died in office, whether under its burdens or under its bullets, in a sense sacrificed their lives for it. Woodrow Wilson, before departing on his fateful and fatal speaking tour in 1919, remarked that he was willing to die in this struggle for his country and humanity. As Commander-in-Chief, he had ordered thousands of young men onto the battlefield, where they had laid down their lives. He was prepared to lay down his life on the political battlefield, and in a sense he did.

CHAPTER XIV

Politician-in-Chief

"The most successful politician is he who says what
everybody is thinking most often and in the loudest voice."

THEODORE ROOSEVELT

POLITICOS ALL

Now that we have dissected the personal qualities that distinguish
the extraordinary from the ordinary Executives, we must turn to
certain indispensable political qualifications. The line between
personal and political is often a fine one, but for present purposes
the distinction ought to be attempted, even at the risk of some
overlap.

The successful President is a successful politician, at a high level.
As the titular head—normally the actual head—of a powerful political
party, he should know the tricks of the game and delight in playing
them. President Washington preceded parties, and then, when they
emerged, endeavored without complete success to rise above the
hubbub. But every one of the other Greats—Jefferson, Lincoln,
Wilson, and Franklin Roosevelt—was a master politician, not to
mention Andrew Jackson and Theodore Roosevelt of the Big Seven
for full measure. They all got their start on the lower rungs of the
political ladder, and then worked up. Lincoln was in fact something
of a "peanut politician" in his younger days: perhaps his crowning

achievement during his four terms in the Illinois legislature was to help logroll the state capital from Vandalia to Springfield.

All of the Greats, except Washington, had a burning desire to attain the coveted office. As for Lincoln, his law partner wrote that "his ambition was a little engine that knew no rest."

Few men have reached the White House without a strenuous political apprenticeship. Conspicuous among the exceptions were the war heroes Taylor, Grant, and Eisenhower, plus the war-hero food administrator, Herbert Hoover. All four probably, and Grant and Eisenhower almost certainly, could have been elected by either major party. None of the four war heroes, except possibly Hoover in the 1920's, had formed any strong party loyalty, had served a political novitiate, or had even voted more than occasionally in a presidential election. Ex-President Truman, who developed a high regard for ex-engineer Herbert Hoover, concluded that "one of his difficulties was that in a political way he started at the top instead of at the bottom. It would be just like my starting an engineering career without knowing anything about engineering."

The Schlesinger experts, in examining the non-political quartet of Taylor, Grant, Eisenhower, and Hoover, awarded no high marks. None of the four ranks above low Average, while Grant is branded a flat Failure. Taft, an amiable misfit, was involved in political life for many years but, like Hoover, always in an appointive office, except for one early election to a judgeship. He did not enjoy his exalted position, but took it with reluctance and misgivings. "Politics make me sick" is the refrain running through his correspondence. He became a good deal sicker when his friend and benefactor, Theodore Roosevelt, finally stabbed him in the back and helped retire him to private life.

PIPELINES TO THE PEOPLE

Politics is essentially the art of dealing with people, of swinging them, whether as voters or legislators, around to one's way of thinking. An aspirant to the highest office who does not like and understand human beings will hardly be a success; certainly he will never receive the highest popular acclaim. Wilson, as we have noted, left the unfortunate impression, which was basically true, that he was more concerned with people in the mass than with people as individuals.

Lincoln and the two Roosevelts, on the other hand, were highly effective in their personal contacts. They conveyed to the common people the conviction that the Man in the White House understood them and sympathized with their aspirations. In 1903, on learning that a large American family had been "blessed" with yet another child, Theodore Roosevelt dashed off the following letter to the proud parents: "Three cheers for Mr. and Mrs. Bower and their really satisfactory American family of twelve children! That is what I call being good citizens."

Herbert Hoover was less gifted in his human relations, even though he had won a well-deserved reputation as the all-time humanitarian in salvaging millions of war-ravaged derelicts. He never succeeded in establishing an intimacy with the people as individuals, especially after the Great Depression cast its dark pall. When the bonus army of bonus-seeking veterans invaded Washington in 1932, a fearful Hoover doubled the White House guard. Franklin Roosevelt, the Democratic nominee, was shocked to learn that the President of the United States was afraid of his own people. The Republic seemed to be reverting to the age of the Russian tsars, who had to be protected from their bomb-throwing subjects.

Without a pipeline to the people, the incumbent is crippled. He is unable to interpret public opinion; he may even make the ruinous mistake of confusing it with pressure-group opinion or minority-group opinion. Without a proper rapport, he cannot know how they will respond to the trumpet call of his leadership in onrushing crises, when galloping events leave no time for a Gallup poll. John F. Kennedy, for example, sensed that he would have the people behind him during the Cuban "crunch" of 1962 with Khrushchev, and he did.

One of Lincoln's crowning virtues was his skill in keeping a sensitive finger on the popular pulse. McKinley was also adept at assessing public currents; he kept a careful ear to the ground, despite the risk, as "Uncle Joe" Cannon sneered, of getting grass-hoppers in it. He sensed that the masses, in an imperialistic mood of wanting to keep up with the German Joneses and other rivals, coveted the Philippines. The people probably did at that time, so he reluctantly scooped up the orphaned islands.

RIDING THE TIDES OF HISTORY

The superior politician-President must have a sense of direction. Not all movement is progress; not all leadership is constructive. The American people discovered this, sometimes to their sorrow, during the zigzagging days of the New Deal. But the country was in such a mood of desperation, following the many anxious months of lagging recovery under Hoover, that it welcomed activity of almost any kind. Will Rogers remarked that if Roosevelt had burned down the capital, the people would say, "Well, at least we got a fire started, anyhow." Under Roosevelt and his try-anything-once mood, the country did not know quite where it was going, but it had a comforting feeling that it was on its way.

A sense of direction must coincide, at least broadly, with the tides of history. This vague term would include contemporary currents, the basic aspirations of the people, the spirit of the age. Hoover, for example, was in tune with the 19th century, while Franklin Roosevelt was in tune with the 20th century.

We associate great revolutions—to use this overused word loosely —with all of the Great Presidents. These overturns were mostly bloodless upheavals or turning points in history. George Washington presided over a conservative counter-revolution which successfully prevented the gains won during the War of Independence from going down the sewer of possible anarchy. Jefferson, capitalizing on the so-called electoral Revolution of 1800, launched a new deal for the forgotten man of the previous century. Jackson, a beneficiary of the electoral overturn of 1828, presided over the enthronement of the new manhood suffrage democracy, with its emphasis on the spoils of office rather than the toils of office. Lincoln, with the most difficult assignment of all, successfully engineered a counter-revolution which preserved the Union and strangled Southern self-determination in the cradle. Wilson, with superlative gifts of constructive leadership, launched the New Freedom revolution with sensational success. Hardly waiting to catch his breath between bills, he shepherded through an often cranky Congress the impressive pile of domestic reforms enacted in 1913–1914.

When Franklin Roosevelt took the inaugural oath during the Depression crisis of 1933, the nation was ripe for change. Europe had surged ahead with enriching programs of social and economic reform. America lagged behind. The Progressive movement and the New Freedom had been sidetracked by World War I, by the delirious prosperity of the gin-and-jazz 1920's, and by the Great Depression. Franklin Roosevelt, despite cries of socialism from the right-wingers, launched his off-the-cuff New Deal. Under the mantle of relief and recovery, he rather subtly engineered a social and economic revolution which enabled America to catch up with the more enlightened nations of the Western world. In this sense the New Deal was an Old Deal. But in no case would the sweeping "revolutions" sponsored by the ablest Presidents have been possible if the spirit of the times had not lent itself to aggressive leadership.

The tragedy of a premature program—one for which the people are not yet ready—is painfully illustrated by the tragedy of Woodrow Wilson. Inspired by his eloquent leadership and the wartime spirit of self-sacrifice, the nation temporarily fell in behind him when he attempted a gigantic leap forward. He strove to turn the nation's back on a century and a half of die-hard isolationism, while embarking upon the turbulent sea of internationalism in a leaky ship christened the League of Nations. In his burning zeal to usher in a better tomorrow, he neglected to launch an adequate campaign from the White House to prepare the public for the epochal change. Perhaps there was not time to shift gears from the crusade against Germany to the crusade for the League of Nations. When disillusionment and drift set in, as they did in 1919–1920, the American people turned against the noble Wilsonian dream.

A SENSE OF TIMING

A sense of timing is so intimately intertwined with a sense of direction that the two, like Siamese twins, can hardly be separated. The President needs delicate antennae, sensitively adjusted to advise him of the possible success of a proposed long-range venture. As regards America's acceptance of the League of Nations, Wilson's sense of direction was sound but his timing, as events unhappily proved, was one world war too soon. Franklin Roosevelt led with success in the same direction, and the result was the United Nations, midwifed in San Francisco in 1945. A leader is often right at the wrong time.

Grover Cleveland, the determined Democrat, was guilty of some bad timing, notably in connection with the Rebel Flag Order of 1887. Finding that a number of captured Confederate standards were gathering dust in the cellar and attic of the War Department, he thought it would be a gracious act, some twenty years after the shooting had stopped, to return these trophies to the South. The announcement stirred up such a tremendous outcry in the North, especially among Republicans and war veterans, that the Man of Courage was forced to back down and rescind the objectionable order. Eighteen years later, when Theodore Roosevelt reigned—as a Republican and a veteran of the Spanish-American War—the flags were quietly returned with scarcely a ripple of protest.

To start a "crusade" when the people are in no mood to fall in behind a crusading leader can be both frustrating and futile. Theodore Roosevelt's Square Deal, Woodrow Wilson's New Freedom, Franklin Roosevelt's New Deal all struck responsive chords and enjoyed spectacular success, especially in the early stages. Eisenhower launched a crusade for Modern Republicanism which would have gilded the ultra-conservative wing of the party with the coloration of liberalism. He was less than successful, largely because his following was not ready for change. Deeply discouraged, he seriously considered forming a new party. Despite his overwhelming personal endorsement at the polls in two successive elections, he was confronted with Democratic majorities in both houses of Congress throughout six of his eight years. This, he ruefully remarked, "was no bed of roses." Nor did his glamor rub off on his belatedly anointed crown prince, Richard M. Nixon.

All this does not mean that a leader should not strive for change if there is danger of defeat. He deserves little credit if he supports only sure things. But he must not get out too far in front. As Franklin Roosevelt once remarked, a leader cannot afford to glance back and find that nobody is following him.

FIRST THINGS FIRST

Closely associated with a sense of direction and a sense of timing is a sense of discrimination. From the smorgasbord of issues displayed in the party platform, the victorious candidate must select the few big ones behind which to throw his weight. Scattering his efforts in all directions is a sure recipe for failure, although concentrating on one goal or on a few goals is no sure guarantee of success.

When the New Frontiersmen rode into power in 1961, they decided to push through a multi-pronged program. It included federal aid to education, medical care for the aged (Medicare), aid to economically depressed areas, the reduction of unemployment, and a halting of inflation. The votes of Southern Democrats were crucial for these objectives; hence a civil rights bill for Negroes was temporarily shoved onto the back burner. The Kennedy administration evidently failed to see that civil rights was the explosive issue, and this oversight accelerated the revolution that burst about its head. President Kennedy got neither a general education bill, nor Medicare, nor civil rights, nor tax reform, nor tax reduction, although he laid the groundwork for all these measures and persuaded Congress to pass some others.

The most effective Executives have been those who came into office with a program—with specific goals for which they were prepared to go to the mat. But the existence of such a program carries with it no certainty of adoption. The New Frontier of Kennedy—launched with fanfare, symbolism, and slogans—quickly ran into lethal opposition in Congress from hatchet-wielding Indians in the shape of conservative Southern Democrats and conservative Northern Republicans.

The success of a program involves a number of other qualities which most of the top-notch leaders have enjoyed. First of all, the President must have foresight, a capacity to look to the future (rather than to the past), as was notably true of Jefferson, Wilson, and the two Roosevelts. The program must accordingly be progressive and reformist, at least in the eyes of contemporaries, rather than regressive and reactionary. The Harding administration is to be condemned not only for the orgy of scandal but perhaps even more for attempting to turn back the clock to the pre-New Freedom days of Wilson. Critics complained that the Old Guard economic policies and ostrichlike foreign policies were attempts to repeal the 20th century.

A successful, creative program requires of its leader many of the personal qualities which we have already discussed. Originality will enable the President to devise or back such wholesome innovations as Kennedy's Peace Corps, which was branded "Kennedy's Kiddie Corps" until it quickly proved its worth. Imagination will enable the President to foresee the beneficial effects of what is proposed, as was notably true of Truman's Marshall Plan for the rehabilitation of post-1945 Europe. A willingness to experiment will enable a Franklin Roosevelt to come up with an atomic bomb—and a new era. Realism and soundness of judgment will also enable a Franklin Roosevelt to reject old war-debt schemes and sponsor new lend-lease devices. Independence of judgment will enable the President, as was true of Cleveland to a high degree, to rise above the needs of the party and keep unerringly in view the needs of the country.

Above all, the incumbent must have a clearsighted concept of a better tomorrow. "Where there is no vision, the people perish," sagely observed the writer of Proverbs.

All of the Big Five were visionaries in the sense that they glimpsed a vision of the nation's future. But they were not idle dreamers. Washington in his Farewell Address envisioned a powerful and completely independent republic. Jefferson in his first inaugural address declared, in a curious overstatement, that the land (even without Louisiana) would last the American people "to the thousandth and thousandth generation." After he had purchased Louisiana, he implemented an earlier plan by sending the explorers Lewis and Clark on a spectacular expedition so that the nation might have a better view of the bargain it had bought. And Lincoln caught a vision of a democratic experiment that would "not perish from the earth."

Wilson, for all of his staring over men's heads as though looking at a star, grasped more than a noble dream in his concept of the League of Nations. But he found, like the Old Testament prophets before him, that cynics stone a man who is too far ahead of his times. If he succeeds, as Wilson did with his New Freedom, we say he has vision. If he fails, as he did with the League of Nations, we say he is a visionary. Franklin Roosevelt, with much the same vision, enjoyed the benefit of superior political know-how and a chastened people who were more mature and more ready to try collective security—and social security as well.

DRIVERSHIP—WITH A LOOSE REIN

The effective Executive must not only have a workable program but the capacity to drive it through. Ex-Professor Wilson, standing over Congress with schoolmasterish ruler in hand, forced that rebellious body (Senator Lodge got ulcers) to pass the main planks of his New Freedom platform. Here we see the activist—the driver. While sailing to Paris in 1919, to negotiate the peace treaty, he urged his small army of experts, "Tell me what's right and I'll fight for it." They did and he did, but only in part—with less than completely satisfactory results.

The leader with a program must be firm, as Washington was in proclaiming and maintaining his neutrality policy in 1793, when war erupted between France and Britain. Yet, as we have seen, he must also be flexible. He must know when to make concessions to achieve the substance of his goals, as Wilson failed to do in 1919 in dealing with the Senate during the League of Nations fight. He must have the courage to be cowardly—to retreat a little here to gain more there.

All the great incumbents have in some degree been greatly inconsistent. As Emerson pithily observed, "A foolish consistency is the hobgoblin of little minds." These Presidents were inconsistent because they had to be opportunists—to take advantage of opportunities as they presented themselves. This was conspicuously true of Jefferson's fortuitous Louisiana Purchase. Here he reluctantly violated a half dozen or so of his most precious precepts, ranging from strict economy to a strict construction of the Constitution. But when the chips were down he had the courage to be inconsistent.

Inconsistency, as veteran politicians well know, is a minor sin. It is quickly forgiven and forgotten by the voters, especially if the results are good, as they clearly were in the case of Louisiana. Thomas Jefferson, the ultra-liberal, became basically a conservative as Chief Executive. Andrew Jackson, earlier a conservative and a stockholder in the Bank of the United States, became a radical as far as his assault on the Monster Bank was concerned. Lincoln, remembered for his house-divided speech, was deemed a radical when he took office. But, a house divided in his own thinking, he came out as a conservative—a conservator of the Union and of slavery, if slavery was needed to save the Union.

Nor does the trail of inconsistencies end here. Woodrow Wilson, after living much of his adult life at Princeton as a conservative, rather belatedly mounted the progressive bandwagon. He then became a flaming liberal with his New Freedom. Franklin Roosevelt, running for the presidency on a platform that called for a balanced budget, less federal spending, and fewer bureaucrats, found himself the biggest budget unbalancer, spender, and bureaucrat up to that point in American history. Seeking to prevent "human erosion," he declared in 1936 that "to balance our budget in 1933 or 1934 or 1935 would have been a crime against the American people."

The most inflexible of the incumbents have in general suffered the most humiliating setbacks. John Tyler, an accidental leader who was determined to crack the whip in his own right, was finally thrown out of the party by fellow Whigs. Andrew Johnson, determined to reconstruct the South with a velvet glove rather than an iron hand, was impeached by the House of Representatives. Grover Cleveland, who would have no truck with the soft-money majority of his party, stood like an oak for his principles. But he left behind him a disrupted Democratic organization that wandered in a wilderness of Republican postmasters for sixteen long years. His successor, McKinley, bending like a willow in the winds of public opinion, retained his commanding position.

Wilson's tragic failure—the attempt to lead an increasingly distrustful America into the League of Nations—grew largely out of an inflexibility that was rendered more rigid by his physical and emotional collapse. James Russell Lowell, speaking through Hosea Biglow, remarked:

> A ginooine statesman should be on his guard,
> Ef he *must* hev beliefs, nut to b'lieve 'em tu hard.

Making due allowance for satire, there is a large kernel of truth in this observation.

CHAPTER XV

Teacher- and Preacher-in-Chief

"It is much easier to make the speeches
than to make the judgments."

JOHN F. KENNEDY, 1962

WINGED WORDS

The most eminent Presidents have generally been eloquent Presidents. They were eloquent with pen, as Jefferson was; or with tongue, as Franklin Roosevelt was; or with both, as Wilson and Lincoln were. George Washington was a conspicuous exception. His prose was pedestrian; his speechmaking painful. When he delivered his semi-audible inaugural address in New York in 1789, the critical Senator William Maclay observed that he was "agitated and embarrassed," thrusting the fingers of one hand and then of the other into his breeches pocket. Maclay regretted that "this great man" could not also have been "first" in speechmaking.

At least four of the five giants, Washington possibly excepted, presented distinguished inaugural addresses. The reasons were varied. Jefferson, Lincoln, Wilson, and Roosevelt were naturally eloquent. All five, except Washington, had come into office as the result of party overturns. All five, including Washington, had "new deals" of one sort or another to launch. Lincoln and Roosevelt (and to some extent Washington) were confronted with crisis situations that generated intense interest.

"Words at great moments of history are deeds," Clement Attlee once said in referring to Winston Churchill. We remember, often in twisted form, Washington's stern admonitions in his Farewell Address against foreign machinations; Jefferson's honest friendship with all—"entangling alliances with none" in his first inaugural address; Lincoln's two inaugural addresses and his Gettysburg tribute to democracy; and the stirring wartime words of both Wilson and Franklin Roosevelt.

Not surprisingly, Bartlett's *Familiar Quotations* honors the most eminent Presidents far more than the less famous ones. Some of these quotes are doubtless included because their authors later rose to the White House, but the quantity is impressive. Judged by the number of lines thus included, the Presidents would rank as follows: Abraham Lincoln, Franklin Roosevelt, Thomas Jefferson, Theodore Roosevelt, Woodrow Wilson, and George Washington. These are the five Greats selected by the Schlesinger experts, plus one Near Great, Theodore Roosevelt. The next five are Harry Truman, John Adams, U. S. Grant, Grover Cleveland, and Andrew Jackson. These men make up the remainder of the Near Great group, except for Polk and for Grant, the alleged Failure. Despite his "genius for silence," he uttered some memorably laconic statements during and after the Civil War.

PROPAGANDIZING ONE'S PEOPLE

The Commander-in-Chief is also the Teacher-in-Chief. If he is to get the wheels to move and "make things happen," in Woodrow Wilson's phrase, he must educate the people regarding the issues and the necessity for taking proper action. Washington's Farewell Address had impressive propaganda value.[1] Though subsequently misquoted to warn against *all* alliances, it educated the people to the dangers of foreign wiles. Jackson's biting veto message on the Bank, fantastic though it may have been financially, had devastating demagogic appeal.

Woodrow Wilson, repeatedly voted the finest lecturer at Princeton, stood in the nation's capital behind the most potent lectern in the world. He was laggard in teaching the lesson of preparedness

[1] Legend to the contrary, the Farewell Address was never delivered as a speech; it was given to a pet newspaper as the scoop of the century.

before 1917, and somewhat slow in teaching that of internationalism after the war ended. But he was superb in proclaiming America's war aims with his Fourteen Points Address and its supplementary principles.

Franklin Roosevelt was a past master in teaching (and softening) disagreeable lessons by resorting to symbolism and oversimplification. He explained federal spending for relief in terms of "priming the pump," which meant pouring in a bucketful of water so that many bucketfuls would flow out. He explained lend-lease aid in terms of lending one's hose to a neighbor, who could use it to put out a fire that was endangering one's own house. When the fire was extinguished, the hose, perhaps a little blackened, would be returned. A skeptical Senator Robert A. Taft demurred that lending a tank or other equipment was like lending chewing gum: "You don't want it back."

The American people will frequently surprise politicians by their willingness to sacrifice when the necessity for doing so is made clear to them. President Truman erred when he failed to explain adequately why hundreds of thousands of American boys were forced to fight in Korea. One of the enigmas of this nasty war is that it was fought to at least a draw by resentful soldiers, vast numbers of whom did not have the foggiest idea of what it was all about. And neither Truman nor Eisenhower nor Kennedy was conspicuously successful in explaining to the American people why they had to spend about $100 billion in foreign aid after World War II. The wonder is that the Congress and the taxpayers did not really revolt until the last days of Kennedy.

THE WHITE HOUSE PULPIT

The Chief Executive is likewise Preacher-in-Chief, if he chooses to be. To a superactive but squeaky-voiced Theodore Roosevelt the presidential podium was a "bully" pulpit, and his pontifical moral judgments echoed throughout the land. Thomas B. ("Czar") Reed congratulated him on his "original discovery of the Ten Commandments," while the British writer John Morley found him an interesting combination of "St. Paul and St. Vitus." Roosevelt assailed "civilized softness," national dishonor, pacifists ("flubdubs and mollycoddles"), plutocrats ("malefactors of great wealth"), corruptionists, impure food ("embalmed beef"), "muckrakers" (he was the chief one), smutty novels, and practitioners of divorce and birth control ("race suicide"). He preached righteousness, national honor, patriotism, honest government, fair play (the Square Deal), the peace of righteousness, preparedness, the strenuous life, good sportsmanship ("clean as a hound's tooth"), progressivism, and phonetic spelling.

So articulate and vehement was the Rough Rider that he virtually drenched Congress with words. Among them the perpendicular pronoun loomed large: the rumor persisted that the Government Printing Office ran out of capital *I*'s soon after Roosevelt began bombarding Capitol Hill with recommendations. Other leaders have learned, as Franklin Roosevelt did, that the "attention span" of Congress holds up better if they send over a succession of short messages, of the rifle-shot type. These are more effective than a few scatter-shot ones, of the blunderbuss variety.

William Howard Taft, in glaring contrast with Theodore Roosevelt, was not a sermonizer, moralizer, stick-waver, palm-pounder, or tub-thumper. Disliking to make speeches, he repeatedly put his foot in his mouth when delivering them. Lacking Roosevelt's dentition and gesticulation, Taft, the ex-judge, sounded ponderous and prosaic to the ordinary farmers. To them ex post facto might well be some newfangled kind of posthole digger.

Most of the high-caliber Executives were noted for high-class evangelism. Lincoln's Gettysburg Address and his second inaugural, with its "With malice toward none; with charity for all," will live as long as the Republic. Woodrow Wilson, himself a lay preacher in the Princeton chapel, used the presidential sounding board for his world-shaking White House sermons. These include his Peace Without Victory Speech to the Senate (and world) in 1917 and his Fourteen Points Speech to Congress in 1918. Franklin Roosevelt, who admired Theodore Roosevelt, once remarked, "I want to be a preaching President—like my cousin." We especially remember the Good-Neighbor Pledge in his first inaugural, the Four Freedoms Address, and the Atlantic Charter, co-authored with Winston Churchill.

ORATORS AND GHOSTLY ORATORS

Eloquence with the pen sufficed in the early days of the Republic, but today it is not enough. George Washington, though first in war and first in peace, was not first in oratory. Thomas Jefferson, with a gifted quill but a weak voice and diffident manner, was no speechmaker. He abandoned the kingly practice, first employed by Washington and Adams, of appearing in person before Congress to read messages—in the ancient manner of a speech from the British throne. Instead, Jefferson sent his manuscript up to Capitol Hill to be read by a leather-larynxed clerk. Not until the days of Woodrow Wilson, himself a moving speaker, was the early practice revived and continued. The Princetonian himself was surprised that the unorthodox Theodore Roosevelt had not thought of this old-new innovation. On his way back from making his first appearance before Congress, Wilson remarked, "I think we put one over on Teddy that time."

Three of America's most eloquent all-time orators are to be found among the five Greats: Lincoln, Wilson, and Franklin Roosevelt. Lincoln suffered from certain handicaps, including a high-pitched voice, a curious mannerism of thrusting his finger at his audience, and characteristic frontier pronunciations ("Mr. Cheermun," "git," "thar," "heered"). But his grotesque appearance seemingly added weight to his words. In 1860 this countryfied Illinois lawyer scored one of the oratorical triumphs of the century when he appeared in New York City, wrinkled black suit and all, before a sophisticated and skeptical audience at Cooper Union. Their applause helped to boost him into the presidency.

Woodrow Wilson was also a speaker of rare persuasiveness. With his penetrating tenor voice, his dignified bearing, his elevated tone, and his impassioned earnestness, he appeared to be one of the elect of God. An admiring newsman remarked that Wilson was the only speaker he ever heard who could be confidential with a crowd; listeners would even be moved to tears. At Paris, while speaking on one occasion for the League of Nations, he pleaded with such eloquence that hard-boiled reporters forgot to take notes.

Franklin Roosevelt, by common consent, was one of the two great English-speaking orators of his age, the other being Winston

Churchill. Despite his Groton-Harvard accent and sophisticated manner, he used his resonantly rich voice and commanding presence (even with painful leg braces) to persuade the masses that he was the forgotten man's man.

Some of the early Presidents, picking other people's brains, secured assistance in the preparation of important messages. But Abraham Lincoln, Theodore Roosevelt, and Woodrow Wilson, all gifted penmen, prepared their own speeches. Wilson was in the habit of blocking them out in shorthand and then transcribing them on his typewriter. Herbert Hoover, laboriously using a lead pencil, appears to have been the last incumbent to rely almost entirely on his own literary talents, which were not exceptional. Lincoln split rails, critics said, but Hoover split infinitives.

The ghost-writer really came into his own in the days of Franklin Roosevelt, who would use as many as twenty-five helpers for one speech. The presidency is now so burdensome an office that we take such ghostly assistance for granted. Provided that the views expressed are the President's own, we can hardly blame him for declining to be a soloist in a task which, if properly performed, could well consume most of his time.

John F. Kennedy, the only President ever to win a Pulitzer prize, had obvious literary gifts, but he too had to lean on ghosts to some extent. At least he had the discernment to employ talented ones, so much so that in 1962 a book of his bons mots was published under the title *The Quotable Mr. Kennedy.* His most glamorous ghost was Theodore C. Sorensen, who overworked the motifs of Lincoln's Gettysburg Address and who published a book of his own in the year of the President's assassination. (One critic remarked that he wrote just like Mr. Kennedy.) Perhaps remembering Franklin Roosevelt's attic full of ghosts, Mr. Sorensen observed that "group authorship is rarely, if ever, successful." He further concluded that "had the Gettysburg address been written by a committee, its ten sentences would surely have grown to a hundred, its simple pledges would surely have been hedged, and the world would indeed have little noted or long remembered what was said there."

THE RADIO AMPLIFIER

The demands on the Chief Executive as the Teacher-in-Chief and Preacher-in-Chief have become more oppressive with the passage of time. Woodrow Wilson, in addressing crowds of ten thousand or so during his ill-starred campaign for the League of Nations, did not even enjoy the crutch of a public-address system. The success that he achieved was a tribute to the carrying power of his voice, exhausting though the effort was. The first President to use the radio, albeit with harsh Vermont twang, was Calvin Coolidge. Although no orator, he presented his annual message of 1924 to Congress over a nationwide hookup, and his effectiveness was heightened by novelty. One of the most intriguing might-have-beens of history is what would have happened if the radio had been available to Wilson. Instead of breaking himself down on an exhausting tour, he could have carried his crusade to the people from the quietness of the White House in several fireside chats. Given the persuasiveness of his voice and manner, he almost certainly would have made his views prevail. He had the message but no radio; Coolidge had the radio but no message—at least not one of comparable significance.

The radio has immensely magnified the voice, but unfortunately not the ideas, of the Pedagogue-in-Chief. For some it has done more than for others. Herbert Hoover was never an outstanding radio performer; though dignified and solemn, he was handicapped by a voice that was flat, tired, monotonous. Truman, especially at first, sounded rather immature, what with an indifferent voice and what he conceded was a "rotten" delivery. But he greatly improved with instruction and experience. He shone most brightly with whistle-stop remarks and rough-and-tumble campaign speeches ("Give 'em Hell, Harry"). Eisenhower was at his best in personal appearances during which his glamor shone through; in radio presentations he tended to fumble the script. Kennedy gave many people the impression, despite his general effectiveness on radio and television, that the written word was his true medium. His broad Boston-Harvard accent—"haalf," "vigah," "Chiner"—did not seem completely grass-rootish.

But for Franklin Roosevelt the radio was made to order. It amplified his self-assured manner, his genius for oversimplification, his matchless voice. Concluding that "they want Poppa to tell them," he introduced and perfected the fireside chat with such sensational success that listeners believed the President was speaking directly to them as individuals. By the subtle use of "we," Roosevelt caused the people to feel that they were a part of the government. Then more than ever the Little Fellow, urged "to tell me your troubles," was sure that he had a friend and champion in high place. In dismay, Republicans moaned that Roosevelt could have swayed the masses merely by reciting the Polish alphabet in his hypnotically rich voice. Obstructionist Congressmen, already battle-scarred, feared the deluge of mail that would pour in on them after a fireside chat. The rumor was that THAT MAN had merely to glance at the microphone to bring them to heel.

But Roosevelt was careful to avoid the dangers of overexposure; he staged only thirty chats over some twelve years, or an average of a little over two a year. The White House even brought pressure to bear on radio mimics of his voice to desist and not blunt the edge of the master's tool.

THE TELEVISION ACTOR

Television has added a startling new dimension, which President Eisenhower was the first to use on a vast scale. His natural gifts were impressive; but reading a speech with smooth eloquence was not one of them. His strong suit was a capacity to radiate an atmosphere of earnestness and sincerity, and this he did with effectiveness, far more so than on radio.

The magic of television requires that the incumbent be not only a good speaker but also a gifted actor. John F. Kennedy, robust and confident, overflowing with facts and figures, triumphed in 1960 partly because he showed to better advantage in the first of his televised joint debates. His opponent, Richard M. Nixon, recently hospitalized and somewhat ill at ease, appeared so haggard and ghastly as to inspire the false rumor that he had been sabotaged by a pro-Kennedy makeup man. Kennedy developed his technique further in "live" television press conferences, and in his supercandid "rocking-chair chat" with newspapermen. "We couldn't survive without TV," he once remarked to Theodore C. Sorensen.

A favorable television image, with all that this implies in acting and speaking, is now a prime prerequisite for the presidential nomination. A rasping voice, a speech impediment, a hooked nose, a harelip, a toothbrush mustache, a diminutive stature—all these can count heavily against the aspirant.

The horrifying conclusion emerges that three of the Greats could not hope to secure the nomination if they were here today and in their prime. George Washington, with his cumbersome dentures, would probably be rejected as a pitiable old man. Abraham Lincoln, with his gawky frame, country-bumpkin manner, high-pitched voice, and back-country pronunciation, might well be laughed off the screen as a hillbilly. The soft-voiced and diffident Jefferson would certainly be passed over in favor of a more aggressive figure.

Two of the Near Greats would also appear to poor advantage on television. Andrew Jackson, hollow-cheeked and hollow-chested, would probably be dismissed as a refugee from a tuberculosis sanitarium, where he may have belonged. Theodore Roosevelt, with his near-falsetto voice, staccato delivery, clenched teeth, flailing fists, and Old Testament dedication, might well draw more laughs than votes.

As for the so-called Failures, another horrible conclusion is inevitable. From the standpoint of the television image, probably the most attractive candidate of all would be the amiable but malleable Warren G. Harding. His handsome profile, distinguished grey locks, well-knit frame, deep voice, and sincere manner would probably fool even more voters than he did in the awesome landslide of 1920. He was the finest imitation of a President we ever had. On the other hand, the television ruined Senator McCarthy by exposing his basic meanness to millions of televiewers. It may do the same thing for future demagogues, provided—and this is an all-important proviso—that they are given rope enough to hang themselves.

Nor can the role of the President as the Great Actor be lightly dismissed, now that he has become a television virtuoso. Franklin Roosevelt, with something of the "ham" in him, would appear to excellent advantage. Early in his own administration General Eisenhower employed a famous Hollywood actor, Mr. Robert Montgomery, to coach him in the techniques of an effective television presentation. Subsequent White House performances have involved the standard makeup devices of Hollywood and the stage.

NEW ORATORICAL FASHIONS

Strangely enough, the American voters have never regarded glittering oratorical gifts as an indispensable qualification for the presidency. Some of the ablest leaders have conspicuously lacked them—men like Washington, Jefferson, Jackson. This was true in the 19th century, when we had oratory of the spread-eagle, buffalo-bellowing, tonsil-straining type. A man without a bullish voice was almost fatally handicapped as a politician. Goldwin Smith, the Oxford don, visited the gallery of the House of Representatives late in the century. He observed that amid the confusion and clamor the only words he could hear distinctly were those of William Jennings Bryan, the Nebraska orator with a silver tongue but a somewhat leaden mind. As we glance back over the pages of American history, we note that great brains and great voices were seldom conjoined.

Even in the heyday of 19th-century oratory, the American people did not elevate to the highest office the most eloquent spellbinders of their successive generations. Where are the Patrick Henrys, the Alexander Hamiltons, the Henry Clays, the Daniel Websters, the John C. Calhouns, the Charles Sumners, the Stephen A. Douglases, the James G. Blaines, the Robert G. Ingersolls, the Roscoe Conklings, and the William Jennings Bryans, to say nothing of a host of others?

The Englishman James Bryce, writing his classic *American Commonwealth* (1888), discusses the interesting question of why the voters did not choose their most eminent statesmen for their most exalted office. He suggests, among various explanations, that the masses instinctively shy away from a leader whose glittering talents set him too high above his fellows. They prefer a "safe" candidate: the bugaboo of the Man on Horseback is never entirely absent. Voters are instinctively distrustful of politicos who are too "smart," but intellectual prowess is less noisy, less obvious, and hence less dangerous than oratorical prowess. Of course, several of the gifted speakers just listed missed the White House by the narrowest of margins. Some were notoriously unlucky; others, like Daniel Webster of New Hampshire and Massachusetts, hailed from politically unimportant states. Still others, like Colonel Robert G. Ingersoll, with his blatant agnosticism, trod on too many toes.

Whatever the explanation, modern miracles have wrought a vast change. Thanks to them, a weak-voiced or otherwise ungifted public speaker can present his message clearly and with a minimum of effort. Franklin Roosevelt would have been a moving orator in any age, so splendid were his vocal and dramatic talents. But the radio and the television were boons to men like Coolidge, Hoover, Truman, and Eisenhower, all of whom, except possibly Eisenhower, would probably have fallen flat before large crowds in the dusty arena of the 19th century.

Even in the days of Washington and Jefferson, the voice of the President, though physically weak, was by far the most powerful in the land. This was true when he spoke only through the printed word, as in the Farewell Address. Today his winged phrases and his visual image—broadcast and rebroadcast, televised and re-televised—enter tens of millions of homes. He is now a guest in the living room, a member of the family, not the far-off phantom of the Potomac. Every word and every move are news. He simply cannot make a purely non-political speech, even if he confines his remarks exclusively to the Red Cross. If he is eligible for re-election and desires it, and if he has been reasonably effective, he begins with an enormous advantage over possible rivals.

In the century since Lincoln was re-elected in 1864, only three incumbents have been defeated for re-election—Cleveland, Taft, and Hoover. Cleveland was re-elected when he tried again, while Taft and Hoover were unlucky: the one a victim of a great political donnybrook, the other of a great economic depression. If the incumbent had a strong appeal in the era before television, he is virtually unbeatable today.

Administrator-in-Chief

"The Presidency is not merely an administrative office. That is
the least of it. It is pre-eminently a place of moral leadership."

FRANKLIN D. ROOSEVELT, 1932

KEEPING SHOP

Administrative capacity is obviously one of the yardsticks by
which we measure presidential competence. The Commander-in-
Chief is Administrator-in-Chief, ensconced on the apex of an immense bureaucratic pyramid. In the "Gay Nineties" the President
had a "billion-dollar Congress"; now he has a hundred-billion-dollar
Congress. The bloating of the budget inevitably raises the question
among hardheaded businessmen, as it was raised in the free-
spending days of Franklin Roosevelt, "Has he ever met a payroll?"

Ironically, some of our ablest administrators have been our poorest
Presidents, and some of our poorest administrators have been our
ablest Presidents, at least in popular esteem. By the test of administrative expertise, Herbert Hoover, himself a hardheaded businessman, would stand at or near the very top of the list. The nation came
to expect miracles in the light of his achievements as feeder of the
Belgians, as feeder of wartime Americans, as feeder of destitute
Europeans, and as perhaps our most aggressive Secretary of Commerce. But the Great Depression deepened, and Hoover was hooted
out of office as the Great Engineer—a stationary engineer at that—

who had "ditched, drained, and dammed the country in four years."
Deeply respectful of facts, he appeared at times to be a pussyfooting
President who ducked decisions by appointing investigative commissions, including the Janus-faced Wickersham commission on
prohibition. At one time there were eight of these bodies at work,
and their deliberations seemed to result in much wordage but little
voltage.

John Adams, though rated a Near Great by the experts, must be
rated a Near Failure as an administrator. His only previous quasi-
executive post was that of Vice President, which he regarded as
"the most insignificant that ever the mind of man did conceive."
Inherited Cabinets invariably spell trouble, and Adams blundered
when he took over bodily Washington's Cabinet. It not only felt no
real loyalty to him, but it actively connived behind his back with
the now-shelved Alexander Hamilton, the dynamo of the party.

Honest John Adams, though a conscientious Puritan, established an all-time record for absenteeism from the nation's capital.
Shrugging off administrative detail and insisting that he could run
the government just as well in Quincy, Massachusetts, as in Philadelphia or Washington, he spent over one fourth of his four-year
term (385 days) at his beloved home. He argued that since the
Cabinet members daily mailed him the details of "all the business
of consequence," and since the "post goes very rapidly" (nine-day
round trip), he had everything under control. Actually, the Cabinet
did not report everything of "consequence" (including their back-
stabbing), the mail carriers did not travel "rapidly" by modern
standards, and Adams was not in complete control of the machinery.
The central government thus lost in leadership and executive impulse during a critical stage in Franco-American relations.[1]

High-class administrators are of course to be found among the
Presidents, some of them with military background. George Washington, with his genius for large-scale plantation management and
with eight years as organizer of the armed forces, was a topflight
executive. He excelled in gathering the essential facts, listening to
able counsel, and then making firm decisions.

Woodrow Wilson, despite a reluctance to welcome advice, was a
top-drawer administrator. One White House employee observed that

[1] In fairness we should note that his wife's illness, combined with yellow
fever in Philadelphia, further inclined Adams to absenteeism.

he demolished a pile of papers as a starving man would demolish a pile of flapjacks. He had behind him many years of university experience, including much bitter academic infighting, plus two years as Governor of New Jersey, including some bitter political infighting. He made a fetish of punctuality, and he organized his day so well that he had ample time for golf and vaudeville. His management of World War I, with its wholesale delegation of responsibility to able subordinates—his "faculty"—was a noteworthy performance, despite blunders resulting from unpreparedness. Some of his war-spawned organizations were forerunners of the depression-spawned alphabetical agencies of Franklin Roosevelt.

In foreign affairs, Wilson shone less brightly. A number of his decisions, notoriously in regard to Mexico, were based on ignorance or faulty information. Some of his third-choice diplomatic agents turned out badly, both in Mexico and Great Britain. "The responsibilities of the President are great," he complained, "and I cannot perform them alone. If I can't have the assistance of those in whom I have confidence, what am I to do?"

POLK AND LINCOLN: ANTITHESES

As a conscientious administrator, both at high and low levels, James K. Polk was in a class by himself, whatever his other shortcomings. This talent partially accounts for his Near Great status. He was the last incumbent to attempt to keep all the strands of government in his own hands. He confided to his diary that, as a faithful President did not dare entrust "the details and smaller matters to subordinates," he preferred "to supervise the whole operation of the Government" himself. He slaved away at his desk through the steaming Washington summers, and when several of the Department heads fled, he shouldered their burdens as well. Secretary of State Buchanan testified that Polk was the "most laborious man" he had ever known, and that in the brief span of four years he had "assumed the appearance of an old man." He died only 103 days after leaving office—an all-time presidential record for what seems to have been slow suicide by overwork.

That transplanted frontiersman, Abraham Lincoln, usually regarded as the greatest of the Greats, has gained this lofty ranking for reasons other than administrative genius. Though boasting limited legislative experience, he came to Washington after having managed nothing bigger than a country store, which failed, leaving him and his whiskey-swilling partner heavily in debt. His law office in Springfield was so untidy that a package of seeds sprouted in the dirt of a corner of his desk. A Springfield associate recalled having seen an envelope which Lincoln had marked, "When you can't find it anywhere else, look in this." He used his stovepipe hat as a filing case for important papers while a circuit-riding lawyer in Illinois, and he continued this slipshod practice after coming to the Executive Mansion.

The Lincoln administration, which was essentially a history of the Civil War, was cursed with much fumbling and bumbling. At the outset the Rail Splitter proved to be green and indecisive, and much too accessible to office seekers. (Caught in the tentacles of the system, he turned out to be more of a spoilsman than Andrew Jackson.) Disturbed by disloyalty in his official family, he was prone to lone-wolfism in counsel, and to trial-and-errorism in the choice of generals. In addition, the machinery of government was ill-meshed. When Secretary of the Treasury Chase wanted to know what was happening, he would send a boy out to buy the latest copy of the *New York Herald.*

Despite such deficiencies at the lower levels, Lincoln was gifted with compensating qualities at higher levels. These included a jealousy of Congressional encroachments, a willingness to expand his war powers, a sensitivity to public opinion, and a singleness of purpose in keeping aloft the banner of the Union. In the big things he was a strong leader; in the routine things he held a slack rein.

COMPETITIVE ADMINISTRATION

Highly controversial is the role of Franklin Roosevelt as an administrator. On the one hand, he could point to a creditable record as an executive—nearly eight years as Assistant Secretary of the Navy and four years as Governor of New York. On the other hand, he privately confessed that he was a "softy" who hated to "fire" incompetent underlings. Secretary of War Stimson, who had also held Cabinet posts under Presidents Taft and Hoover, regarded Franklin Roosevelt as the poorest administrator he had ever served under. He probably was thinking of the annoying procrastination, the blossoming bureaucracy, the overlapping jurisdiction, the competing agencies, and the clashing personalities who carried their feuds to the point of civil war.

Roosevelt was notorious for leaving an unsatisfactory man on the job and appointing another man or agency to do the same work. This duplication of duties seems like a poor way to run a White House, but Roosevelt's admirers argue that the "competitive theory of administration" (like that of the Army and Navy) often sparked fresh ideas and better results. It also had the advantage of attracting to Washington a large corps of ardent and intelligent New Dealers with reformist gleams in their eyes. FDR himself seemed positively to relish the squabbling, bickering, and backbiting that sprang from all this "joyous disorganization."

As the "happy improviser," Roosevelt was gloriously and blithe-somely unconventional. Unlike the orthodox efficiency experts, he refused to put on blinkers and thread his way through channels. Reformers bent on speedy reform must take shortcuts. Besides, there are always bootlickers who feel that the way to promotion and pay is to tell the President only what they think he will find agreeable. Like the cuckolded husband, he is often the last to know.

Roosevelt bypassed the State Department on numerous occasions, employing side-door informants and unofficial agents like the ailing Iowan, Harry Hopkins. He seldom saw, and even more seldom con-sulted, some of his Cabinet members. The results were often confusion, cross-purposes, crossed wires, misunderstandings, and bruised feelings. Distrusting the "cooky pushers" of the professional white-spat brigade, he often served as his own Secretary of State. In his man-to-man dealings with Prime Minister Churchill, he frequently ignored the long-suffering Secretary Cordell Hull, who, in his *Memoirs*, subsequently laid bare his resentment.

Roosevelt's final "torpedoing" of the London Economic Con-ference in 1933—an impetuous and ill-considered act—brought both American policy and performance into global disrepute. The dum-founding finale was merely the climax of a tragedy of errors, which involved the undercutting of Secretary Hull by Brain Truster Raymond C. Moley, and the undercutting of Moley by Secretary Hull. Competitive administration may work out after a fashion in domestic affairs, but it can be disastrous in foreign affairs.

FDR'S ADMINISTRATIVE ARTISTRY

The admirers of Roosevelt naturally defend him as an administrator. They agree with him that, as far as the presidential job was concerned, administration was "the least of it." Low-level leg work should be left to the file clerks and other flunkies, while the Chief focuses his attention on grand strategy. In this respect Roosevelt resembled the far-visioned Thomas Jefferson, who was not noteworthy for managing day-to-day details but who preferred to concern himself with broad objectives.

Robert E. Sherwood, a ghost-writer who saw much of the White House, described Roosevelt as "an administrative artist" who never lost sight of the forest by concentrating on individual trees. Much can be said for his point of view—and has been. Dr. Clinton Rossiter, a highly perceptive scholar, contends that Roosevelt was really a superb administrator, not only as regards design but as regards machinery. He urged on Congress administrative reform that would enable him to correct what he called the "higgledy-piggledy patchwork of duplicate responsibilities and overlapping powers" in "the executive and administrative departments."

Congress belatedly obliged in 1939 with the Revised Reorganization Act, under which the New Dealer issued his epochal Executive Order Number 8248. For the first time, it made provision for a large general staff which was reasonably adequate for the needs of the modern presidency and which since then has proved its worth. This, Dr. Rossiter claims, was "an accomplishment in public administration superior to that of any other President. . . ." Thus Roosevelt not only made his mark as a President but he left an enduring mark on the administrative labyrinth of the presidential office.

Much more can be said in defense of Roosevelt as an administrator. His most spectacular triumph—winning World War II—was achieved with remarkable efficiency, considering the global magnitude of the operation. (Ironically, it pulled him out of his greatest frustration: his inability to whip the Depression.) World War II was the nation's best-fought major war—a judgment that may not reflect high praise on the management of others. But we should remember that America had ample warning after Hitler's lunge into

Poland in 1939. (Wilson had received a similar two-year warning when the Germans lunged into Belgium in 1914, but he had refused to heed it properly.) We should also note that the United States, though ill prepared, was better prepared for World War II than for any of the others. One basic reason was that Roosevelt had involved the nation in the conflict on an undeclared basis for about a year and a half before the bewildering blow at Pearl Harbor.

With Wilson's failures vividly in memory, Franklin Roosevelt also excelled in wartime planning for the postwar world. Avoiding a new quarrel over Allied war debts, he devised his clever lend-lease scheme, which eliminated "the silly, foolish old dollar sign." Averting a new deadlock over a League of Nations, he deferred to the Senate in laying bi-partisan groundwork for America's entrance into the United Nations. Heading off a new partisan split over postwar policy, he spiked the guns of his Republican opponents by bringing them into his camp (and Cabinet). Forestalling an angry dispute with the fallen enemy, he refrained from tieing the United Nations Charter to a punitive Treaty of Versailles. All this was a part of his high-level administrative "artistry."

THE TYRANNY OF THE TRIVIAL

No statesman should lose sight of broad objectives and long-range goals in his preoccupation with paper clips. But ideally he should have some concern for the lower echelons, as well as for the higher. If he cannot supervise both, he must concentrate on the more pressing problems.

Grover Cleveland fell prey to the tyranny of the trivial, although on the whole he was a competent administrator. As a practicing lawyer, he had learned not to sign documents without reading them. (Today the President could not begin to read all papers, including officers' commissions, presented to him for signature.)[2] When hundreds of private pension bills for Civil War veterans came to Cleveland's desk, he read them carefully and vetoed several hundred that he found objectionable. More than that, he laboriously penned individual veto messages detailing his objections. The lights in the White House burned into the wee hours of the morning as he pain-

---

[2] Many documents now bear a President's signature put there by other hands or by mechanical means.

fully decided with ink-stained fingers whether or not William Bishop's disability was service-connected (in many cases it was not), and whether he was entitled to a monthly stipend of twenty dollars or so from a Treasury that was rapidly accumulating a surplus of one hundred million dollars.

Cleveland's cheese-paring economies were unpopular, especially with the veterans. But he was determined to make the pension roll an honor roll and not a muster roll of deadbeats and frauds. His critics complained that he would be a better Executive, and the country would be better off, if he let these minor leakages continue. Instead of playing Boy at the Dike, he could better go to bed for a good night's sleep, and then face the big problems confronting the country the next morning with a steady hand and a clear brain. From a purely administrative standpoint the critics were right. Something is wrong when the President feels that he must labor until two or three o'clock in the morning. "I don't work at night," President Coolidge told Secret Service man E. W. Starling. "If a man can't finish his job in the daytime, he's not smart."

Woodrow Wilson once remarked that every official in Washington "either grows or swells." Some Presidents have grown as administrators, as was conspicuously true of Harry Truman. After the shock of Roosevelt's death in 1945, he recovered his poise and displayed genuine talent as an energetic and decisive administrator.

DELEGATING DUTIES

One of the marks of a superior administrator is his ability to pick able subordinates, and then delegate a substantial share of responsibility to them. The selection of men for key posts, whether as official or as unofficial advisers, has often been largely a matter of luck, as we have seen. Much depends on whether the President can enlist the services of his first choice or his sixth choice. Wilson became so desperate in searching for a Secretary of War in 1913 that his assistant finally resorted to looking up names in a lawyers' directory. This is how they stumbled on Secretary Garrison.

The President's role as a talent scout is no simple one. The capacity to spot a man of top-drawer ability, to persuade him to accept the office, to induce him to remain, and to inspire in him loyal support is not solely luck. Accident alone did not bring Elihu

Root to Theodore Roosevelt's Cabinet as Secretary of State, or William H. Taft as both Secretary of War and troubleshooter-in-chief. Both men were chosen because they were able, loyal, and dedicated public servants—with the emphasis on service.

Ability attracts ability, just as wealth tends to marry wealth. Often the bigness of a leader can be measured by the caliber of the men whom he gathers around him. Many a prospective appointee of the highest quality has declined to risk his reputation and peace of mind by tying himself to the tail of a tainted administration. Men like E. R. Hoar and J. D. Cox, who, by happy accident, landed in General Grant's first Cabinet, finally got out or were squeezed out. They thus mocked Darwinism with the survival of the unfittest. A conspicuous exception was Secretary of State Fish, who held his nose through nearly eight long years and repeatedly offered his resignation.

The presidential office is now so burdensome that no man can hope to do what Polk prostrated himself doing: keep all the important threads of responsibility in his own hands. He must increasingly delegate authority if he is to survive, much less succeed, as an administrator. If he cannot gather around him able subordinates in whom he has confidence, he is in deep trouble. If the appointee forfeits that confidence, the President must have the fortitude to drop him without undue delay, as Wilson did not in the case of Ambassador Page in London. Franklin Roosevelt liked to pose as the tenderhearted politician he often was, but he could be brutally peremptory on occasion, as when he removed William E. Humphrey from the Federal Trade Commission.

The foreign service presents special problems. The diplomats stationed abroad are men and women whom the Executive seldom sees personally and who in turn must delegate responsibility to underlings. Though vastly improved in recent decades, the foreign service has traditionally been something of an ugly duckling. It has been undermined by political pull, low salaries, insecure tenure, bad housing, and other serious handicaps. But the President gets much of the blame when the appointment turns sour, as did Franklin Roosevelt's choice of multi-millionaire Joseph P. Kennedy as "my Ambassador" for the London post in the 1930's. Again we wonder how much of the President's reputation rests on innate ability and how much on pure luck.

Leader-in-Chief

"The first duty of a leader is to lead."
THEODORE ROOSEVELT, 1911

FOR PARTY (AND COUNTRY)

In vivisecting the President as a political animal, we have touched glancingly upon his powers of leadership. This all-important theme requires more detailed treatment, because the White House needs to be the lighthouse that guides the entire nation.

The quality of the incumbent's leadership is the most acid of acid tests. First of all, he should be the undisputed leader of his party; he is the cement that helps hold it together. Next, he must be the leader of his nation. But if he cannot lead his party, he cannot lead his people. The party is the instrument by which he carries his program into effect.

Franklin Roosevelt ascended the throne with no clearly outlined New Deal, but the Democratic platform of 1932 was embarrassingly specific. It pledged an elimination of extravagance, a reduction of federal spending, a balanced budget, a sound currency, and the exclusion of government from private industry. Much of the platform was enacted into law, but not these parts. Franklin Roosevelt, however weighty his other achievements, does not receive an "A" grade on the platform-implementation test.

The more effective Presidents have usually been those who

managed to keep their political army behind them as a fighting unit, whether in Congress or out. One of Andrew Jackson's most enduring claims to fame is that he served as a party catalyst. He reorganized and reoriented a motley grouping—the Democratic party—which still exists as the oldest living thing of its kind in America. Franklin Roosevelt, despite his abortive efforts to purge dissenters, managed to preserve increasingly defiant Democratic majorities in both houses of Congress throughout his twelve-plus years. Woodrow Wilson, though perhaps best remembered as a world leader, was likewise a gifted party leader. For the first six of his eight years he retained Democratic majorities in both houses of Congress.

Lincoln, of all the Greats, was the least successful party leader, primarily because of continuing crises. One of the several civil wars that he had to wage involved a running fight with his Republican majority in Congress. Taking the bit into its teeth, it tried to force more drastic measures on the South than the generous-hearted Emancipator was willing to endorse. A "dump-Lincoln" movement developed among certain Republicans during the pre-convention maneuvering of 1864, but it died aborning. Skillful manipulation and timely military victories resulted in Lincoln's re-election over the deposed war hero and Democrat, General McClellan.

CONTROLLING THE SUCCESSION

One test of forceful party leadership is the ability of the incumbent to handpick his successor, as Jackson did Van Buren and Theodore Roosevelt did Taft. But this does not mean, as we have seen, that forcing such favorites down the throat of the nominating convention is good for the party in the long run.

The high-caliber leader ought at least to keep his political machinery in such smooth working order that he is succeeded by a President of his own party. Among the Greats, two died in office—Abraham Lincoln and Franklin Roosevelt—and such a test is inapplicable. George Washington, a Federalist, was succeeded by John Adams, also a Federalist, and here the Father of his Country, though no dyed-in-the-wool politician, perhaps deserves some credit. Three of the Greats or Near Greats—Jefferson, Jackson, and Theodore Roosevelt—either handpicked their successors or made known their favorites. The remaining five Greats or Near Greats were succeeded by administrations of the opposition party: Woodrow Wilson, John Adams, James K. Polk, Grover Cleveland, and Harry Truman. This tailing off weakens their claim to the highest echelon.

Wilson's physical collapse, followed by the collapse of his vigorous party leadership, paved the way for Harding's landslide victory and the ascendancy of the Republicans. The Democrats wandered disconsolately in outer darkness for twelve long years, when the angry waves of the Great Depression swept them back into Congress and the White House. Wilson was the only one of the so-called Greats who was not succeeded by a man of his own party, and if this test is a valid one, his lofty ranking may be further challenged.

Three of the Near Greats either failed as party leaders, or were less than successful. For this reason we may also question their claim to a high grade. John Adams, unable to manage the warhawk Hamiltonian wing of his Federalist party, was defeated for re-election by Thomas Jefferson, albeit by a wafer-thin margin. His party never thereafter won the White House. Grover Cleveland was unable to control the inflationary, free-silver wing of his own Democratic party; it broke loose from him while he stood doggedly for sound-money policies. The Democratic nominating convention of 1896 paid him the supreme discourtesy of rejecting, by a vote of 564 to 357, a resolution approving his administration. His ruptured party, following the Pied Piper of the Platte (William J. Bryan), went down to defeat in four successive elections, three of them with Bryan, the hardy quadrennial, as the standard-bearer.

Harry Truman, unwanted yet undaunted, split his own party into three parts in 1948. He won re-election by a political miracle, but was at loggerheads with Congress—Democrats and Republicans alike—during much of his turbulent stint. Many of his former followers changed the song "We're Just Wild About Harry" to "We're Just Mild About Harry." When he left office, he shared the unhappy experience of John Adams and Grover Cleveland of being followed by a victorious candidate of the opposition party, in this case the magnetic Eisenhower.

Party bosses are often unsavory, boozy, blowzy, cigar-chomping gentry, but the realistic Executive learns to hold his nose and play ball with them. Lincoln patiently tolerated "Boss" Simon Cameron of Pennsylvania, up to a point. Grover Cleveland, no man's lackey, was much more inflexible, and to this trait we must largely attribute his splitting of the party and his other setbacks. Theodore Roosevelt, who had worked with "Boss" Platt and others, at times abjectly, was of a different kidney. Six days after McKinley's mantle fell on him, he wrote to a friend, "Now, mind you, I am no second Grover Cleveland. I admire certain of his qualities, but I have no intention of doing with the Republican party what he did with the Democratic party."

Franklin Roosevelt, like Theodore a masterful politician, also learned how to hold his nose gracefully. During the heyday of the New Deal, the Democratic party consisted basically of the Solid South plus the big machines of the Northern cities. In supping with the Devil, Franklin Roosevelt had to use a long spoon, but use it he did in associating with characters like "Boss" Ed Flynn of the Bronx and "Boss" Frank ("I am the law") Hague of Jersey City. A President cannot carry out his program, secure re-election, and do his country (and his own reputation) any good unless he has his party behind him. To this end he must play ball with its leaders, no matter how uncouth they may be.

NON-PARTISAN POLITICS

To say that the effective Executive must be a good party leader is not to say that he must be a partisan leader. He must at all times realize, as Franklin Roosevelt put it, that he is President of "all the people"—both Democrats and Republicans—and not President of any one party. Although of necessity *the* party leader, he must at times rise above his party, while not cutting himself loose from it.

Woodrow Wilson, normally a shrewd politician, blundered badly when he issued a narrowly partisan appeal for the election of a Democratic Congress in 1918. Whether as a result or not, he got a Republican Congress and a Pandora's box of woes. If an appeal of any kind was in order—and this is highly debatable—he should have called for the election of Congressmen who would uphold his hands in the delicate peace negotiations that lay ahead.

"Bad politics" often turns out to be "good politics" when the people perceive that the President has uppermost in mind the welfare of the nation. Grover Cleveland's courageous tariff message, submitted to Congress in 1887, was condemned as "bad politics" by the wheel-horses of his party. Although he was barely defeated for re-election, he polled 100,000 more popular votes than his opponent. Four years later he was triumphantly re-elected—the only President ever returned to his office after having been ousted.

The successful party leader in the White House also reveals skill in dealing with the opposition leaders in Congress. Little is gained by making mortal enemies of members on one issue when their support might be normally expected on other issues. President Van Buren, an astute manager of men, saw no reason why political opponents could not be personal friends. Many Presidents, including Franklin Roosevelt and Dwight D. Eisenhower, grasped this basic truth. During the Eisenhower era of Modern Republicanism, leaders of the Democratic majority in Congress, including Senator Lyndon B. Johnson, were constant and on the whole cooperative callers at the White House.

Partisanship has always existed in the presidency, despite efforts in recent decades to promote bi-partisanship in Congress. Partisanship will never die as long as we have the two-party system. Parties elect Presidents, and the party in power will always claim credit for just about everything praiseworthy that happens during its administration.

Woodrow Wilson strove for bi-partisanship during World War I ("politics is adjourned"), and Franklin Roosevelt revived the concept during World War II. The war and the peace were national issues, not partisan planks. President Kennedy, in negotiating the test-ban treaty with Russia in 1963, arranged for two Republican Senators to fly to Moscow, there to join four Democratic Senators in the signing. Second-choice Republicans had to be drafted; first-choice Republicans did not want to be tainted with a Democratic triumph.

The President must never forget that while in a narrow sense he is the leader of a party, in a broad sense he is the leader of all parties. He must speak for every state, every section, every group. He should know no East or West, rich or poor, Catholic or Protestant, black or white, white collar, blue collar, or lack of collar. When John F. Kennedy was shot, one bereaved woman wrote that she had not voted for him, but after all "he was my President."

ACTIVISM IN THE WHITE HOUSE

National leadership of a high order is the one quality above all others that the American people expect in their President. It may be political or moral, preferably both. All of the Greats and Near Greats have provided it—in varying degrees, in varying ways, and with varying success. Sometimes it was flamboyant, as was true of Theodore Roosevelt; sometimes it was quiet yet firm, as was true of Lincoln.

The voters will overlook many personal shortcomings in their Chief Magistrate, and have repeatedly done so. But they will seldom forgive his failure to provide leadership when constructive action is urgently needed. James Buchanan is often rated a failure (rather unfairly) because of drifting during the crisis of 1860–1861, rather than attempting to seize the secession bull by the horns. Hoover was booed by countless thousands, not so much because he failed to vanquish the Depression (Roosevelt failed here also) as because in the later stages he seemed to be doing little or nothing while waiting for the storm to blow itself out. (The truth is that he was bestirring himself more actively than the public realized.)

The American people admire a chieftain who can command their allegiance, unite the sections, placate factions in Congress, inspire them to greater patriotism, and arouse them with a challenge that will appeal to their better selves. Woodrow Wilson and Franklin Roosevelt, both as war leaders and evangels of forward-looking domestic programs, possessed this inspirational quality. "Honest Harold" Ickes, Franklin Roosevelt's Secretary of the Interior, wrote regarding the Cabinet meetings: "You go in tired and discouraged and out of sorts and the President puts new life into you. You come out feeling like a fighting cock."

The voters respect the masterful leader who can rally public opinion behind him, as Andrew Jackson did. Descendants of generations of doers, they dislike having to sweat out a problem. Any action, no matter how misguided, seems better than no action, as the try-anything-once Franklin Roosevelt discovered. They respond to positive, do-something leadership: they are not temperamentally equipped to tolerate the dreamer, the drifter, or the worshipper of the status quo. There was a good deal of the stargazer in both

Jefferson and Wilson, though most of the time they had their feet on solid ground, and both endured brickbats for their presumed impracticality.

Yet not all effective leadership is of a positive nature, even though the constructive statesman is usually more generously praised than the obstructive one. Andrew Jackson is perhaps best remembered for having smashed the Bank of the United States. Grover Cleveland is commended for his stiff-necked determination not to be stampeded by Congress into a clash with Spain over atrocities in Cuba. When a bellicose Congressman reminded him that the Constitution authorized Congress to declare war, Cleveland rejoined, "Yes, but it also makes me Commander-in-Chief, and I will not mobilize the army." Without mobilization and without a commander, there could be no war. Sheer negativism, or the ability to put one's foot down when it ought to be put down, is often commendable in a leader.

But the fruits that we pick, even though somewhat sour, seem more impressive than those we do not. We are more disposed to praise the leader who provides plenty of fireworks than the one who digs in his heels. Of the first four Greats, three, as we have already noted, presided over our three greatest wars.

WARRIOR-IN-CHIEF

Military leadership is thrust upon the President by the Constitution, even though two men were moderate pacifists (Jefferson, Wilson), and one was a Quaker (Hoover). These obligations as Commander-in-Chief obviously become crucial in wartime, and any assessment of White House leadership must take into account how capably they were shouldered.

Madison was a relatively poor leader of the War of 1812. However plausible the excuses offered for his failure, including a near-fatal illness, the results came perilously close to catastrophe. In pushing for a declaration of war by Congress, he ignored a Jeffersonian dictum that "great innovations should not be forced on slender majorities": the vote in the Senate was 19 to 13, in the House 79 to 49. These figures are eloquent in explaining why a divided nation fought so futilely.

Polk was an energetic and indefatigable war leader, and he

emerged, partly through rare good luck, with uninterrupted success. He kept the sole direction of the war in his own hands, from grand strategy to the procurement of mules. A dedicated Democrat, he was distressed to find the ranking generals—Taylor and Scott—both Whigs and potential Presidents. His unsuccessful efforts to substitute the inexperienced Senator Thomas Hart Benton, a Democrat, reflect no credit on either his good sense or his non-partisanship.

The best that can be said for Lincoln is that the North won the Civil War while he was in office. The question as to whether it could have been won a year or two sooner under someone else can never be satisfactorily answered. Like Polk, Lincoln was a rank amateur in military affairs, and like Polk, he became involved in low-level details, including the procurement of horses. Yet he boned up on military tactics, undertook to direct overall strategy, and even contemplated taking the field himself.

Lincoln's fresh approach, combined with natural sagacity, was probably on the whole effective. The brass hats were distrustful of meddling by a civilian, and he had chronic trouble with arrogant and ineffective generals until he found U. S. Grant, who followed his earthy counsel: "Hold on with bulldog grip, and chew and choke, as much as possible." At least one of the leading experts on Lincoln insists that he was a better military strategist than any of his generals. This may or may not be superlative praise.

Other Presidents had their wartime troubles. McKinley gets credit for being the lucky winner of the Spanish-American War, although Secretary of War Alger, an inept orator-politician, had to be thrown to the wolves for his bunglings. Woodrow Wilson was outstanding as commander in chief: he picked his general, John J. Pershing, and backed him with confidence. Pershing delivered. Franklin Roosevelt also excelled as a war leader: he and Churchill kept the grand strategy in their own hands. "It's fun being in the same decade with you," ran one message from the White House to Downing Street. Actually, the two men disagreed more often and more seriously than this airy message suggests.

Harry Truman, like Lincoln in the Civil War, had "general trouble" in Korea. His gadfly was General Douglas MacArthur, the headstrong son of a headstrong general. The war in Korea was waged for limited objectives, and with a desire to avoid wrapping the world in flames at a time when the Soviet threat in Europe seemed to be the main menace to the Western world. General Omar Nelson Bradley, of the Joint Chiefs of Staff in Washington, believed that a major conflict with China would be "the wrong war, at the wrong place, at the wrong time, and with the wrong enemy." General MacArthur, arguing that "there is no substitute for victory," believed that it would be the right war, at the right place, at the right time, with the right enemy. President Truman, his patience finally exhausted, dismissed the strong-willed general in such a brutal manner as to arouse the dogs of partisanship. Critics clamored that a two-bit President had fired a five-star general.

President Truman gleaned few laurels from what Republicans sneeringly called "Mr. Truman's War," which was never formally declared by Congress. Scholars credit him with courage and decisiveness in rushing to the aid of the United Nations when its very existence was in peril. He may well have saved it from going down the old League of Nations road. Political scientists credit him with maintaining the supremacy of the civilian arm over the military in sacking General MacArthur, and in demonstrating that overall policy must be made in Washington and not by the man in the field, no matter how gifted. But the public became thoroughly soured on a "police action" that was being fought, not to military victory but to political stalemate. Americans are an impatient, go-for-broke people, eager for speedy results, and this limited conflict was not in the nation's tradition. There is a "substitute" for evanescent military "victory," General MacArthur to the contrary, and that is an enduring political settlement.

OVERBALANCING THE BALANCES

In any appraisal of leadership, the "strong" Presidents tend to emerge as the "great" Presidents. Perhaps we could better say the "activist" Presidents, like Theodore and Franklin Roosevelt. They were not "caretakers" or "executors" or "constitutional monarchs," as some lesser figures had been. They did not recline in the White House while Congress ran rampant at the other end of Pennsylvania Avenue. They were not more bent on lulling than leading. They did not hesitate to wield the immense powers of their office to achieve their goals. They were take-charge, do-something leaders whose talents were such that they could hasten the course of history and "make things happen." They could sway their party, the Congress, American public opinion, and even world opinion, as both Woodrow Wilson and Franklin Roosevelt did in pursuit of their goals.

The checks and balances of the Constitution are all well and good. But if the checks and balances were at all times in perfect equilibrium, the government would be on dead center and in danger of paralysis. Ordinarily "things" begin to "happen" most spectacularly when the powers are overbalanced in favor of the Executive. If he does not lead, there is no leadership. The nation drifts and Congress tries to seize the helm. A legislative body that is windy, seniority-strangled, tradition-bound, and unwieldy—a debating society—cannot govern, much less lead. At times the public wonders if it can even legislate.

The bare fact that a President was a strong one, or a domineering one, does not necessarily mean that he was a great one or even a good one. The crucial questions arise: Was he strong in the right direction? Was he a dignified, fair, constitutional ruler, serving the ends of democracy in a democratic and ethical manner?

The record of the Greats is reassuring. George Washington was strong, in a quiet, self-assured way, and we honor him for his strength. Thomas Jefferson was strong in a firm, soft-spoken way, while Andrew Jackson was strong in a headstrong, aggressive way. His constructive-destructive achievements, on balance, were probably wholesome. Lincoln was strong in an oddly homespun way, Wilson was strong in a persuasively magisterial way, and Franklin Roosevelt was strong in a suavely masterful way. His mother remembered that he used to order his youthful playmates around, and that when she suggested a division of authority, he replied, "Mummie, if I didn't give orders, nothing would happen."

The stick-wielding Theodore Roosevelt is the classic example of a leader who was strong, noisy, and violent. Even granting that he stirred people up for desirable reforms, he overdid strenuosity. His furious if somewhat ineffectual trust-busting gave Wall Street the jitters, and may well have triggered the disastrous Bankers' Panic of 1907. "Hail Caesar, we who are about to bust salute thee!" ran the caption of one cartoon. A leaven of gentleness and restraint would have helped, but then we would not have had Theodore Roosevelt, who on the whole proved to be an effective President.

At least two men are sometimes accounted strong for the wrong reasons. John Tyler, whom the English scholar Harold J. Laski regarded as a strong President, was in fact only strong willed. An obstinate leader, he failed to make his policies prevail with hostile majorities in Congress. Andrew Johnson was strong in a pigheaded way, but he got nowhere, except perilously close to the impeachment graveyard.

THE WEAKNESS OF STRENGTH

Unusual strength in the Executive is not infallibly the proper test of an administration. Noise is not necessarily progress. Deep waters often run the quietest, as was especially true of Washington, Jefferson, and Lincoln. At times an overstrong leader may be a liability, even a menace. When the genial Warren G. Harding was picked by the Chicago convention in 1920, Senator Brandegee explained somewhat apologetically that the times did not demand "first-raters." The times indeed demanded relaxation from "moral overstrain" but Harding proved to be a third-rater. The hilariously slaphappy 1920's, with their inane theme song, "Yes, We Have No Bananas," were building up to the depression deluge of the threadbare thirties.

Some writers on the presidency are guilty of a puzzling inconsistency. First they pay obeisance to the checks and balances of the Constitution as the mainspring of the governmental apparatus. Then they praise the strong President who violates either the spirit or letter of his inaugural oath by taking undue liberties with the Constitution he has solemnly sworn to uphold. He either rides roughshod over the legislative branch, as the Roosevelts did or attempted to do, or defies the judicial branch, as Jackson did, or refuses to "faithfully execute" laws which he disapproves, as Truman did with the allegedly anti-labor Taft-Hartley law. Those commentators who favor usurpation of power by the President are in effect saying that they really do not believe in the Constitution of the United States.

Advocates of the overmuscled Executive are prone to overlook the operation of a sobering law of political physics. Action generally produces reaction, like the aftereffects of strong drink or a powerful drug. Too often for happenstance, a browbeaten Congress is succeeded by a domineering Congress in the eternal tug-of-war between the Executive and the legislative arms. Too often for happenstance, an activist President is succeeded by a passivist.

Excluding accidental Presidents, the sequence in which the pas-sivists line up is startling. An absentee landlord John Adams fol-lowed Washington; a mousey Madison followed Jefferson; a mild-mannered Van Buren followed Jackson; an amateurish Taylor followed Polk; a hoodwinked Grant followed Lincoln; an insipid Harrison followed Cleveland; a bumbling Taft followed Roosevelt; a wishy-washy Harding followed Wilson; a mark-time General Eisen-hower followed the energetic Franklin Roosevelt-Truman com-bination.

Significantly, the two men popularly regarded as Failures—Grant and Harding—came after two of the strongest wartime leaders, Lincoln and Wilson. In the short run, we often pay a high price for excessive strength in the Executive.

Yet one important compensation must be noted. Lincoln, forced to look back over the heads of Buchanan and other passivist prede-cessors, took off from strong men Jackson and Polk. Wilson took off from strong men Lincoln and Theodore Roosevelt; Franklin Roose-velt took off from strong man (until sick) Wilson. Not all the precedents of the strong Presidents were followed but the ebb and flow has been persistently upward.

STATESMEN MAKE HISTORY

One of the first requisites of a presidential leader is the ability to form sound judgments and then act on them, or not act on them, as the case may be. To this end certain qualities, some of which we have already touched upon, are essential.

The President must first of all have common sense—or horse sense, as it was called in a day when Old Dobbin would pull both the buggy and its drunken owner home. Lincoln had an uncommon amount of common sense, and he rode out the waves of civil conflict. Andrew Johnson, uncommonly lacking in common sense, foundered during the stormy days of Reconstruction.

A close cousin of horse sense is moderation, which Washington and Lincoln exemplified in high degree. They were not extremists, either of the right or of the left, and fortunately so, because the extremist is all too frequently wrong. They were unwilling to push programs that had little prospect of securing the necessary public support, although Jefferson departed from this rule when he backed the desperation embargo. They were men of restraint who realized that a problem will often be solved more quickly if one does not rush at it with both arms flailing. They realized that politics, as well as high-level politics called statesmanship, is the art of the possible, of the attainable, often of the next best. They were men of prudence, yet their prudence was leavened with a degree of boldness, as when Franklin Roosevelt daringly embarked upon the New Deal.

The ablest leaders, on the whole, were distinguished for steadfastness of purpose, as Lincoln and Wilson were in their great wars. Most of them were blessed with a sense of detachment which enabled them to perceive the swell of the sea rather than be misled by the whitecaps of the coast. In 1793 the clamor of the pro-French faction for war with England became so noisy that many anxious citizens feared an overthrow of the infant government. Many people believed, so Vice President John Adams reported, that only the sobering effect of the terrible yellow-fever epidemic in Philadelphia, the temporary capital, averted such a calamity. Yet through it all George Washington imperturbably held the ship of state on the neutral course which he had determined to be in the best interests of the nascent nation.

The American presidency yields abundant proof that men make history, and are not necessarily the playthings of uncontrollable events.

CHAPTER XVIII

Further Tests of Leadership

"It is the business of the President as party leader to do
the best he can to see that the declared party platform purposes
are translated into legislative and administrative action."

CALVIN COOLIDGE, 1929

THE IMPACT-ON-OFFICE TEST

Intimately related to aggressive leadership is the impact of the
incumbent on his high office. Students of government have concluded
that the "strong" President has, in general, had a strong influence in
shaping the powers of the Executive. This, they contend, is a praiseworthy development.

All of the giants fall into the impact-on-office category, partly because they were activists. Only men who bestir themselves leave
"footprints on the sands of time." George Washington, in establishing numerous precedents while getting the ship of state off under
fair breezes, certainly was a Shaping Father of the office. Thomas
Jefferson, who infiltrated Congress and its committees, made the
presidency so strong that he enfeebled it for his less capable successors. They lacked his genius for dominating the legislative branch
without appearing to dictate to it. "King Andrew" Jackson, who
imperiously wielded the veto and who swept over the government
like a "tropical tornado," certainly added new dimensions to presidential power.

The first two high-quality war leaders—Lincoln and Wilson—are illuminating examples of how the office can be expanded in the stress of a national emergency. Lincoln blazed a trail that was followed and improved upon by later comers; he demonstrated what could be done in persuading the people to accept an overstretching of the Constitution in surmounting a crisis. When he was accused of subverting the liberties of the people permanently, he replied in his homely way that the nation was sick and needed desperate remedies. He did not believe that a man, after recovering from an illness, would continue to take vomit-inducing drugs, any more than a nation would commit the same folly.

Woodrow Wilson, the next outstanding war leader, exercised a type of personal leadership during World War I that was unmatched by any of his predecessors. In so doing, he improved upon Lincoln's example. Above all, he was able to avert an elbow-jogging Congressional Committee on the Conduct of the War, which had been one of the Emancipator's many crosses.

Theodore Roosevelt, practitioner of the strenuous life, brought a new concept of aggressiveness to the White House. His predecessors, many of them "literalists," generally believed that they could do only those things that the Constitution literally authorized. The Rough Rider, seeking to provide a Square Deal for the downtrodden masses, proclaimed his famous Stewardship Theory—a theory which must have caused the bones of the Founding Fathers to rattle in uneasy graves. He declared in effect that, as the elected steward of the people, he could do anything that the Constitution and laws did not specifically forbid.

Franklin Roosevelt, indubitably a strong President, ventured further in some respects than anyone else. He was not only bolder than many of his predecessors, but he was confronted with the double-barreled crisis of depression and war. Besides, he probably had a more elastic conscience than any of the other Greats, including Jefferson; and an elastic conscience makes easier an elastic interpretation of the elastic clauses of the Constitution. He borrowed to some extent from Wilson's wartime agencies in setting up the New Deal, and he clearly expanded on Wilson's wartime precedents when he found the nation sucked into the vortex of World War II.

Lesser incumbents, on the other hand, have definitely weakened the White House. Grant and Harding, the dupes of thieves, brought disrepute to their illustrious office. Andrew Johnson, attempting to launch a moderate reconstruction policy in the teeth of immoderate Radical Republicans, was slapped down by the Tenure of Office Act. Under its crippling provisions, the President could not remove Senate-confirmed appointees without again securing, hat in hand, the formal approval of the Senate. This Damoclean sword, although in blunted form, hung over and harassed the five succeeding incumbents.

Yet all this emphasis on the impact on office can be overplayed. The American people are primarily interested in how effective a man is in discharging the duties entrusted to him, and not in how good he is for the office and its subsequent occupants.

THE COURT AND THE EXECUTIVE

The "strong" Presidents—three of them crisis Presidents—have not been Constitution worshippers. Though sworn to uphold the sacred parchment, they have not scrupled to bend, twist, distort, or reinterpret it, provided that the pressure of events required a bold hand. As Franklin Roosevelt said during his first year, "While it isn't written in the Constitution, nevertheless, it is the inherent duty of the federal government to keep its citizens from starvation."

Significantly, all but two of the Schlesinger Big Seven either clashed with the Supreme Court or showed scant respect for it. The fortunate exceptions were George Washington, who handpicked all its members, and Woodrow Wilson, who was plain lucky. All of the others, including at times Washington and Wilson, were accused of subverting the Constitution. Such accusations are almost infallible proof that the incumbent was a "strong" leader. Vigorous actions often mean that the Executive is usurping the powers of the judicial or legislative branches. The story of all our major wars is that the Congress grudgingly permits encroachments, and then when the shooting stops it struggles to regain its lost powers.

The Supreme Court is involved with presidential competence in yet another way. Admittedly the federal judiciary is one of the three coordinate branches, but the President leaves his mark on it through his power of appointment. Perhaps John Adams' chief claim to fame, aside from not fighting France, was his lame-duck appointment of the Federalist anachronism, John Marshall, as Chief Justice of the Supreme Court. Jeffersonian liberals viewed his thirty-four years of anti-democratic conservatism with mounting frustration and fury, but Marshall's towering reputation reflects credit on his appointer.

We think better of Harding and Hoover for appointing two eminent Chief Justices: ex-President Taft and ex-presidential candidate Charles Evans Hughes. Liberals praise Theodore Roosevelt for having made Oliver Wendell Holmes an Associate Justice, and acclaim Woodrow Wilson for having so honored the controversial Jewish reformer, Louis D. Brandeis. Liberals likewise applaud Franklin Roosevelt's long-postponed appointments of men like Associate Justices Black, Frankfurter, and Douglas. President Truman's four quasi-political selections, as well as those to the lower courts, reflect rather unfavorably on him, while President Eisenhower is given a pat on the back for his five generally praiseworthy choices for the Supreme Bench.

But there is more than meets the eye in Supreme Court appointments, to say nothing of others. The President, as we have seen, does not always get his first choice: William H. Taft declined four times before accepting the fifth offer. Traditionally a balance has been maintained among Protestant, Catholic, and Jew. And luck enters the picture. John Adams could hardly have dreamed that John Marshall—initially a fourth choice—would turn out to be the dominating figure he became. Franklin Roosevelt must have had grave misgivings about the now-liberal Mr. Justice Black, especially after the nominee from Alabama had unpenitently confessed on a nationwide radio broadcast that he had once been a member of the Ku Klux Klan.

CONSTITUTIONAL CONSTRICTIONS

The best constitutional lawyers have in general been among the least effective presidential leaders. Such men, brought up to revere the law and to study the Constitution through the lenses of the states'-rights Founding Fathers, have tended to recoil from resolute action. It might impinge upon the Constitution and upset the delicate checks and balances.

The reverse has been generally true of the non-lawyers among the strong incumbents. George Washington, a surveyor and plantation manager, went along with Hamilton's liberal or "loose" interpretation of the Constitution. Presidents Jackson, Wilson, and the two Roosevelts were hardly career lawyers, though all were at least exposed to the law, and without exception they were notorious Constitution stretchers. Jefferson and Lincoln were successful practicing attorneys, though hardly renowned as constitutional lawyers. Both were able to rise above shackling legal principles to achieve what they conceived to be desirable goals. They were judicious without being unduly juridical.

Among the foremost constitutional lawyers to rise to the presidency were James Madison, James Buchanan, Benjamin Harrison, and William H. Taft. None of them is generally rated a strong or even an activist President.

James Madison, the so-called Father of the Constitution, is a prime example. As one who had helped frame that precious document in Philadelphia, and as the one who had kept the most complete journal of the deliberations, he was definitely handicapped. Although desiring war with Britain in 1812, he was betrayed by his scrupulous regard for constitutional principles into taking a weak and compromising course. Temperamentally, he was better fitted to be president of William and Mary College in Virginia than President of the United States in Washington.

William H. Taft, a former judge and future Chief Justice of the Supreme Court, had too respectful a regard for legal principles. If Theodore Roosevelt believed that he could do anything the Constitution did not prohibit, Taft, the literalist, believed that he could not do anything the Constitution did not permit. When Roosevelt allegedly burst out in a Cabinet meeting, "Damn the law, I want the canal built!" Taft's legalistic soul must have cringed. The cautious Ohioan tended to believe that the President was more the servant than the colleague of Congress. When the Progressive movement swelled to hurricane proportions, he was constitutionally (and temperamentally) unable to provide forceful leadership.

Andrew Johnson, though not a lawyer, was a stickler for the Constitution, which he revered. Therein lies the explanation of much of his inflexibility in dealing with Congress. In compliance with his wishes, he was buried with a copy of the hallowed document, the first one he had ever owned, as a pillow.

Not all of the activist Presidents were non-lawyers; the aggressive Polk was a lawyer by profession. Not all of the passivists were lawyers; Harding, for example, was a newspaperman. Some Executives began as passivists and wound up as activists, notably Eisenhower. Sensing his newness to politics, and remembering his textbook civics, he began with much deference to Congress.[1] He would not discipline Senator McCarthy when the latter hounded his own Executive Departments, and at first he would not even express a preference for those Republicans running for Congress who had supported his policies. But with the passage of time, he became less deferential toward Congress, and when Sherman Adams and John Foster Dulles were no longer available as deputies, he began to exercise dynamic leadership—six years too late, said his critics. He even appealed to the country to elect members of his own party to Congress—something that Wilson had been crucified for doing in his October appeal of 1918.

THE LEGISLATIVE BOX SCORE

One of the commonest tests of a President's capability is his success in shepherding his program through Congress. Woodrow Wilson and Franklin Roosevelt both succeeded spectacularly, at least early in their administrations. In 1913, when the controversial Federal Reserve Bill came to a vote, Wilson managed to line up every Democrat in the Senate behind it.

But the test of success with Congress must be applied with extreme caution, and with due regard to changing traditions. During the 19th century the Executive was not supposed to lead Congress, much less dominate it. Andrew Jackson, the military chieftain who resented back talk from the ranks, was an exception. He was commonly pilloried by cartoonists as a tyrant who trampled the Constitution under his soldier's boots. He was the first to wield the veto extensively, although on a miniscule scale judged by modern standards—nine times as compared with 169 for Eisenhower.

Jackson was also the first, as we have observed, to employ the veto against bills that he did not like, irrespective of their presumed unconstitutionality. He did not display a reverence for the delicate checks and balances that was revealed by his predecessors and by

[1] Eisenhower's conception of the checks and balances was rather naive. As he told the National War College, "The President cannot do certain things without checking with the Congress."

many of his successors. Technically, no law passed by Congress is unconstitutional until the Supreme Court so decrees. When a President vetoes a bill on the grounds of presumed unconstitutionality, he is in effect usurping the powers of the judicial arm. He becomes Judge-in-Chief.

Grover Cleveland and Franklin Roosevelt were strong Presidents who made free use of the veto. On occasion Roosevelt would ask his aides for "something I can veto," just to keep Congress from getting too "uppity." In some respects Eisenhower's record is most remarkable of all. Although he was confronted by hostile majorities in both houses of Congress during his last six years, only on two occasions did Congress repass a bill over his 169 vetoes. The constant threat of the General's pen caused the rewriting of much legislation, and in this sense the Commander-in-Chief became Legislator-in-Chief or leader by negation. Occasionally he went even further, as others have done, and declined to administer, with or without prior notice, parts of laws that he did not favor—all in defiance of his oath that the laws be "faithfully" executed.

The President is also, or should be, Lobbyist-in-Chief. Woodrow Wilson complained, when the tariff lobbyists descended on Congress in 1913, that the selfish special interests had plenty of highly paid and expert representation. But the people as a whole had no lobbyist to protect their interests. Senators spoke for their states; Representatives spoke for their districts. But only the President, chosen by a more democratically constituted electorate, could speak for all the people. Even President Eisenhower, who began with a hands-off-Congress policy, later changed to put pressure on the members to pass legislation that his conscience told him was in the public interest. "If that's lobbying," he confessed, "I'm guilty."

Historically, the role of the Executive as Representative-in-Chief has been of immense importance. Many of the states have weighted their representation in Congress to favor the older agricultural areas, leaving the exploding urban centers, with their huge labor force and minority groups, underrepresented or unrepresented. Belated recognition of these slighted masses by the White House dates conspicuously from the days of Franklin Roosevelt and Harry Truman, and partly as a consequence Northern Negroes tend to vote Democratic in impressive numbers.

Not until the 20th century—the era of Modern Presidents—was the concept generally accepted that the Executive was to lead, even drive, Congress. Theodore Roosevelt galloped onto the stage of history whirling his Big Stick, and the government has never quite recovered from the shock. Clenching his fist, he once exclaimed, "Sometimes I wish I could be President and Congress too." Franklin Roosevelt developed his leadership (better "drivership") of Congress to a high point. Early in the days of the New Deal he sent up to Capitol Hill demands for "must legislation," often accompanied by drafts of bills prepared by his brain-truster assistants. Some Congressmen became so badly spoiled by having their homework done for them that they complained when recommendations came up from the White House without the customary draft.

COERCING CONGRESS

The difficulty, not to say absurdity, of comparing Presidents of the 20th century with those of the 18th and 19th centuries is highlighted by changing attitudes toward the legislative branch. In the 1830's many Americans condemned Jackson for overvigorous leadership of Congress; in the 1950's they condemned Eisenhower for undervigorous leadership. Today we are prone to define a "strong" President as one who manages to ram the bulk of his program through Congress. Instead of blaming the legislative branch for its failure to legislate, we blame the Executive.

Presidents who have previously enjoyed long terms in Congress, especially the House of Representatives, generally get along more harmoniously with that unwieldy body than those who have not. William McKinley, who had served thirteen years in the House and who had got the "feel" of the Congressional "club," established an admirable rapport with former colleagues. The Senate, the self-proclaimed "greatest deliberative body in the world," is more assertive. Senator Lyndon Johnson, as Senate majority leader, aped the President in 1959 with his own State of the Union message. Ex-Senators, including Andrew Jackson and Andrew Johnson, seem to adjust less well to Congress after they become President than ex-Representatives.

A conspicuous example is Harry Truman, a ten-year Senator. He is commonly bracketed with the Near Greats for his amazingly long list of soul-racking executive decisions, and not for his masterly leadership of the legislative arm. Relations with his four Congresses —one Republican and three Democratic—were on the whole troubled, at times poisonous. This was especially true of the Republican 80th Congress ("the no-account, do-nothing Congress," he dubbed it) and the Democratic 81st ("eighty worst"). After the Republican National Convention of 1948 had proclaimed its platform goals, Truman cleverly called the Republican Congress back into special session to translate these promising words into deeds. Unwilling to confer on his administration any credit for legislative achievement, the members dug in their heels for thirteen days and finally adjourned. "The damned fools didn't pass one measure," Truman later remarked. "If they had, I would have been licked."

Truman's relations with Congress at length became incredibly bad. He got to the point where he evidently relished preparing resounding veto messages, which he used to promote his political fortunes. He probably did his political stock no harm by vetoing the Walter-McCarran immigration bill; it was loaded against foreign "undesirables" whose countrymen in America wielded many votes. Even more helpful was his earlier veto of the Taft-Hartley labor bill, which he branded a "slave labor" bill and which millions of trade unionists (almost all voters) roundly cursed.

John F. Kennedy, despite his fourteen years in the House of Representatives and in the Senate, likewise had his troubles. A young man in a hurry who was never a member of the Senatorial "club" of insiders, he was not conspicuously successful in leading Congress into the legislative pastures of the New Frontier. "I never realized how powerful the Senate was," he complained, "until I left it and came up to this end of Pennsylvania Avenue." With a touch of whimsey he observed, "I used to wonder when I was a member of the House how President Truman got in so much trouble. Now I am beginning to get the idea. It is not difficult."

In the days of Kennedy the box-score technique—unthinkable in the 19th century—was becoming increasingly popular. It consisted of listing the President's recommendations to Congress, and then computing what percentage of them at that particular time had managed to run the legislative gauntlet. Keeping score in this fashion is certainly in line with the traditions of sports-minded Americans. But it is not in harmony with the checks and balances written into the Constitution by the Founding Fathers, who regarded the President as the head of a coordinate branch and not as a dictator trying to force something upon a subordinate branch.

A natural, built-in-rivalry—not to say enmity—exists between Congress and the Executive, much like that between men and women. In teeter-totter fashion, the influence of the President normally sinks as that of Congress rises, and vice versa. A common pattern is for the legislative branch to be relatively friendly during the "honeymoon" outset of an administration, as both Theodore and Franklin Roosevelt discovered, and more rebellious toward the end. Even the most docile legislators come to resent the lash of leadership.

CRISIS LEADERS

Another test of top-drawer leadership is the firmness and coolness of the incumbent in handling emergencies. One of the pleasant myths of American history, as of British history, is that the great crisis always brings forth the great man.

The facts are otherwise. Thomas Jefferson, when faced with intolerable British indignities in 1807, came up with the self-destructive embargo. In the caustic words of John Randolph, it was like cutting off one's toes to cure the corns. Jefferson's wispy successor, James Madison, not only inherited the same crisis in aggravated form, but managed to lead a divided nation into an unnecessary and humiliating war. Buchanan temporized before the secession crisis, and goes down in history (way down) as the man who did not head off secession—assuming that any mortal man could have wrought this miracle. Lincoln was not doing too well with the same crisis when the Confederates solved his unsolvable problem by bombarding Fort Sumter.

Even economic crises have not customarily called forth heroic leadership. Both Martin Van Buren and Grover Cleveland met the financial panics of their administrations with large doses of do-nothingism. Herbert Hoover, no matter how charitable the explanation, did not display breath-taking leadership in grappling with the Great Depression of the 1930's. A leader, especially one trained as an engineer, cannot easily grasp intangible forces.

Four of the five Greats, on the other hand, show to excellent advantage as crisis Presidents, partly because the magnitude of the crisis has magnified them. George Washington, as we have seen, rode out the neutrality imbroglio of the Anglo-French War in 1793–1794. Lincoln, faced with perhaps the gravest emergency of all, grew steadily in stature and drove the meat-grinding war through to a victorious conclusion. Critics who doubt the greatness of the man can hardly doubt the greatness of the problem. Wilson led his people through the terrible war with Germany. Franklin Roosevelt was a dual-crisis President: first, the Great Depression, and then World War II, with the latter submerging the former.

Among the Near Greats, Andrew Jackson and Theodore Roosevelt can hardly be regarded as crisis leaders. James K. Polk was one only in the sense that he precipitated two crises himself, one with Britain and the other with Mexico. From both of these tense episodes the Republic luckily emerged, with little bloodshed and with vastly expanded boundaries. John Adams was a crisis President who, finally following in the footsteps of Washington, chose an unpopular peace rather than a wasteful war when the showdown came with France in 1798.

Harry Truman, plunged into the cold bath of the Cold War, was a crisis President if ever there was one. This is the basic reason why he lands among the Near Greats. If Franklin Roosevelt was a dual-crisis man, Truman, as previously noted, was a dozen-crisis man. Whatever his other shortcomings, Truman revived faith in the American democratic system by showing that an ex-haberdasher from Missouri could step into the breach and acquit himself creditably. But Truman was not an ordinary man; he was an extraordinary man. Two witticisms of the era only brushed the truth: "Truman proved that anybody can be President," while "Eisenhower proved that we do not need a President."

America's leaders during the supreme war crises—Lincoln, Wilson, Franklin Roosevelt—enjoyed one advantage that the others did not, and this advantage has much to do with their towering reputations. They were not only compelled by events to take strong measures, but the nation was compelled to accept them. In time of war the American people recognize the need of fighting the Devil with fire. They will endure sacrifices, accept unconstitutional infractions of civil rights, and follow resolute leadership to a degree that would not be possible in piping times of peace. If victory comes, blunders are largely forgotten: success is the universal salve.

During the Civil War, Lincoln did little more than muddle

through, in the time-honored Anglo-Saxon tradition. The conflict
was one of appalling blunders. Yet Lincoln surmounted the supreme
crisis—or the nation surmounted the crisis while he was in the presidential chair. As he declared candidly in a private letter in 1864, "I
claim not to have controlled events, but confess plainly that events
have controlled me." Making due allowance for his innate modesty,
this partially describes what happened in connection with his
issuance of the Emancipation Proclamation.

THE AVOIDANCE-OF-BLUNDERS TEST

A negative way of grading a leader is to determine whether or
not he avoided major blunders. This approach again raises the
question of rating a man on the basis of what he did not do rather
than on what he did. Negativism, as we have observed, is not
necessarily bad. Only by knowing the various alternatives confronting the President—say, when Lincoln decided to provision
Fort Sumter—can we form a fair assessment of his statesmanship.

Again the record is instructive. We honor George Washington
and John Adams for what they did not do: in the first case, keeping
out of war with England on the side of France; in the second, keeping out of war with France on the side of England. This constructive negativism may be found in other incumbents all the way
to recent times. Truman passed up an opportunity to atom-bomb
China during the Korean War, with all the risks of global incinera-
tion. Eisenhower passed up an opportunity to intervene in the
Hungarian revolt of 1956, with all the dangers of World War III.

These examples of abstentionism, picked at random, just happen
to involve foreign affairs. In the 18th and 19th centuries, only a
crackpot would have suggested that a test of presidential greatness
was skill in world leadership. There was none by the United States,
which, though a weight in the world balance of power, chose not to
throw its weight around like a world power. The nation was ingrown
and introverted, content to wrap itself in the isolationism of its
encircling seas. If the President had undertaken world leadership—
for example, at the time of the Monroe Doctrine in 1823—the powers
of Europe would have laughed him to scorn. This they did anyhow
when Monroe warned them to stay on their side of the water so
that America might cultivate her own fields in peace. If he had then

proposed world leadership, his own people probably would have regarded him as a dangerous busybody.

As late as 1884, when the Arthur administration reluctantly consented to send a delegate to the Berlin Congress on the fate of the Congo, isolationist critics burst into full cry. One cartoonist showed a meddlesome-Matty Uncle Sam sticking his elongated nose up the Congo River. Three quarters of a century later, the United States under President Kennedy (and the United Nations) had its nose all the way up the Congo River into the mineral-rich Katanga province.

Fashions have changed in world leadership. It was bluntly spurned by old-fogey Grover Cleveland, who would not take even the paradisiacal Hawaiian Islands as a gift. President McKinley, the conservatives' conservative, stepped gingerly into the lukewarm waters of tropical imperialism when he reluctantly scooped up the Spanish Philippines, Guam, and Puerto Rico. But Theodore Roosevelt, the first of the Modern Presidents, perceived that the iron hand of destiny was forcing America onto the world stage. He concluded that the nation would do well to shape events in its own interest rather than drift at their mercy. Alert to all opportunities, he pioneered in using the executive agreement, notably with Japan and Santo Domingo, to bypass the hatchet wielded by the Senate in mutilating or murdering treaties.

Every one of the incumbents since McKinley has been a world leader, some actively, others passively. Even easygoing Taft tried his hand at dollar diplomacy to promote American foreign policy abroad, but with only sporadic success. Harding, Coolidge, and Hoover, all of them in the ostrichlike 1920's, reflected the isolationist tradition, but they were world leaders in spite of themselves. The United States was perhaps the most formidable nation in the world, and power makes itself felt, whether used actively or not. All the later Presidents from and including Franklin Roosevelt had the weighty mantle of world leadership thrust onto their shoulders, whether they wanted it or not.

Again the difficulty of devising yardsticks for measuring greatness becomes obvious. George Washington and Thomas Jefferson are esteemed Great, largely because they were determined to keep out of the broils of Europe and the rest of the outside world. Woodrow Wilson and Franklin Roosevelt are esteemed Great, largely because they led the nation into the broils of Europe and the rest of the outside world. We must learn to judge these men by what was expected of them at the time they wore their crowns of thorns.

A GLOBAL CONSTITUENCY

The Commander-in-Chief, armed with ample constitutional authority, has always been Diplomat-in-Chief, if he chose to be. But more recent events have added the crushing responsibility of leadership of the free world. The transforming force has been the enthronement of powerful and hostile foreign ideologies, beginning with the Communist revolution in Russia in 1917.

The President, as keeper of the peace, now has a world constituency consisting of several billion non-voting non-Americans. The English historian Arnold J. Toynbee put his finger on a startling truth in 1951. "We can't vote for the President of the United States," he said, "but he is the most important executive officer we possess. We can't have any voice in who is to be Secretary of State, but he is the most important diplomatic officer we possess. You didn't ask for it; we didn't ask for it; but that is the situation."

James Bryce, another Englishman, concluded in 1888 that in time of peace the President was more or less a clerk. The truth is that Congress often emerged as the dominant branch, conspicuously in the constant pulling and hauling with the Executive over domestic issues. But now there is perpetual global warfare. It is for the most part a Cold War, but a war nevertheless. As modern miracles shrivel the world, we are jammed tighter and tighter into the same cockpit. As the globe grows smaller, America's role in it grows larger. And with that role the power of the President increases proportionately, whether he elects to use it or not.

The same cannot be said of the Executive's management of domestic affairs. In this arena Congress is more able to hold its own in the eternal struggle over mutual encroachments. Foreign dangers tend to unite the American people, as they were united after Pearl Harbor. Domestic dangers tend to divide them, as was painfully true of the struggle over slavery and the subsequent attempts of the Negro to win equality. In 1963, when the race issue was convulsing Birmingham, Alabama, one American journalist observed, with obvious exaggeration, that President Kennedy was able to exert more power in Birmingham, England, than in Birmingham, Alabama.

DIPLOMAT-IN-CHIEF

All of the five Greats had another trait in common. They were all their own Secretaries of State in shaping major policies and in all other decisions of crucial importance.

George Washington had the experienced Secretary Jefferson at his elbow, but the neutrality policy finally devised was his own. President Jefferson had the alert James Madison near at hand, but Jefferson was the master in the delicate negotiations with the warring powers of Europe.

Abraham Lincoln, more than any of the other four, concentrated on a domestic crisis—welding the sundered states together again. He gave Secretary of State Seward a relatively free hand but not a completely free rein. He squelched the Secretary's insane scheme for picking a fight with certain of the major powers of Europe, in the hope of luring the South back into the Union. In all other critical decisions involving foreign affairs, including the explosive *Trent* quarrel with Britain, the President had the final voice.

Woodrow Wilson, perhaps more than any other Great, was his own Secretary of State. That three-time electoral loser, William Jennings Bryan, was forced on him as Secretary by the unwritten law of politics, and he permitted the frustrated Commoner to bemuse himself with the negotiation of some thirty cooling-off treaties to avert war. But in all major concerns Wilson took command, and even drafted a number of the critical notes that went to Germany over the signature of the Secretary of State. When Bryan resigned in protest, Wilson deliberately chose an underling in the State Department, Robert Lansing, on the mistaken assumption that the latter would serve as a kind of glorified clerk. When the Paris Peace Conference assembled, Wilson went himself to help shape a brave new world.

Franklin Roosevelt had in Cordell Hull a Secretary of State of more impressive stature. A potential presidential nominee, Hull could not be treated as cavalierly as Wilson had treated Lansing. During his first term Roosevelt was so heavily involved with the New Deal that he gave Hull a relatively free rein, particularly in dealing with such seemingly secondary issues as the Good-Neighbor policy and reciprocal trade agreements. As the European crisis deepened, Hull was increasingly elbowed aside, although he continued to have a large hand in the development of Far Eastern policy. After Pearl Harbor the Chief himself took over global diplomacy and strategy at the highest level, dealing directly with Winston Churchill and repeatedly cold-shouldering Hull. The Secretary, who was not taken abroad to any of the summit conferences, resented being turned into a fifth wheel. Yet he did yeoman work in shaping a bi-partisan foreign policy and in pioneering for the United Nations Organization.

Generally speaking, if we find a masterful and dominating Secretary of State, we find a weak and ineffective President. Opposites seem to attract each other. Secretary Seward managed to bring some badly needed luster to the floundering Johnson administration by his astuteness in elbowing the French out of Mexico and by his foresight in purchasing Alaska at a fire-sale price. Secretary Fish contrived to blunt the worst of Grant's blunders, and crown the General's administration with diplomatic laurels at the expense of Britain. The imperious Secretary Hughes completely overshadowed the hesitant Harding, and to a considerable extent the provincial and unimaginative Coolidge.

The usual formula that a strong Secretary equals a weak President does General Eisenhower's reputation no good. Prudently relaxing to conserve his health, he gave John Foster Dulles a looser rope than any other recent Secretary of State has yet enjoyed, at least when big issues were at stake. Richard Goold-Adams, the British journalist, concluded in 1962, "Dulles held more power in his own hands than any modern American except Franklin Roosevelt." While Dulles was "playing God," Eisenhower was "playing golf," writes Rexford G. Tugwell, a former Democratic brain truster, with obvious exaggeration.

In the horse-and-buggy days of the 19th century, few people cared much whether the President or the Secretary of State exercised the controlling voice in foreign affairs. The stage was vastly smaller. Today people care. John F. Kennedy, who believed that diplomacy was much too important to be left solely to the diplomats, used to remark, "foreign policy can kill us." If the President turns over critical decisions to his Secretary of State, he renounces what is perhaps the most important part of his job. If he is content to abdicate his responsibilities in this fashion, he is no longer Diplomat-in-Chief but Figurehead-in-Chief.

CHAPTER XIX

Final Tests of Greatness

"To persevere in one's duty and be silent
is the best answer to calumny."

GEORGE WASHINGTON, 1796

KEEPING HOME FIRES BURNING

The presidential office, at bottom, is involved with domestic problems rather than foreign affairs. The basic obligation of the Executive is to manage the bread-and-butter concerns of tens of millions of fellow Americans. But in recent decades the twilight zone between domestic and foreign affairs has become increasingly blurred, especially in regard to such problems as tariffs, immigration, foreign trade, foreign aid, and international debts.

A glance at the record is rewarding. From the days of George Washington down to the outbreak of World War I in 1914, America experienced only one period when issues involving foreign affairs loomed as large in the public mind as those involving domestic affairs. This was during the wars of the French Revolution and the subsequent Napoleonic upheaval, which ultimately sucked the young Republic into the sideshow War of 1812.

World War I, with the emotional debauch that came with making the world safe for democracy, left America weary of well-doing. She retreated into the storm cellar until Hitler and the other dictators forced her to do the dirty job all over again—at a much higher cost. History *does* repeat itself, some wag has said, but the price goes up each time.

The aftermath of World War II spawned the Cold War. It forced America, in spite of herself, into the costly and uncomfortable position of holding the dike for the free world against Communism. The Gallup pollsters often found their respondents more worried about keeping the peace with Russia than about "gut issues" like housing, the cost of living, unemployment, and race relations.

Even though foreign vexations now tend to be the most worrisome ones, the stubborn fact remains that the President is not elected by foreigners but by Americans. The higher his standing abroad, the lower his standing may be with his own people, especially when he is ladling out billions of dollars in overseas aid. Franklin Roosevelt in the 1940's probably would have run even better in England than in the United States, so grateful were the British for lend-lease largesse and other handouts. John F. Kennedy undoubtedly would have run better in Berlin than in Dallas after proclaiming to a roaring German crowd, *"Ich bin ein Berliner"* (I am a Berliner). Lyndon B. Johnson was hurt rather than helped in 1964 by the overwhelming approval of the European press for him rather than for his opponent, Senator Goldwater.

But a leader must look to the fences in his own backyard if he expects to pursue a successful program abroad. Policy, like charity, begins at home. We naturally applaud spectacular, if hollow, achievements in the foreign arena, like Harding's Washington Disarmament Conference. But we can rate no administration as a distinguished one, or even a successful one, unless the President has managed to keep the home fires burning.

PROSPERITY SPELLS POPULARITY

The maintenance of good times is a test that can make or break any administration. Even Eisenhower's amazing popularity suffered a sharp decline during the recession (Republicans said "dip") of 1958. The crucial question is: Was the incumbent lucky enough to be the beneficiary of an enriching wave of prosperity? Whether he had much to do with it, or little to do with it, or nothing to do with it is all beside the point. He gets credit for boom times, discredit for bad times. Among his numerous roles, many of them recent, is that of Manager of Prosperity or Financier-in-Chief.

Beginning with the paralyzing panic of 1819, depressions blighted the economy almost precisely every twenty years. They came with such cyclical regularity as to indicate that the White House had no control over them, and consequently should receive neither denunciation for depression nor approbation for prosperity. But as Dwight W. Morrow said of the Republicans in 1930, the party which takes credit for the rain must expect discredit for the drought.

Only two of the eleven Greats or Near Greats are regarded (rather unfairly) as panic Presidents. This statement in itself contains volumes, for it prompts the obvious conclusion that to attain an exalted reputation the incumbent must be lucky enough to avoid hard times.

The first of the unlucky duo was Grover Cleveland, the die-hard old Democrat. He inherited a depression from his predecessor Benjamin Harrison, for which he was not responsible but for which he was bitterly blamed. Fortunately for Cleveland's political future, he had already been re-elected, and the voters could not turn him out at the polls. But they did in a figurative sense when, in 1896, they vented their wrath against the Democratic nominee, the golden-tongued freesilverite, William J. Bryan.

Franklin Roosevelt, the topmost among the Greats or Near Greats in the sheer size of his personal following, was definitely a Depression President. But the black pall had descended some three years before he entered office, after the collapse of the Big Bull Market early in the unhappy days of the hapless Hoover. About eight of Roosevelt's twelve toilsome years were spent in a rather fruitless but financially expensive effort to pull the Republic out of the Depression doldrums. Yet if he could not be fairly blamed for getting the country into the morass, he was blamed for getting it in deeper or not pulling it out sooner. Herbert Hoover then believed, and in later years repeatedly charged, that the threat of the erratic New Dealer's election in 1932 plunged a recovering nation back into the depths. He iterated and then reiterated the charge that Roosevelt's spendthrift, socialistic, collectivistic policies impeded rather than speeded recovery.

Yet if adversity can break a President, prosperity can make him. George Washington was fortunate in this respect. Folklore has it that the intrepid Father of his Country, plus the new Constitution, plus the financial wizardry of the boy-wonder Secretary of the Treasury Hamilton, ushered in an era of prosperity and thus rescued the infant Republic from bankruptcy. The truth is that in the mid-1780's the nascent nation was wallowing in the trough of a depression, and that returning prosperity helped to save both the new Constitution and the new government.

George Washington was marked as a darling of the gods even before two horses were shot under him and four bullets zipped through his coat on Braddock's bloody field in 1755. Washington's luck continued throughout his presidency. If the nation had been sucked into the war with England, as it almost was in 1793–1794, the customs revenues, predominantly from British imports, would have dwindled to a trickle. Hamilton's top-heavy financial structure might have crashed in ruins, and the gifted young financier might have gone down in history not as the "greatest Secretary of the Treasury" but as the last. Luckily the United States, in pursuance of Washington's wise policy of playing for time, managed with a supreme effort to remain neutral. In succeeding years the Americans fattened as feeders while the Europeans famished as fighters.

Another related test of presidential competence is sound management of the nation's economy, particularly the federal budget. Every one of the Big Five, each a crisis President, was confronted with a burdensome national debt. Except for a few years beginning with 1834, America has always had a national debt, but it must be measured in the light of the size of the population and of the gross national product.[1]

The Washington-Hamilton team deserves high praise for reviving the corpse of public credit and putting the finances of the federal government on a sound and self-liquidating basis. Thomas Jefferson, though not himself distinguished in the field of finance, both preached and practiced rigid economy. He joined with the Geneva-born Albert Gallatin ("the greatest Secretary of the Treasury since Hamilton," another foreigner) to bring penny-pinching to bucolic Washington. But the visionary Virginian went too far when he undertook to slash naval expenses by investing in cut-rate gunboats

---

[1] Technically there has always been a "total gross debt," which embraced matured obligations that had not yet been presented for redemption but for which there were sufficient funds.

rather than in expensive frigates. This so-called mosquito fleet proved to be virtually without bite in the war that was later waged with Britain in 1812–1815.

Abraham Lincoln, Woodrow Wilson, and Franklin Roosevelt were the other members of the Big Five to be confronted with oppressive financial problems. They all rank high among the freest spenders and the greatest inflaters of the national debt. But each of them had a frightful war on his hands, and in the case of Roosevelt a war plus a Depression. No sane President, thinking of both the national welfare and his own reputation, is willing to lose a war to balance a budget.

THE ABUSE-IN-OFFICE TEST

The ablest Executives have all been savagely abused by large segments of the press and the public. Scandal loves a shining target; there is little point in showering filth on personages who are not eminent and hence not newsworthy. Small minds derive much satisfaction from trying to bring distinguished figures down closer to their own mean level. A kind of political law seems to operate: the greater the President, the greater the abuse. To put it another way, if he was not vilified by at least a considerable minority of his own people, we may doubt that he was really an eminent President.

Even aristocratic George Washington was not immune. Pilloried as a dictator and as the Stepfather of his Country, he bitterly regretted ever having consented to enter public life. He complained to Thomas Jefferson that he was abused "in such exaggerated and indecent terms as could scarcely be applied to a Nero; a notorious defaulter; or even to a common pickpocket." "Damn George Washington!" cried John Randolph of Virginia in a public toast at the time Washington was supporting the unpopular Jay's Treaty with England. When the President retired, the grandson of Benjamin Franklin (himself a disappointed office seeker) let fly a venomous blast in his editorial columns. He rejoiced that Washington's name would no longer "give a currency to political iniquity and... legalize corruption." But such views were those of a carping minority, and when Washington died nearly three years later a deluge of eulogies washed away the residue of bitterness.

Thomas Jefferson, an outspoken champion of free speech, suffered

acutely from overfree speech. He was libelously accused of being
the son of a half-breed Indian squaw by a Virginia mulatto father,
and, as we have seen, of having sold his own ill-begotten mulatto
children into slavery. The thirteen-year-old poet, William Cullen
Bryant, in his first published verses (*The Embargo*), merely repeated what his Federalist elders in New England were saying:

> Go, scan, Philosophist, thy * * * * * * charms
> And sink supinely in her sable arms.

The precocious poet later excluded this schoolboy indiscretion from
his published works.

Andrew Jackson, aside from being called a despot, was earlier
accused of being an adulterer, married to an adulteress. For good
measure the hatemongers charged that his pious mother was a
prostitute who had married a Negro, and that his eldest brother
had been sold as a slave. A President, or a candidate for the presidency, cannot reply publicly to such foul libels or fight duels.
Privately fuming, Jackson declared that "was not my hands tied,
and my mouth closed, I would have soon put an end to their
slanders."

If the virulence and variety of abuse are a test of greatness, then
Lincoln towers over all rivals. Bitterness was at a boil, as Americans
slaughtered Americans by the tens of thousands. Much of this
venom was directed, both North and South, at the presumed author
of these woes. He was the Illinois Ape, a baboon, a gorilla, and an
orangutan. More charitably, he was an unsuccessful abortion resulting
from the lust of some footloose and fancy-free Southern gentleman,
or some other gentleman—all told numbering at least seventeen.

A partial alphabetical list of the epithets hurled at Old Abe would
include: assassin, bastard, blackguard, braggart, bully, butcher,
coward, despot, drunkard, fiend, filthy-story teller, head ghoul, idiot,
ignoramus, imbecile, jokester, liar, monster, mulatto (Abraham
Africanus I), murderer, obscene clown, perjurer, robber, savage,
scoundrel, slave hound of Illinois, stallion, thief, tyrant, and un-
principled usurper. The District Attorney of New York, the Honorable (?) A. Oakey Hall, publicly charged President Lincoln with a
score or so of crimes, including treason, homicide, arson, burglary,
robbery, perjury, kidnapping, blasphemy, profanity, obscenity,

bribery, embezzlement, forgery, and mayhem. If, as Jonathan Swift said, "Censure is the tax a man pays to the public for being eminent," Lincoln was heavily taxed.

BRICKBATS FOR REFORMERS

Woodrow Wilson, a simon-pure Presbyterian, maintained platonic relations with several women. He was inevitably accused of illicit affairs, including one with Mrs. Mary Hulbert Peck, from which the Princetonian emerged as "Peck's Bad Boy," after a humorous novel by that name. He loftily ignored such scandalmongers. When he suffered a paralytic stroke and confinement to the White House, the tongue of gossip wagged viciously about insanity resulting from the ravages of tertiary syphilis.

Franklin Roosevelt probably ranks next to Lincoln as a target of slander. Like Lincoln, he was a prolonged-crisis President; and great crises generate great bitterness. Some malicious gossips had "that cripple in the White House" regularly visited by mistresses; others had him completely paralyzed below the waist. Still others revived the hoary charge against Theodore Roosevelt that the original family name was a Jewish "Rosenvelt." An elaborate genealogy was published under the title *Roosevelt's Jewish Ancestry.*

No normal person likes to be smeared, especially if he is doing only his duty under severe difficulties and at considerable personal sacrifice. Washington, ordinarily imperturbable, did not suffer mud-flingers gladly. Jefferson, whose dedication to a free press was less resolute than is commonly supposed, wryly concluded that the Federalist calumniators ought to be protected "in the right of lying and calumniating." Lincoln remarked that "if the end brings me out right," then the attacks "won't amount to anything." But "if the end brings me out wrong, ten angels swearing I was right would make no difference."

One test of eminence is to observe how philosophically the incumbent rose above libelous assaults. Here Lincoln attains true greatness. No man should aspire to be President unless he has a thick skin and a light heart. In this respect Herbert Hoover was seriously handicapped: he wasted too much time and energy fretting over what people said about him. The successful President needs not only the stamina of a bull moose but the hide of a rhinoceros.

A basic reason for the name-calling directed at the giants is that they all undertook democratic reforms, and reform always treads on the corns of vested interests. Their voices are not only influential but they are amplified by the power of wealth. Newspaper publishing in America has increasingly become a big business, and big business is basically conservative. It tends to align itself with the more conservative Republican party, and hence Democrats get their full share of partisan criticism.[2] In every one of his elections Franklin Roosevelt had an increasing majority of the newspapers against him.

As newspapers become bigger and fewer—there are now many one-newspaper cities—the press generally becomes more anti-Democratic. Harry Truman, among various Democrats, had complained that we now have a one-party press, which in effect is a paper curtain. To a degree this is true, but a breakthrough is achieved by syndicated columnists of a pro-Democratic bent, and by commentators and candidates on both radio and television.

Of one thing we can be certain. If a President, like Calvin Coolidge, is content to stand pat, he will receive friendly treatment at the hands of the big-business newspaper press. If he turns out to be a Hercules bent on cleansing the stables, he is in for a roasting. After President Kennedy had launched his reformist New Frontier, he was asked to comment on the press treatment of his administration. "Well," he replied, "I'm reading more but enjoying it less."

THE PRESS CONFERENCE IMAGE

A more recent test of competence, if not greatness, is how skillfully the incumbent handles his press conferences. This image-projecting device is of such recent vintage that it is clearly one of the many yardsticks not applicable to Executives of the oxcart era. Formally started by Wilson in 1913, it was first conducted on a cut-and-dried basis, with the correspondents submitting their written questions in advance. Newsman Warren G. Harding, though guilty of at least one bad blunder, on the whole projected a favorable image through his press conferences. Silent Cal Coolidge belied his

---

[2] An exception is the Johnson-Goldwater campaign, in which the Republican Goldwater was so erratically conservative—even radical—as to cause many Republican newspapers to support Johnson.

nickname by proving to be unexpectedly garrulous in dealing with the press. Clever enough to help the newshawks out with their stories, he succeeded remarkably well in keeping his personality, rather than his policies (if any), in the limelight. Therein lay the secret of much of his popularity. The harassed Herbert Hoover, who insisted on written questions, remained on rather chilly terms with the newsmen, and he finally abandoned the regular sessions altogether.

With Franklin Roosevelt the press conference, supplementing the fireside chat, emerged as a major medium for self-advertising and policy promotion. Meeting some two hundred correspondents twice a week, and abandoning the stuffy written questions, he staged about five times more conferences during his first term than Hoover had held. Gay, bantering, parrying probes, scoring with ripostes, delighting in the contest of wits, and flattering "the boys" with confidential off-the-record remarks, he maintained warm relations with the newsmen, especially in the early days. Many of them were employed by anti-New Deal newspaper proprietors, whose prejudices were partially offset by "the working press." Roosevelt actually did more than perfect the press conference as an instrument for projecting his personality and policies. Through it he added a new dimension to the art of democratic governing that was comparable, some admirers claimed, to parliamentary questioning in England.

Succeeding Presidents developed their own "style." Truman was self-assured, cocky, sometimes a bit quarrelsome, but on the whole informally informative. A more formal Eisenhower, despite confusing sentence structure and perplexing platitudes, held up surprisingly well: his personality often came through more clearly than his ideas. He was stronger on sincerity than syntax. Kennedy, likewise prone to less precise rhetoric when speaking extempore, made a major feature of press conferences, which he handled with increasing mastery. Some of them were televised "live" with virtuoso effect. Lyndon Johnson, at first a bit gun-shy, would hold "quickie conferences," more or less on the hoof, and once from a bale of hay on his Texas ranch. He gradually slipped into a more conventional pattern.

The press conference, as now perfected, is a uniquely American institution. It is a remarkable manifestation of democracy at work, roughly in the town-meeting tradition. No other head of state will subject himself to this kind of third degree, answering off the top of his head complicated and often tricky questions that involve the fate of hundreds of millions of people. Slips of the tongue, if not of the brain, are inevitable. They have resulted, on a number of embarrassing occasions, in hasty cover-up explanations.

The Presidents naturally take the ordeal of the press conference seriously. It is now so much a part of their job as to be almost a part of the unwritten Constitution. Often they subject themselves to dry-run briefing sessions, in which they are primed on questions most likely to arise; sometimes they arrange for "planted" questions, as Kennedy did on a few occasions. Their subsequent appearance on the air is consequently not so much of a gamble as it may seem. President Eisenhower, who obviously resented the critical references to his scrambled syntax, took pride in having made no major blunders.

The televised press conference is thus a major shaper and sharpener of the presidential image. Despite the pitfalls lurking in an exhibition that is presented "live," a glib and knowledgeable Executive can create the impression that he is a "smart" leader who knows what he is doing. A well-ringmastered press conference adds immeasurably to his "style"—a subject of growing interest to students of the office.

GREAT CHALLENGES FOR GREAT MEN

Grave crises do not necessarily bring forth great men to grapple with them, as we have observed in the case of Buchanan and others. Yet the so-called Greats have all lived in great times, or perhaps better, in greatly troubled times. These in turn have inflated their reputations.

Shortly after World War II, one of America's naval heroes was asked how one became a famous admiral. First, he replied, get into the navy; then get to be an officer; then get a command; then have a command in time of war; then become involved in a great naval battle; and then win it (preferably with a ringing slogan). Many a naval officer of the highest ability has retired an unknown sailor simply because this entire chain of prerequisites was not present. He had the misfortune, at least for his reputation, not to have lived greatly in great times. Admiral W. F. ("Bull") Halsey is quoted as saying: "There are no great men, only great challenges that ordinary men are forced by circumstances to meet."

The fate of American Vice Presidents, traditionally those faceless timeservers, is instructive. Until recent years, they have been chosen by weary conventions, more or less as the sweaty delegates were packing their bags, but with due regard for geographical and ideological "balance" or antithesis on the ticket. As we glance over the twenty-six Vice Presidents (excluding those who later gained the White House), we immediately conclude that the group consisted of a lot of third-rate Throttlebottoms. We are inclined to agree with Prince Otto von Bismarck's supposed jibe that God looks after "fools, drunkards, and the United States of America."

But let us not dismiss the vice presidential "unknowns" too lightly. Four of the "accidental eight" Presidents were subsequently elected in their own right, all of them in this century: Theodore Roosevelt, Calvin Coolidge, Harry Truman, and Lyndon Johnson. Both Theodore Roosevelt and Calvin Coolidge could easily have been honored with "third terms," counting the unexpired years of their predecessors. Harry Truman chose not to run for a "third term" in 1952, though he alone would have been eligible under the newly adopted Twenty-second Amendment. (He was clever enough not to press his luck and tangle with the dazzling General Eisenhower.)

The record of the eight accidental Presidents is more than just respectable. The Schlesinger experts rank none of them a Failure. Yet suppose that a capricious fate had instead tapped eight others at random—including Daniel D. Tompkins, Richard M. Johnson, William A. Wheeler, Levi P. Morton, and Charles W. Fairbanks. Is it not reasonable to suppose that these ticket-balancers would have done about as well, mediocre though they seem to be, as the eight presumed nonentities who, by the grace of God, were catapulted into the White House? In early November, 1963, Vice President Johnson was more or less a forgotten man ("Whatever happened to Lyndon Johnson?"). A month or so later the Gallup pollsters found him to be the most admired man in America.

This kind of speculation leads one a bit further. If some of the lesser Presidents had lived in more stressful times—say, Rutherford B. Hayes during the Civil War—they might have risen to the same echelon in the public esteem that Lincoln attained. If hard-luck artists like Hoover had served ten years or so earlier, they almost certainly would rank much higher. We shall never quite know with precision whether great times make great men or great men make great times, or both.

IMPACT-ON-HISTORY TESTS

The rock-bottom test of a President's leadership is not so much the impact on his office as the impact on his times. What was his influence, both short run and long run, on his own generation and on the far reaches of history? Did he give voice and shape to an epoch? Was an age named after him—such as the Age of Jackson? If so, who did the naming: his worshipful contemporaries or some latter-day scholars who happened to discover currents that may not have been discernible to contemporaries?

The distinction between short run and long run is crucial. At the time of the fight over the League of Nations, Woodrow Wilson declared, "I would rather fail in a cause that I know will one day succeed than succeed in a cause that I know will one day fail." Coolidgean prosperity became a byword, and if the historians had passed judgment in March, 1929, when the complacent Vermonter left office, he would probably have been esteemed one of the ablest Presidents. But when the speculative bubble popped in October—a bubble that Coolidge had actively encouraged—the judgment was different.

The impact on one's times must, of course, be for good. A near-maniac Hitler, who was responsible for monstrous misery and death, could hardly be called an eminent statesman, though his impact was world-shattering. Andrew Jackson had a profound impact on his times, but it continued to be reflected in tens of thousands of bank failures, which as late as 1933 were occurring at the rate of about four thousand a year. Woodrow Wilson, a towering world leader, had a tremendous impact on his era. Although he failed in a cause that he hoped would one day succeed, the United Nations was erected on the ruins of the old League of Nations, after mankind had committed the insanity of World War II.

Whatever the impact, popularity is no guarantee that an administration was distinguished or even successful.[3] But we have observed that all of the Big Five, plus Jackson, were re-elected, though in Wilson's case by a breathlessly narrow margin. The two so-called Failures in fact enjoyed unusual popularity. Grant was re-elected in a landslide over the grotesque Greeley, and he was a powerful contender for a third nomination and a third term in 1880. Handsome Warren Harding, the hail-fellow-well-met, was a well-liked figure at the time of his death, which plunged the nation into deep mourning. Then came the overflooding cesspool. Poker-faced Coolidge was an unusually popular President who could have had a third term if he had not uttered his most famous words: "I do not choose to run in 1928." Yet the experts rank him close to Failure. General Eisenhower, who enjoyed phenomenal personal popularity and who probably could have had a third term but for the Twenty-second Amendment, is rated only two notches above Below Average.

The presidency is not a popularity contest, and in a sense Dr. Gallup renders us a disservice by his repeated polls on popular standings. Excessive acclaim, while personally gratifying, may be a bad sign as far as eminence is concerned. President Washington, though first in war and first in peace, was not first in the hearts of many of his countrymen at the end of eight years. Presidents like Cleveland, who were loved for the enemies they had made, had the courage to scorn popularity. Presidents who achieved reforms, like Wilson and Franklin Roosevelt, were bound to make foes among the dislodged. President Eisenhower was so popular as to raise the suspicion that he had not disturbed enough entrenched interests.

Generally speaking, the most eminent Executives have not been unduly popular. Supported or tolerated by the many, they have been resented by a vocal minority which at times sounded like a majority.

PRESIDENTS IN PERSPECTIVE

A final test of distinction is to determine how the incumbent was regarded by his contemporaries, at home and abroad, in his lifetime and after.

[3] The pollsters found that Eisenhower's popularity shot up spectacularly after the U-2 spy-plane blunder of 1960, as did Kennedy's after the Bay of Pigs fiasco in Cuba in 1961. These were two of the worst bungled episodes of their respective administrations, yet the public evidently displayed a rally-behind-the-President sentiment.

The Big Three of the early years all attained international stature. Washington and Jefferson, especially Washington, were renowned and respected in two hemispheres before becoming Chief Magistrates. Much less prominent before attaining the White House was Abraham Lincoln; his fame came with his war leadership and his martyrdom. From London to New Delhi to Tokyo he was ultimately hailed as a major prophet of democracy. Emperor Hirohito kept a bust of Lincoln in his study, just as Emperor Napoleon I had kept a bust of Washington on display.

Not until the dawn of the 20th century did the White House loom large in the thinking of foreign statesmen and peoples. World leadership, grasped for the first time by the United States, inevitably brought international influence to the presidency. Theodore Roosevelt, basking in the limelight of two hemispheres, was undoubtedly the first American President to be acclaimed a global leader during his incumbency. A dominating figure, he incurred the hostility of many Russians and Japanese by serving as the honest broker who led them to the peace table at Portsmouth and induced them to compromise.

Woodrow Wilson suffered a cruel fate. At first a messianic leader during World War I, he became a fallen angel after his disappointing role at the Paris Peace Conference and his failure to shepherd the United States into the League of Nations. Disgruntled Germans, disappointed Frenchmen and Britons, and disillusioned American liberals all turned savagely against him.

Presidents Harding, Coolidge, and Hoover—the Republican trio tinged with isolationism—were not highly regarded abroad during their terms. Hoover was a partial exception; he gained some luster as a pioneer of the Good Neighbor Policy in Latin America. Provincial Republican policies of the 1920's, which featured lofty tariff barriers and a dunning of the war debtors, generated enduring bitterness abroad.

Starting with Franklin Roosevelt, who ushered in an exciting new era of internationalism, the President again became a shining world leader. The New Dealer won immense popularity in Latin America with his Good-Neighbor policy, and in the Allied countries with his flagrantly unneutral assistance. The British erected a statue to him in London. Even the Russians, the beneficiaries of eleven billion dollars' worth of lend-lease, spoke kindly of him, in contrast to his successors. The defeated Axis nations were less appreciative.

Harry Truman, the momentarily bewildered little Man from Missouri, overnight became a world figure. He enjoyed immense popularity in Greece, with his lifesaving Truman Doctrine, and also in western Europe, with his life-giving Marshall Plan. (The Communist world naturally denounced his "dollar imperialism.") Eisenhower was popular outside the Communist orbit, and his goodwill tours, in Latin America, India, and elsewhere, evoked incredible displays of admiration, even adoration. This regard was not shared by the Communist world, particularly after the U-2 spy-plane revealed the amiable General as a "fishy friend" of Khrushchev. John F. Kennedy was able to inspire much the same kind of acclaim (especially when accompanied by his bewitching wife) in Latin America and western Europe.

But popularity abroad may destroy popularity at home. Much of the esteem that foreigners have displayed for Presidents since Hoover is only dollar-deep. The very attributes that cause pleasure abroad may cause pain at home. And the President can never afford to forget, whether popular or unpopular, that he must dedicate his efforts to the interests of his own country. If foreigners are benefited thereby, all well and good. If they are not, that is their misfortune. He is merely doing his duty.

CHAPTER XX

Summary Reassessments:
Washington to Lincoln

"I believe Washington was, not even excepting Lincoln,
the very greatest man of modern times;
and a great general, of the Fabian order, too. . . ."

THEODORE ROOSEVELT, 1884

FORTY-THREE YARDSTICKS

We have observed that presidential greatness is impossible to determine with satisfying precision. But if we are going to make ratings with even a rough degree of plausibility, we must first set up measuring rods. I have assembled a list of more than one hundred tests which the ideal President ought to pass, but which none has ever passed in all particulars. No statesman has ever been superlative in everything, nor can he ever be.

We may boil down the one hundred or so items to the following forty-three alphabetical listings, which contain most of the more obvious tests. Many of them, as well as some less significant yardsticks, we have already considered in connection with specific Presidents.

A. MAJOR OVERALL TESTS

Achievement. What was the President's record of achievement, at home and abroad, both long range and short range? What allow-

262

ances must be made for the handicaps he faced, for the deeds of others for which he received credit, and for sheer lucky strokes? The world often ascribes wisdom to him who guesses right.

Administrative Capacity. As Administrator-in-Chief, what was his record at both high and low levels? How effective was he in organizing his day, clearing his desk, working with subordinates, and delegating responsibility?

Appointees and Advisers. As Bureaucrat-in-Chief, how successful was he in persuading able men to accept official posts or unofficial advisory positions? To what extent were his ablest appointees the product of discernment and to what extent the result of pure luck? How harmoniously was he able to work with them?

Blunders. Did he avoid blunders, whether of the foot-in-the-mouth variety or of a major caliber? What were his purely negative contributions?

Congress. As Legislator-in-Chief, how adept was he in proposing and promoting legislation, and in working constructively with Congress, whether controlled by his own party or by the opposition?

Crises. What was his record in dealing with recurrent crises, at home and abroad, especially wars and near-wars?

Dignity. As Chief of State, was he able to maintain the dignity of his exalted office without becoming too earthy or too lofty?

Domestic Affairs. How skillful was he in the solution of domestic problems, and how did his record in this respect compare with his management of foreign affairs?

Eloquence. As Spokesman-in-Chief, was he able to inspire his own people to follow his leadership by his eloquent words, whether written or spoken?

Enemies. Did he make enemies of the right sort or were his immediate supporters and close associates cronies of an unsavory stripe?

Ethics. Did he conduct the business of his office with a regard for high ethical standards, and particularly did he avoid giving the nation a bad name abroad by high-handed, devious, or other questionable conduct?

Executive. Did he "faithfully" execute the laws of Congress, as his inaugural oath required, or was he prone to enforce with vigor, if at all, only those that he personally approved?

Fiscal Management. As Financier-in-Chief, did he keep the monetary affairs of the government on a sound basis, and was he able to reduce taxes and balance the budget without sacrificing the national interest?

Foreign Affairs. As Diplomat-in-Chief, how effective was he in handling foreign affairs when he chose to do so, and to what extent was he his own Secretary of State?

Growth. Did he grow conspicuously in his grasp of the office and in the execution of his powers, whether inherited or self-expanded?

Impact. What was his total impact on his own country, on the world, and on history? Was that impact good or bad?

Industriousness. Was he deeply interested in his job and dedicated to working hard at it?

Integrity. Did he place the national welfare above personal popularity, and did he have the courage to say "no" to whatever was questionable or dishonest?

Judiciary. Were his appointments to the judiciary, especially the Supreme Court, of the highest possible quality? If the appointments were good ones, were they lucky shots? Were his relations with the Supreme Court harmonious, and if not, were the clashes to his credit?

Leadership. What was the quality of his leadership? Was it buttressed by such virtues as courage, a capacity to fight for the right, decisiveness, a good sense of timing, common sense, flexibility, sound judgment, equanimity of spirit, magnanimity, moderation, patience, persistence, steadfastness, tolerance, and vision? Did he meet problems head on, or was he inclined to duck them?

Military. As Commander-in-Chief of the armed forces, how successful was he in making the necessary preparations for national defense, in leading the nation in war, and in utilizing his war powers, with or without the approval of Congress?

National Interest. Did he rise above special interests in his pursuit of the national interest?

Partisanship. Did he avoid unnecessary friction with the political opposition? To what extent did he succeed in enlisting its support for bi-partisan programs? Did he place country above party?

Party Leader. As Politician-in-Chief and head of his party, how successful was he in leading his followers toward an achievement of goals?

Peace. Was he lucky or skillful enough to keep the peace, and, if so, how high a price did he have to pay to maintain it?

Popularity. Was he highly regarded by his own people, and did he receive a popular endorsement of his administration by re-election?

Presidential Office. Did he expand or contract the powers of the Executive so as to strengthen or weaken the office for his successors?

Prestige. Did he preserve the prestige of the nation at home and abroad at a high level?

Program. Did he have a constructive program of a forward-looking nature? If so, how fully did he achieve it? Did he bring off a so-called "revolution"?

Prosperity. Was he able to avoid depressions and panics, and if so, was his success due to skill or luck?

Public Opinion. As Opinion-Maker-in-Chief, did he reveal unusual qualities in interpreting, educating, and managing public opinion?

Scandals. Did he avoid major domestic scandals, whether through a sterling character, a wise choice of subordinates, or sheer good fortune?

Sensitivity. Did he have a thick skin or was he so excessively annoyed by criticism as to be unable to preserve the necessary composure?

Succession. Were his control of the party and his popular appeal such that he was able to handpick his successor, or at least witness the election of a successor of his own party? Or did he leave office with his following disorganized and defeated?

Veto. How skillful was he in controlling Congress or shaping legislation by the veto or threat of veto?

B. ADDITIONAL TESTS

(Chiefly for Modern Presidents in the 20th Century)

Activist. Was he an activist who undertook aggressive leadership? By stretching his constitutional powers, did he overtip the balances in favor of the Executive?

Budget Manager. To what extent did he become Appropriator-in-Chief by fixing the limits of the budgetary requests that he submitted to Congress?

Congress. Was he distinguished for his "drivership" rather than his leadership of Congress with "must-pass" legislation? What percentage of his proposals to Congress ("the box score") finally was enacted into law?

Executive Agreements. To what extent was he able to achieve his ends by bypassing the Senate with executive agreements?

Press Conferences. Was he adept in handling his press conferences, and thus strengthening his prestige and marshaling public opinion behind his program?

Radio and Television. Did he project a favorable image into millions of American homes through the airwaves?

Twenty-second Amendment. To what extent did he rise above the handicap of being a partial lame duck as a result of his noneligibility for a third term after 1951?

World Leadership. To what degree did he succeed in assuming and discharging the responsibilities thrust upon the United States as a world leader, especially as General-in-Chief of the alliance network of so-called free nations?

SUBJECTIVE OBJECTIVITY

The above forty-three tests emphasize certain observations previously made, some at considerable length.

To apply to all Presidents the standards that are applicable only to those of the 20th century is grossly unfair to the earlier incumbents. They must all be judged, if judged at all, in the context of their times.

The tests that one must keep in mind simultaneously are so numerous, so complex, so interlocking, and of such varying weight that they simply cannot be employed with complete fairness. This conclusion would be true even if *all* of the experts using them were fully informed about *all* the Presidents, as seems most unlikely.

Finally, such tests cannot be utilized scientifically. Let us suppose that "Achievement" carries a maximum of ten points, "Leadership" a maximum of eight points, and "Administrative Capacity" a maximum of five points. We shall find no agreement among the experts as to these weights. Even if we did, the tests would have to be applied subjectively, and the tester will instinctively overweigh those that he personally regards as the most significant. The subjective application of objective tests still results in subjectivity, just as the multiplication of 10,000,000 by zero still results in zero.

After having thus proved, at least to my own satisfaction, that presidential greatness cannot be measured with even quasi-scientific precision, I should be foolish indeed if I were to make a list of the Presidents in the descending order of their eminence. I do not even believe, as I have made clear, that they can be fairly separated into five neat categories, and I am especially reluctant to use such terms as "Great," "Near Great," and "Failure." What I propose to do by way of partial recapitulation is to take what I conceive to be the consensus of scholarly judgment, whether in polls, articles, or treatises, including textbooks. Then, with the forty-three tests before me, I shall indicate in a rough way whether I agree or disagree with the general appraisal. I do even this with considerable reluctance and only because I believe that the reader expects, and perhaps is entitled to, some such general appraisal.

Lest this exercise seem unduly arrogant, I should add that not even the seventy-five Schlesinger experts agreed among themselves; the published polls were merely a tabulation of a wide spectrum of opinion. If the seventy-five had been asked to make up a list of the Presidents in the descending order of their distinction, the mathematical odds would be overwhelmingly against any two lists being precisely the same, barring collusion. In conversation and correspondence with some of these historians, I have discovered that none of them, not even Dr. Schlesinger himself, agreed completely with the final consensus, and some objected emphatically to certain ratings. Perhaps I may be pardoned for reserving the same privilege for myself.

The following thumbnail sketches represent in part, but only in part, a summation of certain points previously made. If space permitted, much more could be said both pro and con in each instance.

GEORGE WASHINGTON (1789–1797)

If we must rank Presidents, Washington, in my judgment, deserves the place at the very top. He not only passes most of the standard tests with flying colors, but in several significant respects is in a class by himself.

First, the Constitutional Convention, over which Washington had presided, specifically tailored the presidency to fit him, in the hope and expectation that he would accept the high office. The resulting Constitution, which was narrowly ratified anyhow, probably would have lost out if the people had not been assured that their beloved general would serve. He could be trusted not to subvert their liberties with these vast new powers, because he had spurned a suggested kingship and had gladly laid down quasi-dictatorial authority when the War of Independence ended.

Second, Washington was the one truly "indispensable man." With his towering prestige, unfaltering leadership, and sterling character, he was the only figure able to command the confidence necessary to get the new ship of state off on even keel. He was perhaps the only man in the history of the presidency bigger than the government itself. Hamilton, Jefferson, and Madison all urged him to serve; and Hamilton and Jefferson, in agreement on little else, insisted that he subject himself to a second term. Even Vice President Adams, though eaten with envy and in line for the office himself, privately conceded that Washington had to be drafted again. The Republic was not yet sufficiently united to fall in step behind a New England sectionalist like Adams.

Third, the absence-of-blunders test leaves Washington with a uniquely high mark. Although his every move could be deemed a potential precedent binding generations unborn, his foot did not slip once. He made no major mistakes—something that cannot be said of any of his successors who served long enough to make a mistake. The Irish-British historian W. E. H. Lecky, writing of Washington's leadership during the Revolution, concluded that "of all the great men in history," the august Virginian was the most "invariably judicious." Perhaps his only real failure, at least administratively, was his failure to mix fire and water, that is, to persuade Hamilton and Jefferson to work together harmoniously in his Cabinet.

Washington has been criticized for having been too aristocratic, too monarchical, too friendly to legislation favoring the wealthy bigwigs. But statesmen must be judged in the context of their times, and the monarchical, aristocratic past was too recent to permit a clean break. Even if Washington had been disposed to do so, which he was not, he could not have ushered in Jacksonian democracy or even Jeffersonian democracy. He admittedly "packed" the federal offices with conservative-minded Federalists who were favorable to the Constitution. He would have been criminally derelict in his duty if he had done less. The Constitution was going to get off to a wobbly enough start at best, and it almost certainly would have been scuttled if entrusted to the hands of its enemies. As for the charge that Washington used undue force in crushing the Whiskey Rebellion in Pennsylvania, he was determined to establish the authority of the new government once and for all, and that he did.

If, as Henry Lee's eulogy proclaimed in 1799, Washington was "first in war, first in peace, and first in the hearts of his countrymen," in more ways than one he was first among the Presidents. I have no quarrel with the experts who put him in the Great category, only I would place him ahead of Lincoln in the premier position.

JOHN ADAMS (1797–1801)

John Adams, temperamentally unfitted to be President, is over-generously rated a Near Great by the Schlesinger experts. In some respects he was a flat failure.

We have been thrown off the track by his undeniably valuable services to the Republic during the Revolutionary years, by the magic name of one of America's most distinguished families, and above all by his "courageous" handling of the X Y Z crisis with France in 1798. He dramatically opted for peace in the teeth of violent opposition from the Hamiltonian wing of his own Federalist party, and he later suggested for his epitaph: "Here lies John Adams, who took upon himself the responsibility of peace with France in the year 1800." [1]

Adams' management of the French crisis has been extravagantly overpraised. The masterly policy of George Washington and the other Founding Fathers was to remain neutral and stall for time while our weak and divided nation grew strong and our birthrate fought our battles for us. When we had attained sufficient strength, we could stand up to the major powers of Europe. But Adams, swept off his feet by the anti-French hysteria of 1798, led the nation

[1] The epitaph finally used was: "John Adams, Signer of the Declaration of Independence, Framer of the Constitution of Massachusetts, Second President of the United States, 1735–1826."

to the brink of hostilities—an early exercise in "brinkmanship"—and then recoiled when he looked over the edge of the abyss. His enthusiasm for war further cooled when he perceived that Alexander Hamilton, his scheming and ambitious rival, was seeking to milk the maximum military glory from it. Adams finally decided, with George Washington approving, to do what he should have done in the first place: patch up the ridiculous quarrel with France.

If an outfielder badly misjudges a fly ball and then makes a desperate shoestring catch, we cheer him wildly while forgetting that if he had played his position properly, there would have been no need for heroics. It took considerable courage for Adams to plump for peace while the warhawk wing of his own party was clamoring for war. But it took perhaps more courage to go to war, with a large element in the country—probably a majority—clamoring against it. Adams may even have concluded that his political fortunes would be best promoted by giving the country the peace that it so urgently needed. In any event, we do not ordinarily praise men for doing their plain duty after having departed so irrationally from its path.

Obstinate, opinionated, vain, ill-tempered, impatient, and lacking in sound judgment, Adams was additionally a poor administrator. He could hardly fail to be when, as an absentee-landlord President, he spent more than one year out of his four at home in Massachusetts. His Cabinet was not so much a Cabinet as a cabal. He was not alert enough at the outset to perceive that it was plotting against him and conniving with Hamilton. He favored the notorious Alien and Sedition Laws, which were an alarming assault on free speech and other civil liberties. He left his Federalist party disrupted and badly demoralized, never to regain control of the national administration. He himself was defeated for re-election, though narrowly. All this does not add up to a highly effective presidency.

On the other hand, Adams demonstrated that the country could muddle along after a fashion without the towering Washington, whom he had the misfortune to follow. He had the good fortune to glean reflected glory from his lame-duck appointment of John Marshall to the Supreme Court several weeks before he slunk out of Washington. As for the notorious Alien and Sedition Acts, they were precautionary crisis measures passed during an undeclared war which was expected to widen momentarily into a full-dress conflict. In this context they do not seem either so hysterical or so tyrannical. And it should be remembered that the record of other war-crisis Presidents on civil rights—Lincoln, Wilson, Franklin Roosevelt—is not one of the proudest chapters in American history. Even so, I would seriously question the Near Great ranking by the experts and rate John Adams, if a rating is called for, no higher than Below Average.

THOMAS JEFFERSON (1801–1809)

Though undeniably a great man and a giant among the Founding Fathers, Jefferson has more difficulty qualifying as a great President. Jack-of-all trades and master of many, he comes close to the 18th-century ideal of a universal genius. In some respects he could more easily rank among the five greatest Americans of all time than among the five greatest Presidents.

The inflation of Jefferson's reputation as Chief Magistrate has grown largely out of two misconceptions. First, that he engineered a democratic overturn which he called "The Revolution of 1800." The "democratic" and "revolutionary" aspects of this narrow electoral victory have been vastly overblown: it was renovation rather than revolution. Second, that by astute diplomacy he managed to purchase all of the vast Louisiana wilderness—an achievement so breathtaking in its ultimate consequences as seemingly to make inescapable the crown of supreme greatness.

The cold truth is that Jefferson was seeking only the mouth of the Mississippi River, together with some adjoining territory to the east. Napoleon, for entirely realistic reasons, suddenly dumped the whole thing into his lap. The President was deeply embarrassed, not only because he was getting vastly more than he had bargained for or really wanted but because he believed that the acquisition of this enormous area by purchase was clearly unconstitutional. But he was less embarrassed to keep the territory than to brush it off his lap, so he reluctantly stifled his constitutional qualms, did the cowardly but expedient thing, and kept Louisiana. In short, if an Aaron Burr or a Ulysses S. Grant had been President, the result would probably have been the same, only they would probably have snapped up the bargain with a good deal more alacrity.

Jefferson's greatest failures came in the field of foreign affairs, an area in which this ex-diplomat was an expert and more than occasionally slippery. One of his basic troubles was that he was unable to "think big." Dedicated to cheese-paring economy in government, he embarked upon cut-rate defense by building cheap gunboats instead of expensive frigates. When the showdown came with Britain and France, he could wield no Big Stick. He either had to endure their cuffs and kicks or seek a substitute for warfare in the form of economic sanctions. His policy of embargoing exports —midway between submission and shooting—virtually ruined the American economy, and proved to be a disastrous failure, at least in the short run. He himself confessed that the experiment was about three times more costly than war, which came anyhow. If a small portion of the money sacrificed by the embargo had gone into a fleet of some twenty or thirty frigates of the *Constitution* ("Old Ironsides") class, Britain almost certainly would not have provoked America to the point of war in 1812. Jefferson would rank higher today if we could only overlook his last fourteen months—those of the embargo—just as Wilson would rank higher if we could overlook his last seventeen months.

Some of Jefferson's most unfortunate legacies were the defects of his virtues. No one can deny that he was a superb political organizer—but this talent led to the introduction of the baleful spoils system for the first time on a considerable scale in Washington. Nor can one deny that he was a master in leading, even dominating, Congress (until the closing days of his second term). He was so skillful in infiltrating that body—its committees and its caucuses— that he actually weakened the presidential office because his immediate successors, less skilled than he, could not bend the bow of Ulysses. Not until twenty years later, with the advent of Andrew Jackson, did the presidency regain its former power.

All this is not to begrudge Jefferson the glory of forming a new political party, of infusing it with a more refreshing concept of democracy, of strengthening the two-term tradition, of standing up to the Tripolitan pirates, or of promoting the exploration of the West, conspicuously by the Lewis and Clark Expedition through the Louisiana country which he had so reluctantly accepted. But black marks cancel out white marks, and we are entitled to doubt if this great man really gave us a great presidency. I would here part company with the experts, who label him a Great, and put him somewhere in the Near-Great niche.

JAMES MADISON (1809–1817)

A near-dwarf physically but a giant intellectually, James Madison was a first-rate constitutional theorist, legislator, and Cabinet member, but, at best, a second-rate President. The Schlesinger experts rank him a couple of notches below Near Great; actually he merits little better than Near Failure. We have been misled by his other and more successful roles, notably as one of the leading "demigods" of the Constitutional Convention of 1787. Irresolute and lacking commanding influence, this "withered little applejohn" (Washington Irving's phrase) simply was not cut out to be a dynamic leader of men.

The deepening crisis with England, including war, dominated and bedeviled his first six years. On the eve of the conflict he did not bestir himself actively enough to save the expiring and badly needed Bank of the United States. With President Jefferson's powerful hand gone, Congress seized the tiller from the indecisive Madison, notably in the persons of Speaker Henry Clay and his warhawk colleagues.

Madison himself abandoned the delaying tactics so urgently counseled by other Founding Fathers. Befooled by France and rebuffed by Britain, he became himself a moderate warhawk. He realized that the country was unprepared and disunited, but threw forward the flag in the hope that rebellious New England would spring forward and keep it from falling. To lead a disunited people into war in the hope that fighting will unite them is about as risky as marrying a drunkard in the hope that matrimony will reform him. Most New England Federalists were content to let the Stars and Stripes lie in the mud.

Given the current state of unpreparedness (which was largely the fault of Congress), not even a Napoleonic genius could have escaped embarrassments—and Madison was no Napoleon. In his defense we may note that on paper the invasion of Canada should have succeeded, that he was gravely ill for many weeks during a critical period of the war, and that there was blame enough to go around. But he took at least six months to weed the worst incompetents out of the various Departments, and a year or so to locate the more capable generals. When the invading redcoats approached Washington, he joined the defenders as commander in chief in an officiously inept fashion and was almost captured. He was lucky to get off with only a burned-out capital. But the clouds of gunsmoke arising from Andrew Jackson's glorious battlefield at New Orleans obscured the fact that the war was almost lost when the end came, and that the administration was additionally menaced by the dual threats of bankruptcy and secession.

As one of the ablest of the Founding Fathers, Madison had demonstrated that he could write an admirable constitution but that in a crisis such as confronted him in 1812 he was incapable of implementing one effectively. He had the ill luck to be thrust into the one job for which he was the least fitted. Fortunately, his last two years in office were bathed in the golden afterglow of New Orleans, and if we could remember only these two years, as we tend to forget the last two of Jefferson and Wilson, the "withered little applejohn" loses many of his wrinkles. Even so, he remains Below Average.

JAMES MONROE (1817–1825)

In the popular view, Monroe seems to be somewhat overrated; in the expert view, somewhat underrated. The Schlesinger panel ranked him low Average, between Van Buren and Hoover. In my judgment he could more fairly be placed among the high Average.

As for the popular view, Monroe was one of the Founding Fathers who walked and talked with statesmen like Washington and Jefferson. As the last and least gifted of the Virginia Dynasty, he may not have been a giant himself, but he rubbed elbows with giants. He died most appropriately on the Fourth of July, as did Jefferson and John Adams—and the hand of God has been seen therein. His name is associated with the Monroe Doctrine, and though most Americans do not know what it means, they assume that it must be something epochal because it has lasted for more than a century and a quarter. The author of any policy that enduring must have been a great man.

We all recognize that Monroe's administration was dubbed the Era of Good Feelings, for there was only one political party actively in the field. We also know that Monroe, though somewhat colorless, was extremely popular, and that when re-elected he lacked only one vote of unanimity in the Electoral College—an honor still reserved to Washington in his two elections. We are likewise aware that Monroe is one of the few Presidents to enjoy the distinction of leaving office more popular than when he entered. Sandwiched between the irresolute Madison and the anachronistic Adams, he looks good by comparison.

But the experts are too knowledgeable to be taken in by all this. They know that Monroe was not brilliant; that he was not eloquent with either tongue or pen; that his mind worked slowly; and that his strong point, like Washington's, was deliberate and sound judgment. They also know that his diplomatic record before becoming President was erratic, and that he had revealed inordinate ambition. They concede that he was an able administrator, better than Jefferson or Madison. But they also point out that the diplomatic achievements of the Monroe administrations—including the Monroe Doctrine, the acquisition of Florida, the treaty of 1818 with Britain—were largely the handiwork of a superlative Secretary of State, John Quincy Adams. They know that Monroe made no real effort to lead Congress, which rather overshadowed him, and that he ostensibly abdicated all leadership of it during the fearsome debate in 1820 over admitting slave-owning Missouri. They likewise know that his old-school hostility to using federal funds for roads and other internal improvements blocked essential progress.

Above all, the experts are aware that the so-called Era of Good Feelings was largely fictional. It might better have been called the Era of Inflamed Feelings, for when there is only one major party, the inevitable result is that it breaks into factions which fight among themselves.

All this is true. But let us give Monroe credit for having chosen the ablest possible Secretary of State, and for having worked hand-in-glove with him. The diary of John Quincy Adams, though acid in its comments on others, is remarkably friendly to Monroe. As for his unwillingness to lead Congress, this was partly the reaction to Jeffersonian domination, and it became the norm during the 19th century. Hence, when we consider the mood of the times and what had to be done, Monroe emerges as one of our more effective Presidents—High Average.

JOHN QUINCY ADAMS (1825–1829)

Like his father before him, flinty John Quincy Adams was less than a success as President; in many respects he was a complete disappointment. The Schlesinger experts rank him a couple of notches below Near Great; actually he merits little better than Near Failure.

Adams came into office blackened by the so-called Corrupt Bargain with Henry Clay which, at the very best, did not avoid the appearance of evil.[2] Gloomily introspective and chilly, he refused to play the game of politics by rewarding his supporters with the loaves and fishes of office. He made only twelve removals in four years, and retained an Attorney General who was supporting Andrew Jackson for President. He was unwilling to lead Congress, and Congress reciprocated by being unwilling to be led. During his second two years the leadership passed into the hands of the political opposition. A world-renowned expert on foreign affairs, he bungled foreign affairs, notably in taking too stiff a position with Britain regarding the West Indian trade and in mishandling the ill-starred Panama Congress.

Most ineptly of all, Adams proposed an extreme nationalistic program at government expense, including voyages of discovery, at a time when the mood of the country was swinging away from yeasty nationalism of the post-1814 era toward divisive sectionalism. If few things are stronger than an idea whose time has come, few things are flabbier than an idea whose time has passed. Finally, with the two-party system again crystallizing, Adams was caught in the middle of partisan brick-throwing. Unwilling to stoop to conquer, and unable to command popular support, he was defeated by Jackson for re-election.

Why have the experts been so overgenerous in their appraisal of Adams? For one thing, there is an aura of greatness about the Adams

[2] During the disputed election of 1824–1825, Speaker Henry Clay threw his support to John Quincy Adams, who then made Clay his Secretary of State. This arrangement was assailed by the Jackson men as a "Corrupt Bargain," but at the worst it was a political "deal," now so common in American politics. Lincoln's nomination was secured in 1860 by trading future Cabinet posts for votes; Franklin Roosevelt's nomination was assured in 1932 by promising the vice presidency to John N. Garner for Garner votes.

name, and John Quincy Adams was undeniably a great man, though not a great President. His exceptional experience abroad as a diplomat justifies his lasting place in the diplomatic Hall of Fame. His high-mindedness as a Massachusetts Senator in defying his Federalist constituents and supporting Jefferson's embargo cost him his seat in the Senate but won him a chapter in John F. Kennedy's *Profiles in Courage*. His brilliant record as Secretary of State (when teamed with President Monroe) entitles him to serious consideration as the ablest man ever to hold that office. His postpresidential career in Congress, during which he fought the proslavery forces with withering sarcasm and invective, endeared him to the abolitionists, who in turn colored much of our early history writing.

Yet all of these distinctions are wholly unrelated to the presidency. If by their fruits ye shall know them, Adams, as President, fell far short of effectiveness.

ANDREW JACKSON (1829–1837)

Andrew Jackson, in my judgment, is overrated as President, and does not belong in the highest echelon, where the Schlesinger experts at first put him. They later dropped him to the top of the Near Greats; actually, he should rate not better than high Average, if that.

Much depends on one's tests and their relevancy. Jackson was a great national hero, a great popular leader, a great party catalyst, and a great public figure. He had a powerful impact on the presidential office and on his times, but not all of the controversy and head-cracking were for the best. Woodrow Wilson, writing as a conservative in 1896, declared, "He came into our national politics like a cyclone from off the Western prairies. Americans of the present day perceptibly shudder at the very recollection of Jackson."

Specifically, he provided two-fisted presidential leadership, which his enemies branded as capricious and dictatorial. As a beneficiary of the New Democracy, he led the West and the underprivileged in politics, and left the White House even more fanatically popular than when he had entered. He revived, strengthened, and reoriented the present Democratic party. He fought the plutocrats in the interests of the democrats. He upheld the Union against the nullifiers of South Carolina, although his so-called victory was such a barren one that the still-defiant state could have been voted the one most likely to secede. (In 1860 it led the exodus.)

Jackson was the first to promote on a significant scale the concept that the President was the only elective officer of all the people—the representative-at-large—and that he should consequently uphold their interests against a sectionalized Congress. He dominated that body and was the first to use the veto for reasons of expediency rather than unconstitutionality. In a sense he remade rather than revived the presidential office. But in so doing he overtipped the constitutional checks and balances in favor of the Executive at the expense of the legislative and judicial branches.

All this sounds overwhelming until we examine the other side of the ledger. Jackson's official Cabinet was so weak that he turned to an unofficial Kitchen Cabinet, which helped with "managed news." He purged his regular Cabinet and almost wrecked his administration near the outset by his prolonged and quixotic battle over the premarital chastity of Peggy Eaton, wife of the Secretary of War. He further entrenched the spoils system on a large scale, and bullheadedly appointed scoundrels like Samuel Swartwout to high office. He vindictively crushed the Bank of the United States, when curbing would have sufficed, and launched the nation upon more than a century of unsound finance that brought untold misery to hundreds of thousands of innocent people. Favoring the small businessman over the nabobs, he lowered the tone of public life by helping to drive the aristocrats into private life, where they have generally stayed since then. Personalizing politics, he intensified the class conflict between the plowholder and the bondholder.

Nor is this all. He defied the Supreme Court on the issue of Indian lands in Georgia, and attempted to make himself co-equal with the judicial branch in determining the constitutionality of legislation. He did manage to wring a concession from Britain on West Indian trade (here the experienced President John Quincy Adams had failed), but he skated perilously close to the brink of war in forcing the French to pay their overdue obligations.

Paradoxically, Jackson made the presidential office so strong that he weakened it, as Jefferson had done. His successors until Lincoln, who was prodded by military necessity, were unable to don his dictatorial mantle. He was a great American in many respects, especially when we consider his educational and cultural limitations, but hardly a great President, at best Above Average. One such man in a century was about all that the country—and the Constitution—could stand.

MARTIN VAN BUREN (1837–1841)

Martin Van Buren was a better President than he is generally esteemed, especially by the popular mind, which is influenced by textbooks often written by non-historians.

A shrewd judge of men and affairs, cheerful and witty, he was one of the most accomplished politicians of the century—and democratic politics (and government) cannot function without politicians. Blessed with a well-trained legal mind, he revealed genuine courage and statesmanlike vision while in the presidency and while ex-President. Unfriendly to the extension of slavery, he opposed the annexation of Texas as unconstitutional and as liable to provoke war with Mexico. He established a landmark in labor history by proclaiming a ten-hour day on public works, and he rescued public money from the clutches of politicians by backing the Independent Treasury System.

Then why has Van Buren been downgraded? For one thing, he followed the noise and fury of Old Hickory, and the people felt let down. He was determined to be a "constitutional President," and not ride roughshod over the Congress, in the Jacksonian manner. As a candidate handpicked by Jackson and machine-made by the party, he was long associated with the spoils system, which, in fact, was not all bad, especially in that era. Worst of all, he was a depression President. Given the current hands-off philosophy, he could do nothing but let the distressed people sweat out the Panic of 1837, and he earned an undeserved reputation for aristocratic coldness and callousness.

Worst of all, Van Buren was the victim of cruel caricature. His smoothness as a politician won him many nicknames, including the Red Fox of Kinderhook, and the impression lingers that he was only a superslick politician whose administration went to the dogs. The hoopla, log-cabin, hard-cider campaign of 1840 did him lasting harm, for he was pictured in enduring campaign song as a simpering dandy. Although washed out of the White House in a tidal wave of apple juice and electioneering froth, he was almost renominated by the Democrats at Baltimore four years later. He won a simple majority on the first ballot, but his sly opponents, knowing that he opposed the annexation of Texas, outfoxed him by introducing the two-thirds rule.

The combination of hard times and hard cider was enough to tarnish the reputation of an abler man than Martin Van Buren. Yet he turned out to be a reasonably competent President. The experts give him a median Average rating, and this is about where he belongs.

WILLIAM HENRY HARRISON (1841)

Even the most dyed-in-the-wool President-raters fight shy of Harrison, who apparently did nothing important during his one month in office except die. He enjoys the dubious distinction of having delivered by far the longest inaugural address and having served by far the shortest term.

A posthumous prognosis is that this overballyhooed war hero would have been no ball of fire if he had lived out his term. The real leaders of the Whig party, Henry Clay and Daniel Webster, evidently expected to steer him around by the military coattails. With an indifferent record in public life, he was the first President to be elected not because he was a statesman but because he had not taken a strong position on controversial issues. Issueless and hence relatively enemyless, the old man—he was an all-time sixty-eight when inaugurated—was expected to be "an Old Gentleman in Leading Strings."

But the indications are that Harrison was determined to be his own man. "Old Tippecanoe," had he lived, might have developed some of the independence for which "Tyler too" became notorious.

JOHN TYLER (1841–1845)

John Tyler, the genteel but iron-willed Virginian, is generally downgraded as a President by both the historians and the general public. The experts rate him Below Average.

The older textbooks unfairly picture this proud patrician as something of a political apostate, not too many removes from Benedict Arnold. A turncoat Democratic wolf in Whig clothing, they relate, he accepted the vice presidency on the Whig ticket. When Harrison died, Tyler blocked the Whig program, was read out of the party, and ended his inherited term in complete deadlock and futility.

The facts must be interpreted somewhat differently. Although a latter-day convert to the Whig party, Tyler belonged to the minority states'-rights wing. His views were well known in 1840, while the majority group (Clay, Webster) artfully concealed theirs. He was put on the ticket primarily because he held those views and presumably could attract the votes of Southern states'-righters. When Harrison died, Tyler strengthened the presidential office by boldly assuming the title of President. (This precedent has stood, even though the Constitution stipulated that the Vice President should take over the *duties* but not the *title* of the President.)[3] Tyler attempted to work out an accommodation with Clay, who peremptorily tried to push through his own nationalistic program. Tyler then stubbornly vetoed a substantial part of it.

But this is not the whole story. Tyler was an able administrator. He managed to steer through Congress a commendable sheaf of non-partisan measures, including a reorganization of the Navy. He cooperated closely and effectively with Secretary of State Webster in negotiating the air-clearing Webster-Ashburton Treaty with Britain. By clever management he brought off the annexation of Texas in 1845, which in itself was no mean achievement.

A man who falls into an office to which he was not elected and could not have been elected, is handicapped at the start. This is true of all act-of-God Presidents. Tyler proved, in reverse, that effective government is party government, and that no President can do his job properly who is not working with his party. Ideally, Tyler should have resigned and permitted majority rule when he saw how events were shaping up; instead his entire Cabinet resigned, except Daniel Webster, who remained temporarily.

Tyler was a cultured Virginian, the scion of a family of influence and affluence, whose genial exterior concealed a steely interior. He had a sense of humor—and needed it. At the final gala affair in the White House, he remarked, "They cannot say now that I am a President without a party." One could properly rescue him from the Below Average category and make him at least low Average.

[3] The proposed Twenty-fifth Amendment to the Constitution, now in the process of ratification, specifically corrects this deficiency by making the Vice President the President.

JAMES KNOX POLK (1845–1849)

For more than half a century after his death Polk was bitterly condemned and routinely underrated. Then, with the publication in four volumes of his presidential diary (1910), the pendulum began to swing strongly in his favor. Today he is generally overrated. The experts made him a Near Great, ranking just below Andrew Jackson and Theodore Roosevelt.

A pallid personality, Polk was handicapped at the outset by being the first "dark-horse" President. He was also the whipping boy of anti-slavery historians, particularly the Whig-Republican school of New England. The war that he waged with Mexico not only reconfirmed the annexation of slave-state Texas but additionally acquired vast areas from Mexico that presumably might become slave territory. In pursuing his program of expansion, he gave the United States a moral black eye by the brazenness of his rapacity and by his twisting of the truth to cover his aims and motives.

The Polk diary and other sources soften somewhat the harsh anti-slavery interpretation. The controversial President emerges as a competent administrator, a gluttonous worker unable to delegate responsibility, a leader able to manage Congress with unusual success (even though he had a hostile Whig majority in the House during his last two years). He was clearly the strongest President between Jackson and Lincoln, although admittedly the competition was not too keen. On questionable authority, he was reported to have entered the White House with four "great measures" in view: a lowered tariff, the Independent Treasury System, the annexation of California, and the settlement of the Oregon dispute.[4] He pro-

---

[4] If a marksman announces in advance the four bull's-eyes he is going to hit, his performance is more impressive than if he shoots first and then claims that the four he hit were the four he was aiming at. Polk did not announce publicly early in the game that these were his four "must" objectives; in fact he ultimately recommended to Congress a number of measures that were not adopted. Forty-two years after the event, Polk's Secretary of the Navy, George Bancroft, then eighty-six years of age, wrote an interesting letter to the historian James Schouler. Bancroft's recollection was that shortly after inauguration Polk told him of his "four great measures." Considering the frailty of human memory, the advanced age of the witness, and the lapse of time, one can hardly cite this letter as conclusive evidence. See James Schouler, *History of the United States of America* (1889), IV, 498.

ceeded to tick them off one by one, we are told, with a thousand percent batting average.

A closer look at Polk raises certain doubts. The Oregon boundary was compromised with Britain during his presidency but he deserves scant credit for this achievement. In his saber-rattling inaugural address he had demanded all of the Oregon Country, but he undertook no serious preparations for war. He then permitted the negotiation of a treaty that settled on the present boundary, or roughly one half of the boast. Ducking criticism, he rather weakly dumped the treaty onto the Senate, which was instantly placed on the hot seat: rejection would bring the onus of spurning a fair compromise, while approval would bring the onus of yielding too much. The Senators wisely approved the treaty, and a slippery Polk gets the credit. Critical historians in recent years have referred to him not as Polk the Mendacious but as Polk the Braggart and Polk the Buck Passer.

As for California, Polk tried to buy it from Mexico. When she refused to sell, he provocatively ordered General Taylor's tiny army into disputed territory on the Rio Grande, where the Mexicans were goaded into an attack. This was several weeks before the settlement of the Oregon boundary. If Britain had joined Mexico in the war against the Americans, as seemed entirely probable, the British fleet in the Pacific almost certainly would have gobbled up California. Polk gambled desperately on not losing this prize, which he desired above all others, and the Senate saved him by accepting the Oregon treaty.

After much mismanagement and rare good luck, the war with Mexico was finally won by Generals Taylor and Scott without a single defeat. But if Polk could have had his way, he would have replaced them with the unfitted politician Senator Thomas Hart Benton. He finally tried to bribe the Mexicans into making peace, and when his agent, Nicholas P. Trist, disobeyed instructions and negotiated a treaty, Polk rather reluctantly submitted it to the Senate, which again took him off the hook. And again the President gets the credit.

Polk evidently did not have the vision to foresee that the fruits of victory would be apples of discord. He apparently believed that the burning issue of slavery in the territories would be settled by the iron hands of geography, topography, and meteorology. Instead, it was settled by several million soldiers, over half a million of whom died. Mexico got belated and bloody revenge.

Polk was a relatively strong President, at times a doer and at others a drifter, at times a leader and at others a laggard. He comes out with a better image than he deserves, and partly for the wrong reasons. He may not brush the margins of greatness, but on the whole he does rank as an efficient, industrious, single-minded, and aggressive Executive. My own appraisal would demote him from the Near Greats and leave him little better than Average.

ZACHARY TAYLOR (1849–1850)

Often pictured as a coarse-featured, uncouth, semi-literate frontier fighter and slaveholder, Taylor has popularly been downgraded beyond his deserts. The historical fraternity, after the sad experience with General Grant, has developed an ingrained antipathy toward professional soldiers in the White House. Taylor was forty years a soldier and sixteen months a President—hardly a long enough period to work up a good head of steam. Politics is an intricate art, and General Taylor was a political rookie. He had never voted for a President before he ran in 1848, and evidently he did not vote then, not even for himself.

Descended from a distinguished Virginia family, Taylor was a man of more than average intelligence. He grew in statesmanlike stature under the new responsibilities of his presidential office, despite a money scandal involving three members of his Cabinet. Perhaps his most distinguishing trait was firmness, which his enemies called mulishness. He refused to be pushed around by Henry Clay and other fellow Whig leaders; their pressures hardened him in his opposition to the crucial Compromise of 1850 over slavery. In addition, he displayed honesty, forthrightness, self-reliance, industry, and stubborn devotion to the Union. He showed no favoritism toward his native South, whose threats of impeachment and secession aroused his military ire. He could no more yield to Southerners or to Henry Clay than he could to Santa Anna on the battlefield of Buena Vista.

During the slavery-extension crisis of 1850, Taylor declared his determination to "Jacksonize" the Texans—that is, to take the field himself and prevent their invasion of the disputed area in New

Mexico. In this sense, he was a "strong" President—perhaps over-strong. He died at the critical moment, and Vice President Fillmore willingly signed into law the compromise measures (the Compromise of 1850) that Taylor seemed determined to veto.

Any solid assessment of Taylor depends on the flimsiest of conjecture. If one believes that the Compromise of 1850 postponed the Civil War for a decade—a decade in which the North grew preponderantly stronger and consequently triumphed—then one must conclude that Taylor rendered his country a final signal service by dying when he did. But if one believes that Taylor could have solved the problem of secession by chastising Texas, as seems unlikely, then he rises in stature and his death becomes a calamity.

Taylor's biographers praise not only his native intelligence but his good sense. If he had possessed only a modest amount of good sense, he would never have taken on a burden for which he was grossly unprepared. He did better than one might have expected, but few thinking men could have expected much. The experts rated him first in the Below Average group, and one is hard put to find reasons for boosting him much higher.

MILLARD FILLMORE (1850–1853)

The three forgotten men of the 1850's—Fillmore, Pierce, and Buchanan—are among the least colorful, least well known, and the most misunderstood of all the Presidents. They are generally regarded, if mentioned at all, as near failures or outright failures.

It is unfair to criticize this drab trio for not having been two-fisted men of the Jackson type who would use strong-arm methods to head off secession. The North and the South quivered in uneasy equipoise; violence would upset it. The Union had been forged in 1787–1788 by compromise; it had been held together repeatedly by compromise; and when compromise broke down, the Union broke up.

Fillmore, Pierce, and Buchanan were all dedicated to conciliation and concession in their determination to preserve the Union. They were not always fortunate in their attempts at compromise, but they at least recognized that therein lay the path of statesmanship. Lincoln himself was still trying conciliation when the Confederates opened fire on Fort Sumter, and to the very end he put the preservation of the Union above any specific settlement of the slavery issue. Why blame Fillmore, Pierce, and Buchanan for attempting to do what Lincoln did?

Urbane and gracious Millard Fillmore, President-by-deathbed and the "last of the Whigs," deserves better treatment at the hands of historians than he has received. Disapproving of "fanatics and disunionists" both North and South, he not only signed the compromise measures of 1850, but had a large hand in breaking the logjam by proposing that Texas be indemnified for yielding her claim to New Mexican territory. In an attempt to deal fairly with the South, he also approved the Fugitive Slave Act of 1850; and faithful to his inaugural oath, he attempted to enforce it. These two acts damned him forever in the eyes of the abolitionists and abolitionist-oriented history.

Fillmore was an accidental President who was never elected to the office but who filled it with reasonable competence after Taylor died. He merits somewhat more acclaim from posterity than he has received, including the median Below Average ranking of the Schlesinger experts. In my judgment he could more properly lodge in the Average group, although in the lower ranges.

FRANKLIN PIERCE (1853–1857)

Handsome, genial, magnetic Franklin Pierce, traditionally stereotyped as a putty man, was certainly not a strong President, but he has been condemned somewhat unfairly. He was plainly in beyond his depth, as anyone would have been in the sectional quagmire of the 1850's, including the two defeated major candidates, Winfield Scott (1852) and John C. Frémont (1856). Even Lincoln was floundering about when the Southerners ended his indecisiveness by seizing the sword.

A small-town lawyer from New Hampshire, Pierce was the darkest of dark horses. His name did not even turn up until the thirty-fifth ballot of the Baltimore convention that nominated him. The threadbare charge that he lacked vigor as President is only partially true. He showed vigor against the abolitionists, who branded him and his associates as "tools and lickspittles" because they tried to uphold the Constitution and the laws, including the hated Fugitive Slave Law. Abolitionist-oriented historians have since then continued to belabor him. He showed considerable vigor as an expansionist. He promoted the opening of Japan, achieved commercial reciprocity with Canada, stood up to the "British landgrabbers" in Central America, recognized the pro-slavery filibustering regime of William Walker in Nicaragua, acquired the Gadsden Purchase from Mexico, and vainly attempted to purchase or seize slaveholding Cuba. Here he was blackened by the leaked-out Ostend Manifesto, which was never adopted by his administration but which was the top-secret recommendation of headstrong subordinates who were prepared to seize Cuba.

Pierce stumbled into his hottest water when he tried to be fair to both North and South, at a time when neither side really wanted fairness. Seeking to preserve the profitable relationship between cotton-growing Southerners and cotton-consuming Northerners, he strove to keep the anti-slaveryites and the pro-slaveryites from rocking the boat. The way of the honest broker is hard, and the abolitionists indelibly labeled Pierce a "doughface"—or a pro-slavery Yankee. His greatest blunder—a catastrophic blunder—was in supporting the Kansas-Nebraska Act of 1854, which repealed the Missouri Compromise of 1820 and undid the sectional truce. But the Kansas-Nebraska Act was in itself a substitute compromise, adopted on the fifty-fifty assumption that Kansas would become slave and Nebraska free. The initiative was seized by the Congress, with Democrats like Senator Douglas calling the tune, and the Democratic Pierce felt obliged to go along in the hope of securing other legislation. He also sought to promote the Pacific Railroad, which presumably would be facilitated by the Kansas-Nebraska Act. Striving to allay sectional bitterness, he evidently did not perceive how violently the anti-slavery North would react to the Kansas-Nebraska compromise. But neither did Senator Douglas and other members of Congress who presumably were bigger men than the President.

Pierce is a tragic figure. He suffered from an overfondness for alcohol and a violent allergy to it. On the eve of inauguration his only surviving child, the eleven-year-old Bennie, was mangled before his eyes and those of his wife in a railroad wreck. He thus lost his son physically, his wife nervously, and himself emotionally. Tossed by the riptides of expansion, he was caught up in the crosscurrents of nationalism and sectionalism, of abolitionism and nativism. A big frog in the New Hampshire puddle, he was a small frog

in the turbulent sea of national politics. Less than a success, he was
not wholly a failure. The experts put him near the bottom of the
Below Average group, almost a Failure, but perhaps we can push
him up a few notches higher. If there was a failure, it was that of
the American political system in turning up such a pleasant mediocrity at a time that demanded giants. And what solution would the
giants have found, assuming that they existed, for the sections that
were hell-bent on a collision course?

JAMES BUCHANAN (1857–1861)

James Buchanan, though one of the most experienced statesmen
of his generation, fell conspicuously short of being a successful
President. Yet he has been grossly maligned, like Franklin Pierce,
and for many of the same reasons. The threadbare adjectives scattered through the textbooks are "weak," "feeble," "timid," "indecisive," "vacillating," "senile," "time-serving," "legalistic," "pro-Southern," and "traitorous." He serves as a foil for the towering Lincoln,
under whom the Civil War erupted but for which Buchanan gets
the blame. He is further blamed for not using powers which 19th-
century Presidents were not supposed to exercise in peacetime but
which Lincoln did exercise as a part of his crisis-born war powers.
To compare Buchanan unfavorably with Jackson is to overlook the
fact that Jackson was dealing with nullification in South Carolina,
not secession.

Weakness was no doubt present in the Buchanan administration,
but it was more in the Union—"the sacred balance"—than in Buchanan. His chief weakness was perhaps not weakness at all but
at times an overstrong adherence to mistaken policies, notably in
backing the outrageous pro-slavery Lecompton Constitution for
Kansas. He showed marked vigor when he had clear authority, as
in sending some fifteen hundred troops into Utah in 1858 to force
the polygamous Mormons to abide by federal laws. He also displayed some vigor in foreign affairs, notably when his administration
secured epochal treaties with both Japan and China, blocked the
British in Central America, doomed the filibustering William Walker
in Nicaragua, and successfully challenged the British on the issue
of visit and search in the Caribbean. As regards secession, he had a
policy which he pursued consistently and which Lincoln adopted

and followed for many weeks: conciliation and compromise rather than coercion and clash, and no firing unless fired upon. This has been called "drift," but the alternative was immediate disaster. And if Buchanan was a drifter and appeaser, so was Lincoln until Fort Sumter was bombarded. Certainly Buchanan's policy of accommodation was far more respresentative of the national will than the views of the extremist minorities, North and South. Above all, he managed to keep four of the fifteen slave states in the Union, namely the crucial Border States.

When seven states seceded following the election of Lincoln in 1860, Buchanan was already handicapped by events with which he had little or nothing to do: the Panic of 1857, the John Brown raid and martyrdom, and the election of Lincoln. As a lame duck, Buchanan was reluctant to commit his successor to embarrassing or drastic courses, and he did not. His Cabinet, which included some scheming Southerners, was a house divided. Five members ultimately resigned; others threatened to follow them; and one (Stanton) was a stool pigeon for the opposition Republicans. With a reconstituted Cabinet, the President assumed a firmer stance during his last few weeks in office.

As a lawyer and a constitutionalist, Buchanan was technically correct in concluding that he had no legal authority to act in seceded South Carolina. The federal officials there had resigned, and the Senate flatly refused to confirm his nominee as customs collector. Until a federal official requested assistance, Buchanan could not, he believed, lawfully send it. He repeatedly appealed to Congress for laws, money, and militia to do the job, but Congress further lamed the aged lame duck by spurning his proposals. The Republican members flagrantly played politics by voting solidly against him. After thus tying his hands, they blamed him for not using his hands.

A non-legalistic Buchanan might have resorted to dictatorial decrees, as a war-vexed Lincoln did later, to stem secession and try to force the states back into the Union. But Congress was not in session when Lincoln ran his ten-week dictatorship, and it was in session during Buchanan's lame-duck ordeal of 1860–1861. If he had promulgated laws from the White House when the lawmaking body was a mile away on Capitol Hill, he would have subverted his beloved republican form of government and subjected himself to impeachment. He had no army with which to crush the South, and if he had tried to raise one by illegal means, how could he have prevented the Civil War by starting it? Until the guns began to boom, there was always the last-ditch hope of a peaceful settlement. Lincoln's call for troops after Fort Sumter merely added four more states to the seven that had seceded.

Buchanan was a moderate-minded man in a decade when conciliation was the only alternative to a catastrophic clash. This "indecisive" President flatly refused to abandon Fort Sumter, despite great pressure to do so, and sent the *Star of the West* with some two hundred troops to *reinforce* the outpost, even though the ship was beaten off. This was a more decisive action than Lincoln took when he touched off the fireworks by merely undertaking to *provision* the fort. During the pre-Sumter weeks Lincoln not only followed Buchanan's basic policies but even borrowed some of his phrases. And the strategy of delay may in the long run have saved the Union by permitting pro-Union sentiment to crystallize in the North.

The allegedly supine Buchanan showed considerable firmness in enforcing the Fugitive Slave Law and in opposing the abolitionists. These zealots wanted him to enforce (without enforcement officials) the federal laws in the South, while not enforcing the federal Fugitive Slave Law in the North. They got their long-term revenge against Buchanan in the abolitionist-tinged history books.

When Buchanan left office, no brother's blood had been shed, though seven states had peacefully seceded. When a murdered Lincoln left office, eleven states had seceded, and more than half a million men lay mouldering in their graves. Unblessed are the peacemakers, for they shall not inherit statues. Perhaps the "irrepressible conflict" was irrepressible, but by one of the curiosities of history Buchanan is the goat and Lincoln the hero. We judge Buchanan chiefly by his last four months in office, and render the verdict of vacillation; we judge Woodrow Wilson by ignoring his last months of office, and render the verdict of greatness. Surely "Buchanan the Blunderer" is deserving of at least a few notches better than the lowest slot among the Below Average or Near Failure, which the experts accord him. The real failure was in the breakdown of the American democratic system—of the American people themselves.

CHAPTER XXI

Summary Reassessments:
Lincoln Through McKinley

"So far as one who is not a great man can model himself upon one who was, I try to follow out the general lines of policy which Lincoln laid down."

THEODORE ROOSEVELT, 1904

ABRAHAM LINCOLN (1861–1865)

So many layers of adulation, idolatry, and mythology cling to the homely frame of Abraham Lincoln that one is puzzled to know how much is left when they are all chipped away. He was unquestionably one of the strongest Presidents. He had to become one, despite his modest nature, if the Union was to be preserved. The path to glory lay in simply doing what plain duty forced upon him. Congress was not in session during the crucial ten weeks after Fort Sumter, and the American people will gag down strong medicines for critical national ills. His career beautifully illustrates the axiom that nothing succeeds like success, no matter how much fumbling there may be on the road to victory. And he was shot at the perfect time for his reputation.

The Man of Sorrows and "velvet steel" was undeniably a great man. He was great in spirit, in humility, in humanity, in magnanimity, in patience, in Christlike charity, in capacity for growth, in political instincts, in holding together a discordant political following, in interpreting and leading public opinion, and in seizing with bulldog grip the essential ideal of preserving the Union.

But the record is not all star-spangled. Lincoln remained too silent during Buchanan's lame-duck period when he might have tried to reassure the South and promote conciliation. He actually spurned the last-chance Crittenden Compromise for reasons, including narrowly partisan ones, that are not altogether satisfying to many historians. After shilly-shallying, he botched the negotiations over Fort Sumter. He permitted too much arrogance, disloyalty, and even corruption (Secretary Cameron) in his Cabinet. He rode roughshod, no doubt necessarily, over civil rights, even to the extent of suppressing newspapers and imprisoning dissenters arbitrarily. He interfered in military affairs, sometimes clumsily; he tolerated too much insolence from prima-donna commanders; and he was agonizingly slow in finding the right general. On top of that he was a sloppy administrator who wasted too much time with politicians and casual visitors.

Lincoln is praised by students of government, even by those who acclaim the checks and balances, as a shining example of what the President may do by expanding his war powers. He made the office so strong that, like Jefferson and Jackson, he weakened it for his successors in the inevitable morning after. He violated his oath to support the Constitution, so as to save the sacred parchment; he unconstitutionally exercised a half dozen or so powers that are the sole prerogative of Congress, including the appropriation of funds. (Men have gone to prison for less.) Taking little direct initiative in framing legislation, he was unable to lead Congress with conspicuous success, if at all. He also had to tolerate the snooping Congressional Committee on the Conduct of the War, and he was heading into serious trouble with Congress over reconstructing the South when Booth's bullet laid him low. He signed important Congressional measures under protest, and, contrary to his inaugural oath, declined to execute faithfully some of them, including a scheme for emancipation (Second Confiscation Act) that went beyond his own. He used the veto sparingly, and stands as the weakest of the "strong" Presidents in managing Congress. As an inheritor of the hands-off Whig tradition, he more or less ignored it.

Lincoln's fame as the Great Emancipator is both overblown and overdramatized: the Rail Splitter simply did not split the shackles from the legs of three and one-half million slaves with one stroke of the pen. Never an abolitionist, he finally issued the Emancipation Proclamation, after much pulling and hauling, as an act of sheer military necessity. It lacks any expression of moral indignation or any appeal to the rights of men, and consequently is about as inspirational as a bill of lading. Technically it freed no slaves whatever. Yet Lincoln deserves real credit for having backed the Thirteenth Amendment, which in 1865 legally freed all slaves.

Lincoln acted greatly in great times: he possessed the inner fortitude to see the horrible ordeal through to the last corpse. The task of bringing the South back into the Union was overpowering enough, but he had to complete it under incredibly harrowing conditions. Imagine a captain in a hurricane whose ship, nearly broken in half, is being blown rapidly onto the rocks. Below in the cabin his beloved son lies dead and his wife is having hysterics. On deck, nearly half of the crew is firing mutinous shots; the rest of the crew is firing back; many of the passengers are screaming contradictory orders; others are demanding a new captain or conspiring to take his place; while still others are below trying to scuttle the ship. Yet, "My Captain," in Walt Whitman's words, "weather'd every rack," and came safely to port, "cold and dead," past the shoals of secession and emancipation and the rocks of Copperheadism and disunion.

Lincoln's reputation lies perhaps not so much in what he did as in what he endured. He remains a classic symbol of union, democracy, and presidential presence in an hour of supreme crisis. We can hardly deny him a place somewhere among the Greats, though he may not have been a super-great.

ANDREW JOHNSON (1865–1869)

If ever a President failed on his job, it was Andrew Johnson. He was confronted by an enormous task: to bring the Southern states back into the Union and reconstruct them on a fair and reasonable basis. A stickler for the Constitution, he finally adopted the pro-Southern view, shortsightedly forgetting that no victors, after four years of bloody fighting, ever killed the fatted calf for still-unrepentant brothers who had allegedly forced the fighting on them. Largely through tactlessness and bullheadedness Johnson first lost control of himself and then of the Republican Congress. That body, representing the victors, then proceeded to impose its bayonet-supported military reconstruction on the South, and the result was a cup of bitterness which to this day has not been fully drained. On top of all that, Johnson was accorded the supreme insult of being impeached by the House of Representatives, though the Senate acquitted him by a single vote.

Andrew Johnson proved again, as "accidental" President Tyler had already proved, that a President cannot drive an ambitious program through Congress if he is at loggerheads with his own party or is in the wrong party. (Johnson, as a Democrat placed on the ticket of the Union party with Lincoln in 1864, was never a Republican.) The President may be eternally right, but he simply cannot get the job done. Johnson was undeniably a man of intelligence, integrity, courage, and devotion to the Union and the Constitution. But his impatience, lack of self-control, ill temper, bad taste, and boorishness proved his undoing.

Some students of government praise Johnson for having stood up to Congress (futilely), and for having strengthened the presidency by offering himself as a sacrificial goat and proving how difficult the impeachment process is. This is somewhat like saying that World War I was a boon because it enabled medical science to make giant strides in plastic surgery. Granting that Johnson strengthened the office by getting himself impeached, his hollow triumph hardly compensates for the woes that he visited upon millions living and unborn, white and black, by bungling reconstruction.

The myth persists that Johnson was "crucified" for Lincoln. President Johnson himself helped midwife it when he declared in 1866, "And I say here tonight that if my predecessor had lived, the vials of wrath would have poured out upon him." In 1959 ex-President Truman, an amateur historian who rated the ex-tailor "a great President," told Columbia University students, "If Lincoln had lived, he would have done no better than Johnson."

This borders on the preposterous. Lincoln would have had trouble with Congress, which was already kicking up its heels. But as a victorious war leader, the unquestioned head of his own party, a masterful politician, a shrewd interpreter of public opinion, a statesman of tact and common sense, Lincoln almost certainly would have done better. It is unthinkable that he would have managed to get himself impeached. The very qualities in which Lincoln was strong—especially tact and common sense—were notably lacking in Andrew Johnson, a square peg in a round hole. He was confronted with difficulties, as are all Presidents, yet he failed to overcome them. They overcame him. Dour, determined, dedicated, and disastrous, he simply did not measure up to the demands of the office, to which he could not have been elected in the first place.

Johnson as President was a failure—if we must use such a low grade. Yet the Schlesinger experts boosted him to the bottom of the Average group, no doubt feeling sorry for the misguided and misunderstood man who had nearly lost his official life by walking the impeachment plank.

ULYSSES S. GRANT (1869–1877)

Grant was an ignorant and confused President, and his eight long years in blunderland are generally regarded as a national disgrace. But the hero-worshipping American people, who pushed him into the presidential chair, must shoulder much of the blame. John Tyler and Andrew Johnson, both square-peg Presidents, were never elected to their high office. War-hero Grant was twice nominated unanimously on the first ballot by the Republicans, and twice honored by election, the second time by a far wider margin than the first. In 1880, in his formidable attempt to break the two-term tradition after a four-year interlude, he led all other nominees on the first thirty-five ballots, and, if he had been nominated, might well have been elected. If Grant was a flat failure, he and millions of his fellow countrymen evidently did not think so.

Postwar corruption characterized the Gilded Age, during which big-business moguls ran off with much of the gilt. Scandals would have developed in any event, but with some of the more notorious Grant was not even remotely connected. Yet the horse-loving general had no political horse sense, no experience with civilian office, no grasp of politics (he had voted only once for President), and no real comprehension of the powers and duties of the high office, already muddied by Johnson's prolonged warfare with Congress. Unduly impressed by rich men, Grant named several to his crazy-quilt first Cabinet. Fanatically loyal to cronies, he shamefully tried to cover up for his private secretary and a Cabinet member when, among others, they became involved in noxious scandals.

He not only debased the civil service by appointing questionable characters to important offices but likewise took care of his relatives, both blood relations and in-laws. The management of Indian affairs in his administration was something of a scandal, but so it was during most of the 19th century, as well as later.

Life grinds on even under the worst Presidents, and the country lurched forward, without much help or hindrance from Grant. He explicitly denied any intent to lead Congress and the party, although he did strengthen the Executive somewhat following the Johnson debacle. During Grant's regime the South was reconstructed by bayonet (as a result of policies previously laid down by Congress). Inflationary pressures were squelched at the expense of the debtor (perhaps they should not have been). A major panic was surmounted and the credit of the government was put on firm foundations. The electoral crisis of the Hayes-Tilden election was resolved without civil war. Once-embittered relations with Britain were placed on a friendlier footing, thanks largely to Secretary Fish. Grant's one real venture (misadventure) in foreign affairs was a dogged but futile attempt to annex Santo Domingo by treaty. He who had whipped General Lee was whipped by the Senate oligarchy, which was to ride high for decades to come.

Grant almost commands our sympathy. He did not know enough to know that the job was too big for him or that he had bungled it. Having little interest in government or politics, he failed to do his homework and relied too heavily on the party bosses. Thin-skinned, he regarded criticism as unwarranted or partisan, and he interpreted his election over bizarre Horace Greeley in 1872 as a ringing vindication. Woodrow Wilson concluded that "he combined great gifts with great mediocrity." The great gifts related to war; the great mediocrity to government.

It is fashionable to flunk Grant as President, and the experts (mostly Democratic academicians) lodge this war-hero Republican with the Failures. A lot of others failed, if Grant did, and some of the other more highly regarded Presidents had less to show for their administrations. Perhaps we are unduly swayed by the scandals: actually the Republic has suffered far more from ignorance and stupidity than from quiet grafting. Eliminate those crooks for whom Grant was not directly responsible, and he is entitled to a Below Average rating, a few notches better than complete Failure.

RUTHERFORD BIRCHARD HAYES (1877–1881)

A symbol of rectitude in government, "His Honesty" Hayes is not fully appreciated. Actually he proved to be a more effective incumbent than the average, and must be reckoned among the strong Presidents as far as invigorating the office is concerned.

A middle-class, middle-road conservative, he came to Washington under grave handicaps. Having run nearly 300,000 popular votes behind the Democrat Tilden in a disputed election, he was declared the winner after an electoral commission had cut the Gordian knot of a complicated dispute. One of the ironies of history is that this man of sterling honesty should have been the beneficiary of perhaps the most dishonest presidential election in our history. The dishonesty was shared by Republicans as well as by frustrated Democrats, who never forgave Hayes for "robbing" their man. Yet he resolutely took office and chose an outstanding Cabinet, which included one ex-Confederate. He courageously carried out his pre-election bargain and withdrew the last federal troops that were propping up carpetbag Southern governments. If the Democrats never forgave him for accepting the presidency, die-hard Republicans never forgave him for letting the Solid South solidify. Democrats also berated him for rewarding with high office unsavory politicians in Louisiana and Florida who had connived at his irregular election. Here Hayes received what was perhaps his blackest black mark.

Hayes was unable to drive a constructive program through Congress. At the outset, he was forced to alienate the Republican bosses in the Senate by a successful battle for civil service reform in New York. The Democrats controlled the House during his entire four years, and the Senate during his last two years. But he vigorously fought for and strengthened presidential prerogatives that Congress had usurped since Lincoln's day, thereby benefiting his successors.

Hayes richly deserved re-election, but he was an avowed one-termer and he had antagonized the party bosses. His great contribution was to restore faith in the integrity of the Washington regime and to prove, despite the Grant orgy, that a Republican could be honest, courageous, and a roadblock to designing thieves. He swept

away the fetid moral atmosphere of the White House, and permitted
his prohibitionist wife to install an era of aridity. He paved the way
for genuine civil service reform. He fought not only for sound
government but also for a sound dollar. He vetoed (futilely) silver-
purchase legislation, and presided over the restoration of the gold
standard, suspended since 1861. He left the country more prosperous
than when he had entered office, and his Republican successor was
elected by a plurality of ten thousand votes.

The Schlesinger experts rank Hayes as high Average, with only
Madison and John Quincy Adams between him and the Near
Greats. That is roughly where he belongs, but in my judgment he is
so much more deserving of this honored place than either Madison
or John Quincy Adams that they ought to move over and yield
their places to him.

JAMES A. GARFIELD (1881)

The most charitable assessment of Garfield is that his truncated
term of six months did not give him a fair chance to display his
talents. A genuine dark-horse candidate, he was not really wanted
by either the Conklingite or the Blaineite factions of the Republican
party, and he failed to harmonize their differences. Overwhelmed
by office seekers, hating to say "no," pulled first toward one faction
and then toward the other, this beloved and warmhearted man
revealed little strength as President. To add to his burdens, scandals
of long standing were erupting in the Post Office Department. When
shot by a disappointed Conklingite, he was involved in a disgraceful
squabble with the Republican Senate oligarchy over the prize
patronage plum known as the Collectorship of the Port of New York.

Garfield has been much overpraised for his so-called fight for
civil service reform. The blunt truth is that the quarrel with the
Senate flared forth when he removed a meritorious Hayes appointee
in New York so as to reward a notorious Blaine supporter and thus
spite Garfield's enemies of the Conkling faction. This was not
furthering civil service reform; it was old-fashioned spoilsmanship
of the most vicious sort.

But Garfield did promote civil service reform by getting shot. The
nation was shocked into a realization that something had to be done
to clean up the unsavory patronage mess. Harsh though this judg-

ment is, Garfield's greatest service to his country was to die in these tragic circumstances. "The Martyred President" became the unwitting father of the epochal Civil Service Reform Act approved two years later.

The experts routinely refrain from ranking Garfield because of his partial term. The weaknesses of this amiable man were such that he had his feet firmly planted on the road to failure when Charles Guiteau's bullet ended his spectacular log-cabin-to-White House career.

CHESTER ALAN ARTHUR (1881–1885)

Traditionally downgraded as a dandified mediocrity, Arthur was brushed aside by Professor Woodrow Wilson as "a nonentity with side-whiskers." Dismissed for objectionable political activity from the only civilian office he had ever held before coming to the vice presidency, he was elevated by one voter—the pistol-bearing Charles Guiteau. The country was horrified, for we have traditionally elected Vice Presidents in haste and repented at leisure.

"Power corrupts," concluded Lord Acton—and it often does. But power sometimes stimulates and elevates and ennobles. Perhaps shocked by the cold bath of his new responsibilities, Arthur rose commendably to the challenge and gave the American people a far better administration than they deserved for having elected him to high office in the first place. This turncoat spoilsman cold-shouldered his spoilsmen cronies of other days, supported the Pendleton Civil Service Reform Act of 1883 with vigor, and implemented it with faithfulness. He showed vision in launching the new steel Navy, honesty in prosecuting post-office frauds, conscience in vetoing an immigration exclusion bill that violated a treaty with China, and courage in vetoing a notorious pork-barrel bill. One of the ablest of the deathbed Presidents, he deserved to be nominated and elected "in his own right," but his courage and independence had infuriated the party bosses, and he was turned out to pasture. Even so, he had won the respect if not the affection of the voters.

Cultured, intelligent, charming, Arthur was an able administrator, if not an imposing leader of men. A sterling champion of sound money, he gave the country a sound administration and, Arthurian legend to the contrary, surely deserves to rank among the more effective Chief Magistrates. The experts rate him as low Average, but in my view he deserves to rise at least a few notches higher.

GROVER CLEVELAND (1885–1889; 1893–1897)

By most meaningful tests Grover Cleveland, though an outstanding character, was not an outstanding President. He left office at the end of his second term with the economy panic-riddled, the Treasury in the red, his party disrupted, his Republican opponents triumphant, and himself formally repudiated by his Democratic following.

Provincial and narrow-visioned, Cleveland had never been to Washington prior to going there to take the inaugural oath. A great President is in tune with his times, but "Old Grover" never fully grasped the significance of the vast social and economic changes that were convulsing the country. He scrutinized too critically minor pension bills while ignoring major economic ills. With dubious legality he used the army to break the Pullman strike in Chicago, over the vehement opposition of the Governor of Illinois and laboring men in general. He turned his broad back on the New Manifest Destiny and refused to take the idyllic Hawaiian Islands as a gift. Then, misled by Venezuelan propagandists, he almost went to war with Britain over a boundary dispute in the steaming Orinoco jungle land —all without undertaking serious preparations for war. In taking this position he seriously overstrained the original Monroe Doctrine, yet the United States, having stared down the British lion, emerged with enhanced standing among the powers of the world.

Why then is Cleveland generally rated as one of the ablest Presidents? The basic answer is that he showed a degree of independence and courage—his foes said bullheadedness—so rare in public life as to obscure serious shortcomings. His ablest biographer, Allan Nevins, eloquently concludes that to have given the country "such an example of iron fortitude is better than to have swayed parliaments or to have won battles or to have annexed provinces." He battled candidly and courageously for tariff reform, but achieved only patchwork success. He stood inflexibly for deflation and the gold standard, at a time when the nation probably needed some moderate inflation. He broke up his party over the silver issue, but judicious compromise might have averted disaster. He saved millions of acres of forests from the predatory interests; he kept us out of war with Spain over Cuba (temporarily); he gave the country a truly *national* administration by putting Southerners in his Cabinet. Finally, he proved that the Confederate-tainted Democratic party could be trusted to govern in the interests of the nation as a whole.

Cleveland was admittedly conscientious, incorruptible, and courageously indifferent to popularity—but his courage has been overplayed. Despite substantial progress toward civil service reform, he betrayed weakness in yielding to enormous patronage pressure and in permitting Adlai Stevenson, Sr., to lop off the heads of thousands of Republican officeholders ("Adlai's Axe"). He backed down after a storm of opposition had greeted his order to restore Civil War battle flags to the Southern states. Fearing to lose the election of 1888 (which he did anyhow), he bundled the interfering and blundering British Minister Sackville-West off to London with indecent haste. He weakly (and angrily) permitted the log-rolled Wilson-Gorman Tariff Act to become law without either his signature or his veto. All of which suggests that even the most courageous statesmen have to make concessions on occasion to political expediency.

Cleveland, Allan Nevins concedes, "was too conservative to be a great constructive statesman." His record is heavily one of obstruction rather than construction; he was strong in the way in which he dug in his heels. If the most effective Presidents make things happen, then Cleveland will not qualify: he evidently got his keenest satisfaction not in making good things happen but in making bad things not happen. He opposed overgenerous pensions for the veterans, land for the railroads, gravy for the spoilsmen, tariffs for big business, handouts for drought victims. The two conspicuous occasions when he tried to lead Congress—on the tariff and the silver purchase repeal—resulted in disaster for his party and himself.

As an ultra-conservative worshipper of the status quo, lawyer Grover Cleveland was a Hamiltonian Democrat and, like Hamilton, a "traitor" to the non-affluent class from which he had risen. Also, like lawyer Hamilton, he was more concerned with law, order, and property rights than with human rights. It is odd that historians, with their liberal leanings and their penchant for progress, are so friendly to an illiberal figure who stood stolidly and solidly in the path of change. But present-day American historians are largely

Democrats, and Cleveland was the only Democrat in the White House between 1861, when Buchanan bowed out, and 1913, when Wilson bowed in—a total of fifty-two years. When Wilson came to Washington, he claimed that he, not Cleveland, was the first Democrat since Buchanan. "Cleveland," he told a group of Senators, "was a conservative Republican."

Cleveland was well above the average in his courageous negativism, but below average in a number of other qualities that we value more highly. If he was the ablest President between Lincoln and Theodore Roosevelt, the others must have been an indifferent lot indeed. The experts acclaim him a Near Great; I would rank him no better than Average.

BENJAMIN HARRISON (1889–1893)

Lackluster Harrison, something of a party hack, is usually written off as a run-of-the-mill President. He was the Republican caretaker type, which was precisely what the country then expected and evidently wanted. As a recent member of the high-riding Senate oligarchy, he could be counted on not to ram legislation down Congressional gullets; in fact, he had fought eloquently in Congress to curb President Cleveland's authority to remove presidential appointees. A halfhearted civil service reformer, he pleased neither the spoilsmen nor the do-gooders.

Harrison's coldness is overstressed; no one this side of the morgue could have been as chilly as legend pictures him. Though a graceful and effective public speaker, he was dignified and standoffish; his searching gray eyes had a disagreeable effect on self-seeking visitors. He was almost completely colorless, except for the Civil War bloody shirt which he and his supporters vigorously flapped. But if his administration lacked flamboyance, it was at least clean and respectable.

During Harrison's four years Congress passed red-letter legislation regarding trusts, tariffs, pensions, and silver, but the President did little more than affix his signature. The Republican party organization came fairly close to running the government. A pet of the politicians, pensioneers, and big-business predators, Harrison was a conservative—a kind of whiskered Cleveland—at a time when the radical forces of Populism were beginning to work up an angry head of steam. Secretary of State Blaine, the uncrowned king of the party, was expected to shine in foreign affairs, and this he did in convening the first International Conference of American States in Washington in 1889. But Blaine was ill during much of his secretaryship, and Harrison took the initiative in aggressive dealings with Chile and Germany. The old Civil War general, reverting to nostalgic days, rattled his saber alarmingly. On the other hand, he arranged for arbitration of the quarrel with Britain over Bering Sea seals.

Harrison's troubled administration ended on a note of frustration and failure. The Treasury surplus had melted away (thanks to prodigal pensions and tariff tinkering), panic was rumbling in the wings, labor disorders were mounting, and the sons of the soil were raising "less corn and more hell." Harrison, moreover, had been defeated for re-election. A medium-sized man with perhaps better than medium-sized abilities, he had given the country a mediocre, mark-time administration. The experts lodge him almost in the middle—that is, near the middle of the Average category—but he seems to slip more comfortably into the top of the Below Average group.

WILLIAM McKINLEY (1897–1901)

Traditionally downgraded as an indecisive weakling, the martyred McKinley has rebounded—perhaps overrebounded—after more mature assessments by biographers and other scholars. He was clearly abler than the ordinary run of Presidents in the 19th century.

The cartoonists and other myth-makers have given us a puppet (which he was not), the tool of "Dollar Mark" Hanna and big business (which he was not), an irresolute and indecisive creature (which he was not), a slavish follower rather than a leader of public opinion (which was only partly true), and a "chickenhearted politician" who kept his ear glued to the ground (which was only partly true). His backbone, said his critics, was of jelly; his legs were of flannel.[1]

No one can deny that the platitudinous McKinley was amiable,

---

[1] Both Theodore Roosevelt and Representative T. B. Reed are supposed to have accused McKinley of having "no more backbone than a chocolate éclair." No proof that either made this statement has been forthcoming.

genial, courteous, imperturbable, and impeccable. Dignity and girth added inches to his short frame. Looking for all the world like a benign undertaker, he embalmed himself for posterity. Never permitting himself to be photographed in disarray, he would change his white vests, when wrinkled, several times a day. So great was his self-control that he seemed not to perspire even during the muggiest Washington weather. His wonderfully warm handshake, his remarkable memory for names and faces, his ready accessibility, his patient listening, and his red carnation for the visitor's buttonhole all revealed the common touch. A compassionate man, he was a martyr not only to his office but to an epileptic wife as well. As a personality, he was probably the most beloved President during his lifetime that the nation had thus far had.

A consummate interpreter of public opinion, McKinley believed in democracy. He felt that the people, not the President, should rule. Yet on occasion he was prepared to oppose the popular will, notably when he resisted great pressure from the Civil War veterans to fire an upright Commissioner of Pensions. (President Roosevelt later let him go.) The masses demanded war with Spain, and they evidently wanted an overseas empire at its end. McKinley's implementation of their will in both instances has been condemned by second-guessers. He finally gave a fight-thirsty Congress the war with Spain, but he deserves some credit for having held out as long as he did. He also gave the people the Philippines and other overseas pickings. Perhaps he should not have, but the alternatives were all disagreeable and some were dangerous. The crucial mistake was probably not so much in taking the Philippines as in refusing (Congress' fault) a guarantee of independence in the discernible future.

The conciliatory McKinley, who had served thirteen years in the House of Representatives, showed remarkable skill in closing the breaches of his own party, to say nothing of his skill in managing opposition Democrats. He was the first President in a long succession to provide Congress with active and effective leadership. One has to go back to Andrew Jackson for a comparable performance; to Jefferson for as velvet-gloved a performance. In leading Congress, he served as a kind of halfway house: the last of the old-fashioned caretakers and the first of the new-fashioned drivers.

The stereotype of indecisiveness must also go into the ashcan. McKinley was cautious and, like George Washington, slow in making up his mind. But once he had made it up, he held firmly to his decision. Flanked by an able Secretary of State, John Hay, he made the United States an active force in world leadership on a considerable scale for the first time. The theater extended from Cuba and Puerto Rico to Hawaii, the Philippines, and even China. There he intervened by participating in the Boxer expeditionary force and in promulgating the Open-Door policy. The fateful decision to take the Philippines, after generously sampling public opinion, was largely his own.

McKinley was not a top-bracket President, but he served capably in stirring times and gave the country a creditable administration. His name is associated with prosperity, sound money, an uninterruptedly victorious war, a triumphant re-election, and a substantial closing of the bloody chasm between North and South. The experts rank him high Average, and there I would leave him.

CHAPTER XXII

Summary Reassessments:
Theodore Roosevelt to Johnson

"A President's hardest task is not to do what is right, but to know what is right."

LYNDON B. JOHNSON, 1965

THEODORE ROOSEVELT (1901–1909)

One of the most puzzling Presidents to appraise is Theodore Roosevelt. At times he had the mark of greatness; at others, concluded his English friend, Ambassador Spring-Rice, he was a six-year-old child (and a spoiled child at that). But if the Rough Rider was not the greatest of the Presidents, he was indubitably the noisiest. His favorite saying, "Speak softly and carry a big stick," is thoroughly misleading. He carried a Big Stick, all right, but the soft speaking resembled the bellowing of a bull moose during mating season. He had a "bully time," but not everyone else did.

Roosevelt is warmly praised by students of government for having used his dynamic leadership—often a bulldozing kind of leadership—to strengthen, even overbalance, the presidency. As the first of the Modern Presidents, he was undeniably a strong Executive. On occasion he would lead Congress (always a Republican Congress) or drive it or dominate it or deceive it or circumvent it, generally with considerable success. He evolved his all-embracing "Stewardship Theory," that is, the President may take any action in the public interest not forbidden by the laws and the Constitution. He short-circuited the Senate by entering into executive agreements behind its back, notably in dealing with Santo Domingo and Japan, and he led the nation far deeper into the chill waters of internationalism than had the reluctant McKinley. He was in fact the first President to operate in the grand manner on the world stage.

As heads cracked, Roosevelt the Reformer permitted few dull moments. Whether a radical conservative or a conservative radical, he acted as a kind of lightning rod to deflect or absorb radical movements, and may have headed off socialism with a noisy if overrated dose of reformism. Seeking a Square Deal for the forgotten man, he marshaled, moulded, and muddied public opinion. Sullying the good name of America, he "took" the Panama Canal Zone and got the dirt to flying, though more kinds of dirt finally flew than he had anticipated. He beefed up the Navy, and sent the big white battleships steaming around the world with one grand flourish. He embarked upon a furious crusade for the conservation of natural resources, and although he was not the first conservationist, as many believed, he was certainly the loudest, most aggressive, most energetic, most dedicated, and most effective.

Yet the demerits cut him down to size. The noise was not commensurate with the accomplishment. As a trustbuster, he was something of a "bust": at best, the trusts were only temporarily curbed, though substantial progress was made—or better, some lost ground was regained. His pugnacity and bellicosity were almost pathological. His impatience and impetuosity brought on the Brownsville blunder involving the dismissal of an entire Negro detachment. His deviousness led to his abetting the Panama coup and rigging the trumped-up Alaska boundary "arbitration." His intemperance of speech caused the formation of the Ananias Club, after the New Testament liar, by those whom he publicly branded liars, including newsmen. It was a large, flourishing, and expanding organization. His capacity for exaggeration evidently caused him to overstate his role in the Venezuela crisis of 1902 and the Far Eastern crisis of 1904, and hence earn the distrust of historians. His unconventionality led him to pervert the Monroe Doctrine, use it as a tool of American imperialism, and intensify the Bad-Neighbor policy.

Partly because he was clever enough to sidetrack the tariff issue,

Roosevelt got along reasonably well with Congress, especially the House, until his closing months. Then an unseemly row broke out over his use of the Secret Service to "shadow" members. He was reportedly seeking information, for legislative blackmail purposes, about their alleged patronage of prostitutes. The House, in an unprecedented display of resentment, formally rebuked him by a vote of 212 to 35. In the end, Roosevelt, like Eisenhower after him, failed to impose his own brand of Republicanism on his party. His record of legislative accomplishment was not particularly impressive.

Roosevelt was a great personality, a great activist, a great preacher of the moralities, a great controversialist, a great showman. He dominated his era as he dominated conversations. Sometimes people wondered whether they had an administration or a circus. He was a great egoist, a great self-glorifier, a great exhibitionist, a great headline catcher, so much so that some critics felt he had degraded the dignity of his high office. But the masses loved him; he proved to be a great popular idol and a great vote getter. A consummate politician, he was also a great opportunist and withal a great leader. Yet, on balance, Roosevelt fell short of being a Grade-A President; at best he was B plus, or a Near Great, as the experts have decreed.

Had a major war come during Roosevelt's incumbency, and he had won it, he no doubt would rank higher. The irony is that this disciple of Mars, sobered by responsibility, sidestepped several glorious opportunities for war. He was in fact hailed as the premier peacemaker of the Russo-Japanese War, indeed of his day (Nobel prize). If he had been better balanced, he would have been a greater man and a greater President. But then he would not have been Theodore Roosevelt—the perpetual adult-adolescent.

WILLIAM HOWARD TAFT (1909–1913)

Leaving office in 1913 as the worst defeated incumbent up to that time, Taft is commonly regarded as considerably less than a success. Theodore Roosevelt's sneering compliment that he meant well but that he meant well feebly has clung to his outsized frame. But in more recent years, lengthened perspective, guilty consciences, and friendly biographers have pushed the portly President up to an echelon perhaps higher than he deserves.

Taft looks somewhat better when we consider the handicaps

under which he labored. A slow-moving judge by temperament and training, he disliked politics, and was never cut out to be President. He was prone to play his cards face up. Lacking "fire in his belly," he was not an aggressive leader, either of Congress or of public opinion. He fumbled the baton of dynamic leadership (modern presidency) which Roosevelt passed on to him but which Wilson in turn seized. He seemed to regard his office as a kind of glorified clerkship, and himself (in Roosevelt's words) a servant of Congress. An able assistant President, he was lost in the driver's seat. Selecting a middle-of-the-road route, he soon discovered that the middle is the most dangerous place. Unwilling or unable to make effective concessions to the liberal elements in his Republican party, he was finally run over and flattened by the Progressive firetruck. He was a mild progressive who would probably have passed as a liberal in 1900, but by 1912 the Progressive procession had got out in front of him. Handpicked by Roosevelt, and oversold by him, he retained enough Rooseveltism to arouse the Rough Rider's numerous enemies, but not enough to please the Rough Rider himself. Each one finally tried to kick the other out of the Republican bed. The result was that Taft left his party badly disrupted, and the opposition Democrats in the seats of the mighty.

Roosevelt's was a tough act to follow, and an aura of fumble, bumble, and stumble clung to Taft. Almost nothing seemed to go right for him. Unlike Roosevelt, he forthrightly tackled the tariff, and then defended the resulting "sham revision" with indecent zeal and an inept exhibition of foot-in-mouthism. On the issue of conservation, which he helped along significantly, he was forced to dismiss Gifford Pinchot and finally ease out Secretary of the Interior Ballinger, amidst a frightful administrative row.

In foreign affairs, the Taft record is disappointing, although his much-criticized dollar diplomacy was adopted and expanded by the succeeding Wilsonian Democrats. Secretary Knox's plan for neutralizing the railroads of China's Manchuria was rebuffed by both Russia and Japan; Canadian reciprocity was hurled back in Taft's face by the Canadians; the Russian commercial treaty was cavalierly terminated by the House over his objections; his pet arbitration treaties were emasculated by the Senate and then dropped; the Lodge corollary to the Monroe Doctrine was forced on him by the Senate; and the Panama Canal Tolls exemption, which

Taft the legalist had supported, was repealed by the next Congress.

But the Taft story is not all bleak or black. On paper his record as a trustbuster is even more impressive than that of Roosevelt himself. As a conservationist he set aside millions of acres for Americans yet unborn. He pressed for and secured from Congress the postal savings bank (fought by bankers) and parcel post (fought by express companies). His legislative record compares not unfavorably with that of his predecessor. He achieved a four-nation pact for saving the North Pacific seals and a treaty with Britain for ending the century-old controversy over the North Atlantic fisheries. Finally, he had the good judgment, despite heavy public pressure, not to send troops into revolution-torn Mexico. That baby he left on Wilson's doorstep.

Taft, the conservative progressive, was personally popular. The experts boost him into the upper half of the Average group, but he probably belongs a few notches lower.

WOODROW WILSON (1913–1921)

Like Jefferson, Wilson is easier to tab as a great man than as a great President. Both served long enough to see their early laurels wither during their last months in office. Until his collapse in September, 1919, Wilson had rung up an amazing record as a leader. With unprecedented energy he propelled through Congress an impressive legislative program implementing his New Freedom—a precursor of the New Deal. As a wartime evangel, he led the nation on a holy crusade with spectacular success, considering his lack of military preparedness. A great leader (of the lone-wolf type), a great politician (the "regulars" were not too happy), a great phrase-maker, a great idealist, a great orator, a great preacher-moralist, he was also a great failure—at least in the short run. Instead of leading his people into the promised land, he led them into the fog and bog of disillusionment and frustration, where they fell under the spell of false prophets like Harding. His campaign to educate the masses to their new responsibilities had been too little and too late. The peace treaty which he co-authored, but which his own people refused to accept on his own terms, bred another war from whose ashes the United Nations rose. In this sense, Wilson, like Columbus, was a successful failure—a temporary failure but a success twenty-five years and millions of war dead later.

Wilson left his own party disorganized and defeated, partly as a result of his mistakes in peacemaking and partly as a result of his irrational vendetta with Senator Lodge. The ablest Presidents have usually passed the office on to their successors as a sharper tool: Wilson passed it on to Harding as a duller tool, with the old Senate oligarchy once more in the ascendancy and with the Republic convulsed by the aftermath of the Big Red Scare.

Wilson, like the other Virginia idealist Jefferson, was a bundle of inconsistencies. Coming into office as a foe of Republican dollar diplomacy, he made the old dollar diplomacy, in the words of one critic, look like ten-cent diplomacy. A stern moralist, he waged a personal feud with President Huerta of Mexico, and though a non-doctrinaire pacifist, twice invaded Mexico. In 1913 he warned the bewildered American bankers to pull out of the Chinese railroad consortium, and later in 1917 urged them to go back in.

When war erupted in Europe, Wilson proposed an impossible neutrality in thought; he opposed preparedness because it might involve us; he belatedly and rather halfheartedly got onto the preparedness bandwagon; and then when the German submarine challenge came, he had no Big Stick. Holding Germany (but not the Allies) to "strict accountability," he refused to ban American passengers from belligerent ships in the war zones. This, he argued, would be dishonorable, although lopsided majorities in Congress found it quite honorable in the 1930's. He issued a blank-check ultimatum to Berlin after the *Sussex* torpedoing, in effect promising war if the Germans reopened their merciless attacks. They filled in the blank with their unrestricted submarine warfare, and he was compelled to ask Congress for a declaration of war. Preaching self-determination for Europe, Wilson denied it to marine-occupied Haiti and Santo Domingo. In Paris, he was forced to compromise away many of his Fourteen Points to save the League of Nations; in Washington, he drew the line at compromising enough with Lodge to save the League of Nations.

Speaking of the Treaty of Versailles, Jan C. Smuts concluded that Wilson had not failed; it was "the human spirit" that had failed. To a degree this was true, but a statesman must learn to deal with people as they are, not as they ought to be. Great men are generally judged by what they achieve—make happen—rather than by what a benighted populace failed to support. A leader can no more flog an emotionally exhausted people into further self-sacrifice than a jockey can flog a physically exhausted horse into winning a race.

Wilson's spectacular successes at home are substantially cancelled out by his failures abroad, including his supreme failure as a peace-maker. He belongs with the Greats, where the experts put him, if we consider his first six years. He rises no higher than Near Great, if that high, when we consider all eight years, including the two when he was a shadow President broken on the wheel of fate.

WARREN GAMALIEL HARDING (1921–1923)

The three Republicans of the 1920's—Harding, Coolidge, and Hoover—are generally downgraded by the experts, themselves largely Democrats who admire Wilson and the League of Nations which Harding spurned. These critics are perhaps not so much condemning the incumbents as the "treadmill" Republican phi-losophy which they espoused. We have earlier noted that Republican Presidents were supposed to be the caretaker type—modest medi-ocrities and harmonizers like Harding—rather than dynamic leaders or intellectually arrogant reformers like Wilson, bent on rocking the boat of big business and browbeating Congress. This is what the Republicans wanted, and since they were the majority party by a wide margin in the 1920's, this is what the country got. All three of the "prosperity presidents" of the 1920's were personally popular; the Hoover of the 1930's is a different story.

Harding is reckoned a rock-bottom Failure by the experts, and this view is so commonly held that for an historian to argue other-wise is rank heresy. The voluminous Harding papers were not opened to researchers until 1964, so we must conclude that these judgments have been based on incomplete evidence, not to say badly biased testimony, including the flippant observations of William Allen White and Alice Roosevelt Longworth.

Amiable, genial, companionable Warren Harding was not a Joseph as far as conventional sexual morality was concerned, but neither was Grover Cleveland with his "woman scrape." Harding's scandalous sex relationships (one is fully documented) occurred before he became President, as was true of Cleveland. He did have liquor in his living quarters in the White House, although prohibition was the law of the land, but more sterling public servants than Harding flouted the Eighteenth Amendment as an unwarranted invasion of personal liberty. Legend to the contrary, he was not the clear choice of the Senate bosses at Chicago in 1920; they did not control the convention; and he was not nominated in a smoke-filled hotel room but in an open assembly, where he was the second or third or fourth choice of the delegates after the favorites had killed one another off. As a back-slapping politician of the Rotarian type and an arm-flailing orator of the tear-jerking school, he had made a host of friends. He was not the "creature" of his Attorney General, the small-town Harry M. Daugherty; rather the reverse. The slippery Daugherty lived to tell his side of the story, but the overloyal Harding carried his to the grave.

Harding was no "brain," as he was the first to admit. But he promised to gather about him the "best minds," and his Cabinet did contain Hughes, Hoover, and Mellon. (They were offset in part by two sleazy characters, Daugherty and Fall.) Harding's public speeches were fuzzy and contradictory; his inaugural address was described by a British critic as the most illiterate statement ever made by the head of a civilized government. He and his successors pursued a short-sighted political isolation (though not economic isolation) regarding Europe, but this course was plainly what the country desired. Harding did show some little gumption when he came out for joining the World Court, despite the predictable outcry from bitter-enders in the Senate.

His blackest eyes came from unfortunate appointees, partly as a result of bad luck and partly as a result of bad judgment of character. A generous man, he delighted in giving his personal friends, even though lowly placed ward heelers, highly placed federal jobs. The multi-million-dollar Forbes scandal in the Veterans Bureau came to light some five months before his death, but he took care of that himself. Then followed a sorry succession of suicides and jailings. The Teapot Dome scandal broke after his death, and above all else belatedly besmirched his name. He had signed the transfer of the oil lands, from the Navy Department to Secretary Fall's Interior Department, knowing what he was doing. Incredibly enough, what Fall did in making his back-alley deal with Sinclair and Doheny was to some degree in the public interest, for private oilmen were draining adjacent oil pools, the money-pinched Navy needed refined oil, and Doheny did build the enormous storage tanks at Pearl Harbor that were of inestimable value to the Navy during World War II. But the one inescapable fact is that Fall accepted bribes and was jailed.

At first unsure of himself, Harding gradually developed some confidence, worked harder at his desk than most Presidents (he needed more time than some). At the end he thought he was doing a good job. He stood up to the Senate with increasing stubbornness (including Henry Cabot Lodge), and insisted upon the excellent appointments of Hughes and Hoover. He officially summoned the Washington Disarmament Conference, but had little directly to do with it: the idea was Senator Borah's rather than his. The disarmament part proved illusory (thanks largely to American lassitude) but the general air clearing was praiseworthy, and may have averted war in the Pacific for a decade. This was perhaps the only one of America's much-ballyhooed international conclaves of the 1920's and 1930's to achieve really significant results.

Harding (or his administration) is also credited with making separate peace treaties with the enemy of World War I, with passing an immigration law to stem the war-ravaged hordes of Europe, with initiating the first of the war debt agreements (that with Britain), with sending relief to famine-racked Russia, with concluding the Panama heart-balm treaty with Colombia, and with improving relations with Mexico. At home, Harding was ultimately responsible for a revised tariff law (better in some respects than Hoover's Hawley-Smoot), for inaugurating the efficient Bureau of the Budget, for cutting war taxes drastically (especially for the rich), for engineering one of the largest debt reductions in our history, for vetoing a Treasury-raiding soldiers' bonus bill, for expanding employment and prosperity, for securing some aid for depressed farmers and disabled veterans, for courageously urging political rights for the Negro in a Birmingham speech (in the interests of Republican votes), for appointing Taft as Chief Justice, for releasing Debs from the federal penitentiary for overfree speech during the war, and for personally arranging for an eight-hour day in the steel industry in place of the man-killing twelve-hour day.

This is only a partial list, and some of the so-called achievements were of dubious merit. Yet for any other administration most of these items would add up to a record of substantial accomplishment. But then there are the scandals, financial and sexual, that came out later. Overall, Harding's administration—a faithful reflection of the times—was not so much of a failure as that of Andrew Johnson or John Quincy Adams or even James Madison, to whom the experts give good marks. The affable Ohioan was regarded as a "cinch" for renomination, and almost certain of re-election. Several biographies, based on the newly available papers, are in the works, so let us extend to Harding the Christian charity (or was it good politics?) that he showed Debs, and lodge him, at least temporarily, low in the Below Average category.

CALVIN COOLIDGE (1923–1929)

Tightfisted Calvin Coolidge, a subtle master of self-advertising, was acclaimed a highly successful President when he left office early in 1929. He was clearly the most popular since Theodore Roosevelt. But late in 1929, when the speculative bubble burst, much of his fame began to evaporate, and he must now be accounted less than effective.

The shy, pinchpenny Vermonter, whom Woodrow Wilson dismissed as "no one in particular," was a spectacularly successful politician at the lower levels who came to the White House by a series of flukes. Acclaimed as the Massachusetts Governor who broke the Boston police strike (his role was belated and exaggerated), he was nominated for the vice presidency when the Chicago convention suddenly revolted against the presumed choice of the Senate oligarchy. "I thought I could swing it," he later twanged about his unexpected elevation to the White House.

The dour-faced Yankee (Alice Roosevelt Longworth quipped that he had been "weaned on a pickle") had many of the standard virtues of reliable New England bank clerks. He was honest, thrifty, punctual, conscientious, cautious, conservative, moral, and religious. He believed in both God and mammon—with mammon represented by business, invested capital, and wealth. The son of a small storekeeper-farmer, he had absorbed the businessman's point of view, and one of his famous banalities, "The business of America is business," rings down through the ages—rather hollowly.

Coolidge was what Americans rather prize as a "character." As a

sober offset to the flapperized 1920's, he appealed to older citizens
who felt that the dogs had finally caught up with the younger
generation. As a sharp, cash-on-the-barrelhead Yankee, he would not
be outslickered, as Wilson presumably had been, by the white-
spatted and scheming European debtors. "They hired the money,
didn't they," he is supposed to have remarked in connection with
making the debtors pay up. Coolidgean complacency not only
fitted the times perfectly but also Republican philosophy, which
amounted to about the same thing. The country (except farmers)
was reveling in Coolidge "prosperity," though a spotty and feverish
prosperity, and those twin roadblocks to progress, Laissez Faire and
Status Quo, were goddesses to both the President and the nation.

Yet Coolidge was almost totally deficient in powers of leadership.
Lacking both energy and foresight, he kept fit, as he later confessed,
"by avoiding the big problems," including prohibition. Respecting
the Congressmen as colleagues also elected by the people, he made
no sustained effort to use his popularity to coerce or even coax
them. Dozens of his recommendations they ignored; he was forced
to sign unpalatable immigration and tax bills; he was overridden
on the soldiers' bonus bill. The Senate kicked his shins by rejecting
two of his major appointments, including an Attorney General. He
was distressingly slow—nearly six months—in authorizing an investigation of the notorious Teapot Dome scandal, and he seemed to
regard the Senate investigators as unwelcome boat-rockers, as
indeed they were in a political sense. (Silent Cal broke his silence
on this issue only when pressured by public opinion.) He not only
actively encouraged stockmarket speculation but raised no effective
protest against the billions that were being poured abroad for
investment. He turned the Federal Trade Commission, designed to
police business, into a prop of business. Evidently believing that it
was more important to kill bad legislation than to promote good
legislation, he vetoed two farm-aid bills and the Norris Bill (precursor of the Tennessee Valley Authority).

Coolidge is credited with having helped to launch the Good-
Neighbor policy by sending his Amherst classmate, Dwight W.
Morrow, to Mexico as Ambassador, but he left foreign affairs
largely to his able Secretaries of State, Hughes and Kellogg. Former
Secretary Elihu Root remarked that "he did not have an inter-
national hair in his head." On occasion he was rudely taciturn (he

may have been part Indian); on other occasions he was positively garrulous in his harsh, nasal, New England monotone. Such was Silent Cal.

As a reluctant refugee from the 19th century, symbolically sworn in by his farmer-father by the light of a kerosene lamp, Coolidge reflected that era's homely virtues. A rugged individualist and hack politician, embodying "the genius of the average," he lacked both imagination and idealism. "He had no ideas," wrote H. L. Mencken, "but he was not a nuisance." At times it seemed as though his mental visibility rose no higher than his native Green Mountains. The myth of the strong, silent President must be discarded: he was neither strong nor silent. I am not prepared to quarrel with the experts who place him Below Average in effectiveness.

HERBERT CLARK HOOVER (1929–1933)

If Hoover had never entered the White House, his admirers would say, "What a splendid President he would have made." But when the Great Depression came in the door, the Great Engineer's reputation gradually leaked out the window. The oversold Miracle Worker-Superman ran into bad luck, as all incumbents do to some extent. We judge Presidents by how effectively they grapple with the difficulties that confront them, not by how well they would have done if there had been no bumps in the road. Repudiated by humiliating majorities in 1932, Hoover must be regarded as less than a successful President. His much-heralded New Day never dawned.

As an efficiency expert and boy-wonder, Hoover suffered from unusual handicaps. Billed with much fanfare as the Great Humanitarian and a McKinleyesque Advance Agent of Prosperity, he got caught in the cogs of a Depression in which his basic humanitarianism clashed with his old-fashioned ideas of "rugged individualism." Accustomed most of his life to quick success and to giving orders, he was baffled and annoyed by back talk from strong-willed politicians, some of them intellectually his peers. Never previously elected to public office and never an astute politician, he was a Johnny-come-lately to the professionals who had elbowed their way up. He was also excessively thin-skinned regarding criticism, and he was never Lincolnesque in a readiness to admit errors, as his *Memoirs* abundantly attest.

Depressingly shy, dignified, and ponderous, whether on the platform or on the radio, Hoover not only detested demagoguery but lacked color and warmth. Gutzon Borglum said he looked as though a rose would wilt if put in his hand. He also lacked cleverness with words. His 19th-century high collar, stiffly starched, matched his 19th-century laissez-faireism and rugged individualism, even though his support of both prohibition and the tariff squared with neither. He was pained to have to adjust his time-tested views, at least partially and belatedly, to depression-cursed conditions. Impressively overflowing with figures, he seemed to believe that with hard work and hard facts all political and economic problems, such as the Depression, could be solved as one could solve the problem of building a dam.

The Republican party, now split into right and left wings, added more hairs to his hair shirt by splitting under him. The liberal Republicans in the Senate, including the "wild jackass" insurgents, combined with the Democratic minority to harass him. This is a not uncommon pattern. During his last two years he had in addition a Democratic majority in the House, but it cooperated surprisingly well in supporting his anti-Depression measures.

On the debit side, Hoover blundered by calling a special session of Congress on the tariff, and then failed to provide aggressive leadership. He signed the backward-looking and disturbingly high Hawley-Smoot Tariff in the teeth of vehement protests from American economists and foreign exporters. He shared the narrow and self-defeating views of the general public on war debts and reparations. A non-fighting Quaker and a citizen of the world who had become basically an isolationist, he shied away from the League of Nations and from involvement with Japan over the Manchurian crisis of 1931, at a time when the mikado's warlords might have been halted. Instead, he claimed credit for launching, if not authoring, the slap-on-the-wrist Hoover-Stimson non-recognition doctrine. Prone to vacillate by appointing numerous fact-gathering commissions, he took what was decried as a "pussyfooting" stand on a number of public issues, especially prohibition. (One critic suggested a Hoover Commission to investigate Hoover.) Finally, he bunglingly drove the bonus army out of Washington. Even before the Depression descended, critics charged that his mishandling of the tariff, prohibition, and the farm problem was enough to brand him a failure.

On the credit side, Hoover markedly improved relations with Latin America, and thus foreshadowed Roosevelt's vaunted Good-Neighbor policy. He fought for and secured the flexible tariff provision of the otherwise objectionable Hawley-Smoot Tariff. He vigorously supported and praised the London Naval Conference, even though the results rang hollow as regards both economy and disarmament. He eased the debt problem by proclaiming a one-year moratorium, which led predictably and inexorably to outright default by all the debtors except "brave little Finland."

Legend to the contrary, Hoover was not a do-nothing President but a true activist, within the confines of his rigid ideology. Departing sharply from the Harding-Coolidge ideal of drift, he boldly and speedily bestirred himself with rational proposals and measures when the crash came in 1929. Complaints about his handling of the Depression did not become general for about two years. But he was too prone to blame foreigners for what had happened, too obsessed with a balanced budget at the expense of the human budget, and too determined to let local relief agencies handle relief when they had no relief to handle.

Hoover finally departed so far from his time-honored principles as to urge Congress to appropriate millions for public works and other schemes to reduce unemployment, even at the distressing cost of an unbalanced budget. Fearing the character-undermining effect of direct doles (we now see better what he meant), he belatedly and at first reluctantly supported the Reconstruction Finance Corporation. It would bail out the big banks, which in turn would help recovery by the trickle-down process. Other measures championed by Hoover definitely foreshadowed the deficit-spending relief-and-recovery program of the New Deal. Without these intermediate steps, Roosevelt's giant-boot strides probably would not have been possible. Hoover at least proved that local relief was not enough, and that no federal government could humanely and safely permit its people to starve in the midst of abundance. His apologists went so far as to claim that the essentials of the Hundred Days legislation of the New Dealers were all enacted in his administration. But Hoover condemned those selfsame measures as paternalistic, socialistic, collectivistic, fascistic, and communistic.

Hoover offered active leadership but not effective leadership: his own party and his own people did not provide followership. He was not so much a do-nothing President as he was one who apparently did nothing that worked to stem the tidal wave of depression. Yet the nagging question remains: Who could have done better? The political leader of every other major democratic nation was also blackened by the Depression: Ramsay MacDonald in Britain, Pierre Laval in France, and Heinrich Brüning in Germany. Franklin Roosevelt needed eight years, a twenty-billion-dollar deficit, and the outbreak of a world war to conquer the Depression. Hoover's great sin was failing to achieve the impossible goal of preserving the status quo for which he had been elected and which he had more or less promised.

The experts, perhaps rebounding guiltily from earlier low assessments and remembering Hoover's other extraordinary public services, leave him almost in the middle of the Average group. I would regard him as in many ways a remarkable man but a Below Average President.

FRANKLIN DELANO ROOSEVELT (1933–1945)

As great men are reckoned, Franklin Roosevelt was undeniably a great man. His impact on history was enormous. Inspiriting the American people and causing them to recapture faith in themselves and in their democracy, he engineered a sweeping social and economic revolution known as the New Deal. He led with magnificent self-assurance, buoyancy, and grace. He intervened successfully and decisively in a global war. He was the chief architect of the United Nations. Demonstrating anew the power of aggressive presidential leadership, he may have saved the American free-enterprise system from an anti-capitalistic upheaval, and he probably saved American democracy and much of the world's freedom from the dictators. What more can be said of any other figure in American history?

Like Jefferson, Roosevelt can more easily be labeled a great man than a great President. In his case, as in that of Jefferson, the black marks cancel out many of the white marks. He was a great leader, a great politician, a great activist, a great innovator, a great vote getter, a great personality, a great showman, a great actor, a great hope-inspirer, a great idealist, a great optimist, a great reformer, a great voice, a great humanitarian, and a great liberal (with other people's money, the critics jibed). Yet does all this add up to a great President?

Roosevelt lived greatly in great times, but he made many mistakes, some of them near-catastrophic blunders. Of course, he had a better opportunity to make costly mistakes, and a longer time in which to make them. Only great men are in a position to err greatly. Part resolute lion and part sly fox, Roosevelt at times was so devious as to reveal a basic lack of faith in democracy. Hoover called him "a chameleon on plaid." The New Deal, a coalition of the disinherited and underprivileged, promoted class strife, confusion, and contradiction. Whatever the necessity, Roosevelt encouraged the masses to develop their wishbones more than their backbones. At a cost of some twenty billion dollars and six years of agony, the "Happy Borrower" did not cure the Depression: he merely administered aspirin and sedatives.

Though a master politician, Roosevelt the Fox made a half dozen or so blundering political missteps. Conspicuous among them were his boomeranging attempts to purge the Supreme Court of moss-backs in 1937 and the Congress of recalcitrants in 1938. In so doing he accelerated the coalition between conservative Southern Democrats and Northern Republicans which successfully stymied all his major reforms after 1938. He overstrengthened the presidency by his early "constitutional dictatorship" and by his later shattering of the two-term tradition. One result was the posthumous anti-third-term amendment, which, political scientists are virtually unanimous in agreeing, permanently weakens the presidency.[1]

In foreign affairs, Roosevelt's record is spotty. He got off on the wrong foot by impulsively torpedoing the London Economic Conference, but supported the tariff-lowering reciprocal trade agreements and brought the Good Neighbor policy to an all-time peak of felicity. He reluctantly approved the head-in-the-sands neutrality legislation of the 1930's but actively supported the purblind embargo

[1] My own view is that this weakening, though real, is exaggerated. See the discussion of lame ducks earlier, pp. 110–113. As Eisenhower testified in 1962, the President has plenty of powers, if he will but use them judiciously, and they are increasing with new devices and vastly improved means of communication and transportation. But his problems and responsibilities are increasing at an even faster rate.

on arms to the Spanish loyalists, who became the unwitting victims of a dress rehearsal for World War II. If he had used his magnetic gifts as a leader to induce the American people to avoid strait-jacket neutrality and to build up their arms to a point commensurate with the danger, he might have been able to head off World War II altogether. His bold Quarantine Speech of 1937, followed by a backdown, revealed a politician more willing to drift along with public opinion than to lead it into unpopular whirlpools. At times he even lagged conspicuously behind public sentiment.

Roosevelt was caught asleep at the Pearl Harbor switch, even though there were ample signs of an impending Japanese strike somewhere. He was actually easing the nation into war by less than candid means when the paralyzing blow fell. The uprooting of tens of thousands of American citizens of Japanese ancestry, at his order, turned out to be a gross violation of civil liberties. Reposing undue confidence in the Russians, he provided mountains of lend-lease aid, even after the suspicious Soviets had shown no intention whatever of following America's policies of collective security after the war. Taking a short-run military view of the conflict, and not looking far enough beyond at the political consequences, he appeased the dictators in France and Spain, proclaimed a policy of unconditional surrender which begot unconditional resistance, and counted too heavily on Russian pledges of good faith at Yalta. He naively over-estimated his capacity to charm a steely Stalin, wishfully regarded China as a major power, and idealistically (if ignorantly) sought to break up the colonial empires of his allies.

This bill of indictment, of course, lists many arguable items. Roosevelt felt the pressure to win the war before the dictators de-veloped unbeatable secret weapons, as they almost did. The alterna-tive to being friendly to the Russians was certain hostility, at a time when friendship seemed worth a gamble. The American public took a short-run view of the war, and was determined to "whip the bullies" and bring the boys home before the fire was really out. But a great leader will strive mightily and persistently to persuade the people to do what they ought to do for their own long-range good.

On the basis of impact alone, Roosevelt can hardly be denied a place in the highest echelon of American Presidents. But one could still wish that there had been more of the lion and less of the fox.

HARRY S TRUMAN (1945–1953)

Cocky, spunky, and outspoken, Truman was undeniably a "strong" President in the Jackson-Roosevelt tradition. He is the only Executive in our history to wind up one major war, lead the nation through a major reconstruction, fight another war (our third largest), and then embark anew upon reconstruction. Meanwhile, he was fighting a third war—the Cold War—in his determined and generally successful efforts to stem Soviet aggression. And he left the country pulsatingly prosperous.

Truman's boss-ridden beginnings were inauspicious. A small-town alumnus of a notorious Missouri machine, he was first thrust into the vice presidency and then catapulted into the White House. Unbriefed by President Roosevelt, he later said he felt that he had "lived five lifetimes in my first five days as President." Yet this seemingly ordinary high-school graduate boned up on his homework, assembled the facts, consulted advisers, delegated authority, made the key decisions, and did an extraordinary job, considering his limitations. He was clearly a clean-desk administrator who helped establish important advisory agencies, including the National Security Council. Modestly pooh-poohing all talk about being a "great" President, he later remarked that the only accolade he desired was: "He did his damndest."

All this is not to say that Truman shone in all areas. Generally big in the big things—the White House Truman—he was often small in the small things—the Courthouse Truman. His loud sport shirts, his quick-mouthed remarks, his blistering S.O.B. letters, among other shockers, debased presidential dignity. A victim of "cronyism," he proved distressingly loyal to his wartime buddies of the Missouri gang when they got caught with their hands in or near the federal till.

Few Presidents have hung up a worse record of getting along with Congress, whether controlled by their own party or not. Twelve of his vetoes were overridden—a setback not equaled since the days of floundering Andrew Johnson. Many of his key recommendations were spurned. Most of his dozen or so "great decisions" were executive acts which did not require the approval of Congress (Berlin airlift) or which more or less committed Congress to implementation

(Truman Doctrine). A peppery partisan and a courageous fighter for what he believed right, he split his party into three parts over the civil rights issue in 1948. "Stuck with Harry," the Democrats reluctantly renominated him, and only by a political miracle did he manage to win re-election in his own right and largely by his own efforts. The so-called "mess in Washington," including "influence peddling" by Truman's cronies, became a rallying cry for the Republicans when they swept into power with the eye-catching Eisenhower in 1953. "Corruption" at home and "courage" abroad were the labels commonly used by journalists.

Not all of the "great decisions" were necessarily the correct ones, especially in the light of information now available. "To err is Truman" became a current quip. In retrospect, the dropping of the atomic bomb, though approved by expert advisers, does not seem to have been the only statesmanlike alternative. The abrupt cancellation of lend-lease aid to allies was a blunder which Truman later admitted was made in haste and on the basis of improper information. The "dumping" of Chiang followed an unrealistic effort to induce the Nationalist Chinese lamb to lie down with the Communist wolf. The decisions to create the state of Israel and then recognize it on a rush-order basis were taken in defiance of the "overeducated" advisers in the State Department and the long-range interests of America in the oil-rich Arab world. The dismissal of General MacArthur represented an upholding of the powers of the presidential office, but it was carried out with the finesse of a punch on the nose. The withdrawal of American troops from South Korea and Secretary of State Acheson's announcement that its defense was a responsibility of the United Nations probably helped trigger the Korean War. Truman presumably saved the United Nations by intervening, but he cannot avoid some responsibility for having created a situation that seemingly made intervention imperative.

Truman had the intestinal stamina to make the unprecedented series of decisions, without shilly-shallying, that he felt had to be made. Succeeding a popular idol who was widely regarded as an indispensable man, he renewed faith in American democracy by demonstrating anew that our government can be run by a plain-speaking, middle-weight, middle-class man—one who could rise to tremendous challenges without any special gifts except decisiveness, "guttiness," and a capacity for growth. He was unique in his commonness. He lacked the grand manner, whether in word or deed, but he left no doubt who was President. The experts call him a Near Great, four notches below Great, but his greatness lies largely in having done greatly better than anyone had any reason to anticipate. Balancing his remarkable record in foreign affairs against his rather barren record in domestic affairs, I would say that this seemingly average man turned out to be no better than an average President. "Haberdasher Harry" was competent rather than eminent, but even this is a compliment.

DWIGHT DAVID EISENHOWER (1953–1961)

A five-star war hero, Eisenhower came to the office a political greenhorn. Yet, after prolonged on-the-job training, he gradually developed into a fairly sophisticated politician who gave the country a far better administration than it had any right to expect from such a novice. Unlike many another ageing military man in civilian office, he proved to be humble, modest, teachable, susceptible to growth, and endowed with common sense. He was not power-hungry. Even more popular at the end than at the beginning, he left the country prosperous and peaceful: his proud boast was that no American soldiers had lost their lives fighting on foreign soil during his eight years. Yet he held the containment line against Communism with reasonable success from Berlin to Formosa, although his flamboyant Secretary of State Dulles spoke extravagantly of "liberation" and "rollback."

Eisenhower restored dignity to his exalted office, while often appearing to be above the battle, as though politics were too dirty for a clean old soldier. He was a conciliator and accommodator, an apostle of the middle way, rather than a critic and crusader; a tranquilizer rather than a stimulant. American soldiers are trained to defend things, not uproot them; the Army does not ordinarily produce flaming liberals.

The retired general was something of a split personality. On the one hand, he was a liberal in international affairs and human relations; on the other, a middle-of-the-road Kansas conservative in domestic affairs and economic relationships. A businessman's ideal, he was obsessively concerned with balancing the budget—"fiscal responsibility" was one of his favorite watchwords. ("Better dead than in the red," said critics.)

As a moderate, Eisenhower answered the need for a breathing-spell President and a father image after the prolonged crisis years under Roosevelt and Truman. His non-politicalness actually appealed strongly to many voters who were fed up with the goings-on in Washington. He failed to impose his own brand of liberal conservatism (Modern Republicanism) on his recently adopted party, but he helped preserve the two-party system at a time when repeated defeats had threatened the Republicans with the fate of the Federalists and the dodo. He also helped to prevent the party from reverting to the shortsighted isolationism or quasi-isolationism of Harding, Coolidge, and Hoover.

The other side of the ledger is somewhat disturbing. Unsure of himself on a new job, he was at first prepared to lean on Congress rather than lead it. In this sense he was a caretaker and not one of the Modern Presidents at all. He refused to crack down on McCarthyism, even when his own Departments were unfairly assailed. He was forced to deal with unprecedented Democratic majorities in both houses during his last six years, though the liberal Democrats cooperated with him more wholeheartedly than the conservative Republicans. (Senator Lyndon B. Johnson, Democratic majority leader, was known as the second most powerful man in Washington.) Eisenhower finally developed his veto technique to the point where he restored something of a balance between the Legislative and the Executive.

Like Grant, Eisenhower was not interested in the boring details of his job, which he found "fatiguing" as well as "intriguing," and he did not give it everything he had. He ordinarily read newspapers only on weekends. His staff-system methods, which were carried over from military days and which featured one-page summaries of lengthy memoranda, left him with much free time for golf. But they also left a disturbing amount of power in the hands of non-elected officials like Secretary of State Dulles and Assistant President Sherman Adams.

Oddly enough, one of the areas in which Eisenhower was most vulnerable to criticism—the military—happened to be the one in which he could claim the most expertise. He was inclined to tailor the armed forces to the budget rather than to the nation's commitments, and to rely too exclusively on "massive [nuclear] retaliation." In the absence of adequate ground forces and a "flexible response," the alternatives could have been holocaust or humiliation.

The most persistent criticism of Eisenhower is difficult to parry. With remarkable powers of leadership and unprecedented popularity, at first he simply refused to lead, or at any rate to lead dynamically. Generally satisfied with the status quo, as Republican Presidents have traditionally been, he was described as "the bland leading the bland." Though a fighter by profession, he ducked a mud-spattering fight with low-blow Senator McCarthy. Given to preaching high-sounding moralities, he tended to blur major issues. He often revealed that in politics, as in golf, his backswing was stronger than his follow-through. Mildly favoring civil rights for the Negro, he abdicated moral leadership by failing to fight for them, and finally the Little Rock crisis caught up with him.

A great personality, Eisenhower hoarded his popularity rather than expending it to achieve his ends. Re-elected by the largest popular-vote margin up to that point in our history, he could have brought much greater pressure to bear on Congress than he did. He almost certainly could have swung the election of Richard M. Nixon as his successor if he had come out for him earlier and more emphatically, though he did more than was initially planned. The result was that he left his adopted party in the hands of the opposition—what he later called a "hit in the solar plexus with a ball bat." His feat of winning re-election in 1956 by an overwhelming margin while the Republicans were losing both houses of Congress would indicate that the voters were not voting for party government at all, but for a father figure—or the Cult of Personality. "Ike" was so likable as to raise doubts as to the toughness of his moral fiber. He was a soothing-syrup President who promoted a dangerous feeling of complacency and euphoria by radiating goodwill and good intentions, while sweeping certain bothersome problems under the rug.

It is unfair to say that the only command the dazzling general ever gave was to mark time, and that he "benignly ruled" over the Great Postponement. About halfway through his eight years he was stricken with three major illnesses, and did not have the vigor thereafter to be more than a part-time President. After the departure of Dulles and Adams, the "New Eisenhower" put on a commendable display of energy in his last two years, and with growing self-assurance did more governing and less golfing. He became his own President. If he achieved no sensational successes, he made no catastrophic blunders, not even in grossly mishandling the U-2 spy-plane affair. His latter-day goodwill tours elicited fantastic out-pourings of adoration from India to Europe, but stirred up un-realizable expectations of aid. Critics argued that stagecraft was no substitute for statecraft—tough, old-fashioned negotiation.

The Democratic jeer about "eight long years of golfing and goofing," of puttering and putting, is palpably cruel. As a "constitu-tional monarch," Eisenhower reigned too much and ruled too little. But he turned out to be a competent President, far better than his fellow West Pointer, U. S. Grant, the only other Republican ever to serve two full terms. The pity is that he might have been, had he chosen to be, a truly distinguished leader who "made things happen" in the fields of education, civil rights, health insurance, and other areas. Historians will almost certainly never give him as high a mark as the voters did,[2] but perhaps we ought to be grateful that this untrained soldier and popular idol turned out to be an eminently respectable and respected President, remembered for his dignity, decency, and dedication. The Schlesinger experts, with their Demo-cratic coloration, put him near the bottom of the Average group, just above blundering Andrew Johnson. In my judgment, he belongs at least several notches higher.

JOHN FITZGERALD KENNEDY (1961–1963)

Perspective is too short, the term was too short, the shock of death was too great, the growth of the legend too rapid to permit a satisfying evaluation of Kennedy. If he had served eight full years, as seemed in the cards, he probably would be ranked by the experts (mostly fellow Democrats) as one of our more successful Presidents, perhaps a Near Great or even a Great.[3] He grew visibly and im-

[2] Rexford G. Tugwell, distinguished political scientist and earlier one of FDR's brain trusters, records: "Neither Truman nor Eisenhower had the re-motest chance of being listed in the future as among the more competent Presidents. . . ." *The Enlargement of the Presidency* (1960), p. 461.

[3] Arthur M. Schlesinger, Jr., in his *A Thousand Days* (1965), refrains from a categorical evaluation, though his admiration is evident. Theodore C. Sorensen, in his *Kennedy* (1965), p. 758, concludes that "the man was greater than the legend," and that he could not be ranked below "any of the great men who have held the Presidency in this century." This would include Wilson and Franklin Roosevelt.

pressively before our eyes during his turbulent Thousand Days
(actually 1,037). As a thoughtful intellectual rather than an arm-
flailing activist, as a man of ideals as much as of deeds, he was a
symbol of what might have been rather than what actually was.
His reach, like Wilson's, exceeded his grasp; he planted seeds of
hope but did not live to reap the full harvest. One fellow Harvard
man remarked that he was great not for what he did but for "what
he was about to do."

As fate would have it, the Kennedy administration did not fully
measure up to the eloquent pronouncements associated with the
New Frontier. There were always roadblocks in the form of "special
circumstances." The Congress was strongly Democratic, but conservative Southern Democrats locked arms with conservative
Northern Republicans in an "unholy alliance" to block some of
Kennedy's most urgent reformist legislation. The "Box Score," as
published in the *Congressional Quarterly,* shows that by October 9,
1963 (six weeks before the shooting), when the first session of the
88th Congress might normally have adjourned, it had approved
only 37 of Kennedy's 405 legislative requests. Some of the bogged-
down bills no doubt would have passed in time, but the tax-reduc-
tion and tax-reform bill (with reform neatly excised) was bottle-
necked in a seniority-strangled Congress. So was the crucial civil
rights legislation. The foreign aid authorization bill was being
butchered. Federal aid to education had resulted in only patchwork
legislation, while medicare for the aged, already defeated in the
previous Congress, was neatly shelved, to Kennedy's deep mortifica-
tion. A Gallup poll had only 55 percent of the respondents approving of his stewardship shortly before his murder.

All this emphasis on the Box Score is not only misleading but
downright harmful. A President who is unduly sensitive about his
batting average will be tempted to recommend only reasonably sure
things. Kennedy, who realistically concluded that proposals had to
be put into the pipeline if they were ever to emerge as laws, presented an extraordinary number of requests—1,054 in three years.
Perhaps too much emphasis has been placed on his disappointments.
His two Congresses were not do-nothing Congresses. They passed a
surprising amount of constructive legislation, especially if one
counts the measures enacted after the shock of his death. But

Kennedy was clearly losing momentum at the end, in part because
the more pressing measures had already been passed.[4]

It is true that Congress was cantankerous, but Kennedy, never in
full rapport with it, did not dangle the carrot and apply the stick
with consummate skill. He prodded rather than led. He demanded
both a tax cut and tax reform, and then scuttled reform before the
battle was fairly joined. He requested foreign aid, but indicated that
he would settle for a bone-deep cut (which he got). His angry
outburst against the steel companies for collusively raising their
prices was understandable and to a large degree justifiable, but it
had the unhappy effect of unsettling and antagonizing the business
community. He favored civil rights, but rather too quietly and too
late, because of the delicate political balance in Congress. The
Negroes finally took to the streets and a full-throated revolution
burst about his head.

In foreign affairs, the Bay of Pigs fiasco in Cuba got the administration off to an incredibly bad start, and probably convinced
Moscow that the young man lacked nerve. He faced down one of the
periodic Soviet bluffs over Berlin by calling up the reservists, perhaps unnecessarily, and thus intensified the crisis atmosphere. He
backed the United Nations in its much-criticized anti-Communist
operation in the Congo. His Alliance for Progress in Latin America
was an imaginative and neighborly concept which at first progressed
only limpingly, but his Peace Corps proved to be a resounding
success, and a relatively inexpensive one at that. Probably his most
momentous long-range decision was the one in 1961 to implement
further the Eisenhower policy and commit a sizeable number of
military "advisers" to South Vietnam. Virtually all of the chronic
crisis points remained when he was shot, only the spotlight had
shifted from Berlin to Southeast Asia.

Kennedy's finest hour came when he manfully faced up to nuclear
annihilation by the Soviets during the Cuban crunch of October,
1962, which was probably brought on in part by his fumbling of the
Bay of Pigs. He then came of age as a statesman. But when the

[4] The *Congressional Quarterly* (November 22, 1963, the day of Kennedy's
death) shows that of 25 "major" proposals, final action had been taken on only
6. Much depends on who defines "major." A summary prepared under Democratic auspices concludes that of 53 "major" recommendations in 1961, 33 were
enacted into law; of 54 in 1962, 40 were enacted into law. See *Senate Document* No. 53, 88th Cong., 1st sess.

dust had settled, Cuba was more firmly under the Communist heel than ever. The nuclear test-ban treaty and the "hot line" to Moscow, both of which followed the October sigh of relief, were steps forward, but they had no technical relation whatever to disarmament. Kennedy's grand design for an economically integrated United States of Europe, with the United States of America as senior partner, was bound to run into France's President de Gaulle sooner or later. But Kennedy's solo dealings with Britain over nuclear weapons, to the exclusion of France, could hardly fail to raise Gallic hackles.

Yet the youthful President had brains, wit, elegance, and gallantry to such a degree that foreigners, hardly less than Americans, mourned his death. Both he and his wife were glamorous thoroughbreds. He proved that a Catholic can be trusted to govern the nation in the interests of the American people and not of the Vatican: mass was held in the White House only once, the day of his funeral. He will be remembered perhaps more for what he championed than for what he achieved: the obligation to public service, the welfare of the underprivileged, the dignity and equality of man, the relaxation of tensions among nations, and an end to the mass insanity of war. His tragic death shocked the nation and the Congress into greater movement, and to this extent his influence extended—and will continue to extend—beyond the grave.

LYNDON BAINES JOHNSON (1963–   )

As for Lyndon Johnson, we lack both perspective and a complete record. Only a tentative assessment is possible.

The tall Texan has displayed an almost pathological desire to be judged great, and if he does not suffer another heart attack or break himself down with overwork, he may well attain his goal. Although a half-forgotten Vice President in 1963, he grasped the falling torch from Kennedy and engineered an amazingly smooth transfer of power—all in good taste. As usual, the office dignified the man, and Johnson's hog-calling oratory, which hitherto had tended to be of the "howdy, you-all" type, took on greater sobriety and dignity, as befitted a reflective statesman. He lacked the photogenic glamor of a Franklin Roosevelt or a John F. Kennedy, but he was effective on television in projecting the image of a prudent, humble, compassionate, and knowledgeable leader who knew where he was going. Yet many Republican critics found his presentations too patronizing, too evasive, too emotional, too pious, too honey-mouthed, too "corny."

Johnson, the White House whirlwind, answered every definition of a "strong" President. He shone as the activist, the man in motion, rather than the man of meditation. If Kennedy made men think, Johnson made them act. As "Mr. Maneuver," he coaxed, flattered, prodded, and arm-twisted Congress into action. Within an incredibly short time he induced that balky body to pass an impressive number of Kennedy's key measures that had been bottled up for many months. (Possibly he was determined to show up his predecessor and invite comparisons with Franklin Roosevelt's marvelous One Hundred Days, as indeed he did.) An able administrator who chose able appointees, he proceeded to "Johnsonize" and Texanize his inherited regime and burn the LBJ brand on it. No one could doubt who was President: in fact, critics complained of the one-man rodeo. So impressive was his initial constructive leadership that eleven months after having inherited the office he was elected in his own right by an unprecedented popular majority, accompanied by overwhelming majorities in Congress. The result, of course, was in part due to an ineffective, Goldwaterized opposition.

A middle-of-the-road-hog, Johnson left only the gutters for the extreme right and the extreme left. Ever striving for a "consensus"— a "Consensuscrat" rather than a Democrat—he proclaimed himself to be President of all the people. He achieved his goal so spectacularly in 1964 that he united behind him not only labor but a large part of the Republican business community. Relatively few loathed him; relatively few really loved him. Ever-friendly, folksy ("howdy, folks"), and accessible, he snake-charmed unbelievers in a series of White House dinners and other mammoth social affairs, at which he danced coltishly with the lady guests. His compulsive desire to be liked led him to old-fashioned baby kissing while on the campaign trail, as well as to overeager "pressing the flesh," despite bleeding hands and the risk of assassination.

Johnson's capacity to secure constructive action through compromise, perfected during his many years as Senate majority leader, carried over to the presidential chair. "Come now, and let us reason together," was his favorite admonition (from Isaiah 1:18). Much of his high-powered legislative engineering was done over the telephone; indeed, Johnson's unstinted use of the instrument established new records. All these devices enabled him to win party leadership and national leadership to a degree that invited comparison with the nation's Greats. He even contrived an aid-to-public-education bill which, after nearly twenty years of deadlock, was acceptable to the supporters of Catholic parochial schools.

On the debit side lay his excessive attention to detail, his prodigal expenditure of energy, and his intensity of emotion. He was so determined to "range boss" almost everything that he reminded one of Polk, who had virtually killed himself with overwork. His days were push, push, push. But Johnson so loved his job that he derived inspiration and relaxation from it: it was his consuming hobby. His frenetic movements bothered the press corps, who were hard put to keep up with him, as did his excessive thinness of skin regarding criticism. The newsmen were also disturbed by his withholding news (bombings of Laos) and by his sugarcoating or warping disagreeable news regarding Vietnam. All this was in the manner of his political "daddy," Franklin Roosevelt, whose old-fashioned New Deal he spectacularly expanded, especially in his elected term.

A superb professional politician, worthy to be bracketed with the greatest, Johnson retained some of the superslickness of the Senate majority leader—"the Johnson treatment." Critics could not completely forget his reputation as a wheeler-dealer in the Senate, and his lack of candor in later covering up the Bobby Baker scandal and other embarrassments. Enough dirt was swept under the White House rug, charged Senator Goldwater in 1964, to qualify for the soil bank.

Johnson's compulsion to be loved, always to win and to win big, resulted in an unseemly amount of self-advertising. Eager to squeeze every ounce of credit for his achievements, and evidently not fearing the dangers of "overexposure," he would rush to the television camera at the drop of a ten-gallon hat. The classic case, on the eve of the election of 1964, was the air strike against North Vietnam, which, to the possible advantage of the enemy, he advertised an hour or so before it happened. In these operations he undertook the backbreaking task of being both field marshal and top sergeant.

In foreign affairs, Johnson was evidently less at home than in domestic affairs, as was true of Lincoln, Washington, and most others, and here he suffered his heaviest criticism. He had the intellectual capacity, when he had the time, to do his homework. His widening of the war in South Vietnam, to which he was largely committed by his two predecessors, received strong initial backing in Congress and with the public, despite vehement protests from the intellectuals, pacifists, and the left-wing world.

The dogs of criticism were also aroused in 1965 by Johnson's sudden dispatching of troops to Santo Domingo, probably more to avert a possible Communist take-over than to protect American lives. Such iron-knuckled treatment was in plain violation of America's solemn commitments under the United Nations Charter and the Organization of American States, but time was precious, and Johnson appears to have been grievously misled by American officials on the scene. This reversion to "gunboat diplomacy," with its reversal of the non-interventionism proclaimed by his "daddy" Franklin Roosevelt in 1933, resulted in another vehement outcry, especially in Latin America and the Communist world. But Johnson, with an unwavering eye on the polls, mustered 76 percent support, according to Dr. Gallup. The American people evidently preferred, with Castro's Communized Cuba just over the horizon, to shoot first and ask questions afterward, in the quick-draw Texas tradition. Johnson himself declared that he was not going to sit back in a "rocking chair"—perhaps a Freudian reference to Kennedy and the Bay of Pigs—and let another Cuba come into being. Here was the Churchillian man of action—no appeaser of Communism—and semi-ironic cheers arose from the Goldwaterites, whom the Johnsonites in 1964 had accused of being "trigger-happy."

Presidents are more likely to be judged great if they contrive catchy brand names. Johnson came up with the Great Society—presumably borrowed from the Englishman Graham Wallas' socialist book, *The Great Society* (1914)—in which there would be less poverty and more equality. Great Presidents generally have had big wars, and with the escalation of bombing and shooting in South Vietnam, Johnson may enjoy this added advantage as he eagerly seeks an honored place beside Lincoln, Wilson, and Franklin Roosevelt. "What Lyndon wants, Lyndon gets," it was said. And if he can avoid a physical breakdown or an economic depression, he may conceivably get there yet. If crisis times make great men, he is well on his way to greatness.

This is the record. It is cne of which America on the whole can be proud. Even though scholars cannot measure presidential greatness with exactitude, or even agree that it has existed in certain Presidents, we must concede that the roster includes an impressively large number of able men. Some of them were conspicuously weaker than others, but none was an outright scoundrel. Even the scandal-smirched Grant and Harding never profited personally, so it seems, from the thievery that went on under their insensitive noses.

The record is all the more remarkable when we note that in a population of about two hundred million there are only a few thousand men who could even be seriously considered as presidential timber. Almost everybody is automatically ruled out by the Constitution, political tradition, or voter preference. Specific barriers include youth (pre-thirty-five), foreign birth, female sex, dark color, physical and mental disabilities, colorless or offensive personality, dubious character, lack of oratorical talents, unpopular religion, distasteful ideologies, unsuitable occupations, unsavory business connections, insufficient education, inadequate political experience, small-state or sure-state residence, and minority party affiliation. Only a relative handful of men—a survival of the fittest—can clear all these hurdles, plus others.

The Founding Fathers of 1787 wrought wiser than they knew when they created the presidential office.

The Bias of Historians

As a kind of follow-up to the Schlesinger polls, I conducted an informal poll of my own. I made contact with friends or acquaintances in the history departments of some thirty leading universities, either personally or by letter. I asked whether a majority of the instructors teaching American history in these institutions were Democrats or Republicans. With the exception of one evenly balanced department and one pro-Republican department, in every instance a clear majority of the teachers presenting American history was Democratic. In many cases the majority was overwhelming; in several cases the group was unanimously Democratic. Even where the members were Republicans, they were inclined to be liberals and to favor Hamiltonian means to achieve Jeffersonian ends.

My next query was: Why should there be this disproportion of Democrats? I received many acute observations and a few plain guesses.

Historians are inclined to applaud progress, including experimentation: without movement or change there can be little history to record—or teach. The Democratic party is more actively identified than its chief rival with sweeping programs of social and economic betterment, whether New Freedoms, New Deals, Fair Deals, New Frontiers, or Great Societies. Not since Theodore Roosevelt thundered out of the White House in 1909 have we had a Republican administration zealously dedicated to reform. Certainly the conservative administrations of Harding, Coolidge, and Hoover were enough to alienate those voters who were concerned with social and economic change.

Many of the teachers of American history today were impressionable, even impoverished, youths in the depression era of Franklin Roosevelt; some were direct beneficiaries of federal relief measures. New Deal nostalgia further promotes the conviction that the Democratic party is the party of progress—the refuge of the humanitarian, the reformer, and the thinker who has caught a vision of a better tomorrow.

The Republican party, with its big-business orientation, is more inclined to be anti-intellectual. We recall President-General Eisenhower's definition of an intellectual as "a man who takes more words than necessary to tell us more than he knows." From the days of ex-Professor Wilson's New Freedom, beginning in 1913, the Democratic party has enjoyed a strong appeal to the intelligentsia. This was especially marked in the heyday of Franklin Roosevelt's New Deal and John F. Kennedy's New Frontier, when brain trusters and other egghead professors were welcome in Washington.

Historians also tend to be internationally minded. The isolationist Republican party of Harding, Coolidge, and Hoover turned its back on the internationalism of Republicans like James G. Blaine, John Hay, and Theodore Roosevelt. This was conspicuously true of the Republican reaction to the League of Nations, which generally attracted the intellectuals. The Democratic party of Woodrow Wilson, Franklin Roosevelt, Harry Truman, John F. Kennedy, and Lyndon B. Johnson displayed a higher degree of outer-world mindedness than its opponent.

Nor are academicians immune to economic motivations. The Republican party, with considerable warrant, has long been regarded as the rich man's party. Will Rogers, the rope-twirling "poet lariat" of the prosperous 1920's, once quipped that when a Democrat scraped together ten dollars he became a Republican. Teachers in the relatively low-salaried academic world, especially the lower ranks, tend to identify themselves with the party of the forgotten man, who was a special concern of Democrats like Thomas Jefferson, Andrew Jackson, and Franklin Roosevelt. The observation is frequently made that university schools of law and business, often with higher salaries than those in the social sciences, generally line up with the Republican party. Well-paid college administrators, many of them resolute Republicans cultivating rich Republican donors, likewise arouse resentment among ill-paid and often overworked underlings.

Other influences also operate. Historians in the South, especially those born and reared there, have associated most comfortably with the Democratic party. Ever since the days of Thomas Jefferson and his opposition to the Alien Law of 1798, the Democrats have tended to roll out the welcome mat for immigrants. Foreign-born scholars, some of the Jewish faith, find the Democratic party more hospitable. The deep concern—or at least politically profitable concern—of the New Deal for minority groups, including Negroes, has also borne belated fruit.

Whatever the reasons, many college teachers of American history unquestionably cherish a strong pro-liberal, pro-Democratic bias, whether subtle or overt. "History professors are notoriously pink," wrote one of my students who had probably come from an ultra-conservative Republican home. The historian Dr. Samuel E. Morison observed in 1950 that fifty years earlier practically all general histories of the United States presented the "Federalist-Whig-Republican point of view." Fifty years later practically all espoused the "Jefferson-Jackson-F. D. Roosevelt line." *American Historical Review,* LVI (January, 1951), p. 272.

Political scientists reveal the same general pattern. A systematic questioning of 213 of them revealed that about three fourths are Democrats; this trend has been especially marked since the days of Herbert Hoover. In general Democrats are younger, have lower academic rank, and teach in larger institutions. The same can evidently be said of American historians. See H. A. Turner, C. G. McClintock, and C. B. Spaulding, "The Political Party Affiliation of American Political Scientists," *Western Political Quarterly,* XVI (1963), 650–65.

Is the Presidency a Killing Job?

Alarmists often describe the presidency as a killing job—a virtual death sentence, or at least a shortener of life. They point a warning finger at the undeniable fact that the early incumbents, especially those to the 1840's, lived considerably longer on the average than those of the 20th century, even though life expectancy at birth was much less. (In 1789 it was about thirty-four years for white males; now it is about double that figure.) The implication is that today only Presidents with the constitution of an ox can survive, much less do a creditable job.

One drawback is that we do not yet have an adequate sample from which to draw conclusions. Only twenty-eight Presidents have died of natural causes; and three more are still living (counting Lyndon B. Johnson) and pushing the recent average age up to a more reassuring level.[1] Of the first eight, only George Washington, who died at sixty-seven, failed to live beyond his life expectancy at the time of inauguration. (In 1789 he was fifty-seven, and should have lived about seventeen more years; he actually lived only ten.) The seven who succeeded him all died in their seventies or eighties, except John Adams, who set an all-time record of ninety years plus 297 days.

These figures reveal that by the luck of the draw the nation just happened to get seven exceptionally tough men among the first eight. Their average life span was seventy-nine, although, as we have noted, life expectancy at birth in 1789 was less than half that figure. The first eight incumbents outlived the members of the First Congress by an average of more than ten years. Not until the eleventh President, James K. Polk, did we have one whose life span did not exceed that of his Vice President. The first eight were inaugurated at a considerably later average age than subsequent Presidents, and if a man lived to be sixty in those disease-

[1] The figures used in this section exclude Presidents killed in office. In the comparisons with Vice Presidents I have also excluded men who served both as Vice President and President.

ridden days, the chances were rather good that he would reach his seventies. Indeed, life expectancy at age sixty was almost the same in 1789 as it is today, even with vastly improved medical science.

In the 20th century, and also by the luck of the draw, we managed to elect some stock that was less tough. This was notably true of men like Wilson (a frail youth), Harding, and Coolidge. Theodore Roosevelt was a sickly child, and probably would have been put to death as an infant in ancient Sparta. The average for the later comers is rising, for Hoover attained ninety, Truman was eighty-one in 1965 (his mother died at ninety-four), and Eisenhower, at seventy-five in 1965, was still remarkably vigorous (his mother died at eighty-four and his father at seventy-nine).

Certain other statistics raise doubts as to the "killing" nature of the office.

On the average, the Presidents who died natural deaths exceeded the life span of their Vice Presidents by a considerable margin. Seven Vice Presidents have died in office of natural causes, but only three Presidents.

By a narrow margin, more Presidents than not have exceeded the life span of their chief rival of the opposition party. (Here we take into account their first election to the presidency.)

If we single out the front-runner on the first ballot in the convention that nominated the winning candidate, we find that about as many Presidents outlived their chief rival as did not.

The Presidents, by a nearly two-to-one margin, have surpassed the life span of their wives, including second wives in four cases. Yet since 1789, when reliable statistics were first kept, women have enjoyed an increasingly longer life expectancy than men.

The Presidents, by nearly a two-to-one margin, have lived beyond the average age of their two parents.

No President has died of ulcers, or is even known to have suffered from them.

Overweight is supposed to shorten life, yet the two most corpulent— Grover Cleveland at about 260 pounds and William H. Taft at 350— lived to respectable old ages, seventy-one and seventy-two, respectively. Despite the double burdens of their bodies and their office, they exceeded life expectancy at the time of inauguration (not the time of birth) by a modest margin.

Exercise is supposed to prolong life. But Theodore Roosevelt, preferring to burn out rather than rust out, burned himself out at sixty. Franklin Roosevelt, who was virtually immobilized by poliomyelitis for the last twenty-four years of his life, outlived his cousin by three years.

Overwork and little exercise are supposed to shorten life. Yet probably no incumbent worked harder under more stress than did Herbert

Hoover, who lived past his ninetieth birthday and came close to surpassing John Adams' all-time record. Calvin Coolidge took life casually, napped often, exercised a little on an electric horse, and died at sixty, twelve years short of life expectancy at inauguration.

Frustration and disappointment are also commonly supposed to shorten life. This may explain why the Vice Presidents and the defeated candidates did not live longer than the Presidents themselves, who had the moral tonic of accomplishment and success. Yet two of the unhappiest and most frustrated of the Presidents were John Adams and Herbert Hoover, to say nothing of James Madison and John Quincy Adams. The first two reached ninety, and the other two lived to be eighty-five and eighty, respectively.

No Presidents evidently enjoyed their job more than Theodore Roosevelt and Franklin Roosevelt, yet both fell eight years short of life expectancy at the time of their first inauguration. The second Roosevelt, one should add, served more than twelve years under unprecedented strain.

Again we must note that twenty-eight Presidents are too small a sample from which to draw satisfying conclusions. But enough data are available to challenge the cliché about the lethal nature of the job. The manager of a Chinese laundry can kill himself if he does not take time out for proper food, rest, relaxation, and medical care.

A politician might well live longer as President than as an unsuccessful candidate. His White House day is well organized, he has a large staff to attend to his needs, and minor frustrations are reduced to a minimum, with limousines, ships, helicopters, and airplanes. In addition, regular periods are normally set aside for relaxation, whether on presidential yachts or hideaway Shangri-las (Hoover's Rapidan, Eisenhower's Camp David). How many business tycoons can take a two-hour nap whenever they desire? To top it off, a White House physician rides constant herd on the President, who has on tap, at government expense, the finest medical technicians in the country. Without them, the stricken Wilson and Eisenhower might well have died in office. Eisenhower's opponent in 1952 and 1956, Adlai Stevenson, died at an early sixty-five, while the ageing ex-President, whose early demise Stevenson had foreseen in 1956, continued to enjoy life.

The daily challenges and high-pressure activities of the presidency may actually act as a desirable kind of stimulant. Physicians are constantly urging retired businessmen, among others, to keep active. There are too many tragic cases of topflight executives who fall to pieces after retiring to a life of carpet-slipper ease.

But the Chief Magistracy *is* a killing job when we consider the danger from an assassin's bullet or bomb. Four incumbents have been shot, all fatally. At least four other Presidents or Presidents-elect have been shot at or narrowly escaped would-be assassins. Presidents-elect Hayes and Franklin Roosevelt experienced close calls, and President Lincoln had his stovepipe hat shot off on one occasion. President Jackson was attacked at point-blank range by a would-be assassin whose two pistols failed to discharge. The chances of a dual misfire have been reckoned as one in 125,000. A guard protecting President Truman was killed during an assassination attempt by Puerto Rican assailants. Nor does this list take into account the numerous bombs that have been intercepted in the White House mail room.

Perhaps the most killing part of the job is really not a part of the job at all. Especially exhausting are the grueling primaries and the inhumanly overlong presidential campaign, as Kennedy, among others, discovered.

On presidential assassinations, see R. J. Donovan, *The Assassins* (1952). Material on presidential longevity appears in Louis I. Dublin, *et al., Length of Life* (rev. ed., 1949); Metropolitan Life Insurance Company, *Statistical Bulletin,* No. 10, Vol. 27, October, 1946; F. L. Griffin, "Mortality of the U.S. Presidents and Certain Other Federal Officers," *Transactions of the Actuarial Society of America,* XLI (October, 1940), pp. 487–91. The present writer's researches resulted in conclusions that differ from some of these findings.

APPENDIX C

General Bibliography and Notes

The following titles represent a distillation which emphasizes the approach of the historian rather than that of the political scientist. They may serve as an index to the kinds of materials used by the author and as a guide to further reading.

Valuable overviews are Louis W. Koenig, *The Chief Executive* (1964); Clinton Rossiter, *The American Presidency* (rev. ed., 1960); James M. Burns, *Presidential Government* (1966); Wilfred E. Binkley, *The Man in the White House* (1958) and *The Powers of the President* (1937); Edward S. Corwin and Louis W. Koenig, *The Presidency Today* (1956); and Francis H. Heller, *The Presidency: A Modern Perspective* (1960). A full-length older classic is Edward S. Corwin, *The President: Office and Powers* (4th ed., 1957). More interpretive are Sidney Hyman, *The American President* (1954); Harold J. Laski, *The American Presidency* (1940); and Louis Brownlow, *The President and the Presidency* (1949). Old but still of some use is Norman J. Small, *Some Presidential Interpretations of the Presidency* (1932).

The subject is approached from special viewpoints by Herman Finer, *The Presidency: Crisis and Regeneration* (1960); Rexford G. Tugwell, *The Enlargement of the Presidency* (1960) and *How They Became President* (1965); C. P. Patterson, *Presidential Government in the United States* (1947); John C. Long, *The Liberal Presidents* (1948); E. E. Cornwell, Jr., *Presidential Leadership of Public Opinion* (1965); and S. G. Brown, *The American Presidency: Leadership, Partisanship, and Popularity* (1966).

D. B. Johnson and J. L. Walker, eds., *The Dynamics of the American Presidency* (1964), contains many choice items, chiefly articles. A. B. Tourtellot, *The Presidents on the Presidency* (1964), consists mainly of short quotations from the Presidents themselves on key topics.

Eugene H. Roseboom, *A History of Presidential Elections* (rev. ed.,

.1964), outmodes Edward Stanwood's *History of Presidential Elections* (1884).

Entire issues of the following journals are devoted to articles on the presidency: *American Heritage*, Vol. XV, August, 1964; *Annals of the American Academy*, Vol. CCCVII, September, 1956; *Current History*, Vol. XXV, September, 1953, and Vol. XXXIX, October, 1960; *Journal of Politics*, Vol. XI, February, 1949; *Law and Contemporary Problems*, XXI (Autumn), 1957.

Chapter I.   PRESIDENTIAL CULTS AND CULTISTS

General references are Dixon Wecter, *The Hero in America* (1941); Sidney Hook, *The Hero in History* (1943); Gerald W. Johnson, *American Heroes and Hero Worship* (1943); Marshall W. Fishwick, *American Heroes* (1954); Holman Hamilton, *White House Images and Realities* (1958); William B. Brown, *The People's Choice: The Presidential Image in the Campaign Biography* (1960); Bernard Mayo, *Myths and Men* [Washington, Jefferson] (1959). Relevant articles are Dumas Malone, "When a Legend Becomes a President," *New York Times Magazine*, February 22, 1953, and the same author's "Was Washington the Greatest American?" *ibid.*, February 16, 1958; Reginald C. McGrane, "George Washington: An Anglo-American Hero," *Virginia Magazine of History and Biography*, LXIII (January, 1955), pp. 3–14; C. P. Nettels, "The Washington Theme in American History," *Proceedings of Massachusetts Historical Society*, LXVIII (1952), pp. 171–98; Esmond Wright, "Washington: The Man and the Myth," *History Today*, V (December, 1955), pp. 825–32. On Statuary Hall, consult, "Compilation of Works of Art in the United States Capitol," Joint Committee Print, 82nd Cong., 2nd sess. See also references herein in Biographical Appendix D under Washington, Jefferson, Lincoln, Jackson, Wilson, the two Roosevelts, and Kennedy; and particularly William A. Bryan, *George Washington in American Literature, 1775–1865* (1952).

Chapter II.   THE PEOPLE'S CHOICE

The best book on the subject is Gilbert C. Fite, *Mount Rushmore* (1952). On the New York University Hall of Fame consult Louis A. Banks, *The Story of the Hall of Fame* (1902); Robert U. Johnson, *Your Hall of Fame* (1935); and Theodore Morello, ed., *The Hall of Fame for Great Americans at New York University* (1962). The quotations from Arthur H. Vandenberg, *The Greatest American: Alexander Hamilton* (1921) may be identified by the index. The survey by J. M. Cattell appears as "A Statistical Study of Eminent Men," *Popular Science*

Monthly, LXII (1903), pp. 359–77. The poll on great living Americans appears in *Fortune,* XXVI (November, 1942), p. 14, and is reproduced in Hadley Cantril, ed., *Public Opinion, 1935–1946* (1951), p. 559, where the Gallup poll of January 31, 1945, is also reprinted (pp. 562–63), as is the National Opinion Research Center poll of July, 1945 (p. 565). A Gallup poll published in 1946 (January 3) rated the four greatest Presidents as F. D. Roosevelt (39 percent), Lincoln (37 percent), Washington (15 percent), and Wilson (5 percent) (Cantril, *op. cit.,* p. 590). The abortive Gallup poll of January 20, 1956, was provided by the courtesy of Dr. Gallup. A refinement of the same poll appears in J. M. Burns, *Presidential Government* (1966), p. 100.

Chapter III. THE EXPERTS' CHOICE

The two Schlesinger polls appear in *Life,* XXV (November 1, 1948), pp. 65–66 and later, and in the *New York Times Magazine,* July 29, 1962. They are here reproduced by the courtesy of Dr. Schlesinger. Additional commentary may be found in A. M. Schlesinger, *Paths to the Present* (1949), Chapter V, and in his autobiography, *In Retrospect: The History of a Historian* (1963), pp. 108–10. For a brief but trenchant commentary see C. A. Amlund, "President-Ranking: A Criticism," *Midwest Journal of Political Science,* VIII (1964), pp. 309–15. Personal judgments of the Presidents, without categorical ratings, may be found in R. G. Tugwell, *The Enlargement of the Presidency* (1960) and in Holman Hamilton, *White House Images and Realities* (1958). Relevant also is a series of articles published in 1936 by L. W. Ferguson in *School and Society,* in which the author discusses the changing attitudes of a class at Stanford University toward the ten incumbents from Benjamin Harrison to Franklin Roosevelt. The students came with a partisan bias which was weakened after ten weeks of study. Dr. Clinton Rossiter rated the Presidents in *American Heritage,* VII (April, 1956), pp. 28ff., but his conclusions are somewhat confused by accompanying portraits of the Presidents, the size of which is roughly equated to their greatness. One cannot tell whether these portraits reflect accurately the judgment of the author or the convenience of the layout man. For his more mature conclusions, see Clinton Rossiter, *The American Presidency* (rev. ed., 1960).

Chapter IV. MEASURING THE UNMEASURABLE

The *New York Times Magazine* has published a valuable series of articles on presidential qualifications. Notable among them are H. S. Commager, "What Makes for Presidential Greatness" (July 22, 1945) and "Yardstick for a Presidential Candidate" (October 5, 1947); James Reston, "The Qualities a President Needs" (October 31, 1948); T. V. Smith, "What It Takes to be a Great President" (July 20, 1952); J. M. Burns, "The One Test for the Presidency" (May 1, 1960); Richard Hofstadter, "The Right Man for the Big Job" (April 3, 1960); Sidney Hyman, "Qualities that Make a President" (December 1, 1963). See also Harold Laski, "Qualifications for the Presidency," *Current History*, LI (May, 1940), pp. 28–30; V. L. Albjerg, "Qualities a President Needs," *ibid.*, XXIII (September, 1952), pp. 129–34; Sidney Warren, "How to Pick a President," *Saturday Review*, XLVII (July 4, 1964), pp. 10–13; and Dwight D. Eisenhower, "Six Qualities that Make a President," *Time*, LXXXI (June 14, 1963), p. 28.

Chapter V. THE BARRIERS OF BIAS

On political postage stamps see Douglass Adair, "Trivia III," *William and Mary Quarterly*, 3rd ser., XII (1955), pp. 332–34. For the episode on Wilson at the meeting of the American Historical Association, see *Time*, XLIII (January 10, 1943), p. 23, and the *New York Times*, December 31, 1943, p. 9. Scholarly unobjectivity in World War I is discussed in James R. Mock and Cedric Larson, *Words that Won the War* (1939), Ch. VII, with bibliography. Many books of cartoons are relevant to the presidency but the most useful ones for present purposes are Roger Butterfield, *The American Past* (1947); Ralph H. Gabriel, ed., *The Pageant of America* (15 vols., 1925–1929), especially Vols. VIII and IX; Albert Shaw, *Abraham Lincoln; His Path to the Presidency* (1929) and *Abraham Lincoln; The Year of His Election* (1929); Stefan Lorant, *Lincoln: A Picture Story of His Life* (1957) and *The Life and Times of Theodore Roosevelt* (1959); Albert Shaw, *A Cartoon History of Roosevelt's Career* (1910); and Allan Nevins and Frank Weitenkampf, *A Century of Political Cartoons* (1944). A good defense may be found in R. S. Kirkendall, "Presidential Libraries—One Researcher's Point of View," *American Archivist*, XXV (October, 1962), pp. 441–48. See also H. F. Graff, "Preserving the Secrets of the White House," *New York Times Magazine*, December 29, 1963.

Chapter VI. PRE-PRESIDENTIAL HAPPENSTANCE

For the log-cabin tradition consult William B. Brown, *The People's Choice* (1960) and R. G. Gunderson, *The Log-Cabin Campaign* [1840] (1957). On the importance of a name see H. F. Graff, "Life with Father, the President," *New York Times Magazine*, July 14, 1963. Religion is treated in Berton Dulce and Edward Richter, *Religion and the Presidency* (1962); Michael Williams, *The Shadow of the Pope* (1932), Edmund A. Moore, *A Catholic Runs for President* [1928] (1956); Ruth C. Silva, *Rum, Religion and Votes: 1928 Re-examined* [statistically] (1962). Slanted toward the 1960 campaign are P. H. Odegard, ed., *Religion and Politics* (1960) and Patricia Barrett, *Religious Liberty and the American Presidency* (1963). On the physical size of great men, consult Enoch B. Gowin, *The Executive and His Control of Men* (1915). The literature on the First Ladies is extensive: among the more useful recent publications are Marianne Means, *The Woman in the White House* (1963); Bess Furman, *White House Profile* (1951); Mary O. Whitton, *First First Ladies, 1789–1865* (1948); and Amy L. Jensen's picture book *The White House and Its Thirty-three Families* (1962). For full references on the Presidents' health, see Chapter X.

Chapter VII. PRE-WHITE HOUSE CAREER

For general references consult Biographical Appendix D, especially under Washington, Jackson, Harrison, Taylor, Grant, Eisenhower. See also Dorothy B. Goebel and Julius Goebel, Jr., *Generals in the White House* (1945); F. J. Cavaioli, *West Point and the Presidency* (1962); R. J. Donovan, *PT 109: John F. Kennedy in World War II* (1961); S. P. Huntington, *The Soldier and the State* (1957); A. A. Ekirch, Jr., *The Civilian and the Military* (1956); and Louis Smith, *American Democracy and Military Power* (1951). W. B. Brown, *The People's Choice* (1960), deals with civilian life, including law, against which there has been some prejudice. The value of the governorship as a runway is discussed by D. S. Broder, "What's the Best Road to the White House? (Senator or Governor)," *New York Times Magazine,* September 22, 1964. The writings of the Presidents are listed in J. N. Kane, *Facts About the Presidents* (1959), pp. 286–89 and in A. B. Tourtellot, *The Presidents on the Presidency* (1964), pp. 471–85. For the disputed election of 1824, consult Samuel F. Bemis, *John Quincy Adams and the Union* (1956); for that of 1876, C. V. Woodward, *Reunion and Reaction* (1951). See also Biographical Appendix D for individual Presidents.

Chapter VIII. PRESIDENTIAL FORTUITIES

Consult the listings under the more distinguished Presidents in the Biographical Appendix D. On the accession of Vice Presidents, see P. R. Levin, *Seven by Chance* (1948); L. C. Hatch, *A History of the Vice*

Presidency . . . (1934); Edgar W. Waugh, *Second Consul* (1956); Irving G. Williams, *The Rise of the Vice Presidency* (1956); Donald Young, *American Roulette: The History and Dilemma of the Vice Presidency* (1965). A useful pamphlet bibliography is Dorothy L. C. Tompkins, *The Office of the Vice President* (1957). See also Margaret L. Coit, "Great Presidents Are Lucky Accidents," *Look*, July 14, 1964. On presidential advisers, consult Louis W. Koenig, *The Invisible Presidency* (1960); Richard F. Fenno, *The President's Cabinet: An Analysis in the Period from Wilson to Eisenhower* (1959); likewise the older Mary L. Hinsdale's *A History of the President's Cabinet* (1911); Henry B. Learned's *The President's Cabinet* (1912). See also A. L. and J. L. George, *Woodrow Wilson and Colonel House* (1956); Robert E. Sherwood, *Roosevelt and Hopkins* (1948); Sherman Adams, *Firsthand Report* (1961). On misplaced credit for Hoover, consult G. D. Nash, "Herbert Hoover and the Origins of the Reconstruction Finance Corporation," *Mississippi Valley Historical Review*, XLVI (1959), pp. 455–68. On the background of the Twenty-second Amendment see Charles W. Stein, *The Third-Term Tradition* (1943); Fred Rodell, *Democracy and the Third Term* (1940). For an abortive attempt to repeal the Twenty-second Amendment see *Senate Report*, No. 1200, 86th Cong., 2 sess., and the accompanying *Hearings Before a Subcommittee of the Committee on the Judiciary, United States Senate*, on S.J. Res. 11, Parts I, II. Public opinion, favoring strong Presidents but fearing dictatorship, continues to support the Twenty-second Amendment.

Chapter IX.   THE POST-PRESIDENTIAL GLOW

For individual Presidents, consult Biographical Appendix D. The only general treatment of post-presidential careers is A. E. Martin, *After the White House* (1951). On obsequies, consult Dixon Wecter, *The Hero in America* (1941). For memoirs, see Andrew Hacker, "When Presidents Take Pen in Hand," *New York Times Magazine*, August 27, 1961. See also the autobiographical listings in A. B. Tourtellot, *The Presidents on the Presidency* (1964), pp. 472–85. The fullest list of nicknames may be found in Joseph N. Kane, *Facts About the Presidents* (1959), pp. 279–81. For log-cabin imagery, consult the bibliography for Chapter VI. By far the best collection of campaign slogans appears in George E. Shankle, *American Mottoes and Slogans* (1941). See also Carl Scherf, "Slang, Slogan and Song in American Politics," *Social Studies*, XXV (1934), pp. 424–30; Alice Aycock, "Campaigning with Catchwords," *New York Times Magazine*, November 29, 1959; and H. F. Graff, "From Tippecanoe to Scranton, Too," *ibid.*, July 5, 1964.

Chapter X. BODY AND BRAIN

On health generally, consult Dr. Rudolph Marx, *The Health of the Presidents* (1960) and Dr. Karl C. Wold, *Mr. President—How Is Your Health?* (1948). See also Appendix B: "Is the Presidency a Killing Job?" On hobbies, see Joseph N. Kane, *Facts About the Presidents* (1959); Don Smith, *Peculiarities of the Presidents* (1938).

Anti-intellectualism is discussed briefly in W. B. Brown, *The People's Choice* (1960), and in Richard Hofstadter, *Anti-Intellectualism in American Life* (1963).

Chapter XI. THE TEST OF CHARACTER

Richard L. Tobin's *Decisions of Destiny* (1961) deals journalistically with ten courageous Presidents, including Chester A. Arthur. On the spoils system, gifts, and scandals, see Leonard D. White's exhaustive four volumes on the administrative history of the presidency to 1901. Harding's major scandal is exposed in J. L. Bates, *The Origins of Teapot Dome* (1963) and Burl Noggle, *Teapot Dome* (1962). Sherman Adams' defense of his gift taking may be found in his *Firsthand Report* (1961), Chapter 21. J. Q. Adams' "Corrupt Bargain" is analyzed fully in Samuel F. Bemis, *John Quincy Adams and the Union* (1956). For lack of candor in Polk and Roosevelt, note the titles by McCormac and Burns in Biographical Appendix D. Consult also Sidney Hyman, "What Makes a 'Strong' President?" *New York Times Magazine,* December 13, 1953. See qualifications for Presidents in bibliography for Chapter IV.

Chapter XII. THE PRESIDENTIAL PERSONALITY

For individual Presidents, consult Biographical Appendix D. See also Sam Rayburn, "The Speaker Speaks of Presidents," *New York Times Magazine,* June 4, 1961. On gaffes, read Beverly Smith, Jr., "Things They Wish They Hadn't Said," *Saturday Evening Post,* CCXXXII (September 19, 1959), pp. 26–27, 139–42. Personal revelations by White House employees or associates are in I. H. Hoover, *Forty-two Years in the White House* (1934); Edmund W. Starling, *Starling of the White House* (1946); Ira R. T. Smith and J. A. Morris, *Dear Mr. President* (1949); Edith Helm, *The Captains and the Kings* (1954); and Theodore G. Joslin, *Hoover Off the Record* (1934). There are dozens of books by journalists and others who had personal contacts with the Presidents; for most of them check Oscar Handlin, *et al., Harvard Guide to American History* (1954).

Chapter XIII. TESTS OF TEMPERAMENT

See references for the preceding chapter. For complaints about the burdens of the office, consult A. B. Tourtellot, *The Presidents on the Presidency* (1964), especially Chapter 8. See also R. B. Morris, ed., *Great Presidential Decisions* (rev. ed. 1965), which consists of state papers. For techniques under Kennedy, consult T. C. Sorensen, *Decision Making in the White House* (1963); under Truman and Eisenhower, R. E. Neustadt, *Presidential Power* (1960). Relevant articles are H. J. Morgenthau, "Alone with Himself and History," *New York Times Magazine*, November 13, 1960; Henry Brandon, "Schlesinger at the White House," *Harper's Magazine*, CCXXIX (July, 1964), pp. 55–60. On Congress, consult references for Chapter XVIII and W. E. Binkley, *President and Congress* (1947); A. B. Tourtellot, *The Presidents on the Presidency* (1964); James M. Burns, *The Deadlock of Democracy* (1963); E. Pendleton Herring, *Presidential Leadership: The Political Relations of Congress and the Chief Executive* (1940); Henry C. Black, *Relation of the Executive Power to Legislation* (1919); Joan C. MacLean, ed., *President and Congress* (1955) [bibliography]. For humor, see Herbert Hoover, *Fishing for Fun* (1963); Maxwell Meyersohn, ed., *The Wit and Wisdom of Franklin D. Roosevelt* (1950); Gerald Gardner, ed., *The Quotable Mr. Kennedy* (1962); Bill Adler, ed., *The Kennedy Wit* (1964) and *More Kennedy Wit* (1965). Relevant articles are R. B. Morris, "Presidential Sense of Humor," *New York Times Magazine*, April 30, 1961; H. F. Graff, "Quipmasters of Politics," *ibid.*, September 17, 1961. See also the references on tests for Presidents in Chapter IV.

Chapter XIV. POLITICIAN-IN-CHIEF

Consult individual Presidents in Biographical Appendix D and also General Bibliography at the beginning of this Appendix, especially Wilfred E. Binkley, *The Man in the White House* (1958), Ch. VI, and C. P. Patterson, *Presidential Government in the United States* (1947). Other relevant books are A. B. Tourtellot, *The Presidents on the Presidency* (1964); H. J. Carman and R. H. Luthin, *Lincoln and the Patronage* (1943). Relevant articles are N. A. Graebner, "Political Parties and the Presidency," *Current History*, XXV (September, 1953), pp. 138–43; L. G. Seligman, "The Presidential Office and the President as Party Leader," *Law and Contemporary Problems*, XXI (Autumn, 1956), pp. 724–34; P. H. Odegard, "Presidential Leadership and Party Responsibility," *Annals of the American Academy of Political and Social Science*, CCCVII (September, 1956), pp. 66–81; E. A. Helms, "The President

and Party Politics," *Journal of Politics*, XI (February, 1949), pp. 42–64.
See also the references on qualifications for Presidents in Chapter IV.

Chapter XV. TEACHER- AND PREACHER-IN-CHIEF

See references for Chapter XIII on the Presidents' wit and wisdom.
For presidential messages to Congress, consult S. H. Fersh, *The View
from the White House* (1961); Edward Boykin, *State of the Union*
(1963). See also Louis Filler, ed., *The President Speaks: From William
McKinley to Lyndon B. Johnson* (1964). On ghost-writers, see S. I.
Rosenman, *Working with Roosevelt* (1952). A revealing article is J. H.
and LaWanda Cox, "Andrew Johnson and His Ghost Writers," *Mississippi
Valley Historical Review*, XLVIII (1961), pp. 460–79. A specialized
study is C. A. H. Thomson, *Television and Presidential Politics* (1956).

Chapter XVI. ADMINISTRATOR-IN-CHIEF

See general references at the beginning of this bibliographical Appendix, and consult Leonard D. White's classic four volumes on the
administrative history of the presidency to 1901. Other useful books are
E. Pendleton Herring, *Presidential Leadership* (1940); James Hart, *The
American Presidency in Action, 1789* (1948); and L. L. Henry, *Presi-
dential Transitions* (1960). On presidential disability, see Richard
Hansen, *The Year We Had No President* (1962); Ruth C. Silva, *Presi-
dential Succession* (1951); Richard M. Nixon, *Six Crises* (1962); Gene
Smith, *When the Cheering Stopped* (1964); and Sherman Adams, *First-
Hand Report* (1961).

Chapter XVII. LEADER-IN-CHIEF

See relevant titles for previous chapter. Note also J. P. Harris, *The
Advice and Consent of the Senate* (1953); George F. Milton, *The Use
of Presidential Power, 1789–1943* (1944); and R. E. Neustadt, *Presi-
dential Power* (1960). On the military side, 'see Clarence Berdahl, *War
Powers of the Executive* (1921); Howard White, *Executive Influence in
Determining Military Policy in the United States* (1924); Clinton Rossiter,
Constitutional Dictatorship (1948); Nathan Grundstein, *Presidential
Delegation of Authority in Wartime* (1961) [World Wars I and II];
Louis W. Koenig, *The Presidency and the Crisis: Powers of the Office
from the Invasion of Poland to Pearl Harbor* (1944); Ernest R. May, ed.,
The Ultimate Decision: The President as Commander-in-Chief (1960).
On Lincoln, consult T. Harry Williams, *Lincoln and His Generals* (1952);
B. J. Hendrick, *Lincoln's War Cabinet* (1946); Robert V. Bruce, *Lincoln*

and the Tools of War (1956). Useful articles are Esther Albjerg, "Our Changing Concept of Leadership," *Current History*, XXV (September, 1953), pp. 157–62; Allan Nevins, "Leadership: A Mysterious Quality," *New York Times Magazine*, August 9, 1953; Andrew Hacker, "When the President Goes to the People," *ibid.*, June 10, 1962; Douglass Cater, "How a President Helps Form Public Opinion," *ibid.*, February 26, 1961.

Chapter XVIII. FURTHER TESTS OF LEADERSHIP

On the Constitution, see R. P. Longaker, *The Presidency and Individual Liberties* (1961); J. G. Randall, *Constitutional Problems Under Lincoln* (rev. ed., 1964); Clinton Rossiter, *The Supreme Court and the Commander-in-Chief* (1951); G. A. Schubert, *The Presidency in the Courts* (1957). On Congress, see references for Chapter XIII and also consult L. H. Chamberlain, *The President, Congress, and Legislation* (1946) and N. W. Polsby, *Congress and the Presidency* (1964). On the veto, refer to C. J. Zinn, *The Veto Power of the President* (1951). On foreign affairs, see E. S. Corwin, *The President's Control of Foreign Relations* (1917); Alexander DeConde, *The American Secretary of State* (1962); P. H. Nitze, "The Modern President as a World Figure," *Annals of the American Academy of Political and Social Science,* CCCVII (1956), pp. 114–23. The most recent book is Robert Rienow and Leona T. Rienow, *The Lonely Quest: The Evolution of Presidential Leadership* (1966).

Chapter XIX. FINAL TESTS OF GREATNESS

Sidney Warren's *The President as World Leader* (1964) ranges from Theodore Roosevelt to recent times. The best book on abuse is D. C. Coyle, *Ordeal of the Presidency* (1960); on the press generally, James E. Pollard, *The Presidents and the Press* (1947). See also E. E. Cornwell, Jr., *Presidential Leadership of Public Opinion* (1965). The press conferences are dealt with in Merriman Smith, *"Thank You Mr. President"* (1946). See also Douglass Cater, "The President and the Press," *Annals of the American Academy of Political and Social Science,* CCCVII (September, 1956), pp. 55–65. The myth of the silent Coolidge is disposed of by E. E. Cornwell, Jr., "Coolidge and Presidential Leadership," *Public Opinion Quarterly,* XXI (1957), pp. 265–78. Consult also Sidney Hyman, "Presidential Popularity Is Not Enough," *New York Times Magazine,* August 12, 1962. For the Vice Presidents, refer to the bibliography for Chapter VIII.

For Chapters XX–XXII, see Appendix D: Biographical Appendix.

Biographical Appendix

The following list is highly refined. The printed letters, public papers, and other published writings of the Presidents are generally not included, except for diaries. For a complete list of such materials, published and unpublished, see Arthur B. Tourtellot, *The Presidents on the Presidency* (1964), pp. 471–85; for the published writings of the Presidents, see Joseph N. Kane, *Facts About the Presidents* (1959), pp. 286–89.

Useful brief assessments of Jefferson, Jackson, Lincoln, the two Roosevelts, Wilson, and Hoover appear in Richard Hofstadter, *The American Political Tradition and the Men Who Made It* (1948); of Washington, Jefferson, Jackson, Lincoln, Grant, and the two Roosevelts in Dixon Wecter, *The Hero in America* (1941); of Washington, Adams, Jefferson, Jackson, Polk, Lincoln, Cleveland, Wilson, and the two Roosevelts in Morton Borden, ed., *America's Ten Greatest Presidents* (1961); of Wilson, Harding, Coolidge, Hoover, the two Roosevelts, Truman, and Eisenhower in *Current History*, XXXIX (October, 1960), pp. 198–236; and of Hoover, Roosevelt, Truman, and Eisenhower in Walter Johnson, *1600 Pennsylvania Avenue: Presidents and the People, 1929–1959* (1960).

GEORGE WASHINGTON. A penetrating brief appraisal is Marcus Cunliffe, *George Washington: Man and Monument* (1958); the most detailed biography, D. S. Freeman, *George Washington* (7 vols., 1948–1957, the last volume having been completed by J. A. Carroll and Mary W. Ashworth). The older one-volume lives by John C. Fitzpatrick (1933), Louis M. Sears (1932), and Nathaniel W. Stephenson and W. H. Dunn (1940) are still of some value. The myth breeding biography by Mason L. (Parson) Weems, first appearing in 1809, is still in print. Frankly debunking are the lives by W. E. Woodward and the three volumes by Rupert Hughes, which reach 1781 and become increasingly favorable. See also paragraph two of Appendix D (above) and the references (above) for Chapter I.

JOHN ADAMS. The best one-volume life is Gilbert Chinard, *Honest John Adams* (1933); the best two-volume life is Page Smith, *John Adams* (1962). Special aspects are treated in S. G. Kurtz, *The Presidency of John Adams* (1957); Manning J. Dauer, *The Adams Federalists* (1953); and Zoltan Haraszti, *John Adams and the Prophets of Progress* (1952). See also paragraph two of Appendix D (above).

THOMAS JEFFERSON. An excellent one-volume biography is Gilbert Chinard, *Thomas Jefferson* (1929); see also Nathan Schachner, *Thomas Jefferson* (2 vols., 1951). The multi-volume life by Dumas Malone, the first volume of which appeared in 1948, has in its third volume (1962) reached the presidency. Claude Bowers' trilogy is highly favorable to Jefferson: *Jefferson and Hamilton* (1925); *Jefferson in Power* (1936); and *The Young Jefferson* (1945). Leonard W. Levy, *Jefferson and Civil Liberties* (1963) is severely critical. Revealing studies are M. D. Peterson, *The Jefferson Image in the American Mind* (1960) and Charles M. Wiltse, *The Jeffersonian Tradition in American Democracy* (1935). See also paragraph two of Appendix D (above).

JAMES MADISON. The six-volume life by Irving Brant (1941–1961) is exhaustive but worshipful. The most recent one-volume biography is Abbot E. Smith, *James Madison: Builder* (1937); that by Gaillard Hunt (1902) is outmoded. Irving Brant has a highly favorable analysis of Madison as a war leader in the *American Heritage*, X (October, 1959), pp. 46–47 and later; Marcus Cunliffe treats the same theme more soberly in Ernest R. May, ed., *The Ultimate Decision* (1960).

JAMES MONROE. The best biographies are William P. Cresson, *James Monroe* (1946) and Arthur Stryon, *The Last of the Cocked Hats* (1945).

JOHN QUINCY ADAMS. The two brilliant biographical volumes by Samuel F. Bemis—*John Quincy Adams and the Foundations of American Foreign Policy* (1949) and *John Quincy Adams and the Union* (1956)—supplant the older accounts by Bennett C. Clark (1932) and John T. Morse (1882). The diary-memoirs of J. Q. Adams, edited by C. F. Adams in twelve volumes (1874–1877), are indispensable.

ANDREW JACKSON. The best biographies are both two-volume works: those by Marquis James (1937–1938) and by John S. Bassett (1911). Penetrating interpretations are Arthur M. Schlesinger, Jr., *The Age of Jackson* (1945) and Marvin Meyers, *The Jacksonian Persuasion* (1957). For ideological impact, consult John W. Ward, *Andrew Jackson: Symbol for an Age* (1955) and Harold C. Syrett, *Andrew Jackson: His Contribution to the American Tradition* (1953). An important bibliographical article is C. G. Sellers, Jr., "Andrew Jackson Versus the Historians," *Mississippi Valley Historical Review*, XLIV (1958), pp. 615–34.

See also A. A. Cave, *Jacksonian Democracy and the Historians* (1964) and paragraph two of Appendix D (above).

MARTIN VAN BUREN. The best lives are by Holmes M. Alexander (1935) and Denis T. Lynch (1929), which supersede Edward M. Shepard's biography (1899). See also Robert Vincent Remini, *Martin Van Buren and the Making of the Democratic Party* (1959).

WILLIAM HENRY HARRISON. The best lives are by Dorothy Burne Goebel, *William Henry Harrison* (1926) and Freeman Cleaves, *Old Tippecanoe* (1939). See also Robert G. Gunderson, *The Log-Cabin Campaign* (1957).

JOHN TYLER. The best lives are by Oliver P. Chitwood, *John Tyler* (1939) and Robert Seager II, *And Tyler Too* (1963). See also Robert J. Morgan, *A Whig Embattled: The Presidency Under John Tyler* (1954).

JAMES K. POLK. The only creditable full-length biography is the older study by Eugene I. McCormac (1922). Charles G. Sellers, *James K. Polk, Jacksonian, 1795–1843* (1957) has not yet reached the presidency. Of value is Charles A. McCoy, *Polk and the Presidency* (1960). Polk's presidential diary, edited in five volumes by M. M. Quaife (1910), is indispensable. See Norman A. Graebner's appraisal in Morton Borden, ed., *America's Ten Greatest Presidents* (1961).

ZACHARY TAYLOR. The fullest biography is the two-volume work by Holman Hamilton (1941, 1951); more succinct is Brainerd Dyer's one-volume life (1946). See also Silas Bent McKinley and Silas Bent, *Old Rough and Ready* (1946).

MILLARD FILLMORE. Robert J. Rayback, *Millard Fillmore* (1959) supersedes the volume by William E. Griffis, *Millard Fillmore* (1915).

FRANKLIN PIERCE. By far the best work is Roy F. Nichols, *Franklin Pierce: Young Hickory of the Granite Hills* (1958), a complete revision and resetting of the earlier edition of 1931.

JAMES BUCHANAN. The meritorious biography by Philip S. Klein, *President James Buchanan* (1962) supersedes that by G. T. Curtis (1883). The rehabilitation by Klein is in some degree foreshadowed by F. R. Klingberg's "James Buchanan and the Crisis of the Union," *Journal of Southern History*, IX (1943), pp. 455–74, and especially P. G. Auchampaugh, *James Buchanan and His Cabinet on the Eve of Secession* (1926).

ABRAHAM LINCOLN. The best short account is Benjamin P. Thomas, *Abraham Lincoln* (1952), though R. H. Luthin, *The Real Abraham Lincoln* (1960) is more compendious. The richest multi-volume scholarship may be found in J. G. Randall, *Lincoln the President* (4 vols., 1945–1955), the last volume of which was completed by Richard N.

Current. Less profound but more colorful is the poet Carl Sandburg, *Abraham Lincoln: The War Years* (4 vols., 1939), preceded by his *Abraham Lincoln: The Prairie Years* (2 vols., 1926). Recent revisionism is well represented by Richard N. Current, *The Lincoln Nobody Knows* (1958) and David Donald, *Lincoln Reconsidered* (1956). Consult also Roy P. Basler, *The Lincoln Legend* (1935); Lloyd Lewis, *Myths After Lincoln* (1940); and Benjamin P. Thomas, *Portrait for Posterity: Lincoln and His Biographers* (1947). The most complete compilation is Jay Monaghan, *Lincoln Bibliography, 1839–1939* (2 vols. 1943–1945). See also paragraph two of Appendix D (above).

ANDREW JOHNSON. The full-length lives are all too laudatory to be satisfactory: Lloyd P. Stryker, *Andrew Johnson* (1929) and Robert W. Winston, *Andrew Johnson* (1928). Earlier works on the presidential struggle are Claude G. Bowers, *The Tragic Era* (1929); George F. Milton, *The Age of Hate* (1930); Howard K. Beale, *The Critical Year* (1930). Their favorable slant toward Johnson, especially Bowers', must be corrected by the strong revisionism of Eric L. McKitrick, *Andrew Johnson and Reconstruction* (1960). See also David M. De Witt, *The Impeachment and Trial of Andrew Johnson* (1903) and Milton Lomask, *Andrew Johnson: President on Trial* (1960). A recent summation is Albert Castel, "Andrew Johnson: His Historiographical Rise and Fall," *Mid-America*, XLV (1963), pp. 175–84.

ULYSSES S. GRANT. The standard life is William B. Hesseltine, *Ulysses S. Grant, Politician* (1935). Sketchy but comprehensive is Bruce Catton, *U. S. Grant and the American Military Tradition* (1954), which makes out a case for Grant as President. Frankly debunking is William E. Woodward, *Meet General Grant* (1928). Valuable sidelights on the general appear in Allan Nevins, *Hamilton Fish: The Inner History of the Grant Administration* (1936).

RUTHERFORD B. HAYES. Harry Barnard, *Rutherford B. Hayes and His America* (1954) is the standard life, though the earlier biographies by H. J. Eckenrode (1930) and Charles R. Williams (1914) are still worth consulting. A useful new edition is T. Harry Williams, ed., *Hayes: The Diary of a President, 1875–1881* (1964). On philanthropic activities, see H. L. Swint, "Rutherford B. Hayes, Educator," *Mississippi Valley Historical Review*, XXXIX (1953), pp. 45–60.

JAMES A. GARFIELD. The best one-volume life is Robert G. Caldwell, *James A. Garfield, Party Chieftain* (1931); much fuller is Theodore C. Smith, *The Life and Letters of James Abram Garfield* (2 vols., 1925).

CHESTER A. ARTHUR. The only solid biography is George F. Howe, *Chester A. Arthur* (1934).

GROVER CLEVELAND. By far the best life is Allan Nevins' favorable *Grover Cleveland: A Study in Courage* (1932). Still useful are Denis T. Lynch, *Grover Cleveland* (1932), and Robert McElroy, *Grover Cleveland* (2 vols., 1923), an "authorized" biography. In brief compass is Horace S. Merrill, *Bourbon Leader: Grover Cleveland and the Democratic Party* (1957). See also Morton Borden, ed., *America's Ten Greatest Presidents* (1961).

BENJAMIN HARRISON. Aside from General Lewis Wallace's hasty campaign biography (1888), there is no full-length life worthy of mention. Harry J. Sievers has brought Harrison's career through his election in 1888 in two volumes (1952, 1959), with the presidential years yet to come. See also Benjamin Harrison, *Views of an Ex-President* (1901).

WILLIAM McKINLEY. The standard life is now H. Wayne Morgan's favorable *William McKinley and His America* (1963), which supplants the earlier biographies by Charles S. Olcott (1916) and William C. Spielman (1954). See also Margaret Leech, *In the Days of McKinley* (1959), and the essay on McKinley as Commander-in-Chief by Ernest R. May, ed., in his *The Ultimate Decision* (1960).

THEODORE ROOSEVELT. The most recent full-length biography of merit is William H. Harbaugh, *The Life and Times of Theodore Roosevelt* (1961), which is much more friendly than Henry F. Pringle's debunking *Theodore Roosevelt: A Biography* (1931). Roosevelt's *An Autobiography* (1913) and the authorized two-volume life by Joseph B. Bishop (1920) are still useful. Consult also John M. Blum, *The Republican Roosevelt* (1954). For an important bibliographical summation, see D. W. Grantham, Jr., "Theodore Roosevelt in American Historical Writing, 1945–1960," *Mid-America*, XLIII (1961), pp. 3–35. See also paragraph two of Appendix D (above).

WILLIAM HOWARD TAFT. Henry F. Pringle's full and friendly *The Life and Times of William Howard Taft* (2 vols., 1939) supplants the earlier biography by Herbert S. Duffy (1930).

WOODROW WILSON. Perhaps the most useful of the numerous one-volume biographies is John A. Garraty, *Woodrow Wilson* (1956); of the two-volumes, Arthur Walworth, *Woodrow Wilson* (1958); of the multi-volumes, Ray Stannard Baker, *Woodrow Wilson: Life and Letters* (8 vols., 1927–1939). Arthur S. Link, the foremost Wilson scholar, is supplanting Baker with his multi-volume life, now carried in five volumes (1947–1965) into 1917. See also John M. Blum, *Woodrow Wilson and the Politics of Morality* (1956). On peacemaking, consult Thomas A. Bailey's *Woodrow Wilson and the Lost Peace* (1944) and *Woodrow Wilson and the Great Betrayal* (1945). Many appraisals were sparked by the centennial of 1956, notably Earl Latham, ed., *The Philosophy and Policies of Woodrow Wilson* (1958). A capital bibliographical article is R. W. Watson, Jr., "Woodrow Wilson and His Interpreters, 1947–1957," *Mississippi Valley Historical Review*, XLIV (1957), pp. 207–36. See paragraph two of Appendix D (above).

WARREN G. HARDING. The only full-length biography, based on the recently opened Harding papers, is Andrew Sinclair's favorable *The Available Man* (1965). Several others are in preparation.

CALVIN COOLIDGE. A laudatory biography is Claude M. Fuess, *Calvin Coolidge: The Man from Vermont* (1940); a debunking treatment is William A. White, *A Puritan in Babylon* (1938). Coolidge's own autobiography appeared in 1929. Various appraisals are in Edward C. Lathem, ed., *Meet Calvin Coolidge* (1960). See also paragraph two of Appendix D (above).

HERBERT HOOVER. Partly because of severe restrictions on his papers, Hoover lacks a satisfactory biography. The most recent one, Eugene Lyons, *Herbert Hoover* (1964), is an adulatory updating of a previous adulatory effusion. The best full-length assessment of Hoover's administration (without benefit of the private papers) is Harris G. Warren, *Herbert Hoover and the Great Depression* (1959). Incisive and fair is C. M. Degler, "The Ordeal of Herbert Hoover," *Yale Review*, LII (1963), 563–83. Hoover's self-justifying *Memoirs* of the presidency in two volumes (1951, 1952) tell the story as he wished to have it remembered. See also paragraph two of Appendix D (above).

FRANKLIN ROOSEVELT. The best one volume is James M. Burns, *Roosevelt: The Lion and the Fox* (1956). Of the multi-volume works, Frank Freidel's projected six-volume study has progressed in three volumes to the presidency (1952, 1954, 1956); and Arthur M. Schlesinger, Jr., has carried the story through the election of 1936 in *The Crisis of the Old Order* (1957), *The Coming of the New Deal* (1959), *The Politics of Upheaval* (1960). Journalist John Gunther is friendly in *Roosevelt in Retrospect* (1950); Edgar E. Robinson is critical in *The Roosevelt Leadership, 1933–1945* (1955), while John T. Flynn, *The Roosevelt Myth* (1948) is a "smear" book. Evaluations by close associates are Frances Perkins, *The Roosevelt I Knew* (1946); Robert E. Sherwood, *Roosevelt and Hopkins* (1948); Rexford G. Tugwell, *The Democratic Roosevelt* (1957); and Raymond Moley, *After Seven Years* (1939). See also paragraph two of Appendix D (above).

HARRY S TRUMAN. A useful biography is Alfred Steinberg, *The Man from Missouri* (1962). See also Jonathan Daniels, *The Man of Independence* (1950), necessarily incomplete on the presidency. William Hillman, *Mr. President* (1952) includes some interesting documents.

Truman published his *Memoirs* in two volumes (1955, 1956), and has presented other views informally in *Mr. Citizen* (1960) and in *Truman Speaks* (1960). See also paragraph two of Appendix D (above).

DWIGHT D. EISENHOWER. It is too early to expect satisfactory biographies. Useful for a starter is Robert J. Donovan, *Eisenhower: The Inside Story* (1956) and Merlo J. Pusey, *Eisenhower: The President* (1956), both campaign biographies. Marquis W. Childs, *Eisenhower: Captive Hero* (1958) is highly critical. "Inside" accounts are the friendly Sherman Adams' *Firsthand Report* (1961) and the unflattering kiss-and-tell revelations of Emmet J. Hughes in *The Ordeal of Power* (1963). The first volume of Eisenhower's presidential memoirs, *Mandate for Change, 1953–1956,* appeared in 1963; Vol. II, *Waging Peace, 1956–1961,* in 1965.

JOHN F. KENNEDY. The best early account was Hugh Sidey, *John F. Kennedy, President* (1963), which is devoted entirely to the presidential years. James M. Burns, *John Kennedy: A Political Profile* (1960) is an able campaign biography. Victor Lasky, *J.F.K.: The Man and the Myth* (1963) is such a venomous attack that the publishers withdrew it for several weeks after the assassination. Theodore C. Sorensen, *Decision-Making in the White House* (1963) is a revealing analysis by Kennedy's close associate and ghost-writer. His personalized account of the "Thousand Days" was published late in 1965 under the title, *Kennedy;* Arthur M. Schlesinger, Jr.'s *A Thousand Days,* also personalized and even more revealing, appeared in 1965. See R. E. Neustadt, "Kennedy in the Presidency: A Premature Appraisal," *Political Science Quarterly,* LXXIX (1964), pp. 321–34; and W. G. Carleton, "Kennedy in History: An Early Appraisal," *Antioch Review,* XXIV (1964), pp. 277–99.

LYNDON B. JOHNSON. Perspective is so short that we must rely heavily on campaign biographies, of which W. S. White, *The Professional: Lyndon B. Johnson* (1964) is an excellent example. See also Jack Bell, *The Johnson Treatment* (1965) and the perceptive little book by the British journalist Michael Davie, *LBJ: A Foreign Observer's Viewpoint* (1966).

Index